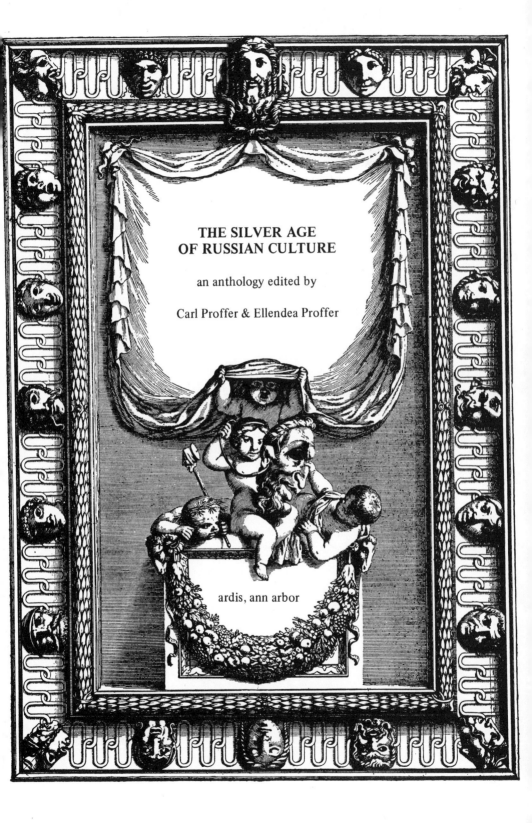

THE SILVER AGE
OF RUSSIAN CULTURE

an anthology edited by

Carl Proffer & Ellendea Proffer

ardis, ann arbor

891.73
P964a
1975

CONTENTS

ARTICLES

APPENDIX - RUSSIAN TEXTS

ILLUSTRATIONS

PREFACE

To the list of adjectives describing the Russian Silver Age—
elegant, effete, morbid, aristocratic, melodious, hyperesthetic,
experimental, elitist, colorful, pseudoclassical, mystical, erotic,
perverse, non-utilitarian, irrationalist, imitative, disingenuous—
one has to add, as with everything else, exciting and boring,
passionate and cold. But while the ballet, music and even the
art of the Russian Silver Age are relatively familiar to the Western reader, until quite recently his knowledge of the modernis-
tic literature of the period from 1894 to 1917 (beyond thin selections in thick anthologies) was limited primarily to a few
classics such as Bely's *Petersburg,* Sologub's *The Petty Demon,*
and Blok's *The Twelve.*

The discovery of Mandelstam's poetry and prose, thanks to
the memoirs of his widow and the erudite work of Clarence
Brown, has led the way in the opening of the Silver Age for the
English-speaking world. In the last five years, in addition to
translations of virtually all of Mandelstam's poetry and prose,
there have been three volumes of Akhmatova in translation,
three books about Akhmatova, translations of Bely's *Kotik Letaev* and *The Silver Dove* (and two books about him), the plays
of Nikolai Evreinov, the stories and diaries of Zinaida Gippius,
anthologies of the poetry and prose of Gumilev and Kuzmin,
and the first English monographs on Merezhkovsky, Gippius,
and Bryusov. English versions of Sologub's *Bad Dreams* and his
complete trilogy *The Created Legend,* a new translation of
Petersburg, the critical prose of Gumilev, Symbolist plays, and
Annensky's poetry are all forthcoming.

When all of this is done, in spite of the considerable problems involved in translations from Russian poetry and poetic
prose, the English reader will be in a fairly good position to
evaluate the Russian contribution to world literature during the
old regime's last cultural renaissance. To this date the best written evaluation of this period is D. S. Mirsky's *A History of*

Russian Literature (New York: Knopf, 1958), pp. 407-503. We assume that most of the people who read this anthology will be doing so in courses of Russian literature where Mirsky's classic is basic reading and where a teacher will be familiar with the items translated here. Rather than repeat Mirsky, we will only add a few words of caution about his rather short comments on developments after Symbolism, and particularly after the October Revolution. While at the time Mirsky was writing Symbolism was far enough in the past to be seen clearly, the writers who began as Acmeists still had much of their major work ahead. Largely suppressed after the Revolution, Mandelstam and Akhmatova were not published in good editions until the 1960s, and then only outside the USSR. There are many readers and critics now, both in the USSR and in the West, who would maintain that Mandelstam is more important than Akhmatova, and that both of them are far more important in the history of Russian letters than any of the Symbolist poets, including Blok. Furthermore, Russian Symbolist poets generally are likely to suffer by comparison to non-Russian poets writing at the same time or even earlier. Thus, while Blok is almost universally regarded as the best Russian Symbolist poet, few people would put him in the same class with Baudelaire, Yeats, or Rilke. And much of the belles-lettres and criticism of the Russian Symbolists is more on the level of Swinburne, Symons, and La Forgue. In the realm of ideas the Symbolists' achievements have worn even less well. We should not forget that their period was the time when Rudolf Steiner and Madame Blavatsky passed as "thinkers."

This anthology is composed largely of items which appeared in the first ten issues of *Russian Literature Triquarterly,* but some important works, such as the almost complete translation of Mandelstam's book *Tristia,* the selections from Annensky's *The Cypress Chest,* and two facing translations of *The Twelve* (with the Russian in an appendix), are published here for the first time. Of course, if translations of other important works were available, our ideal anthology could be twice this size. For example, Futurism, which began at the same time as Acmeism, might justifiably be included in this anthology, but as revolutionary art it does look forward in the century and is better suited to an anthology of the avantgarde Twenties.

We have included Mandelstam's essay "Storm and Stress" because it discusses all of these various schools and transitions. The basic chronological limits of the selections here are 1898-1918, with some major exceptions, such as *Tristia* (published in 1922), and Akhmatova's *A Poem without a Hero* (begun in 1940 and worked on virtually until the poet's death), which deserves to be included because it is a meditation on and a summation of the Silver Age. We have included essays on two of the major periodicals of the Silver Age—*The World of Art* and *Apollo*. These add an important dimension to our picture of Russian culture in this period, showing how closely related the arts became around the turn of the century—a new condition in Russian life, but one which would continue almost until the present day.

The reader will find on the next two pages a brief chronological outline of some of the major events of the Silver Age.

CHRONOLOGY

1890 — Minsky, *By the Light of Conscience*

1892 — Merezhkovsky, *Symbols*

1893 — Merezhkovsky, *On the Reasons for the Decline and on the New Tendencies in Contemporary Russian Literature*

1894 — V. Bryusov and A. L. Miropolsky, *Russian Symbolists*

1898 — *The World of Art* founded
1898 — Solovyov, *Three Meetings*

1902 — Bely, *Symphony (Second Dramatic)*

1903 — Balmont, *Let Us Be Like the Sun*
1903 — Bryusov, *Urbi et Orbi*

1904 — Blok, *Verse about the Beautiful Lady*
1904 — Bely, *Gold in Azure*
1904 — *The World of Art* ends
1904 — *The Scales* founded

1905 — Bryusov, *The Republic of the Southern Cross*
1905 — Ivanov's Tower Wednesdays begin

1906 — *The Golden Fleece* founded
1906 — Kuzmin, *Alexandrian Songs*

1907 — Sologub, *The Petty Demon* (written 1892-1905)

1909 — Bely, *The Silver Dove*
1909 — Evreinov, *A Merry Death* premieres
1909 — *Landmarks* (essays)
1909 — *The Golden Fleece* ends
1909 — *The Scales* ends
1909 — *Apollo* founded

1910 — Kuzmin, *On Beautiful Clarity*
1910 — Annensky, *The Cypress Chest*

1911 — Ivanov, *Cor Ardens*

1912 — The Guild of Poets forms
1912 — Premiere of *The Theater of the Soul*
1912 — Rozanov, *Solitaria*

1913 — Bely, *Petersburg*
1913 — Mandelstam, *Stone*
1913 — Akhmatova, *Beads*
1913 — Gumilev, *Symbolism's Legacy and Acmeism*

1917 — Bely, *Kotik Letaev*

1918 — Blok, *The Twelve*

1921 — Gumilev, *The Pillar of Fire*

1922 — Mandelstam, *Tristia*

CRITICISM

dmitry merezhkovsky / ON THE REASONS FOR THE DECLINE AND ON THE NEW TENDENCIES IN CONTEMPORARY RUSSIAN LITERATURE

[excerpts]

. . . In the age of naive theology and dogmatic metaphysics the region of the unperceived was constantly confused with the region of the unknown. People did not know how to separate them and did not comprehend the entire depth and hopelessness of their ignorance. A mystical feeling intruded into the bounds of exact, scientific investigations and destroyed them. On the other hand the vulgar materialism of dogmatic forms enslaved the religious sensibility.

The newest theory of knowledge has erected an indestructible barrier which for ages divided the concrete earth accessible to people from the boundless and dark ocean lying beyond the bounds of our consciousness. And the waves of this ocean no longer can intrude into the inhabited earth, into the realm of exact science. The foundation, the first granite monoliths of cyclopaedic construction—the great theory of knowledge of the nineteenth century—was laid by Kant. From that time, work on it has proceeded without interruption, the barrier is rising ever higher and higher.

Never before has the restricted frontier of science been so sharp and implacable, never before have people's eyes experienced such an unbearable contrast of light and dark. Meanwhile, whereas on this side of appearances the firm soil of science was flooded with a brilliant light, the region lying on the other side of the plane, in the expression of Carlyle "the deeps of holy ignorance," the night out of which we have all emerged and into which we must return with all due haste, is more impenetrable than ever. In former times metaphysics had cast its gleaming and misty veil over it. A primeval legend illuminated, though slightly, this abyss with its murky but comforting light.

Now the final dogmatic veil has been eternally torn away, the final mystical spirit is being extinguished. And here stand today's people, defenseless—face to face with the indescribable gloom, on the dividing line of light and darkness, and now no one can protect his heart any longer from the terrifying cold drifting up out of the abyss. Wherever we might go, wherever we might hide behind the barrier of scientific criticism, we feel with all our being the nearness of a mystery, the nearness of the ocean.

There are no limits!.. We are free and lonely... No enslaved mysticism of a previous age can be compared with this terror. Never before have people felt in their hearts such a need to believe, and in their minds comprehended their inability to believe. In this diseased and irresolvable dissonance, in this tragic contradiction, as well as in the unheard-of intellectual freedom, in the courage of negation, is contained the most characteristic feature of the

3

mystical need of the nineteenth century.

Our time must define in two contrasting features this time of the most extreme materialism and at the same time of the most passionate idealistic outbursts of the spirit. We are witnessing a mighty and all-important struggle between two views of life, between two diametrically opposed worldviews. The final demands of religious feeling are experiencing a confrontation with the final conclusions of the experimental sciences.

The intellectual struggle which filled the nineteenth century could not but be reflected in contemporary literature.

The overwhelming taste of the masses has been realistic up until now. Artistic materialism corresponds to a scientific and ethical materialism. The cliched aspect of negation, the absence of a higher idealistic culture, a civilized barbarism amid the grandiose contrivances of technology—all this has placed its unique stamp on the relationship of the contemporary masses to art. . .

In essence the entire generation at the end of the nineteenth century bears in its soul that same reaction against the suffocatingly dead positivism which lay on hearts like a stone. It is quite possible that they will perish, that they will not succeed in accomplishing anything. But others will come and will carry on, all the same, their work, because this work is vital. . .

Symbols must naturally and effortlessly emerge out of the depth of reality. But if the author unnaturally invents them in order to express some idea or other, they will be transformed into dead allegories which arouse nothing other than repulsion like all that is dead. The final minutes of the agony of Madame Bovary, accompanied by the crude little song of love by the petty charmer, the scene of madness during the first rays of the rising sun, after the tragic night of "Gespenster," are written with a more merciless psychological naturalism, with a greater penetration into reality, than the most outspoken human documents of the positivistic novel. But in Ibsen and Flaubert, together with the flow of expressed words of thoughts, you involuntarily feel another deeper current.

"A thought expressed is a falsehood." In poetry what is not said and yet gleams through the beauty of the symbol, works more powerfully on the heart than that which is expressed in words. Symbolism makes the very style, the very artistic substance of poetry inspired, transparent, illuminated throughout like the delicate walls of an alabaster amphora in which a flame is ignited.

Characters can also serve as symbols. Sancho Panza and Faust, Don Quixote and Hamlet, Don Juan and Falstaff, according to the words of Goethe, are "schwankende Gestalten"

Apparitions which haunt mankind, sometimes repeatedly from age to age, accompany mankind from generation to generation. It is impossible to communicate in any words whatsoever the idea of such symbolic characters, for words only define and restrict thought, but symbols express the un-

4

restricted aspect of truth.

Moreover we cannot be satisfied with a vulgar, photographic exactness of experimental photography. We demand and have premonition of, according to the allusions of Flaubert, Maupassant, Turgenev, Ibsen, new and as yet undisclosed worlds of impressionability. This thirst for the unexperienced, in pursuit of elusive nuances, of the dark and unconscious in our sensibility, is the characteristic feature of the coming ideal poetry. Earlier Baudelaire and Edgar Allen Poe said that the beautiful must somewhat *amaze,* must seem unexpected and extraordinary. French critics more or less successfully named this feature—*impressionism.*

Such are the three major elements of the new art: *a mystical content, symbols, and the expansion of artistic impressionability.*

No positivistic conclusions, no utilitarian computation, but only *a creative faith in something infinite and immortal* can ignite the soul of man, create heroes, martyrs and prophets... People have need of faith, they need inspiration, they crave a holy madness in their heroes and martyrs.

Only the infinite can we love with an infinite love, i.e., love to the point of self-renunciation, to a point of hatred for life itself, for death. But without this sun, without this love, the earth will be transformed into a glacier, even as the ice has become frozen according to geometrical laws of a utilitarian and positivistic mechanism.

Without faith in the divine beginning of the world there is no beauty on earth, there is no justice, no poetry, no freedom!...

Before us is mighty, so to speak, transformative and preparatory work. *From a period which is creative, immediate and elemental, we must proceed to a period which is critical, conscious and cultural.* These are the two worlds between which exists the entire abyss. The contemporary generation has the misfortune of being born between these two worlds, before this abyss. Herein is explained its frailty, diseased anxiety, hungry search for new ideals and a certain fateful impotency in all of its efforts. The best youth and vigor of talent is not expended on vital creativity but on an internal destructiveness and struggle with the past, on the passage across the abyss *to that land, to that shore,* to the frontiers of a free and divine idealism. How many people are perishing in this pasage or are losing their strength irrevocably!. . .

At any rate, even if the contemporary generation is doomed to perish, to it is given the joy which is surely unique on earth, to it is given a glimpse of the very first ray, the sensation of the first quivering of the new life, the first premonition of the great future.

When the Divine Spirit passes over the earth,—none of the people will known when He cometh and whither He departeth... But it is impossible to resist Him.

He is more powerful than the human will and intellect, more powerful than life, more powerful than death itself.

Translated by Samuel Cioran

I

The term "Symbolism and Decadence" implies a new type not so much of poetry as of poetic art, a type that is vastly dissimilar in form and content to all previous kinds of literary endeavor. Having arisen only 10-12 years ago, the Symbolist movement has spread with extraordinary rapidity throughout all the countries of the civilized world, obviously finding a well-prepared soil and conditions favorable for its acceptance everywhere. As specimens of this type of art let us cite two or three poems:

> Corpses illuminated by gas!
> Scarlet ribbon on the sinful bride!
> Oh, shall we go to the window and kiss!
> Do you see how pale the faces of the dead are?
> This is a hospital where children are in mourning...
> These are oleanders on the ice...
> This is the jacket of romances without words.
> Darling, the moon cannot be seen through the window.
> Our souls are the flower in your boutonniere.
>
> (V. Darov)

In a somewhat more lively meter:

> The shadow of uncreated creations
> Flickers in sleep,
> Like the laminae of latania
> On the enameled wall.
> Violet-colored hands
> On the enameled wall
> Sleepily draw sounds
> In the sonorously sounding depths,
> They grow like spangles
> In the azure moonlight;
> The denuded moon rises
> In the azure moonlight;
> Sounds soar sleepily,

6

> Sounds snuggle up to me,
> Secrets of uncreated creations
> Snuggle up to me caressingly,
> And the shadow of latania flickers
> On the enameled wall. (*Russian Symbolists,* Book II)

The two poems cited above are Russian, of native origin; here is a poem by Maeterlinck:

> My soul is sick all day,
> My soul is sick from parting,
> My soul is struggling with silence,
> My eyes encounter the shadow,
> I see the phantoms of longings;
> A half-forgotten track leads
> The dogs of secret desire
> Into the depths of forgetful forests,
> Packs of lilac-colored fantasies race along,
> And yellow arrows—reproaches—
> Slay the deer of mendacious dreams.
> Alas, alas! Everywhere desires,
> Everywhere returning dreams,
> And the breathing is too blue....
> On the heart the moon's visage grows dim.

What is indisputable and understandable about the content of Symbolism is its general tendency toward eroticism. The god as old as Mother Nature, driven once and for all, so it seemed, from the civic poetry of the 1850s—1870s, broke into a sphere that has always belonged to him and that he has loved since time immemorial, but in a strange and mutilated, in a shamelessly bare form:

> Oh, wondrously tender and passionate disease!
> In you lie my whole life and dear ideal!
> You clasped me in your star-like embrace
> Like a mold clasps the earth,
> Like rust the battle-wearied dagger!
> You gave me freedom, I am dread and great
> Not with bilious rudeness, nor strength, nor knowledge;
> Covered with ulcers is my panic-stricken tongue,
> And I can infect with my breath alone
> Vestal virgins, old men, helpless children;
> I can reward all with the naked disease.

7

I despise life, Nature, and people,
I laugh at anguish, at grief and tears.
(Emel Yanov-Kokhansky)

And also in the following poem, which is extraordinarily hideous even in form:

Do not enter, you out there!
Do I not have white legs?
Do I not have arms that entwine?
Do not enter, you out there!
I shall go mad and grow weak
Behind the sable canopy.
I shall twine my serpentine arms,
I shall touch my bare shoulders,
I shall kiss thy swarthy eyes....
Do not enter!..
(A. Dobrolyubov)

This same motif stands out distinctly in prose as well:

What art thou imploring, Bright One? Is it not undivined eyes thou cravest, or the bated breath of passion? Is it not a smile dressed in tears, or the dewy soul of youth?

I shall give thee a virginal body, shameless, bold, legs, intoxicating lips.... Thou hast approached the morning couch, Stern One.

Am I not young? Serpentine arms will intertwine. The pale white night will grow pale from my embraces and will leave the chamber through the window, into the open.

Bright One! I am comfortable.... I am hurt, Bright One! The white night gazeth at thee with fathomless eyes. It doth not leave. Like a widow, the night is sad.... Like a hired mourner, it weepeth. It weepeth over the cemetery morning. I am afraid, Bright One!
(A. Dobrolyubov)

Here Eros is no longer dressed in poetry, no longer hidden or obscured; all the meaning, all the beauty, all the endless torments and joys from which the act of love proceeds, and which (connected with a different kind of poetry and concerns) follow from this act—all that is discarded here; the very face of the beloved person is discarded; this new "poetry" throws a cover upon it, as though it were the face of a patient on the operating table, lest its expression of suffering, horror, and entreaty interfere with something "vitally important" to be carried out here, around it, but without any attention to it. A woman—not only without form but always without name—usually figures in this "poetry," in which the head of the depicted object plays almost as trifling a role as is

8

played by the head of the depicting subject; as we can see, for example, in the following poem (classic in its brevity) whose content is exhausted in one line:

Oh, cover your pale legs! (Briusov)

Here the viewpoint on man and, it seems, on all human relations, i. e., on life itself, is not revealed from above, does not come from the face, and is not imbued with meaning, but rises from somewhere below, from the legs, and is imbued with sensations and desires that have nothing in common with meaning.

II

The birthplace of Symbolism and Decadence is, as is well known, France; and for virtually the first time in its history, in this new "poetry," it has come forth not as the expounder of others' ideas and aspirations, but as the guide and mentor in a certain new kind of "tastes." The homeland of Marquis de Sade has clearly shown, at last, what it indisputably excels in among all the civilized nationalities, and it has nothing at all to learn from them in this regard. Suddenly, but with quite unexpected vigor, it expressed where its interests really lay, at a time when it was seemingly embroiled in political, religious, economic, and other controversies, before the eyes of a thrilled and often delighted world. Art is more sensitive than anything else to the future; it discloses more clearly than anything else the innermost workings of our soul. About four years ago, in the so-called "artistic" section of a French exhibition in Moscow, ingenuous Russians, had they been perspicacious enough, could already have read the "Decadence" conveyed—not in leg-obsessed poems devoid of rhyme, meter, and sense—but in a number of paintings without accessories, without settings, without the light of day or night, without garments, but with the invariable depiction of the female body, insofar as it is revealed from the direction of the heels. It made a strange impression on you, just as you were crossing the threshold of the gallery, to see a long row of canvases in which there was a complete absence of any other subjects: Nature was not portrayed, nor the sea, nor mountains, nor the sun, nor flowers, nor street views, nor domestic scenes, but only female figures stretched up in almost the same manner, with "thighs" and other details, with revoltingly pinched faces that stretched up, as it were, before the painters' "artistic imagination."[1] Obviously, for these artists history has died; and even in their favorite "subjects" the face, name, past, and future of man have died; and out of this dead silence, out of this dark non-existence protruded—just as for the Decadents of our own day—nothing but "pale legs," the fixed idea of their morbidly disposed imagination.

But the absence of faces, not only intelligent-looking, expressive faces, but simply handsome or young and fresh ones, was not the main peculiarity of this gallery of naked bodies. What struck you here was the labored imagination of these artists, which strove yet failed to express more and more of the sphere of "nakedness." Thus, I remember one painting that portrayed the ocean depths, into which a sunbeam fell; on a closer examination you noticed that some horned shell, stretching upwards and entwining itself with the swirling waters, rose to meet this beam, embraced and absorbed it; on a still closer examination you noticed, with a certain surprise and disgust, that this was not the ocean depths, nor the contorted forms of a seashell reaching upwards, but a convulsively contorted, transparent female body wrapping itself around the beam.

One does not have to be a philosopher of human culture to guess, from looking at this painting, what the literature of the country must have been like during these years. Unfortunately, I have not had the occasion to read anything by Maupassant or Zola, but here is an excerpt from the former's work, as it was presented in a critical article about him (Miss N. L.: "Guy de Maupassant," in *The Russian Herald,* Nov. 1894); here we already enter the sphere of Decadence, although this page was written long before the appearance of this famous "school":

....Love, passionate love, is possible only when you do not see the object of your love. To see is to understand, to understand is to despise. You should love a woman drunkenly, as if you were drunk with wine; so drunkenly, that you no longer taste what it is you are drinking . And drink, drink, drink, without catching your breath, day and night.

This (writes the reviewer) is the entry which the hero of the short story made in his diary *before* his marriage; *after* his marriage he continues the diary:

In marrying her I submitted to the unconscious attraction that drives you to a woman.

She is now my wife. While I was only yearning for her in my soul, she seemed to be the embodiment of my unrealizable dream, which was about to come true. But as soon as I clasped her in my embrace I saw in her only a tool that Nature used to defeat my expectations.

Did she (i. e., my wife) defeat them? No. But she has become hateful to me, so hateful that I cannot touch her without feeling indescribable revulsion of a higher order, revulsion toward sexual union in general, which is so loathesome that beings *of a higher organization* should conceal this shameful act and speak about it only in a whisper, blushingly....

I can no longer bear the sight of my wife when she comes up to me, embraces me, beckoning with a smile or glance. Only recently it seemed to me that her kiss would transport me to heaven! Once, for a short time, she was ill with a fever, and I could smell in her breath the light, subtle, almost imperceptible odor of decay; I was horror-struck!

Oh, frail body, enchanting living dung! Oh, moving, thinking, speaking, laughing decay, so rosy, seductive, and beautiful, yet so deceptive as the soul itself!

We sense behind these words a degree of physical enervation that precludes the possibility of real intimacy; and this enervation, as we can see from the brief passage above, results not from lavish expenditure of lavish energies, but from the exhausting work of the imagination on "subjects" of a certain type, long before they come near and become accessible *in re*. And so a walking corpse, who believes, however, that he belongs to a race of "more highly organized" beings (see above) continues in the same *Diary:*

....I love flowers like living creatures. I spend days and nights in a greenhouse, where I hide them, just as women in a harem are hidden. I have a greenhouse where no one intrudes except the gardener and me.

I enter it as though it were a place of secret delights. In a high glass gallery I pass first of all between rows of crown-shaped flowers, which rise in steps from the ground to the roof. They send me the first kiss.

These flowers, which decorate the antechamber of my mysterious harem, are my modest servant girls. Pretty and coquettish, they welcome me with a burst of their splendor and fragrance. Occupying eight steps on one side and eight steps on the other, they are so massed together that they appear to be gardens descending from both sides down to my feet. My heart beats excitedly, my eyes light with passion on seeing them, my blood rushes, and my hands tremble with desire to seize them. But I walk on. At the end of this gallery three closed doors are visible. I can choose. I have three harems.

Most often (continues the critic) he goes to the orchids:

They quiver on their little stalks as if they were going to fly away. Will they fly to me? No, my soul will fly to them and soar above them—the soul of a mysterious male tormented by love.

....Flowers, flowers—in Nature only flowers give forth such wondrous fragrances— these vivid or pale flowers, whose soft hues make my heart beat so wildly and mist my eyes! They are so lovely and tender, so sensitive, half-open, more seductive than a woman's mouth; they are hollow, with pouting, jagged, fleshy lips that are strewn with the germs of life, which arouse in each of them a specific aroma. They, alone in all of Nature, multiply without shame to their inviolate (?) race, diffusing the wondrous scent of their love and their caresses, the fragrance of incomparable flesh that is full of ineffable charm and endowed with an unusual abundance of forms and colors and with the intoxicating allurement of the most diverse aromas.
(*The Russian Herald,* 94 [November] pp. 269-271)

This wedding flight, as it were, to flowers secluded in a greenhouse-harem recalls an analogous event that actually took place in the ancient world, when a certain Greek, inflamed with a similar passion for a marble statue, became so frenzied that once he secretly defiled it. History remembered that event, and the story of it has come down to us; obviously, the pagan Greeks were so astounded by it that they could not pass over it in silence, and not only in conversation and in the public square but also in books; now the imagination of a Christian writer falls to the depths of a similar brutishness, and even lower—to the depths of inanimate Nature, but he not only falls there, he generalizes and legitimizes his fall, couching it in the beauty of literary forms; and finally, he sings a hymn to it to the rapt attention of the "critics" of every land and to the pleasure of an innumerable throng of listeners and readers—only not without detriment to his own health, unfortunately. That, however, is not the main issue.

These fragments from *The Diary,* in their two sections—manlike and animal—represent a vividly expressed cadence of man and his imagination. Before its author got to flowers with fleshy, pouting lips " strewn with the germs of life," while he still preserved a certain semblance of humanity and had not yet fled the society of man, his imagination was active too, and it obeyed the same law as that obeyed by the imagination of those "artists" of the brush who brought their works to show to the Moscow bigwigs: the same absence of details and accessories; the same absence of a *face* on the subject; the same disregard of history; the same ignorance of Nature; there was neither the bustle of the city nor scenes of family life; neither the family's past nor its present *needs* and *hopes*, hopes of having children, for example. The stern Roman *"Matrimonium liberorum quaerendorum causa"* has died; so too the Biblical "Be fruitful and multiply, fill the earth and possess it," and the evangelical "What therefore God hath joined together let no man put asunder." Man has died and only his pants remain. Straightaway after this the degree of fall is even greater: in painting we saw this cadence in the portrayal of a seashell-woman who absorbed a sunbeam into her body; in belles-lettres—in the guise of a "mystic male" fluttering above womanlike flowers. In both cases the hideous has fallen to the absurd, and we feel no surprise and see nothing new when we read after *that* prose the following lines:

> The denuded moon rises
> In the azure moonlight;
> Sounds soar sleepily,
> Sounds snuggle up to me....

Or:

> Corpses illuminated by gas!
> Scarlet ribbon on the sinful bride!
> Oh, shall we go to the window and kiss!

And finally:

12

My soul is sick all day,
My soul is sick from parting,
My soul is struggling with silence,
My eyes encounter the shadow.

All these are nothing but "orchids" quivering on their little stalks, as if they were going to fly away. "Will they fly to me? No, my soul will fly to them and soar above them, the soul of a mystic male tormented by love."

Thus, Symbolism and Decadence are not a *separate new* school, which arose in France and spread throughout all of Europe: they represent the end and culmination of a certain other school whose links were very extensive and whose roots go back to the beginning of the modern age. Symbolism, easily deduced from Maupassant, can also be deduced from Zola, Flaubert, and Balzac, from *Ultra-realism* as the antithesis of the previous *Ultra-idealism* Romanticism and "renascent" Classicism). It is precisely this element of *ultra*—the result of *ultra* manifested in life itself, in its mores, ideas, proclivities, and aspirations— that has wormed into literature and remained there ever since, expressing itself, finally, in such a hideous phenomenon as Decadence and Symbolism. The *ultra* without its referent, exaggeration without the exaggerated object, preciosity of form conjoined with total disappearance of content, and "poetry" devoid of rhyme, meter, and sense—that is what constitutes Decadence.

III

The great self-limitation practiced by man for ten centuries yielded, between the fourteenth and seventeenth centuries, the whole flower of the so-called "Renaissance." The root, usually, does not resemble the fruit in appearance, but there is an undeniable connection between the root's strength and juiciness and the beauty and taste of the fruit. The Middle Ages, it seems, have nothing in common with the Renaissance and are opposite to it in every way; nonetheless, all the abundance and ebullience of human energies during the Renaissance were based not at all on the supposedly "renascent" classical world, nor on the imitated Plato and Virgil, nor on manuscripts torn from the basements of old monasteries, but precisely on those monasteries, on those stern Franciscians and cruel Dominicans, on Saints Bonaventure, Anselm of Canterbury, and Bernard of Clairvaux. The Middle Ages were a great repository of human energies: in the medieval man's asceticism, self-abnegation, and contempt for his own beauty, his own energies, and his own mind, these energies, this heart, and this mind were stored up until the right time. The Renaissance was the epoch of the discovery of this trove: the thin layer of soil covering it was suddenly thrown aside, and to the amazement of following centuries dazzling, incalculable treasures glittered there; yesterday's pauper and wretched beggar, who only knew how to stand on crossroads and bellow psalms in an inharmonious voice, suddenly started to bloom with poetry, strength, beauty, and intelligence. Whence came all this? From the ancient world, which had exhausted its vital powers? From moldy parchments? But did Plato really write his dialogues with the same keen enjoyment with which Marsilio Ficino annotated them? And did the Romans, when reading the Greeks, really experience the same emotions as Petrarch, when, for ignorance of Greek, he could only move his precious manuscripts from place to place, kiss them now and then, and gaze sadly at their incomprehensible text? All these manuscripts, in convenient and accurate editions, lie before us too: why don't they lead us to a "renascence" among *us*? Why didn't the Greeks bring about a "renascence" in Rome? And why didn't Greco-Roman literature produce anything similar to the Italian Renaissance in Gaul and Africa from the second to the fourth century? The secret of the Renaissance of the fourteenth-fifteenth centuries does not lie in ancient literature: this literature was only the spade that threw the soil off the treasures buried underneath; the secret lies in the treasures themselves; in the fact that between the fourth and fourteenth centuries, under the influence of the strict ascetic ideal of mortifying the flesh and restraining the impulses of his spirit, man only stored up his energies and expended nothing. During this great thousand-year silence his soul matured for *The Divine Comedy*; during this forced closing of eyes to the world—an interesting, albeit sinful world— Galileo was maturing, Copernicus, and the school of careful experimentation founded by Bacon; during the struggle with the Moors the talents of Velasquez and Murillo were forged; and in the prayers of the thousand years leading up to the sixteenth century the Madonna images of that century were drawn, images to which we are able to pray but which no one is able to imitate.

From the fourteenth to the nineteenth century we have merely been expending the incalculable treasures discovered then and using up the great supply of energies gathered up to that time. Hence, modern history is the antithesis of the Middle Ages; man no longer wants to keep silent about himself: he hastens to express to others every slightest feeling and every new thought he may have through the medium of colors or sounds and, without fail, by means of the printing press. One might say that just as man studiously effaced himself up to the fourteenth century, so he becomes garrulous once he crosses into that century and all the succeeding ones. Not only what is wise, not only what is noble, but also what is ridiculous, stupid, and hideous in himself he couches in poetry and prose, sets to music, and would very much like, but he is unable, to express in marble and to fix within architectural lines. It is remarkable that architecture—that kind of impersonal art, that form of creation in which the creator is merged with his epoch and people, in which he does not rise above them, nor set apart his own *I* on their background—declines, as soon as we enter modern history, and not once during this period does it rise to the sublime or the beautiful.

Architecture is too selfless a form of art, and furthermore, modern man is absolutely at a loss how, by what means, he might be able to feel selfless. He is becoming more and more unaccustomed to praying: prayer is the turning of the soul to God; his soul, however, turns only to itself. Everything that constrains and constricts him, that hinders the independent display of his own *I*— be this *I* base or noble, profound or shallow—becomes insufferable for him; in the sixteenth century he throws off the Church, saying "*I* am the Church"; in the eighteenth century he throws off the State, saying "*I* am the State"; he proclaims the rights of this *I* (revolution); he poeticizes the depths of this *I* ("Faust" and "Werther," Byron); he says that the whole world too is but the reflection of this *I* (the philosophy of German idealism)—until this *I*, extolled, bedecked, and protected by legislation, on the ruins of all the great unifying institutions: Church, State, and Family—defines itself, towards the end of the nineteenth century, in this unexpectedly brief, yet expressive wish:

Oh, cover your pale legs!

From the exclamation point closing the line and from the empty margins surrounding it we conclude that on this page a certain "subject" has fully expressed all of his inner content.

IV

The religion of this *I*, the poetry of this *I*, and the philosophy of the same *I* that from Poggio and Felelfo to Byron and Goethe produced a number of works astonishing for their profundity and brilliance have finally exhausted its content; and in the poetry of Decadence we see the rapid falling away of the empty shell of this *I*. We remarked previously about the exaggeration without the exaggerated object, and about the precious style without the subject of this preciosity, which characterize this poetry—this is so in regard to its form; in regard to its content Decadence is above all hopeless egoism. The world, as an object of love, of interest, even as the object of indignation or contempt, has disappeared from this "poetry"; the world has disappeared, not only as an object exciting some reaction in this vapid *I*, but also as a spectator and possible judge of this *I*; it is not even *present:*

These are oleanders on the ice,
This is the jacket of romances without words.

That is what has remained of the world in the uncertain, unloving, and incurious recollection of the ravaged and fallen *I*. One can scarcely find a proper noun in all this literature—the name of a city, or the designation of the locality and hour: before the empty *I* pass purely abstract visions, which do not catch onto any existing reality and do not contain anything of the real world, except isolated words, names of objects, and fragments of scenes that alternate

15

capriciously; among these scenes, objects, and words seized by an uncertain re-
collections from the world of reality and rushing on without purpose or sense
occur thoughts, lost and abandoned, as it were, thoughts without development
and even without any necessary connection:

> I see the phantoms of longings;
> A half-forgotten track leads
> *The dogs of secret desire*
> Into the depths of forgetful forests,
> Packs of lilac-colored fantasies race along,
> *And yellow arrows—reproaches—*
> Slay the deer of mendacious dreams.

The italicized lines·are thoughts interjected, as it were, into scenes of reality to which they have no relation; these very scenes, however, are not reality
but fragments of a recollection about it, a recollection that is not very firm,
little necessary in itself, and, it seems, little necessary to the person recollecting.
We observe in this torrent of incoherence a lack of regularity in the subject
himself; the *I* has fallen to pieces after struggling for three centuries against the
great objective institutions and dissolving them with its subjectivism and rejecting in them any law that was sacred and binding on itself.

There is no reason to think that Decadence—obviously an historical phenomenon of great inevitability and significance—has confined itself to poetry;
we should expect in the more or less distant future the Decadence of philosophy
and finally the Decadence of morality, politics, and forms of communal life.
To a certain extent Nietzsche can already be considered the Decadent of human
thought—at least to the extent that Maupassant, in certain "final touches" of
his art, can be considered the Decadent of human emotion. Like Maupassant,
Nietzsche ended in madness; and in Nietzsche, just as in Maupassant, the cult
of the *I* loses all restraining limits: the world, history, and the human being
with his toils and legitimate demands have disappeared equally from the works
of both; both were "mystic males" to a considerable degree, only one of them
preferred to "flutter" above "quivering orchids," whereas the other liked to
sit inside a cave or upon a mountaintop and proclaim a new religion to mankind in his capacity as the reborn "Zarathustra." The religion of the "super-
man," he explained. But all of them, including Maupassant, were already "su-
permen" in that they had absolutely no need of mankind and mankind had absolutely no need of them. On this new type of *nisus formativus* of human culture, so to speak, we should expect to see great oddities, great hideousness,
and perhaps great calamities and dangers.

A few more words on Decadence: we can genetically connect with very
delicate threads the senseless and hideous Symbolism of our day with such an
intellectually deep and resplendently beautiful creation as "Faust."

They both expressed and still do express the notion of "free humanity," only in one this notion lies at the source of its vibrant energy, while in the other it has reached the end and is depleted of energy. But the essence of "freedom" and "humanity" is equally the main and characteristic feature of both. What is more, the second part of "Faust," which proceeds from the same subjective spirit as the first part, but only when the creative energies of this spirit are exhausted, displays all the features of Symbolism and Decadence, but only in the structure of the whole, the parts of which are just as incoherent and fancifully joined together as the lines of Symbolist poems. In "Faust" we already find a few "enameled latania...." We mean to say that Symbolism and Decadence— the negative attitude to which is indisputable to everyone except the "participants"—are genetically connected with everything brilliant and sublime created by the "unbound personality" during this period of time, from the Renaissance up to the development of electrical engineering; contrariwise, the border which they cannot cross is laid down where man understood that he was always "bound." The great continent of history, the continent of real deeds, practical needs, and more than all that, of *received* religion and the *established* Church— that is whose shore this stinking monster can never crawl into, that is where we are fleeing to from it, that is where man can always save himself. Where the monastery wall rises *this* surge of the faithless waves of history—no matter how strong it may become and how far it may spread around—will stop and fall back.

Translated by Joel Stern[*]

NOTE

[1] It was related at the exhibition that the sovereign, Alexander III, who visited the exhibition, went to the artistic section first, but no sooner had he reached the door and glanced into the hall than he turned back, not wishing to see that "French art."

[*]Translated from *Religiia i kul'tura* (St. Petersburg, 1901).

17

konstantin balmont / ELEMENTARY WORDS ON SYMBOLIST POETRY [excerpts]

. . . Realists always appear as simple observers, Symbolists are always thinkers.

Realists are always, as though in the grip of the surf, captives of concrete life, behind which they see nothing—Symbolists, cut off from actual reality, see in it only their fantasies, they gaze upon life from a window. This is because every Symbolist, even the least of them, is older than every realist, even the greatest of them. The one is still in bondage to matter, the other has departed for the realm of the ideal.

. . . In the course of the nineteenth century we see the simultaneous existence of two diametrically opposed literary directions. Side by side with Dickens we see Edgar Allen Poe, side by side with Balzac and Flaubert is Baudelaire, side by side with Lev Tolstoi is Henrik Ibsen. It is impossible, however, not to recognize that the closer we approach the new century, the more insistent resound the voices of the poet-Symbolists, the more tangible becomes the demand for more refined methods of expression of feelings and thoughts that make up the distinctive feature of Symbolist poetry.

How can Symbolist poetry be defined more specifically? This is poetry in which organically, not willfully, two contents merge: a concealed abstractness and a revealed beauty,—they merge just as easily and naturally as in the summer morning the waters of a river are harmoniously united with the sunlight. However, in spite of the hidden sense of one or the other symbolic work, its immediate concrete content is always finished in itself, it possesses in Symbolist poetry an independent existence, rich in nuances.

Herein is concealed the moment which sharply defines symbolic poetry from allegorical poetry with which it is never mixed. In allegory, contrary to symbolism, the concrete sense manifests itself as completely subordinated, it plays an auxiliary role and usually combines with didactic purposes completely alien to symbolist poetry. In the one case we see a natural merging of two senses which is born spontaneously, in the other, a willful combining of them, called forth by some external conception. Allegory speaks in the monotone of the pastor or in the humorously instructive tone of the street singer (I understand this term in the medieval sense). Symbolics speak in a tender voice of the reed, suffused with allusions and mute nuances, or the profound voice of the sibyl which summons forth premonitions. . .

While the poet-realists examine the world naively, like simple observers, subordinating themselves to its material basis, the poet-symbolists, recreating the materialism with their complicated impressionability, rule over the world and penetrate into its mysterium. The consciousness of the poet-realists does not go further than the framework of earthly life, defined with exactness and wearying boredom by mile posts. The poet-symbolists never lose the mysterious thread of Ariadne connecting them with the universal labyrinth of Chaos, they are always enveloped by currents emanating from the realm of the beyond, and therefore, as though against their will, behind the words which they pronounce, the rumble of voices other than their own is apprehended, the speech of the elements is heard, excerpts from the choruses which resound in the holy of holies, in the Universe conceived of by us. The poet-realists frequently give us valuable treasures, but these treasures are of such a nature that having received them we are satisfied—and to a degree something has been concluded. The poet-symbolists present us in their works with a magic ring which gives us joy as something precious and at the same time summoning us to something more, we sense the proximity to us of the unknown, of the new and, gazing upon the talisman, we proceed somewhere farther, ever farther and farther.

And so, here are the basic features of the Symbolist poetry: it speaks in its own special language, and this language is rich in intonations; like music and painting it arouses a convoluted mood in the soul,—more than any other type of poetry it affects our susceptibility to sound and sight, forces the reader to traverse the return path of creativity: the poet, creating his symbolic work, proceeds from the abstract to the concrete, from the idea to the image,—whosoever becomes acquainted with the symbolist's works, proceeds from the picture to its soul, from the immediate images, beautiful in their independent existence, to their inwardly concealed and spiritual idealness which lends them a two-fold strength.

It is said that Symbolists are incomprehensible. In every tendency there are varying degrees, it is possible to reduce any characteristic to the absurd, in every boiling there is a froth. But it is impossible to gauge the depth of a river by looking at its foam. If we are to judge Symbolism according to those untalented people who create impotent parodies, we will conclude that this style of creativity is only a perversion of some healthy sense a perversion of something that is wholesome in its meaning. If we take the genuine talents, we shall see that Symbolism is a mighty power striving to divine the new combinations of thoughts, colors and sounds, and frequently divining them with an undeniable persuasiveness.

If you love immediate impressions, then enjoy in Symbolism the novelty and luxury of its pictures. If you love convoluted impressions, read between the lines,—the secret lines will reveal themselves and will speak with you in beauteous speech.

1900   *Translated by Samuel Cioran*

valery bryusov / **K. D. BALMONT,** *LET'S BE LIKE THE SUN.*
A BOOK OF SYMBOLS

Moscow: "Skorpion," 1903

Our days are exceptional—some of the most remarkable in history. One should be able to evaluate them. Unexpected and marvelous possibilities are being revealed to mankind. That which has for centuries seemed stagnant, dead fundamental matter is beginning to tremble with life in the depths of our souls. It is as though some kind of windows had slammed shut in our existence and some sort of obscure shutters had parted. Like stems of plants we involuntarily, unconsciously turn our faces toward the source of light. Soothsayers of the new are everywhere—in art, in science, in ethics. Mysteries that we have not known heretofore are revealed even in everyday life. Events to which we had been paying no heed now attract our full attention. Through their coarse thickness the radiance of another existence manifestly shines.

But there is no need to exaggerate the power of the movement attracting us. We are the crest of a risen wave, but it will break. It is still far to the sea, although from our height its salty scent is already evident. The caravan of mankind, traveling its course, has ascended to the top of a mountain and descries the goal of its travels. The youths, walking on ahead, are already shouting "Jerusalem! Jerusalem!" and kiss the earth, and weep with joy. But the elders sternly stop them. They know how the desert mirage brings distant vistas closer. They know that they will still have to descend the other side of the mountain, that they will have to pass through another plain, ford rivers, conquer new mountains, again lose their way and fall into despair.

Yes, the route is still long. That in which we now find promise will not soon come to pass. The flowers of mystical contemplation that were on the verge of reviving in us will yet again die and wither. More than once mankind will return in its intellectual designs to what is closest to it, to the earthly, and more than once glorify it as unique.

There have already been epochs like ours in the past. Quite recently, during the years of Romanticism, these same distances were visible which are now being revealed to us—true, from a lesser height and more obscurely. The seventeenth century was such an epoch of enlightenment. Our books, the creations of our art, are fated to experience years of oblivion in the graveyards of immeasurably expanded museums and libraries. It may be that they will have to wait whole centuries for their triumphant resurrection. Rare madmen, chance dreamers for whom life at that time will be stuffy and confining, will begin searching through these dusty covers, these semi-abandoned canvases and bronzes and, drinking in our words and songs, meeting echoes of their own dreams in the distant past, will say with amazement, "They already knew all this! They already dreamed of this!"

But while recognizing this inevitable, albeit temporary, loss of all our hopes, we must scrutinize the present all the more avidly. In it throb the first convulsions of what will unfold completely and perfectly centuries later. In today's man are signs of those cravings and slakings that will fill the souls of our future brothers like a wild whirlwind. We will apprehend these signs. In the man of tomorrow they may not exist. We can perceive and surmise that life, even though we cannot participate in it.

Tyutchev speaks precisely of this:

> Fortunate the man who has visited this world
> During its fateful moments.
> He has been summoned by the gods
> As a guest at their feast.
> He is a witness of their great spectacles;
> He has been admitted into their councils.
> While still a mortal, yet like a dweller of the skies,
> He has drunk immortality from their chalice.[2]

* * *

In few people does this tremor of futurity so clearly and powerfully manifest itself as in K. D. Balmont. Others recognize perhaps more clearly the entire mysterious meaning of contemporaneity, but rarely does anyone carry this contemporaneity within himself, in his personality, or experience it more fully than Balmont. Balmont is first of all a "new man"; there is a new soul in him, new passions, ideals, expectations—different from those of earlier generations. To a certain extent he is already living that "tenfold life" about which another contemporary poet has dreamed. And it is this *new* life that makes Balmont a poet of the *new* art. He did not arrive at it through a conscious choice. He did not reject the "old" art after rational criticism. He does not set himself the goal of realizing an ideal rationally discovered at an earlier time. In forging his verse, Balmont is concerned only about whether it is beautiful in his own mind, interesting in his own estimation, and if his poetry belongs all the same to the "new" art, it happened without his willing it. He simply relates what is in his own soul, but his soul is among those that have only recently begun to flower in our land. It was the same with Verlaine in his day. Hence all the power of Balmont's poetry, all the vitality of its transports, although in the very same quality lies its weakness and limitation.

> In everything I want to do all there is to do
> In order to thrill as long as I live.[3]

In these two lines A. Dobrolyubov expressed what is more inalienable in the new understanding of life. To live means to be in moments, to surrender to them.[4] Let them take the soul imperiously and draw it into their impetuous rush as a whirlpool seizes a small pebble. That which has transpired now is true. What existed before this is already non-existent. Perhaps there will be no future at all. People who harmonize their actions with stable conviction, with plans for their lives, with temperate conventionality, stand somehow outside of life, on the banks. To freely submit to the succession of all desires is the concept. To place the entire fullness of existence in every moment is the goal. To gain an extra glimpse of a star is worth falling into the abyss. One could sacrifice the love of an entire life to kiss just once the eyes of her who, among passers-by, has pleased you. Everything—even pain, even horror—is desirable so long as it has filled the soul with trembling.

"I am consumed to ashes by each moment, I live in each betrayal," confesses Balmont. "Everyone knows how momentary I am," he says in another passage. And in individual images he lets you see as though with your own eyes those moments which absorb the whole world.

> You and I were drunk on the fragrant cherry blooms.
> Suddenly the morning was forgotten.
> Suddenly we stepped into a dream.
> And the morning turned into a shoreless sea—
> Floating clouds, branches, shrubs and greenery.
> Flowers, grass, and grass and trees,
> Seas of flowers, colors, love and you and I.
> Face to face we bent together; hand in hand
> We were suddenly filled with the joy of lightly trembling grass.
> With blinding light the sun shown down
> And there was ecstasy, surprise and you and I.
> The brief hour lived in us,
> Eternity reigned in us,
> Morning waxed for us, for us, for us.
> Dual radiations, we were phantoms of spring—
> Dreams awakened by the fragrant bird-cherry tree.

But in order to yield to each moment one must love them all. Behind the exterior, the appearance of things, one must surmise their eternally beautiful essence. If one sees around oneself only what is accessible to the ordinary human vision, one cannot pray to everything. But from the most insignificant thing there is a passage to the most magnificent. Every event is a boundary between two infinities. Every object is created by myriad wills and is an indispensable link to the future fate of the universe. Every soul is a deity and every meeting with a person reveals a new world to us. Nothing is of small import: all phenomena are like a light fabric covering fathomless abysses. Only one who does not see them, who is blind, boldly walks near them, among them. One able to look into their depths knows the sacred horror before the abysses surrounding life.

22

Sleep, half-dead, withered flowers,
Like the beauties that knew no blooming;
Planted by the Creator beside well-traveled routes,
Crushed by a sightless, heavy wheel.
When everyone is celebrating the birth of spring,
When unrealizable dreams are coming into being,
When everyone can be delirious, and only you cannot—
Beside you spreads the cursed path.

And now, half-broken, you lie in the dust—
You, who could have brightly looked into the distant sky,
You who could have known happiness like everyone—
Lie in feminine, virginal, inviolate beauty.
Sleep now that you've looked upon the fearsome, dusty road;
Your equals may reign, but you must sleep forever—
Dressed by God for a festival of dream—
Innocent of the blooming of beauty, sleep.

The symbolism of this poem attains an all-embracing compass. It forcefully compels us to feel that, close beside us all, that "fearsome" path lies where every person may perish under a fateful, heavy, "sightless" wheel.

Nowhere does the mystical side of the world reveal itself so manifestly as in love. In the moment of passionate confession, in the moment of passionate embrace, one soul peers directly into another. The mysterious roots of love, its sexual beginning, go deep into the very core of the world, sink into the very heart of the universe, where the difference between I and not I, between thou and he disappears. Love is the absolute limit of our existence, and the beginning of a new existence, a bridge of golden stars over which a person crosses to that which is "not man," or even "not yet man"—to God or beast. Love allows, even only for a moment, a breaking away from the conditions of one's existence, an inspiration of air from another horizon, a fusion of all feelings, all thought, all life, the whole world, into one burst of passion.

"Wandering through countless cities, I am always charmed by love alone"; these are Balmont's words. "Like that Sevillian Don Juan" he passes in love from one soul to another in order to see new worlds and their mysteries. His poetry glorifies and celebrates love, all the rites of love, its entire rainbow. He says himself that, going along the path of love, he can attain "too much—everything!" And here love and voluptuousness are incorporated into the image of a poisonous flower—the arum:

Tropical flower, splendid crimson arum.
Your blossoms burn with ecstatically joyful flame.
Your leaves are threatening, they cannot be forgot—

Like lances, made deadly instruments by fate.
Flower-monster, evil-eyed and haughty,
With unkind fire and dual-hued sheath,
Outwardly gleaming with radiance of dawns,
Brightly violet and black inside.
Baneful flower, invincible arum,
I am a votary of your powerful charms.
I know what they lavishly promise me:
To breathe their flaming bane with amorous festivity.

Neither in love nor in other ways, however, is the thirst for the fullness of the moment ever completely assuaged, for by its very nature it is insatiable. It requires each moment to disintegrate into an infinite number of awarenesses, but in man everything is finite, everything has an end. For all the brightness of life, for all its madness, the feeling of hopelessness and fateful dissatisfaction must grip each soul. Only in ecstasies does the soul truly and entirely surrender itself, but it lacks the power to undergo such ecstasies with any kind of frequency. Some portion of consciousness usually remains on guard, spies in a detached way on the whole turmoil of life and destroys the integrity of the moment, splits it in half by its barely perceptible but relentless gaze. From this tormenting awareness envy invincibly arises toward everything that lives without the form of human life: clouds, wind, water, fire. In the elements there is none of our consciousness: they can completely surrender themselves to every moment, without remembering what has flashed by, without knowing what will follow. They do not have to exclaim bitterly, as we do, about every changing moment: "It's not right, not right!"

Songs to the elements are one of the favorite themes in Balmont's lyrics. "I am unfamiliar with what is human," he notes. He writes hymns to Fire, Sun, the planets. An entire section of his book is devoted to the "four voices of the elements." He calls the wind his "eternal brother," and the ocean the ancient "progenitor" of all human generations.

Ocean, my ancient forebear,
Keeper of a millenial dream,
Bright phantom, giver of life, watery avenger,
Horizon going far into the depths!
Mirror of utmost inceptions,
Seer of the first dawn,
Knower of more than we may know—
I am with you; I speak with the deathless!
You are a wholeness forged by no one.
For the heart the world of land is empty and dead,
But you breathe eternally in boundlessness
With myriad youthfully ravenous lips!

Gracefully solemn, quiet, stormy, tender,
You are like life and truth and deception.
Let me be a watery fleck of your sand,
A drop in the eternal... Eternity! Ocean!

Four fundamental currents in Balmont's art are the thirst for the completeness of every moment, the awareness of the abysses surrounding us, the feeling of mystery in passion and mergence with elemental life. They draw all of his impressions into their channels. Indeed, they determine his literary sympathies as well ("We like the poets who are like us"). In quest of the full life, of integral, impetuous characters, he turned to Calderon, to the Spanish drama of the seventeenth century. "The Awareness of Mysteries" makes him akin to the poet of horror, mad Edgar; his attitude toward love, passion and women draws him close to Baudelaire and today's "decadents"; and finally his penetration into the life of the elements allies him with Shelley and Indian pantheism. Adjunctive to the basic currents are secondary ones; these are rather tributaries with semi-independent lives of their own, yet essentially nourished by the same currents. Hence, in consequence of his belief in the possibility of a "full" life, and thus its opposite, he hates life that is lustreless and temperate. This leads him to stinging, barely lyrical satires (e.g., "In Houses"). Hymns to the elements, on the other hand, often resolve into quiet childrens' songs—gentle, meek, and beautiful songs about fields, spring, dawns and snowflakes. But the four voices remain fundamental in Balmont's entire being and in all his poetry. And they all somehow blend into the full-voiced exclamation of his mermaid, who has managed to swim up "from the deep sea floor" and look at the sun, although it burned her eyes:

I have seen the sun, she said:
Does it matter what the future holds?

* * * *

What "we now consider an idle dream"—all manner of presentiments, hypnosis, foretelling and sympathy, all that is now in us feebly and fortuitously—will someday constitute, of course, the real essence of man's psychological life. The present turtle's pace of thought, our causal cognition, will be replaced by an ardent intuition. The limits of consciousness will expand and submerge in that immensity which we now call the subconscious. But in that barely conceivable future these mysterious powers will attain their full flowering and make man in all aspects of life more discerning, more sensitive, more commanding. But now, having barely awakened from a sleep lasting centuries, they cannot replace for us the coarser but more conventional (for us) means of cognizing the world. It is easier for us to move ahead in thought at a crawl from situation to situation, like a worm, than to strive to fly like birds on unsteady wings. Thus a blind person who has just regained his sight still relies on his sense of touch (and rightly so!).

In Balmont the unconscious life predominates over the conscious. But, proud of his bright eye, this blind man who is recovering his sight depends too much on the power of his vision. He dares to venture upon the most forbidden roads, sometimes slipping pitifully and falling where many walk freely with a stick. Wherever there is power in consciousness and clarity of thought, Balmont is weaker than the weak. All of his efforts to achieve breadth of thought, to imbue his verses with broad crystallizations, to encompass centuries in a concise image, end in failure. His epic effort, the long poem "Artist-Devil," except for several beautifully formulated thoughts, and a few truly lyrical fragments, is completely composed of rhetorical commonplaces rising from that scream with which singers strive to conceal vocal insufficiencies. And in his lyrics Balmont can never survey his creations with the impartial view of a critic. He is either in them or hopelessly distant from them. Hence Balmont can never correct his verses. His corrections are distortions. If he fails with a certain verse he rushes on to the next, satisfied—in the interests of association—with any kind of approximate expression. This obscures the meaning of some of his verses and the obscurity is of the most undesirable kind: it is occasioned not by the ambiguity of the content but in the imprecision of the selected expressions. In such cases Balmont is satisfied even with empty, hackneyed phrases that say nothing. For all the subtlety of the general construction of his poems he reaches the limits of banality in individual verses.

* * * * *

In one of his poems Balmont speaks of himself:

I am the rarefaction of the leisurely Russian tongue;
Other poets before me merely forerun.[5]

If Balmont said this with his individual line in view, its musicality, he is right. Balmont's equals in the art of verse have not existed in Russian literature and do not exist. It might have seemed that in the melodies of Fet Russian verse reached maximal ethereality, but where others saw limits, Balmont discovered the boundless. Such an unattainable model of euphony as Lermontov's "On an Ocean of Air" pales completely before the best songs of Balmont. Yes! He was the first to discover "inflections" [uklony] in our poetry, to discover possibilities that no one had suspected, unprecedented "echoes" [perepevy] of vowels blending one into another like drops of moisture, like crystal ringing.

And yet Balmont's verse has retained the whole construction, the entire substructure of conventional Russian verse. One might have expected Balmont, in his impetuous craving for changing impressions, to surrender his verses to the will of the four winds, to shatter them, to cut them up into small glittering pieces, into a pearly dust.

26

But this simply has not happened. Balmont's verse is the verse of Push-kin and Fet—perfected, refined, but essentially the same. The movement that created *vers libre* in France and Germany, which sought new artistic devices, new forms in poetry, a new instrument for the expression of new feelings and ideas, left Balmont almost completely unaffected. Moreover, when Balmont attempts to adopt the features of the new verse from others, his success is poor. His "broken verse" *[preryvistye stroki]*, as he calls his meterless verse, loses all the charm of the Balmontian musicality without acquiring the freedom of the poetry of Verhaeren, Dehmel and d'Annunzio. Balmont is Balmont only when he writes in strict meters, correctly alternating strophes and rhymes, observing all the conventions developed during two centuries of our versification.

And new content far from always fits into the Procrustean bed of these correct meters. Madness, forced into an excessively rational stanza, loses its elementality. Lucid forms impart a vulgarizing clarity to all the vague, chaotic elements with which Balmont attempts to infuse them. It is as though he accepts Pushkin's "Until Apollo calls the poet..."[6] in reverse. The Pushkinian poet's soul awakened like an eagle responding to divine summons. In Balmont it loses something of its power and freedom. Balmont is free and unlimited in life; in art he is fettered by and entangled in thousands of rules and prejudices. He is a "genius of the elements" and a "bright god" (his own words) in life, but in poetry first a man of letters. His transports and passionate experiences pale in passage through his art. For the most part only fading embers remain of the fire and light; they are still fiery and bright for us, but they are already wholly different from the sun that they were.

Such are the limits of Balmont's poetry.

* * * * * *

Let's Be Like the Sun is Balmont's sixth collection of verse (if the one published in 1890 is not counted).[7] His last collection, *Burning Buildings,* was a momentary flare, a glittering display of fireworks. It was almost entirely composed in a few weeks. It had the poignancy and tension of rapture. *Let's Be Like the Sun* is the art of several years. Here Balmont's poetry has spread out to its full expanse and apparently reached its eternal banks. Here and there it has attempted to splash over these banks in a kind of turbid, weak wave, but without success; it is fated to remain under this horizon. But in his own world Balmont will of course reach ever newer depths, for which he now merely yearns.

Let's Be Like the Sun places Balmont immediately after Tyutchev and Fet in the ranks of our lyric poets. He is their nearest and only successor. Among contemporary poets Balmont is indisputably the most significant, both in the power of his elemental gift and his influence on literature. All of his contemporaries will have to be careful first of all not to fall into the orbit of his gravity, to guard their independence. To vie with Balmont in the realm of the pure lyric is a dangerous feat. There is little hope of surviving even as a cripple, like Jacob.

Translated by Rodney Patterson

NOTES

1. Bryusov's article originally appeared in *The World of Art*, No. 7-8 (1903), 29-36. He republished it in his book of literary essays, *Distant and Near* (M. 1912), 73-82. It is interesting as an illustration of Bryusov's struggle to be independent, impartial and correct in his critical judgments, to explain the mystical, voyant aspects of the new literary trends and to cast himself as a stern "elder" of a far-sighted band of "new men." Perhaps of greater import, however, is its role in inhibiting the rise of Balmont's prestige.

Bryusov noted in the second version that he had decided to detach the first section of the original because he could no longer agree with all the views it expressed. What he failed to note, however, was more interesting: he had radically revised his article, altering or removing some of the passages complimentary to Balmont and adding a number of passages tending to belittle or limit Balmont's contributions to Russian literature.

There is not space here to enumerate all of the changes Bryusov made, but the most significant should be pointed out. Deletions include: the entire first section and the opening lines of the second; the listing of the four basic currents of Balmont's art (section 2); most of the third section (some of the material was rephrased and relocated near the end of the revised version); the remarks about *Burning Buildings* in the last part; and the concluding paragraph placing Balmont next to Tyutchev and Fet. Significant additions include: the charge of didacticism (p. 75) and unevenness of technique (p. 79); remarks designed to cast Balmont as no longer a competitor of Fet, Lermontov and others but as their pupil (p. 78). Thus, Bryusov cannot resist inserting this ironic statement: " 'Other poets' are not only Balmont's 'forerunners' in the art of verse but are doubtless his teachers as well" (p. 79). Some of the criticisms of the first version were expanded, e.g., (relative to his use of traditional meters) "His ecstasy becomes too temperate, his intoxication too sober. One senses that much that was in the poet's soul did not get into his flowing stanzas but remained somewhere beyond their bounds" (p. 80); and (regarding his alleged inability to correct his failures), "All of his books are chaotic mixtures of poems that are exceptionally beautiful and very weak . . . . Balmont does not know how to seek and attain, through labor, the perfection of his creations" (p. 81).

The stormy friendship of Bryusov and Balmont began in September 1894. Balmont was already known as a translator of Shelley and as a promising poet *(Under Northern Sky)*. At the same time Bryusov was proud of his own pioneering role in the modernist movement, but had yet to acquire much more than a *succès de scandale*. Balmont's rise in literature was precipitous; the relative slowness with which Bryusov's reputation developed forced him to take a position definitely inferior to Balmont's. They passed nearly a decade like this, alternately dazed by their fraternal love and their temperamental differences. Bryusov wrote to P. Pertsov in June 1896:

Have you noticed that quite recently a school of poetry has begun to form among us? Oh, how pleasing this can be! Just think—the Fedorovs, the Lebedevs and the Tulubs will not be possible then. Then the worst versifiers will have a goal; they will be needed like cement, like a pedestal for a teacher, they will explain his allusions, they will be as translators between him and his age. I am prepared to rejoice with all my heart. Have you guessed what school I am talking about? About the school of Balmont . . . . the formation of such a school should have been expected for a long time; Balmont is the most accomplished of contemporary poets. [P. Pertsov, *Literaturnye vospominaniia 1890-1902 gg.* (M. 1933), 181.]

Bryusov's diary reveals much about their frequent misunderstandings, as in November 1894:

We parted not coldly, but gloomily. I wrote to Balmont today that I would be alone in the evening. He came. I think he wanted to take revenge. He, who so craved to see me . . . . In his letters he had said that he needed only me in Russia. Oh, of course the original is not the same as what one dreamed of! And much of what Balmont is seeking I will never accept. I also changed during this year [1897], but I did not change as he would have liked, perhaps in a way that is incomprehensible to him. He wanted revenge; he maliciously ridiculed all my words.

We spoke of Christ. Balmont called him a lackey, a philosopher for beggars. But is a conversation really carried on in words? There are conversations of souls. And much was said. I felt like weeping. When we parted Balmont half begged my pardon. 'Don't be angry'. [V. Briusov, *Dnevniki 1891-1910* (M. 1927), 30-31.]

Bryusov's diary also reveals his intense struggle to be his own man (December 1894):

Something in our friendship has broken—something that will never again be reestablished. I know myself that I have departed from his ideal of a poet. He would like me to remain 'beautifully dead and sad,' but I . . . have come alive. I live . . . [Briusov, *Dnevniki,* 31.]

That independence was difficult to maintain, however, as Balmont's reputation rose to ever more flattering heights. The critic Volynsky, writing in 1902, asserted:

With few reservations, Balmont enjoys universal recognition; despite the unpopularity of decadent poetry in Russia, the public snatches up and repeats the tender, light sounds of his poetic flute. [Quoted in Ilya Ehrenburg, *People and Life 1891-1921* (New York, 1962), 105.]

In 1903 the two poets joined in what Bryusov viewed as "the battle of Moscow," i.e., the engagement of the "decadents" against the conservatives. Bryusov insisted on viewing himself and Balmont at this time as "venerable," largely because younger modernists such as Bely and Voloshin deferred to them.

In 1903 Balmont's star seemed destined never to wane (he published two major collections *(Let's Be Like the Sun* and *Love Alone),* and although Bryusov had by this time improved to the point of equality, Balmont's productivity, energy and charisma were so overwhelming that the efforts of other first-rate poets seemed dim by comparison. Getting out of Balmont's shadow must have seemed increasingly imperative to the proud Bryusov, who in March 1903 read his "Keys to the Mysteries," providing the modernists with a manifesto and, by implication, the promise of leadership. He published his fine collection of poems *Urbi et Orbi* the same year.

The time was ripe, therefore, for a coup. Whether Bryusov planned it or it was the result of his honest convictions or subconscious desire for vengeance, Bryusov's review of *Let's Be Like the Sun,* ostensibly lauding the book to the point of excess, in reality planted the seeds of Balmont's literary demise—particularly because of Bryusov's artibrary contention that Balmont's poetic waters would expand no more. Less independent writers, relying perhaps too much on Bryusov's discernment and taste, were inclined to view Balmont's subsequent books as substantiating Bryusov's dictum, with the result that Balmont's reputation among critics (if not immediately with the general public) steadily declined. Balmont's own choice of titles for his subsequent books *(Love Alone* and *Liturgy of Beauty)* may have lent weight to Bryusov's assertions.

By 1912 the poet's reputation was at low ebb, yet there was promise of a kind of revival of esteem; his twenty-five year literary jubilee was celebrated at the University of Petrograd by the Neophilological Society. Balmont received high praise from speakers such as Vyacheslav Ivanov, who said:

The triumphal palm and the Delphian laurel truly belong to Balmont, because he is a poet and only a poet—always and in everything—and every breath of his life is poetry, every sound of his pipe is the breath of life; because of his verse, melodious and 'echoing,' full of bliss and the caress of languishing inner harmonies and echoes, light as the melodic rustle of a reed; because, finally, his mad, wandering muse has found the bewitching words of an ecstasy of sunny, stormy intoxication [and these words] have

29

made our first steps across the threshold of the new century brisk, and like a ray of the May sun, have turned our native poetry into a vernal garden, into a garden [vertograd] green. [Viacheslav Ivanov, "O lirizme Bal'monta," **Apollon**, No. 3-4 (1912), 42.]

Bryusov, however, decided to publish his revised review of *Let's Be Like the Sun* that same year. How effective it was in inhibiting Balmont's recovery among critics remains to be established, but there seem to be reasonable grounds to hypothesize a connection between the article and the fact that Balmont's later works were not given serious critical attention. If Bryusov was the most effective voice in shouting Balmont down it was due in part to the insistence with which he attacked: he wrote a number of negative reviews of Balmont's works, and he was constantly snipping away at Balmont's laurels in such asides as this (in a review of Bely's *Urna*): "Andrei Bely need not fear that the source of his inspiration will dry up, as it has, for example, for K. Balmont." By 1913 the two poets were feuding openly on the pages of the newspaper *Morning of Russia* over the propriety of correcting one's published verse. Bryusov contended that a poet should continue rewriting his works as long as improvement seemed possible. Balmont, remaining true to the theory of "moments" which Bryusov himself had articulated earlier, claimed that a poem is a unique statement that can be made only once and if altered becomes false. Each new "moment," he said, required a new poem. It was a battle between Bryusov's "trusty ox" and Balmont's "summer lightning."

Bryusov still felt at least occasional affection for Balmont even as he sought equality with him in literary histories, as witness the statement he wrote for S. A. Vengerov's *Russian Literature of the Twentieth Century* (1914):

[Balmont] was then full of *joi de vivre* and the most diverse literary projects. His ecstatic love for poetry, his refined feeling for the beauty of verse, his entire unique personality made an exceptional impression on me. Much, very much became intelligible for me and was revealed to me only through Balmont. He taught me to understand other poets, taught me really to love life. I mean that he revealed in my soul what was slumbering there, and without his influence it would have slumbered longer.

The evenings and nights I spent with Balmont, when we endlessly read one another our verses and read the verses of our favorite poets to one another—he reading Shelley and Edgar Poe to me, and I reading Verlaine, Tyutchev (whom at that time he did not know) and Karolina Pavlova to him—those evenings and nights, when we talked *de omni re scribi,* will remain forever among the most significant events of my life. Before meeting Balmont I was one person, but I became another after meeting him. Not without pride I might add, incidentally, that I exercised my influence on Balmont. [V. Briusov, "Avtobiografiia," reprinted in **Sovetskie pisateli: avtobiografii v 2 tt.** (M. 1959), I, 190-92.]

In any case the friendship between Balmont and Bryusov seems to have passed the point of resuscitation in 1920. As he was leaving Russia for the last time he shouted to a friend, "Don't get friendly with Bryusov!" and, to Marina Tsvetaeva, "And you, Marina, tell Valery Bryusov that I do *not* send my regards!" [M. Tsvetaeva, *Proza* (New York, 1953), 263 and Andrei Sedykh, *Dalekie, blizkie,* 2nd ed. (New York, 1962), 72.] Tsvetaeva (in *Proza,* 255) remarked with characteristic acumen: "Balmont and Bryusov. You could write a whole book about this. A book has already been written: *Mozart and Salieri."*

2. Bryusov quotes the last part of Tyutchev's "Cicero."

3. Bryusov quotes the last lines of Alexander Dobrolyubov's poem "Na vecherinku uedinennuiu..." in A. Dobroliubov, *Sobranie stikhov* (M. 1900), 48.

4. The passion for a total submission and sensitivity to "the moment" became a commonplace in Russian and Western European Symbolism. Bryusov discussed it in his *O iskusstve* (1899), where he pointed out that the goal of art should be the preservation and communication of the momentary and the transient, that the artist's task was to reveal his soul and all of his moods, for they are never repeated, always unique.

5. Balmont was often accused of immodesty, particularly because of such statements as this. Purely esthetic considerations aside, he was in certain respects justified in making such assertions, for his predecessor in Decadence, D. S. Merezhkovsky, had admitted:

> ...Our speech is daring;
> But fated to die
> Are premature precursors
> Of a premature spring... ("Children of the Night"
> ["Deti nochi"])

6. Opening lines of Pushkin's poem "The Poet" (1827).

7. Bryusov refers to Balmont's privately published collection, *Sbornik stikhotvorenii* (Yaroslavl, 1890). Balmont was ashamed of it as an immature attempt at poetry, which may explain why Bryusov mentions it.

vyacheslav ivanov / THOUGHTS ON SYMBOLISM*

> I met a shepherd mid deserted mountains
> Who trumpeted upon an Alpine horn.
> His song was pleasing; but his sonorous horn
> Was only used to rouse a hidden echo in the mountains.
> Each time the shepherd waited for its coming,
> Having rung out his own brief melody,
> Such harmony then came amid the gorges,
> Such indescribable sweetness, that it seemed
> An unseen chorus of spirits,
> On instruments not of this world,
> Was translating the language of earth
> Into the language of heaven.
> And I thought: "O genius! like this horn
> You sing earth's song to rouse in hearts
> Another song. Blessed is he who hears!"
> From beyond the mountains a voice responded:
> "Nature is a symbol like this horn,
> It sounds for the echo—the echo is god!
> Blessed is he who hears both song and echo!"

If, as a poet, I know how to paint with the word (poetry is similar to painting—"*Ut pictura poesis*"—classical poetics stated in the imitation of Simonides according to Horace), to paint so that the imagination of the listener produces what I depict with the clear visual quality of what is seen, and things which I name present themselves to his soul prominent in their tangibility and graphic in their picturesqueness, darkened or illuminated, moving or motionless, according to the nature of their perceived manifestation;

if, as a poet, I know how to sing with a magical power (for "it is not sufficient that verses be beautiful: let them also be melodious and willfully draw the soul of the listener wherever they so desire," —*non satis est pulchra esse poemata, dulcia sunto et quocumque volent animum auditoris agunto*"— as classical poetry stated in the words of Horace, concerning this tender seductiveness), if I know how to sing so sweetly and so powerfully that the

---

*Ivanov's article first appeared in *Trudy i dni,* 1 (1912), 3-10. In a later version which appeared in his collected essays, *Borozdy i mezhi* (M. 1916), Ivanov expanded the article, particularly with several pages dealing with the refutation of utilitarian art. This translation is drawn from both sources.

soul, entranced by the sounds, follows submissively after my pipes, longs with my desires, grieves with my grief, is enflamed with my ecstasy, and the listener replies with a harmonious beating of his heart to all the tremblings of the musical wave bearing the melodious poem;

if, as a poet and wiseman, I possess the knowledge of things, and gladdening the heart of the listener, I edify his mind and educate his will;

but, if, crowned with the triple crown of melodious power, I, as a poet, do not know how, through all this threefold enchantment, to force the very soul of the listener to sing together with me in another voice than mine, not in unison with its psychological superficiality, but in the counterpoint of its hidden depth—to sing about that which is deeper than the depths revealed by me, and higher than the heights unclouded by me—if my listener is only a mirror, only an echo, only one who receives, only one who absorbs—if the ray of my word does not betroth my silence to his silence through the rainbow of a mysterious covenant:

then I am not a Symbolist poet.

II.

If art is in fact one of the mightiest forces for human union, one could say of Symbolist art that the principle of its activity is above all union, union in the most direct and most profound sense of this word. In truth, not only does it unite, it also combines. The two are combined by the third and highest. The symbol, this third, resembles a rainbow that has burst into flames between the ray of the word and the moisture of the soul which reflected the ray... And in every work of genuinely symbolic art is the beginning of Jacob's ladder.

Symbolism combines states of consciousness in such a way that they give birth "in beauty." The purpose of love, according to Plato, is the "birth in beauty." Plato's depiction of the paths of love is a definition of Symbolism. From enamorment of the beautiful body, the soul, growing forth, aspires to the love of God. When the esthetic is experienced erotically, artistic creation becomes symbol. The enjoyment of beauty is similar to the enamorment of beautiful flesh, and proves to be the initial step in erotic elevation. The meaning of artistic creation as that which has been experienced is itself inexhaustible. The symbol is the creative principle of love. Eros the leader. Between the two lives—that one incarnated in creation and that one creatively joined to it (creatively because Symbolism is the art which transforms whoever accepts it into a co-participant in creation)—is achieved what is spoken of in the ancient naive profundity of the Italian ballad where two lovers arrange a rendezvous on the condition that a third person will also appear together with them at the appointed hour—the god of love himself:

Pur che il terzo sia presente,
E quel terzo sia L'Amor.

III.

"L'Amor/ che muove il Sole/ e l'altre stelle"—"The love that moves the Sun and other Stars..." In this concluding verse of Dante's *Paradiso* images are composed into myth and music gains wisdom.

Let us examine the musical structure of this melodic line of verse. In it there are three rhythmic rests produced by the caesuras and underlining the words: *Amor, Sole, Stelle*—for on them rests the *ictus*. The radiant images of the god of Love, the Sun and the Stars seem blinding as a consequence of this word arrangement. They are separated by depressions in the rhythm, the obscure and undefined *"muove"* (moves) and *"altre"* (others). In the intervals between the radiant outlines of those three ideas is the gaping night. Music is embodied in a visual manifestation: the Apollonian vision emerges above the gloom of the Dionysian frenzy: indivisible and yet divided is the Pythian dyad. Thus, the starry firmament is imprinted, boundlessly and overwhelmingly, in the soul. But the soul, as the beholder of the mysteries, is not abandoned without some instructive direction clarifying that which is beheld by consciousness. Some hierophant standing over it intones: "Wisdom! Thou seest the movement of the radiant and heavenly vault, thou hearest its harmony: know then that it is Love. Love moves the Sun and other Stars." This sacred word of the hierophant *(ieros logos)* is the word as logos. Thus Dante is crowned by that triune wreath of melodious power. But this is not yet all that he achieves. The shaken soul not only accepts, not only echoes the omniscient word: it discovers within itself and out of the mysterious depths painlessly gives birth to its consummating inner word. The mighty magnet has magnetized it: it too becomes a magnet. Within itself is revealed the universe. What it espies in the heights above is unravelled in it here below. And within it is Love; for after all it already loves. *"Amor"*...at this sound which affirms the magnetism of the living universe its molecules arrange themselves magnetically. And within it are the sun and the stars and the harmonious tumult of the spheres moved by the might of the divine Mover. It sings in harmony with the cosmos that self-same melody of love that it sang in the soul of the poet when he prophesied his cosmic words—Beatrice's melody. The line of verse under discussion (which is examined not merely as the object of pure esthetics, but in realtion to the subject, as the perpetrator of the soul's emotion and inner experience) proves to be not simply filled with an external musical sweetness and an inner musical energy, but is polyphonic as well, the consequence of the consummating musical vibrations summoned forth by it and the awakening of overtones clearly perceived by us. This is why it is not only an artistically perfect verse, but a symbolic verse as well. This is why it is divinely poetic. Being composed, moreover, of symbolic elements insofar as its separate words are pronounced so powerfully in the given connection and the given combinations that they appear as symbols in themselves, it represents in itself a synthetic pronouncement in which for the   subjective symbol (Love) the poet's myth-creating untuition finds the effective word (moves the Sun and the

Stars). And, thus, before us is the myth-creating climax of Symbolism. For the myth is the synthetic pronouncement where the predicative verb is joined to the subjective symbol. The sacred word, *ieros logos,* is transformed into the word as *mythos.*

If we had dared to give an evaluation of the afore-described effect of the concluding words of the *Divine Comedy* from the point of view of the hierarchy of values of a religio-metaphysical order, we would have had to recognize this effect as being theurgic. And with this example we might have tested the already frequently pronounced identification of a genuine and exalted Symbolism (in the above-designated category of examination, by no means, incidentally, unnecessary for the aesthetics of a Symbolist art)—with theurgy.

IV.

And thus I am not a Symbolist if I do not arouse in the heart of the listener with intangible nuance or influence those incommunicable sensations which resemble at times some primeval remembrance (and "for a long time on earth the soul languished, filled with a wondrous desire," "and the monotonous songs of earth could not replace for it the heavenly sounds"), at times a distant, vague premonition, at times a trembling at someone's familiar and long-desired approach—whereby this remembrance and this premonition or presence we experience as the incomprehensible expansion of our individual personality and empirically restricted self-awareness.

I am not a Symbolist if my words do not summon forth in the listener feelings of the connection between that which is his "ego" and that which he calls his "non-ego," —the connection of things which are empirically separated; if my words do not convince him immediately of the existence of a hidden life where his mind had not suspected life; if my words do not move in him the energy of love towards that which he was previously unable to love because his love did not know of the many abodes it possessed.

I am not a Symbolist if my words are not equal to themselves, if they are not the echo of other sounds about which you know nothing, as though of the Spirit, whence they come and wither they depart—and if they do not arouse this in the labyrinths of souls.

V.

I am not a Symbolist, then, for my listener. For Symbolism designates a relationship, and the Symbolist work in itself, as an object removed from the subject, cannot exist.

Abstract aesthetic theory and formal poetics examine an artistic work for itself; in this regard they have no knowledge of Symbolism. About Symbolism one can speak only by studying the work in its relationship to the perceiving subject and to the creating subject as to undivided personalities. Hence the following conclusions: (1) Symbolism lies outside all aesthetic categories; (2) Every artistic work is subordinated to appraisal from the point of

Symbolism; (3) Symbolism is connected with the wholeness of both the individual as the author himself, as well as the one who experiences the artistic revelation.

Obviously the Symbolist-artisan is inconceivable; just as inconceivable is the Symbolist-esthete. Symbolism deals with man. Thus it resurrects the word "poet" in the old meaning—of the poet as a person *(poetae nascuntur)*—in contrast to the colloquial use of the word in our time which strives to lower the value of this elevated name to the meaning of "a recognized artist—versifier talented and refined in his technical area."

VI.

Is the symbolic element required in the organic composition of contemporary creativity? Must a work of art by symbolically effective in order that we consider it complete?

The demand of symbolic effectiveness is just as non-requisite as the demands of *"ut pictura"* or *"dulcia sunto..."* What formal characteristic is at all unconditional in order that a work be considered artistic? Since this characteristic has not been named even in our day, there is no formal esthetic even in our time.

To make up for it there are schools. And the one is distinguished from the other by those particular seemingly superrequisite demands which it voluntarily imposes upon itself, as the rules and vows of its artistic order. And thus the Symbolist school demands of itself more than the others.

It is clear that those very same demands can be realized unconsciously outside of all rules and vows. Each work of art can be tested from the point of view of Symbolism.

Since Symbolism designates the relationship of the artistic object to the two-fold subject, creating and receiving, then upon our reception essentially depends whether the given work appears to be symbolic for us or not. We can, for instance, accept in a symbolic sense the words of Lermontov: "From beneath the mysterious, cold demi-mask I heard your voice..." Although in all probability for the author of these verses the foregoing words were equivalent to themselves in their logical extent and content and he had in mind simply an encounter at a masquerade.

On the other hand, examining the relationship of the work to the integral personality of its creator we can, independently of the actual reception itself, reconstruct the symbolic character of the work. Of this sort we find in any case Lermontov's confession: "You will not meet the answer/Amid the noise of this world./ Out of flame and flight/ Is the word born."

Manifest is the effort of the poet to express in the external word the inner word and his despairing of the accessibility of this latter word to the reception of the listeners which nonetheless is necessary in order that the flaming word, the radiant word not be enveloped by darkness.

Symbolism is magnetism. The magnet attracts only iron. The normal state of molecules of iron is non-magnetic. And that which is attracted by the magnet becomes magnetized...

And thus we Symbolists do not exist if there are no Symbolist-listeners. For Symbolism is not merely the creative act alone, but the creative reciprocal action, not merely the artistic objectivisation of the creative subject, but also the creative subjectivisation of the artistic object.

"Has Symbolism perished?"—reply others. Better were it for them to know whether Symbolism has perished for them. But we who have perished, bear witness, whispering in the ears of those celebrating at our funeral that there is no death.

VII.

But if Symbolism has not died, then how it has grown! It is not the might of its bannermen that has waxed strong and grown—I wish to say,— but the sacred branch of the laurel in their hands, the gift of the Muses of Helikon that bade Hesiod to prophesy only the truth—their living banner.

Not long ago many took Symbolism as the level of poetic depictiveness, related to Impressionism, formally capable of being carried over into the category of stylistics concerning tropes and figures. After the definition of the metaphor (it seems to me that I am reading some entirely modish textbook on the theory of philology that is quite in the process of being realized and yet not realized)—under the paragraph concerning the metaphor I envisage an example for grammar school pupils: "If the metaphor consists not of a single part of speech but is developed into an entire poem, then it is acceptable to call such a poem symbolic."

We have diverged significantly from the Symbolism of the poetic rebuses, of literary device (again merely device!) that consisted in art of summoning forth a series of conceptions capable of arousing associations, the coincidence of which forces one to guess at and, with special power, to perceive the subject or experience, purposely obscured, not as being expressed in their direct meaning, but having to be deciphered. This fashion, beloved in the period after Baudelaire by the French Symbolists (with whom we have neither an historical nor an ideological reason for joining forces) does not belong in the circle of Symbolism as outlined by us. Not only because this is merely device; the reason lies deeper. The goal of the poet becomes in this case—to afford the lyrical idea an illusion of greater compass, in order, little by little, to encompass the greater extent, to materialize and condense its content. We are becoming disillusioned concerning *"dentelle"* and *"jeu supreme"* and so one,— but Mallarme wants only that our thought, having described wide circles, alight on a single point designated by him. For us Symbolism is, on the contrary, energy, liberating itself out of the bounds of the present, lending the soul movement like a revolving spiral.

We wish, in opposition to those who call themselves "Symbolists," to be true to the purpose of an art that is modest in its presentation, yet is mighty in its creation, and not vice versa. For such is the humility of an art that loves modesty. It is more characteristic for genuine Symbolism to depict the earthly than the heavenly: the power of the sound is not important to it, but rather the might of the echo. *A realibus ad realiora. Per realia ad realiora.* Genuine Symbolism does not tear itself away from the earth; it desires to combine roots and stars and spring forth as the starry tower out of the native roots at hand. It does not replace things, and speaking of the sea, means the earthly sea, and by snowy heights ("And what age gleams whitely there, on the snowy heights but the dawn, the today the light of fresh roses is upon them,"—Tyutchev), is understood the peaks of earthly mountains. As art it strives towards one thing: the elasticity of the image, its capacity for inner life and vastness in the soul whither it falls like a seed which must give rise to the seed-pod. Symbolism in this sense is the affirmation of the vast energy of the word and of art. This vast energy does not avoid intersection with spheres that are heteronomous to art, for example with religious systems. Symbolism, as we expound it, does not fear a Babylonian Captivity in any of these spheres; it alone realizes the truly genuine freedom of art; it alone believes in its genuine might.

Those who have called themselves Symbolists, but did not know (as at one time Goethe, the distant father of our Symbolism, knew) that Symbolism speaks of the universal and the collective—they led us by the path of symbols through the radiant valleys in order to return to our prison, to the cramped cell of the insignificant "ego." Illusionists, they did not effect a return to that divine and broad expanse and knew only the broad expanse of fantasy and the enchantment of slumberous daydream out of which we awoke to find ourselves in a prison. Genuine Symbolism poses a completely different task for itself: the liberation of the soul *(katharsis)* as a development of inner experience...

From the time of Goethe, the striving for the symbolic basis of art was definitely noted in the history of the artistic consciousness. With particular intensity and distinctness this striving was manifested in modern Russian philology. I shall restrict myself to the mention of Tyutchev in the sphere of verse, of Dostoevsky in the area of prose. I speak of their victories when I speak of the triumph of Symbolism and not of my contemporaries. I do not defend either our school, or our practices and canons, but I believe that in praising Symbolism I proclaim the dogma of the orthodoxy of art. And by expressing myself in this manner I hope that I shall not be accused of disrespect for that source from which I draw my comparison; for art is in truth a sacred thing and collectivity *[sobornost']*.

The protests directed against dogma will consequently be called heresy. There are various forms of esthetic heresy: alive until our day for example—however wondrous such longevity may be—is the heresy of social utilitarianism which found its final champion in Russia I believe in the person of D. S.

Merezhkovsky. But he is too much a self-deluding person for one to easily believe in the wholesome sincerity of his demagogic outbursts on the similarity of Tyutchevism and Oblomovism and other similar comparisons and considerations. It is not the content of this preaching that is interesting, but rather its psychology; how is the phenomenon itself of Merezhkovsky, the Symbolist, seeking to awaken suspicions against Symbolism psychologically possible? The answer to this question adds a characteristic feature to the portrait of Symbolism in general—the feature of a positive knowledge in spite of all the lifeless monstrosity of its manifestation in the given individual instance. Characteristic of Symbolism is the desire to go beyond its actual boundaries. The form and likeness of higher realities, imprinted on the symbol, make up its living soul and moving energy; the symbol is not a dead copy or idol of this reality but semi-inspired bearer and participant. However, it is only half-inspired and would be completely so; it seeks to be united completely with the reality which is itself expressed by it. The symbol is the word which is in the process of becoming flesh, but is incapable of becoming it; if it did, it would then no longer be a symbol but theurgic reality itself. Thus, this *eros* of Symbolism for effectiveness is holy, but the cause for which Symbolism hungers is not mortal and human, it is immortal and divine. Merezhkovsky, however, seeks to pour the wine of his religious pathos, which he has newly pressed out, into the antique skins of the ancient irreligious radicalism of the times of Belinsky and the 1860s.

Another and more widespread esthetic heresy is the thoughtlessness of "art for art's sake." This opinion on the ultimate separation of art from the roots of life and its profound heart presents itself in an age of decline, in an age of superficial estheticism, and is founded essentially on misunderstanding. I shall express my relation to this heresy briefly.

The single task, the single object of all art is Man. Not man's benefit, but his mystery. In other words—man taken in the vertical, in his free growth into the depths and heights. The name of Man written with a capital letter defines in itself the content of all art; it has no other content. This is why religion always finds its place in great and genuine art; for God is in the verticalness of Man. The supine benefit of everyday life has no place in it, but only in the horizontalness of man, and the physical longing for utilitarianism immediately curtails all artistic activity. The more intently we peer into the nature of heresies, the more obvious the truth of true esthetic will become.

Translated by Samuel Cioran

zinaida gippius / PEREDONOV'S LITTLE TEAR
(What Sologub Doesn't Know)

Once a long time ago, while discussing the subject of rhyme, we discovered that the most profound Russian words are "solitary"—unrhymable. *Pravda* (truth) is solitary, *istina* (truth) is solitary.

There and then Bryusov attempted to write a poem with a rhyme for *istina* and produced these lines:

> Неколебимой истине
> Не верю я давно,
> И все моря, все пристани
> Люблю, люблю равно... и т. д.

The poem is beautiful and remarkable in that nowhere else has Bryusov expressed himself with such precision, vividness and truth. Nonetheless, the rhyme for *istina* turned out to be quite inexact.

I had better luck. True, my poem was written partly in jest and not for publication. I had forgotten it long ago, and I recall excerpts from it now not for the sake of rhyme (albeit for the sake of truth), but because I want to speak about Sologub, to whom the poem was dedicated:

> "...воду извлек,
> Воду живую он из стены,
> Но не увидел, мудрец и пророк,
> Собственной истины..."

Perhaps—and this may even be a good thing—Sologub himself fails to understand his own hero Peredonov *(The Petty Demon)* and to relate to him as he should. Here I am not concerned with whether this is good or bad. I am only establishing the fact that both the author and the public, which was enthusiastic about *The Petty Demon*, understood and interpreted Peredonov in exactly the same way—and further, that such an interpretation was simple, understandable and natural. In the foreword to the recently-released second edition of the novel the author seems to be arguing with his readers about Peredonov; but the essence of the argument is the question of who is depicted in the figure of Peredonov: Fyodor Sologub, or his contemporaries. The readers, apparently, assumed that the author, in a penitent spirit, had presented himself in the figure of his hero; the author clarifies this matter: "No, my dear contemporaries, it is about *you* that I have written my novel of the petty demon and his sinister "nedotikomka," of Ardalion and Varvara Peredonov... About you."

Here the offended reader might catch Sologub: "How can you write about us and not about yourself, if you yourself have many times declared that there is no such thing as 'we,' but only 'I'—that is, you? This means that Peredonov is your own 'I' too, and it is about this 'I' of yours, about yourself, that you have written... Please, don't deny it..."

But I am not an offended reader and have no intention of engaging in such semantic hounding of Sologub. No matter how we settle the argument of who is depicted in the figure of Peredonov, the central issue remains unchanged. For this argument is peripheral. *The Petty Demon* remains a "satire," a venomous tangle of snakes; it is a magic mirror *which exposes* defects...whether of all people or almost all matters little. What is important is that it *exposes*. Incidentally, the author himself mentions a mirror in his foreword.

And indeed *The Petty Demon* was received in precisely this way—as an artful exposure of hidden Peredonovisms. The author himself acknowledges that this is how he regards his Peredonov: "Look, folks, look at yourselves in this faithful mirror; shudder, be repelled, hate Peredonov and...please change yourselves if you can." True, the author is not moralizing, but that doesn't prevent anyone from turning over a new leaf.

It should be said that in no way do I deny this primary accusatory and repelling aspect of the novel or the mirroring quality of Peredonov. The novel supports this interpretation and may be understood in this sense. It is difficult, very difficult to pass beyond the thrice-locked doors, deep into that region where even the father of Peredonov and the *nedotikomka* has not penetrated. But in the final analysis it is impossible not to go there.

I remember my first meeting with Peredonov many years ago. I remember the stack of blue student notebooks from Polyakov's store, covered with Sologub's high, clear script. There were a good many of them, but it was impossible to stop before reading through all of them. At that time the novel still contained a number of coarse spots, later omitted by the author; but Peredonov stood as he stands today: in his full stature. And—one must be truthful—my first impression was identical with that received by almost everyone who reads the novel today. I was enchanted by Ludmila and the symphony of spirits; I was horrified by the revolting truth, the living filth of Peredonov. What could be more hateful than a vulgar fool going out of his mind? Yes, yes, here is an object truly worthy of our hatred, and if, in each of us, there sits this indecent fool who will certainly go mad, then we have all the more reason to hate him. I was delighted by the author's disinterested art, excited by a sordid hatred towards the living Peredonov. And I experienced then the strong conviction that Peredonov exists, not only somewhere in ourselves, partially, but that he is alive and actual—complete, real. If he does not exist today—he will exist tomorrow, he existed yesterday. In a word, he *can* exist.

The years passed. Peredonov "appeared" in literature several times— *The Petty Demon* was first printed in a magazine, then in separate editions. But since the time of the blue notebooks I felt no need to re-read the novel. I thought I knew Peredonov as many know him today; oh, of course, he is the most absolute, most revolting "image of evil." How could one not hate him?

Finally, I open the book. The author's brilliant foreword prepares me for the familiar feelings. I wait for them—and I read.

Here he is, the dirty and dull Ardalion in all his obscenity, rotting and stinking, not even going upright out of his mind, but creeping off its edge. He lies clumsily, plays dirty without disguise. He is hated, not only by the reader, but by everyone who has dealings with him: Varvara deceives him, Ludmila gaily ridicules him, the Director knits his brows and shudders... Nothing goes right for Peredonov, the *nedotikomka* slowly sucks him in; he feels that he is drowning, that everyone is against him...and is it madness that makes him feel this? Such feelings can drive one mad, of course, but Peredonov is not yet mad, for in actual fact everyone and everything *is* against him.

A strange, new, as yet inarticulate feeling for Peredonov stirred within me. And the last thing it resembled was hatred. Not the printed pages of the story about Peredonov, but Peredonov himself, with his gray, embittered face, passed before me. And I fervently wished *that things had happened differently,* that Varvara had not deceived him, that the Director had not thrown him out, that the *nedotikomka* had been caught and killed. It is impossible not to wish this. You can wish not to wish—but you will wish it anyway. Why the devil do we say "satire," "embodiment of evil," when a living man, yesterday's, tomorrow's Ardalion Peredonov finds himself in such desperate, unparalleled misery! Before misery like this all the horrors so laboriously heaped up by Leonid Andreev are mere trifles. In Andreev's novel, first the son of Father Fiveysky drowns, then his wife becomes a drunkard, then an idiot is born to them, then his wife is burned to death in a fire that destroys his home, then...what next? He flips out and performs unnatural rituals over the body of a dead peasant, flees along the road during a storm and dies in the dust. (Lightning or something like that?) Apart from the fact that Fiveysky is entirely invented, that we don't believe in him and therefore don't give a damn about him—leaving all this aside—can we compare Fiveysky's misery with Peredonov's? Fiveysky was created for everyone to sympathize with and pity; Peredonov receives the just hatred and contempt of all. Ivan Karamazov suffers; but he is intelligent, he has a luminous strength of spirit; an old woman in the country suffers, the hanged man in his noose suffers—but surely they are guiltless, someone loves them, wrings his heart for them. A child suffers, shedding "buckets of tears," but he is charming, he is dear, he is holy. Dostoevsky isn't the only one who will demand a justification for the tears of this child, Ivan Karamazov isn't the only one who will intercede for him. In all suffering there is hope; but in Peredonov's there is none. No one will intercede for him. He is ugly, evil, dirty and dull; he has nothing, nothing at all. And nevertheless he is created, he *is;* he is an "I" like any other "I," he matters first to himself and is everything to himself. The gray, slowly contracting ring has seized him, is suffocating him, and he cannot do anything; he possesses nothing beyond the agony of suffocation.

The little tear of the tormented child, the troubles of Vasily Fiveysky—all this is still within the boundaries of our human understanding of justice and injustice. Perhaps one might say, from this point of view, that Peredonov suffers *justly,* that he deserves his torment... But then it becomes clear that every human heart is broader than justice. Peredonov's misery is not just, but somehow *extremely unjust.* It is incumbent upon us to justify the "little tear of the tormented child" because we must know: for what crime? why? for what purpose? But similarly, it is incumbent, strongly incumbent upon me to justify each of Peredonov's elephant tears, each of his shudders at the sight of the *nedotikomka,* each heel blow against his physiognomy, which he "justly" receives from a good man, each of his shrieks and wails in the madhouse where he will inevitably be sent. If we continue to live in and even to love this world full of tormented children and rocks which may fall on our heads tomorrow—it is only because we say our "I do not wish it" and with stubborn, instinctive hope wait for an answer to "for what crime?" "for what purpose?" And our "I do not wish it" stands up even more boldly before Peredonov's complex and unheard-of misery. "I do not wish it"—not in the name of justice, but in the name of that which is higher than justice, whose existence in man is indisputable, whose nature is secret, and which may be called Love. There are very few, however, who understand this word.

Beyond the limits of pure justice, the simple definition of guilt, of human culpability or innocence, disappears. The question "for what crime?" disappears too. We cease to judge Peredonov; we protect him. And, protecting him, we ask: *How did He dare* to create his creature? And how will He *answer for him?*

* * * * * *

Of course, it is another matter entirely if no such person as Peredonov exists, if all this is the fabrication of a talented novelist, if, speaking plainly, Peredonov was created by Sologub. There is no point in turning to such a creator of Peredonov with the question "how did you dare" and "will you answer for him." Clearly, Sologub depicted him against his own desires, does not know him and will in no way answer for him. The feeling of lack of responsibility for his hero is very clear in Sologub's novel. *He does not love* Peredonov and this underscores the fact that he did not give birth to him, but merely found him and exposed him. "I expose—and the deuce take it! I expose—but have no desire to look myself. Who needs it?"

Thank you, nonetheless, for exposing, for remembering him who must be remembered. For, in fact, what does it mean to close one's eyes? Who dares to say, honestly, firmly, that there is not, could not be in this world a single, living Peredonov, with his complex, hopeless Peredonovian misery, a man not only poor in spirit or in other blessings, but *poor in everything?* Who in good conscience can say, "Why, such a woe can never befall a man and has never befallen anyone?"

There are many tormented children, many innocently and guiltily suffering people such as Karamazov and Fiveysky, but the tribe of Peredonovs, suffering hopelessly, poor in everything and cursed by all, is even *more numerous.* We know this, but we think about it only rarely. And when we think—when we see and feel—we stop despising the Peredonovs, we protect them; and protecting them, we ask, "How did You, Creator of Peredonov, dare to create him? How will You answer for him? Tell us, we must know. In the name of love—tell us: we simply must know."

Translated by Sharon Leiter

osip mandelstam / THE MORNING OF ACMEISM[1]

A.

Given the enormous emotional excitement associated with works of art, it is desirable that talk about art be marked by the greatest restraint. The huge majority of people are drawn to a work of art only insofar as they can detect in it the artist's world view. For the artist, however, a world view is a tool and instrument, like a hammer in the hands of a stonemason, and the only thing that is real is the work itself.

To be—that is the artist's greatest pride. He desires no other paradise than existence, and when he hears talk of reality he only smiles bitterly, for he knows the endlessly more convincing reality of art. When we see a mathematician produce the square of a ten-figure number without thinking about it we are filled with a sort of astonishment. But too often we fail to see that a poet raises a phenomenon to its tenth power, and the modest exterior of a work of art often misleads us concerning the monstrously condensed reality that it possesses. In poetry this reality is the word as such. Just now, for instance, while I am expressing my thought in the most exact way that I can, but certainly not in a poetic way, I am speaking essentially with the consciousness, not with the word. Deaf mutes understand each other perfectly and railroad signals perform their extremely complicated function without any recourse to the word. Therefore, if one is to regard the sense as the content, then one must regard everything else in the word as a simple mechanical appendage that only impedes the swift transmission of the thought. "The word as such" was slow aborning. Gradually, one after the other, all the elements of the word were drawn into the concept of form; only the conscious sense, the Logos, is still to this day regarded erroneously and arbitrarily as the content. There is nothing but detriment for Logos in this needless honor; Logos requires only to be on an equal footing with the other elements of the word. The Futurist, since he could not manage to cope with the conscious sense as creative material, thoughtlessly threw it overboard and repeated essentially the same crude error as his predecessors.

For the Acmeists the conscious sense of the word, the Logos, is just as splendid a form as music is for the Symbolists.

And if, among the Futurists, the word as such is still creeping on all fours, in Acmeism it has for the first time assumed a more dignified vertical position and entered upon the stone age of its existence.

B.

The sharp edge of Acmeism is not the stiletto nor the sting of Decadence. Acmeism is for those who, seized with the spirit of building, do not cravenly renounce their own gravity, but joyously accept it in order to awaken and use the forces architecturally sleeping in it. The architect says:

I build—that is to say, I am right. For us the consciousness of our rightness is dearer than all else in poetry, and—scornfully discarding the jack-straws of the Futurists, for whom there is no pleasure more exquisite than hooking a difficult word on the tip of a knitting needle—we are introducing the Gothic into the relationships of words, just as Sebastian Bach established it in music.

What sort of idiot would agree to build if he did not believe in the reality of his material, the resistance of which he must overcome? A cobblestone in the hands of an architect is transformed into substance, and the man who does not hear a metaphysical proof in the sound of a chisel splitting rock was not born to build. Vladimir Soloviev experienced a special kind of prophetic horror before gray Finnish boulders. The mute eloquence of the granite mass disturbed him like an evil enchantment. But Tyutchev's stone, which "having rolled down from the mountain, lay in the valley, torn loose of its own accord or thrown down by a sentient hand," is the word. In this unexpected fall the voice of matter sounds like articulate speech. This challenge can be answered only with architecture. Reverently the Acmeists pick up this mysterious Tyutchevian stone and lay it in the foundation of their building.

The stone thirsted, as it were, for another existence. It was itself the discoverer of the dynamic potential concealed within it—as if it were asking to be let into the "groined arch" to participate in the joyous cooperative action of its fellows.

C.

The Symbolists were not good stay-at-homes, they liked to make journeys; but they did not feel well, did not feel quite themselves in the closet of their own organisms and in the universal closet which Kant constructed with his categories.

The first condition of successful building is a genuine piety before the three dimensions of space—to look upon them not as a burden or unlucky accident but as a God-given palace. Really, what is one to say about the ungrateful guest who lives off his host, makes use of his hospitality, and all the while despises him in his soul and thinks only of how to outwit him? It is possible to build only in the name of the "three dimensions," since they are the condition of all architecture. That is why an architect has to be a good stay-at-home, and the Symbolists were poor architects. To build means to fight against emptiness, to hypnotize space. The fine arrow of the Gothic belltower is angry, for the whole idea of it is to stab the sky, to reproach it for being empty.

D.

The particularity of a man, that which makes him an individual, is tacitly grasped by us and forms part of the far more significant concept of the organism. Acmeists share their love for the organism and organization with the physiologically brilliant Middle Ages. In its chasing after refinement the nineteenth century lost the secret of genuine complexity. That which in the thirteenth century seemed the logical development of the concept of organism—the Gothic cathedral—now has the aesthetic effect of something monstrous; Notre Dame is a festival of physiology, its Dionysian debauch. We do not wish to divert ourselves with a stroll in the "forest of symbols," because we have a more virgin, a denser forest—divine physiology, the boundless complexity of our dark organism.

The Middle Ages, defining in their own way the specific weight of a man, felt and acknowledged it for each man completely regardless of his merits. Men were styled Master readily and with no hesitation. The humblest artisan, the very least clerk, possessed the secret of impressive grandness, of the devout dignity so characteristic of that age. Yes, Europe has passed through a labyrinth of delicate open-work culture, when abstract being, totally unornamented personal existence, was treasured as a sort of heroic accomplishment. Hence the aristocratic intimacy which united all people and which is so alien in spirit to the "equality and fraternity" of the French Revolution. There is no equality, no competition—there is the complicity of those united in a conspiracy against emptiness and nonexistence.

Love the existence of the thing more than the thing itself and your own existence more than yourself: that is the highest commandment of Acmeism.

E.

A A: what a splendid theme for poetry! Symbolism languished and longed for the law of identity; Acmeism makes it its slogan and offers it instead of the dubious *a realibus ad realiora.*

The ability to feel surprise is the poet's greatest virtue. But how then is one not to be surprised by that most fruitful of all laws, the law of identity? Whoever has been seized with reverential surprise before this law is undoubtedly a poet. Thus, having acknowledged the sovereignty of the law of identity, poetry receives life-long feudal possession of all that exists without condition or limitation. Logic is the kingdom of the unexpected. To think logically means to be continually amazed. We have come to love the music of proof. For us logical relationship is not some ditty about a siskin but a choral symphony with organ, so difficult and inspired that the director must exert all his powers to keep the performers under his control.

How persuasive is the music of Bach! What power of conviction! One must prove and prove endlessly: to accept something in art on faith alone is unworthy of an artist, it is easy and tiresome.... We do not fly: we ascend only such towers as we ourselves are able to build.

F.

The Middle Ages are dear to us because they possessed to a high degree the feeling of boundary and partition. They never mixed various levels, and they treated the beyond with huge restraint. A noble mingling of rationality and mysticism and the perception of the world as a living equilibrium makes us kin to this epoch and impels us to derive strength from works which arose on Romance soil around the year 1200. And we shall prove our rightness in such a way that the whole chain of causes and consequences from alpha to omega will shudder in response; we shall learn to carry "more easily and freely the mobile fetters of existence."

Translated by Clarence Brown

---

[1] Although not published until 1919 in a bi-monthly in Voronezh, this manifesto of Acmeism was apparently written at about the same time as Gumilev's essay translated above.

NIKOLAI GUMILEV AND ACMEIST CRITICISM
(Translator's Preface)

The twenty-fifth of August marked the fiftieth anniversary of Gumilev's death at the age of thirty-five before a firing squad. Although his monarchist politics were no less anachronistic in the early years of Soviet rule than were his poetics, Gumilev nonetheless succeeded in founding, guiding, and contributing to a movement which still represents the acme of Russian poetic craftsmanship today. Aristocratic, elitist, and neoclassical in inclination, Acmeism in the theory and practice of its "honorary syndic" marked a return to the tradition of Pushkin, a reintroduction of movement into a poetry become stagnant in the contemplation of mystical symbolisms, and a reinstatement of a masculine principle where the misty, feminine, Lermontovian element had dominated for so long. Together with Akhmatova, Mandelstam, and several other poets, Gumilev created a cult of the word in itself, a perception not so much of its mystical qualities as of its function as a complex union of concrete and associative meanings. Thus Acmeism challenged the transcendent visions of Symbolism with a scrupulous insistence upon finite perceptions: the mysteries which Symbolism claimed to experience spontaneously and directly, Acmeism confronted only through concrete, tangible images. The Acmeist Sergei Gorodetsky claimed: "We wish to admire a rose because it is beautiful, not because it is the symbol of mystical purity." Economical in their means, chaste in their use of words, precise and genuine in expression, they sought the secret of a "beautiful clarity."

As a critic Gumilev provided Acmeism with its fundamental theory and principles. The articles translated below,   typical of the movement in their conciseness, represent two fundamental aspects of the poet's criticism: Acmeism present both as an esthetic *Weltanschauung* and as a set of practical principles governing the poet's skill. In the first article, *Symbolism's Legacy and Acmeism (Nasledie simvolizma i akmeizm),* Gumilev attempts to justify the formation of a new movement by showing its distinctive view of life in general terms. The second and third articles—analyses of Akhmatova's *Beads (Chetki)* and Mandelstam's *Stone (Kamen')*—expound the particular virtues and devices of the practicing Acmeist poet.

Symbolism's Legacy and Acmeism is one of three manifestoes heralding the appearance of a new movement in 1913: Sergei Gorodetsky's *Several Trends in Contemporary Russian Poetry (Neskol'ko techenii v sovremennoi russkoi poezii)* appeared in the same issue of *Apollo* with Gumilev's article, while Mandelstam's *The Morning of Acmeism (Utro akmeizma)* was to appear only in 1919. The formidable task of Gumilev's article was to assert the preeminence of Acmeism over the Symbolist movement which had dominated Russian poetry since the turn of the century. Compared to the violently assertive manifestoes which had characterized Russian journalism for a century or more, Gumilev's manner seems genteel and reserved. He is not the systematic adversary of Symbolism that Belinsky was of Romanticism, that Chernyshevsky was of aestheticism, or that Merezhkovsky was of Naturalism; and unlike them he does not seek to expunge this major movement from the history of poetry. Rather, he renders it homage in complete sincerity. The legacy of Symbolism is Acmeism itself: the new poets were trained in the Symbolist poetics and world-view. His fellow Acmeists certainly could have claimed of themselves as Gumilev did in his 1910 article *The Life of Verse (Zhizn' stikha)*: Symbolism "shall appear old only when mankind rejects this thesis [that the world is our notion of it] ... I leave it for philosophers to judge when this will happen. For now we cannot but be Symbolists."

Gumilev's articles on Akhmatova and Mandelstam—his only "extensive" criticism of his most prominent fellow Acmeists—appeared in 1914 and 1916 as part of the series of nearly forty *Letters on Russian Poetry (Pis'ma o russkoi poezii)* which he wrote for seven years beginning in 1909. In this series of reviews Gumilev developed the canons of taste and craftsmanship which became Acmeism. Perhaps because this is the criticism of a poet and not simply a theoretician or a publicist and promoter of Acmeism, Gumilev seems stinting in his praise of the movement's most popular poets. (Still, Gumilev's limited praise must have pleased Akhmatova, to whom he was married from 1910 until 1918, and whose poetry he considered no more than "the fancy of a poet's wife," despite the fact that she was near the pinnacle of her fame in 1914.) In Gumilev's reviews the concept of poet reverts etymologically to artisan or craftsman. The poet as craftsman is dependent upon and confined by the material with which he creates: Akhmatova by a rosary, a worn string of beads filled with reflective, penitent, exalted associations; Mandelstam by stone, by a heavy, ponderous material which only a brilliant architect can transform into soaring towers with a deceptive lightness of style. Likewise Gumilev's reviews are bound by the material with which the poet-critic works: his restrained, strict, and laconic judgements reflect the style and images he seeks in the works under review. In this sense, then, Gumilev's criticism not only expounded and explained the theory and practice of Acmeism, but it also adopted the movement's economy, precision, and clarity of expression, thereby demonstrating the application of Acmeist poetics to the manner and aims of literary criticism itself.

nikolai gumilev

SYMBOLISM'S LEGACY AND ACMEISM

To the attentive reader it is clear that Symbolism has completed its cycle of development and is now declining. And it is clear that Symbolist works scarcely ever appear anymore, and if they do appear, they are extremely weak even from the point of view of Symbolism; and that there have appeared Futurists, Ego-futurists, and other hyenas which always follow the lion.* Taking Symbolism's place is a new movement, however it may be called—whether Acmeism (from the word *acme*, the highest degree of anything, the flower, florescence) or Adamism (a manfully firm and clear view of life)—in any case it is a movement which demands a greater balance of forces and a more precise knowledge of the relationships between subject and object than was the case with Symbolism. However, in order for this trend to establish itself completely and become a worthy successor to that which precedes it, it must accept the legacy of its predecessor and reply to all the problems previously posed. The fame of one's forefathers entails obligations, and Symbolism has been a worthy father.

French Symbolism, the wellspring of all Symbolism as a school, brought to the fore purely literary problems, free verse, a more unique and protean style, metaphor elevated above all else, and the notorious "theory of correspondences." The latter completely divulges its non-Romanic and consequently non-national, superficial basis. The Romanic spirit loves far too much that element of light which distinguishes objects, which sharply outlines; this very Symbolist melding of all forms and things, this inconstancy of their images could have been born only in the murky gloom of Germanic forests. A mystic might say that Symbolism in France was a direct consequence of Sedan. But at the same time this disclosed in French literature an aristocratic thirsting for the uncommon and the difficult to attain, and in this way saved it from an ominous, vulgar naturalism.

As Russians we cannot avoid coming to terms with French Symbolism, even if only because the new trend of which I was speaking above yields a decisive preference to the Romanic spirit over the Germanic. In like manner as the French sought a new, freer verse, the Acmeists strive to smash the bonds of meter by the omission of syllables, by a transposition of stress freer than ever before, and there are already poems written according to the

---

*The reader should not think that with this phrase I have dispensed with all the extreme aspirations of contemporary art. A special article in one of the next issues of *Apollo* will be devoted to an analysis and evaluation of them.

51

newly conceived syllabic system of versification. The dizzying quality of Symbolist metaphors has conditioned Acmeists to audacious turns of thought; the instability of those words to which they lent an attentive ear motivated them to search in our living national speech for new words with more stable content; and bright irony, which does not undermine the roots of our faith (an irony which could not help but emerge, however infrequently, in Romanic writers), has taken the place of that hopeless German seriousness which our Symbolists have so assiduously courted. Finally, while highly esteeming the Symbolists for having shown us the significance of the symbol in art, we do not concur in offering up in sacrifice to it all other manners of poetic effect, but seek their complete coordination. Thus we answer the question of the comparative "sublime difficulty" of the two trends: it is more difficult to be an Acmeist than a Symbolist, as it is more difficult to build a cathedral than a tower. And it is one of the principles of the new movement always to travel the line of greatest resistance.

Germanic Symbolism in the person of its originators Nietzsche and Ibsen brought forward the question of the role of man in the universe, of the individual in society, and resolved it by locating some kind of objective goal or dogma which was to be served. This betrayed the fact that Germanic Symbolism has no feeling for each phenomenon's independent value, which needs no external justification. For us, hierarchy in the world of phenomena is only the specific gravity of each of them, whereby the weight of the most insignificant is nonetheless immeasurably greater than the absence of weight, than nonexistence, and therefore upon confrontation with nonexistence all phenomena are brothers.

We would never take it upon ourselves to force an atom to bow to God if this were not in its nature. But sensing ourselves to be phenomena among phenomena, we become involved in a world rhythm, we accept all influences upon us and in turn exert an influence ourselves. Our duty, our will, our happiness, and our tragedy is to guess hourly what the next hour shall be for us, for our cause, for the whole world, and to hasten its approach. And yet, not holding our attention even an instant, as the highest reward there appears to us an image of the final hour, which will never come. To revolt in the name of some existential conditions here, where there is death, is just as strange as for a prisoner to break down a wall when there is an open door before him. Here ethics becomes aesthetics, expanding itself to encompass the area of the latter. Here individualism in its greatest intensity creates society. Here God becomes the Living God, because man has felt himself worthy of such a God. Here death is a curtain separating us, the actors, from the audience, and in the inspiration of our acting we despise any cowardly peeking to see what will happen next. As Adamists we are somewhat animals of the forest, and in any case we will not give up any of that which is animalistic in us in exchange for neurasthenia. But this is the time to speak to Russian Symbolism.

Russian Symbolism dispatched its main forces into the area of the unknown. Alternately it fraternized with mysticism, with theosophy, and with occultism. Certain of its quests in this direction almost approached the creation of myth. And it has a right to ask of that trend coming up to take its place whether it can boast only of animalistic virtues, and what its relationship is to the unknowable. The first answer that Acmeism can give to such an interrogation will be to point out that what is unknowable, according to the very meaning of this word, cannot be comprehended. The second is that all efforts in this direction are immodest. The entire beauty, the entire sacred significance of stars rests in the fact that they are infinitely far from the earth and through no successes of aviation will they become closer. He demonstrates a poverty of imagination who imagines the evolution of the individual always in terms of time and space. How are we able to recall our former existences (if this is not clearly a literary device), when we were in an abyss where there were myriads of other existential possibilities, about which we know nothing except that they exist? After all, each of them is negated by our existence and in turn negates ours. Child-like, but wise, and sweet to the point of pain is the sensation of one's own lack of knowledge: this is what the unknown gives us. Francois Villon, upon asking where the most beautiful ladies of antiquity are now, answers himself with the mournful exclamation:

Mais où sont les neiges d'antan!

And this gives us a more powerful sensation of the otherworldly than whole volumes of discussions concerning which side of the moon the souls of the departed are found on... Always keep in mind the unknowable, but do not offend the thought of it with more or less probable speculations—this is Acmeism's principle. This does not mean that it relinquishes its right to depict the soul in those moments when it trembles in approaching another; but at that point it should only shudder. Of course, the comprehension of God, the beautiful lady Theology, shall remain on her throne. But Acmeists wish neither to lower her to the level of literature, nor to elevate literature to her diamond-like frigidity. As concerns angels, demons, elemental and other spirits, these are part of the artist's material and should not outweigh by greater earthly gravity the other images taken up by him.

Every new movement experiences a love for one or another artist or epoch. Fond graves bind people more than anything. In those circles close to Acmeism the names of Shakespeare, Rabelais, Villon, and Théophile Gautier are heard most often. Each of them represents a cornerstone for the building of Acmeism, an extreme intensity of one or another of its elements. Shakespeare showed us the inner world of man; Rabelais—the body and its joys, a wise physiologism; Villon told us about life, without in the least doubting in himself and while knowing everything—God, vice, death, and immortality;

Théophile Gautier found in art the worthy raiments of irreproachable forms for this life. To combine in itself these four moments—this is the dream which now unifies those people who so boldly have called themselves Acmeists.

Apollo, No. 1, 1913.

REVIEW OF AKHMATOVA'S *BEADS*
(Petersburg, 1914)

In Anna Akhmatova's *Beads*, on the contrary, the eidolological aspect is thought out least of all.[1] The poetess has not "created herself," has not put in the center of her experiences some sort of external fact by which to unify them. She does not address herself to something known or understandable to herself alone, and this distinguishes her from the Symbolists. But on the other hand, her themes frequently are not exhausted by the limits of a given poem; much in them seems insubstantial because it remains unproven. As with the majority of young poets, in Anna Akhmatova one frequently meets the words: pain, sorrow, death. This youthful pessimism, so natural and therefore so beautiful, has until now been the property of "pen testers," and, it seems, in Akhmatova's verse for the first time it has taken its place in poetry. Everyone has wondered, I think, at the magnitude of youth's capacity and willingness to suffer. Laws and objects of the real world suddenly assume the place of former ones now pierced through by a dream in whose fulfillment he believed: the poet cannot help but see that they are self-sufficiently beautiful, and he is incapable of comprehending himself among them, of coordinating the rhythm of his spirit with their rhythm. But the force of life and love is so powerful in him that he begins to love his orphanhood itself and achieves the beauty of pain and death. Later, when an "inadvertent joy" begins to appear to his spirit, tired of being ever in one and the same condition, he shall feel that man can joyously comprehend all aspects of the world, and from the ugly duckling which he appeared to himself in his own eyes, he shall become a swan, as in Andersen's fairy tale.

To those people who are not fated to achieve such a transformation, or to those who possess a feline memory, which attaches itself to all passed stages of its spirit, Akhmatova's book will seem exciting and valuable. In it a series of beings, mute until now, acquire a voice—women in love, cunning dreamy, and rapturous, at last speak their own genuine, and at the same time artistically compelling language. That bond with the world about which I spoke above, and which is the lot of every genuine poet, has almost been achieved by Akhmatova, because she knows the joy of perceiving the external and knows how to transmit this joy to us.

Tightly her dry lips are shut,

Three thousand candles flame hot.
Princess Eudoxie thus lay
On a sapphire and scented brocade.

And tearless, a mother bent low,
Prayed for her blind little boy,
And a voicelessly thrashing hysteric
Strained to gulp air with her lips.

A dark-eyed and humpbacked old man,
Come from a far southern land,
As if at the gate of paradise,
To the darkening step has pressed close.

Here I turn to that which is most significant in Akhmatova's poetry, to her stylistics: she almost never explains; she shows. This is achieved both by a carefully considered and original choice of images, as well as (and this is most important) by their detailed elaboration. Epithets defining the value of the object (such as beautiful, ugly, happy, wretched, and so on) occur rarely. This value is suggested by the description of an image and by the interrelationship of images. Akhmatova has many devices for this. I shall indicate a few of them: the conjunction of an adjective defining color with an adjective defining form:

...And the dark green ivy
Thickly entwined the high window.

Or:

...There a raspberry sun
Over dishevelled grey smoke...

Repetition in two successive lines which doubles our attention to the image:

...Tell me how they kiss you,
Tell me how you kiss them.

Or:

...In snowy branches to black jackdaws,
To black jackdaws refuge give.

Transformation of an adjective into a substantive:

...The orchestra is playing [something] gay...

and so forth.

There are many definitions of color in Akhmatova's verse, and most frequently of yellow and grey, until now very rare in poetry. And perhaps as confirmation of the nonaccidental nature of her taste, the majority of her epithets emphasize in particular the poverty and paleness of objects: a threadbare rug, worn-down heels, a faded flag, etc. In order to love the world, Akhmatova must see it as nice and as simple.

Akhmatova's rhythmics serve as a magnificent support to her stylistics. Paeons and pauses help her to single out the most necessary word in the line, and in the whole book I did not find a single example of a stress falling on an unstressed word, or vice versa, a word stressed in meaning but without a stress. Were someone to take upon himself the task of examining the collection of any contemporary poet from this point of view, he would become convinced that usually the case is quite different. A faintness and brokenness of breathing is characteristic of Akhmatova's rhythmics. The tetrametric strophe (in which almost the whole book is written) is too long for her. Her periods most frequently encompass two lines, sometimes three, even occasionally one. The causal relation with which she attempts to replace the rhythmical unity of the strophe for the most part does not achieve its goal. The poetess must elaborate upon her strophe if she wishes to master composition. A single spontaneous transport cannot serve as a basis for composition. This is why Akhmatova as yet knows only the consecutiveness of a logically developed thought or the consecutiveness in which objects appear in her field of vision. This does not constitute a shortcoming of her verse, but it cuts off before her the path to achieving many virtues.

Compared to *Evening (Vecher),* published two years ago, *Beads* represents a great step forward. Her verse has become firmer, the content of each line—more solid, the choice of words—sparingly chaste, and, what is best of all, the incoherence of thought has vanished, that incoherence so characteristic of *Evening* and comprising more a psychological curiosity than a poetic quality.

Apollo, No. 5, 1914.

REVIEW OF MANDELSTAM'S *STONE*
(Petersburg, 1916)

For about ten years now O. Mandelstam has been known and appreciated in literary circles. But the recently published *Stone* seems his only book, because the little brochure of the same name[2] sold out quickly and scarcely reflected the complex paths of its author's skill.

It is important to note first of all the complete independence of Mandelstam's verse. You rarely meet such complete freedom from any extraneous influences whatsoever. Even if he comes across a theme which has already appeared in another poet (which happens rarely), he reworks it to the point where it becomes completely unrecognizable. His sources of inspiration have been the Russian language, whose most complex turns of speech he has come to study, and not always successfully, as well as his own seeing, hearing, palpating, eternally sleepless thought.

This thought reminds me of the fingers of a typist, so rapidly does it fly over the most diverse images, the most whimsical sensations, extracting the absorbing tale of an unfolding spirit.

The first period of Mandelstam's writing, approximately from 1908 to 1912, passes under the sign of Symbolism, insofar as this elusive word explains anything for us. The poet aspires to the periphery of consciousness, to prehistoric chaos, to the kingdom of metaphor, but he does not harmonize this according to his own will, as do those who believe anything, and he is only frightened by its incompatibility with him. *Silentium* with its sorcerous invocation of preexistence ("remain the foam of Aphrodite and, Word, back to music return") is nothing but an audacious amplification of Verlaine's *L'Art poétique*. In the mysterious he feels a genuine danger for his human ego and fears this with an animalistic terror:

> What if, eternally twinkling
> Over a modish shop,
> Straight through my heart like a pin
> The star were to drop?

Even his metaphor "Oh, the pendulum of souls, strict,/Is swinging silent, straight" acquires almost a zoological existence. However, he is not yet perspicacious, he lives as if in a dream, and he himself defines his state so faithfully with the exclamation:

> Indeed am I real,
> And will death actually come?

The crisis comes in this poem:

> No, not the moon, a clock-dial bright
> Shines for me, and why am I at fault
> For feeling the stars' milky frailty?

> Still, the arrogance of Batyushkov repels:
> What time is it, they asked, pray tell—
> And he, bemused, replied: eternity.

From this moment the poet becomes an initiate of the literary trend known by the name of Acmeism. He beautifully employed his knowledge that a single image has no independent significance, but that it is necessary only in order to expose the poet's soul as fully as possible. Now he speaks of his human thought, love, or hatred and precisely defines their objects. By force of circumstance as a city dweller, he became a poet of the contemporary city, although he never wonders like a visiting country hayseed at the automobiles and streetcars, and when visiting the library he does not sigh over how much people have written, but simply gets the necessary book.

An approaching funeral, an old man looking like Verlaine, Petrograd in winter, the Admiralty, janitors in heavy fur coats—everything rivets his attention, gives birth in him to thoughts so diverse, and yet unified by a single perception of the world.

For him everything is pure, everything is a pretext for a poem: a book he has read, whose content he relates in his own way ("Domby and Son"), the cheap romanticism of a movie scenario ("The Cinematographer"), a Bach concerto, a newspaper article on the *Imyabozhtsy,* country-house tennis, etc., etc.

Although he thinks nonetheless most frequently about architecture, about the ponderous masses of Notre Dame and of the Hagia Sophia, yet this is the avid gaze of a disciple upon the work of a master, of a disciple who dares to exclaim: "From the malignant heaviness someday I will create something beautiful."

But man has the quality of reducing everything to a unity; in this way for the most part he arrives at God. O. Mandelstam arrived at an idol: in love with reality, but not having forgotten his trembling before eternity, he has been captivated by the idea of the Eternal City, the Caesarean and papal Rome. His dreams, tired from eternal wanderings, he carries there, and there he hears the chorus of archangels saying, Glory to God in the highest and on earth peace, good will toward men:

> The dove fears not that thunder
> Which is the church's voice:
> In apostolic chorus: Roma!
> It makes the heart rejoice.
>
> Beneath the heavens' eternal dome
> This name still echoes in my ear,
> Though he who spoke to me of Rome
> In holy dusk has disappeared.

However, Rome is just a stage in Mandelstam's writing, just the first symbol of the power and magnificence of the creative spirit to come to mind. The poet already is finding less common and more effective images for expressing the same feeling:

> Theater of Racine! A mighty veil
> Keeps us separate from this other world;
> Undulating with its deepened wrinkles,
> A curtain hangs between this world and us
> Classicism's shawl falls from its shoulders;

Fused by suffering, its voice is strengthened;
Seared with indignation, its phrase submits
To sorrow-filled and doleful tempering...

I came too late to celebrate Racine!

All this concerns questions of artistic vision. Problems of artistic skill
are contemplated in profound and beautiful poems such as "The grain is
poisoned, the air drunk up" and "I never heard the tales of Ossian," not to
mention the earlier "Why is my soul so melodic."

I have indicated only a few directions in the writing of O. Mandelstam,
but I think this is sufficient to show what a significant and interesting poet
we are dealing with. In *Stone* there are shortcomings, weak and confused
poems, ear-splitting mistakes in language, but one does not wish to think or
speak of this when reading a book so rare in value.

Apollo, No. 1, 1916.

Translated by Robert T. Whittaker, Jr.

NOTES

[1] Gumilev is referring to his previous review of Gorodetsky's *Flowering
Staff (Tsvetushchii posokh)*.

[2] The first edition of *Stone* appeared in 1913.

v. m. zhirmunsky / TWO TENDENCIES OF CONTEMPORARY LYRIC POETRY*

Russian lyric poetry of the last quarter of the (nineteenth) century developed under the banner of Symbolism. Although the overcoming of Symbolism has long been a topic of discussion, it is only recently—just shortly before the (First World) War—that a poetic school has arisen that broke with the precepts of Symbolism in its very foundations. The poetic progenitor of this school was M. A. Kuzmin. The participants in the new movement gave their artistic faith the bizarre and meaningless name of "Acmeism." In their poetic manifestos they renounced the romantic mysticism which had dominated the poetic work and worldview of the older poets. Instead of a poetry of hints, allegories and symbols, the vaguely disturbing quality of which had a musical effect, they demanded clarity, completeness and firmness of poetic images, logical exactitude and concreteness *(veshchestvennost')* in words and word combinations. Whereas the Symbolists loved to repeat the words of Verlaine—"Music above all else!"—the theoretician of the new poetic school, Gumilev, quoted the demand of Théophile Gautier: "Creation is the more perfect/The more passionless the material!/Be it verse, marble or metal..."

In this collision of two literary generations we are not witnessing an accidental competition of minor, uninteresting literary cliques, but rather a deep break in poetic feeling—perhaps still deeper than the transition from the lyric poetry of the 1880s to the art of the Symbolists. Balmont continues the tradition of Fet; Blok is internally connected to the lyricism of Vladimir Solovyov. Balmont and Kuzmin, Blok and Akhmatova, contemporaries by chance who are often close to each other in poetic themes, belong to artistic worlds that differ essentially and represent two types of art that are nearly opposites.

We will attempt to show this difference in a comparison of two poems of Blok and Akhmatova which are similar in theme but differ entirely in thematic treatment; a particular instance of such comparison will serve to

---

*This essay of 1920 was a critical landmark for Russian poetry of the period. It gave substance to the Acmeists' claim to have founded a new poetic school distinct from Symbolism.

Zhirmunsky's ties with formalist scholarship are strongly evident here. The concept of artistic evolution as a reaction against immediate predecessors in favor of more distant ones results in Zhirmunsky uniting Acmeism with Classicism and contrasting the former to Symbolism-Romanticism. *Trans.*

illustrate our general conclusions more convincingly.

Blok's poem is entitled "In the Restaurant."

> Never shall I forget (did it take place or not—
> This evening); in a blaze of dawn
> The pale sky flamed out and was shoved aside,
> And in the yellow dawn were lanterns.
> I sat at the window in the overfilled hall.
> Somewhere were bows singing of love,
> I sent you a black rose in a goblet
> Of "Ai" that was as gold as the sky.
> You looked. Confused and bold, I met
> Your haughty gaze and bowed.
> Turning to your escort, with intentional harshness
> You said: "This one's head over heels too."
> And immediately the strings thundered something in reply,
> The bows sang out hysterically...
> But you were with me in your young contempt,
> In the hardly noticeable quiver of your hand...
> You tore away like a frightened bird,
> You passed—light as my dream...
> And perfumes sighed, lashes dreamed,
> Anxiously silks began to whisper.
> But from the depths of mirrors you cast glances at me,
> And casting them, shouted: "Catch."
> And the necklace tinkled, and the gipsy danced
> And howled to the dawn of love.

Akhmatova's poem is entitled "In the Evening."

> The music grated in the garden
> With such inexpressible grief.
> The iced oysters on the plate
> Smelled freshly and sharply of the sea.
> He said to me: "I am a true friend!"
> And touched my dress...
> How unlike caresses
> Are the touches of these hands.
> As if one were patting cats or birds...
> Or watching graceful circus riders...
> Only laughter in his calm eyes
> Under the light gold of the lashes.
> But the mournful voices of the violins

Sing behind the floating smoke:
"Bless the heavens;
You are alone with your beloved for the first time."

Both poems are written on a similar theme; the country garden, the restaurant, the music, and the meeting with the loved one are repeated in both. The more particular features showing similarity, such as the "voices of the violins" which "sing" ("Somewhere bows were singing of love"), are evidence of a possible influence on Akhmatova, particularly in view of the fact that Blok's poem is one of his more famous ones. But there is a deep underlying difference behind the thematic similarity. Blok is depicting an event of mystical content, saturated with boundless significance; Akhmatova has produced a simple everyday meeting, although it is subjectively significant. What devices are used to create this difference of impressions?

Blok begins with the words: "Never shall I forget (did it take place or not—this evening)." Thus he immediately creates the impression of unity, unusualness, and the exclusiveness of this rendezvous. But is he relating a dream or did this actually happen? The same doubt as to the reality of the image of the beautiful is expressed in "The Stranger" ("Neznakomka"):

And every evening, at the appointed hour,
(Or do I only dream this?)
A girl's figure, swathed in silks,
Moves in the murky window...

And the same consciousness of the singularity of the beautiful object and doubt as to its reality are repeated below: "You passed—light as my dream." Akhmatova, however, knows that this happened, not in a dream, but in living reality, recalled in all its details: "The iced oysters on the plate smelled freshly and sharply of the sea."

Blok frames his poem with the use of the symbolic image of "dawn," with which we are already acquainted from most of his other verse as an accompaniment of the wonderful appearance of the stranger ("Neznakomka"). But this is not the bright dawn of his youthful verses of the beautiful lady— roses and gold in the bright azure of the sky; this is the "sick" dawn of his "gypsy" verses—yellow, smoky, inflamed: "The pale sky flamed out and was shoved aside, and in the yellow dawn were lanterns." The metaphorical verbs, "flamed out" and "shoved aside," lend grandiose mythological outlines to this picture of a yellow sick sky. The same is true of the last lines: "And the necklace tinkled, and the gypsy danced and howled to the dawn of love." In Akhmatova's poem this symbolic framing, repeated in the beginning and at the end, is of course absent. In the composition of her verse, the music "grating in the garden"—"the mournful voices of the violin"—play an identical role.

As has already been shown, these violins are present in both verses. In Blok's, however, they are in the unknown vague distance: "Somewhere bows were singing of love"; and the content of the song is just as unknown and incomprehensible to the poet: "And immediately the strings thundered something in reply...." "Somewhere" and "something" are significant words for the romantic poet. In Akhmatova's poem the expression is exact: "the music grated in the garden," "(violins) sing behind the floating smoke." Exact localization of the sounds corresponds to an exact statement of their emotional content—sad, mournful sounds: "The music grated in the garden with such inexpressible grief." This lyrical empathy with the mood of the song is expressed in the words of common everyday speech. And at the same time, as is always the case with Akhmatova, there is a surprising exactness and individuality in the selection of the epithet and in connecting it (synthetic union) with the corresponding word: "But the mournful voices of violins..."

Both poets describe the subject of their love. Blok says of his loved one: "You tore away like a frightened bird, you passed—light as my dream... and perfumes sighed, lashes dreamed,/ Anxiously silks began to whisper..." Before us again passes the image of the stranger: "She sits down at the window, wafting perfumes and mists. And from her supple silks emanate ancient superstitions." By the same devices the poet accomplishes the transformation of the image of the loved one into a wonderful and magical otherworldly phenomenon which has entered into this world. Also used is a series of animating metaphors and comparisons: "perfumes breathe," "eyelashes dream," "silks whisper anxiously"; she rushed from her place "with the frightened movement of a bird." Also, the comparison which has already been pointed out leads us out beyond the borders of the world of external reality: the stranger is like a "dream." This differs from Akhmatova's description of the loved one. It communicates an intimate and delicate sensual observation in an epigrammatically exact verbal formula: "How unlike caresses are the touches of these hands." "Only laughter in his calm eyes under the light gold of the lashes." Here again the art of Akhmatova is primarily a new and creative combination of words that are simple as far as their logical and material meanings are concerned; as a result the union of the words is irreplaceable, individual, synthetic. The metaphorical images of Blok, however, grow out of a lyrical melodic mood. Hence the repetitions of parts of words and whole words, vowels and consonants, syntactic parallelism, even internal rhymes: "And perfumes sighed, lashes dreamed, anxiously silks began to whisper" particularly in the last strophe.

What composes the factual content of the two verses? When told "in one's own words," in prosaic exposition, one feels that Blok's poem is being exposed, it loses its poetic meaning. The meeting with the unknown woman in the restaurant, the poet addressing her, her "haughty" and contemptuous reply, and—abruptly during the sounds of the music, when their eyes meet in the mirror—the sudden feeling of nearness that seized both of them. Only in poetic treatment will we comprehend the mystic significance of this occurrence for the poet ("Never shall I forget!")—the significance of the appearance of the stranger, the only real loved one, in the earthly image of the unknown beauty. And for this reason the first words signifying this singular meeting ("I sent you a black rose in a goblet of 'Ai' that was gold as the sky") sound so romantically solemn. In Akhmatova's poem the content is simple and easily defined, and the external sense of the story corresponds completely to the internal sense. This is the first meeting with the beloved. She recognizes that he does not love her and never will; he is only a "true friend." "He said to me: 'I am a true friend!' and touched my dress . . . How unlike caresses are the touches of these hands."

On the basis of this example we can express, in general form, the difference between the art of Blok and that of Akhmatova—between the mystical lyricism of the Symbolists and contemporary poetry which has "overcome Symbolism."

The lyrical poetry of the Symbolists is of a primarily mystical nature. The presence of the infinite in each experience inserts a peculiar deeper meaning, communicates a new estimation of everything that occurs. We feel that the experience is somehow born from the very depths of the soul—still whole, undivided—frequently chaotic. With Akhmatova and poets of her circle we observe a return to feeling on a finite human scale; it is complete in itself, as if outlined and limited on all sides. The separateness and distinctness of each emotional experience, the graceful and strict order in "emotional housekeeping" is to be understood in this connection. The Symbolists are typified by an exclusive self-centered quality and an internal adhesion to one's own experience. In Akhmatova we have an interest in the external world, its sensual, objective, visual details, and an ability to exactly observe the external signs of emotional experience; each experience is connected with some external fact as its cause or felt sign.

The peculiarities of poetics are inevitably connected with these peculiarities of poetic feeling. Among the Symbolists music is born from the spirit of music; the words call forth a vague mood with their sounds rather than with their meaning; repetitions of sounds, words, and entire lines are common, as in songs. The words become metaphorical allegories, hints at other meanings; their logical and material sense is clouded, but their emotionally lyrical effectiveness is all the stronger. In the new generation of poets, however, the emotional element in immediate musical expression is absent; and at the same time the peculiarities of melodic, lyrically musical style disappear. In return, the poetic images acquire a graphic defined quality; the logical and material sense of the words is restored to its rights; the connection of words is determined primarily by the meaning and is consolidated by an exact, strict, epigrammatic formula; division and completion are expressed in syntactic construction and in the very composition of the poem. A return to the classical art of Pushkin is being accomplished in the poetics of the new school.

Throughout the nineteenth century the Romantic tradition dominated Russian lyrics, tracing its origins back to Zhukovsky, Tyutchev, Fet, and Solovyov. The Russian Symbolists attached themselves to this tradition. We first observe a return to Classicism in the lyric poetry of Mikhail Kuzmin. In Anna Akhmatova's *White Flock* it is expressed quite clearly. For this reason we assert that in the poetic creation of recent years we see a new poetic art which profoundly differs from the lyric poetry of the Symbolist poets.

Translated by John Glad

osip mandelstam / STORM AND STRESS[1]

Henceforth, readers no longer perceive the body of Russian poetry of the first quarter of the twentieth century as "modernism" with all the ambiguity and the near contempt inherent in that idea, but simply as Russian poetry. What has taken place is what one might call the knitting together of the spines of two poetic systems, two poetic epochs.

The Russian reader, who has lived through not one but several poetic revolutions over a quarter of a century, has learned to seize more or less immediately on what is objectively valuable in the multifarious poetic creation surrounding him. Every new literary school—be it Romanticism, Symbolism, or Futurism—arrives in an artificially inflated condition, exaggerating its unique significance, oblivious of its external, historical limitations. It passes inevitably through a period of Storm and Stress. Only later, usually when the main representatives of the school have lost their freshness and ability to work, does it become clear what their real place in literature is and what objective values they have created. At the same time, after the high-water mark of the Storm and Stress, the literary current has to narrow down to its natural channel, and it is precisely these incomparably more modest boundaries and outlines that one remembers ever after. In the first quarter of this century, Russian poetry twice lived through a very pronounced period of Storm and Stress. One was Symbolism, the other Futurism. Both these main currents showed a desire to stop dead on the crest of their wave, and in this desire they were defeated; for history, which was preparing the crests of new waves, gave them at the appointed time an imperious order to recede, to return into the general maternal lap of language and poetry.

In their poetic development, however, Symbolism and Futurism, which complemented each other historically, were of completely different types. The Storm and Stress of Symbolism should be seen as a stormy and passionate process of making European and world poetry accessible to Russian literature. In essence, therefore, this stormy event had an outwardly cultural sense. Early Symbolism was an intensely strong draft of air from the West. Russian Futurism is much closer to Romanticism. It bears all the traits of a national poetic revival, and its reworking of the national treasury of language and of a deep native tradition makes it once more akin to Romanticism, unlike the alien phenomenon of Russian Symbolism, which was a *Kulturträger,* a bearer of poetic culture from one soil to another.

In accordance with this essential distinction between Symbolism and Futurism, the first is an example of an external, the second of an internal aspiration. The pivotal point of Symbolism was its passion for great themes, cosmic and metaphysical in character. Early Russian Symbolism is the realm of great themes and concepts "with a capital letter," derived directly from Baudelaire, Edgar Poe, Mallarmé, Swinburne, Shelley, and others. Futurism lived for the most part on the poetic device and developed not the theme but the device, i. e., something internal, inherent in language. In Symbolism the theme is held forward like a shield protecting the device. The themes of the early Bryusov, Balmont and others are exceedingly distinct. With the Futurists it is difficult to separate the theme from the device, and the inexperienced eye will see in Khlebnikov, say, nothing more than pure device or naked transsense.[2]

It is easier to sum up the period of Symbolism than that of Futurism because the latter did not come to so distinct a conclusion and was not so abruptly terminated as Symbolism, which was extinguished by hostile influences. Almost imperceptibly, it has renounced the extreme positions of its Storm and Stress period and is continuing on its own to work out, in the spirit of the general history of language and poetry, those elements of Futurism which turned out to be of objective value. It is comparatively easy to sum up Symbolism. Of the early stage of Symbolism, swollen and afflicted with the dropsy of great themes, practically nothing remains. The grandiose cosmic hymns of Balmont turned out to be childishly weak and ineffectual in verse technique. The much praised urbanism of the Bryusov who entered poetry as the singer of the universal city has been dimmed by history, since the sounds and images of Bryusov proved to be anything but inherent in his favorite theme. The transcendental poetry of Andrey Bely proved unable to save his metaphysical thought from becoming passe and decrepit. The case of Vyacheslav Ivanov's complicated Byzantine-Hellenic world is somewhat better. Essentially just as much a pioneer and colonizer as all the other Symbolists, he did not treat Byzantium and Hellas as foreign countries destined to be conquered but rightly saw in them the cultural springs of Russian poetry. But owing to the lack of any sense of proportion, common to all the Symbolists, he weighed his poetry down with an unlikely burden of Byzantine—Hellenic images and myths, which considerably cheapened it. One ought to speak separately about Sologub and Annensky, since they never took part in the Storm and Stress of Symbolism. Blok's poetic fate is bound up in the closest possible way with Russian poetry of the nineteenth century and one ought therefore to speak separately about him also. Here, too, it is necessary to mention the work of the younger Symbolists, or Acmeists, who wished not to repeat the errors of early Symbolism, swollen with its dropsy of great themes. With a much soberer estimate of their powers, they renounced the mania for the grandiose of early Symbolism and replaced it, some by monumentality of device, some by clarity of utterance, with far from equal success.

No poetic heritage ever became so old and so decrepit in so short a time as Symbolism. It would even be more accurate to speak of Russian Symbolism as pseudo-Symbolism in order to call attention to its misuse of great themes and abstract concepts, little trace of which could be felt in its language. The whole of pseudo-Symbolism, that is, a huge part of what the Symbolists wrote, is only relatively interesting for literary history. That which has some objective value lies concealed beneath a pile of stage effects and pseudo-Symbolist rubbish. It was a heavy tribute that the age and their cultural task exacted from the most energetic and the noblest generation of Russian poets. Let us begin with the father of Russian Symbolism—Balmont. Extraordinarily little of Balmont has survived—some ten poems. But what has survived is truly superb. Both in its phonetic brilliancy and in its deep sense of roots and sounds it can bear comparison with the best examples of transsense poetry. It is not Balmont's fault that his undemanding readers turned the development of his poetry aside into the worst direction. In his best poems—"O Night, stay awhile with me" *(O noch', pobud' so mnoi)* and "The Old House" *(Staryi dom)*—he drew from Russian verse new and never-to-be repeated sounds of a foreign, somehow seraphic phonetics. For us, the explanation of this lies in the special phonetic quality of Balmont, the exotic perception of the consonant sounds. It is just here, and not in the vulgar musicality, that we find the source of his poetic power. In the best (non-urban) poems of Bryusov, one feature, making him the most consistent and able of all the Russian Symbolists, will never grow old. This is his courageous approach to the theme, his total power over it, the ability to draw from it   all that it can and must give, to exhaust it completely, to find for it a correct and capacious stanzaic vessel. His best poems are models of absolute control over the theme: "Orpheus and Eurydice," "Theseus and Ariadne," "The Demon of Suicide" *(Demon samoubiistva)*. Bryusov taught Russian poets to respect the theme as such. There is also something to be learnt from his last books, *Distances (Dali)* and *Last Dreams (Poslednie mechty)*. Here he gives examples of the capaciousness of his verse and of the astonishing arrangement of varied, thought-filled words in a space of frugal dimensions. In *The Urn (Urna)* Andrey Bely enriched the Russian lyric with sharp prosaic words from the German metaphysical vocabulary, displaying the ironic sound of philosophic terms. In his book *Ashes (Pepel)* he skillfully introduces polyphony— i.e., a many-vocied element—into the poetry of Nekrasov, whose themes are subjected to an original orchestration. The musical populism of Bely amounts to a gesture of beggarly plastic movement accompanying the enormous musical theme. Vyacheslav Ivanov is more of a populist and in the future will be more accessible than all the other Russian Symbolists. A large part of the reverence for his majestic manner derives from our ignorance of philology. In no other Symbolist poet does one hear so clearly the noise of the lexicon, the powerful clamor of the bell of popular speech, which is surging forward and awaiting its turn, as in

Vyacheslav Ivanov: "Mute night, deaf night" *(Noch'nemaia, noch'glukhaia),* "The Maenad" *(Menada),* etc. His perception of the past as being the future makes him akin to Khlebnikov. The archaism of Vyacheslav Ivanov comes not from his choice of themes but from his inaptitude for relative thought, i.e., for comparing different ages. The Hellenic poetry of Vyacheslav Ivanov was not written after Greek poetry, nor at the same time, but before it; for he never for a moment forgets himself, speaking in his barbarous native idiom.

Such were the founders of Russian Symbolism. Not one of them worked in vain. In each of them there is something to be learnt at the present time. Let us turn to their contemporaries, whose fate from the very beginning was the bitter joy of not sharing the historical errors of the others but also of not taking part in the refreshing tumult of the first Symbolist feasts—to Sologub and Annensky.

Sologub and Annensky had begun their activity, completely unnoticed, as early as the 1890s. The influence of Annensky can be felt with extraordinary force on the Russian poetry that came after him. The first teacher of psychological acuity in the modern Russian lyric, he transmitted the art of psychological composition to Futurism. The influence of Sologub, almost equally strong, found a purely negative expression: having carried to the limits of simplicity and perfection, by means of a lofty rationalism, the devices of the old Russian lyric of the decadent period—including Nadson, Apukhtin, and Golenishchev-Kutuzov; having cleansed these devices of their trashy emotional admixture and bathed them in the light of an original erotic myth, he rendered impossible any attempt to return to the past and for all practical purposes had, it would seem no imitators. With an organic compassion for banality, tenderly condoling with dead words, Sologub created a cult of dead and obsolete poetic formulas, breathing into them a miraculous and terminal life. The early poetry of Sologub and his collection *The Flaming Circle (Plamennyi krug),* a cynical and cruel massacre of the poetic cliche, represent not a tempting model but an ominous warning to any brave idiot who might in the future try to write such verse.

With the same resoluteness as Bryusov, Annensky introduced into poetry the historically objective theme, introduced into the lyric psychological constructivism. Burning with a desire to learn from the West, he had no teachers worthy of his mission and was compelled to pretend to be an imitator. Annensky's psychologism is not a caprice and it is not the brief flash of a highly refined sensibility; it is genuine, firm construction. There is a straight line leading from Anennsky's "Steel Cicada" *(Stal'naia tsikada)* to Aseev's "Steel Nightingale" *(Stal'noi solovei).* Annensky taught the lesson how to use psychological analysis as a working tool in the lyric. He was the real forerunner of the psychological construction so brilliantly headed by Pasternak in Russian Futurism. Annensky has not up to now found his Russian reader and is known only by Akhmatova's vulgarization of his methods. One would like to transfer every poem in his books *Quiet Songs (Tikhie pesni)* and *The Cypress Chest (Kiparisovyi larets)* into an anthology.

If Russian Symbolism had its Virgils and Ovids, it also had its Catulluses, not so much on account of their age as their type of work. Here one must mention Kuzmin and Khodasevich. These are typical younger poets with all the purity and charm of sound characteristic of younger poets. For Kuzmin the older line in world literature would appear not to exist at all. He is completely biased toward it and completely bent on canonizing the younger line, something about on the level of Goldoni's comedy and the love songs of Sumarokov. He rather successfully cultivated in his poetry a conscious carelessness and awkwardness of speech, sprinkled with Gallicisms and Polonisms. Taking his fire from the younger poetry of the West, from, say, Musset—cf. his "New Rolla" *(Novyi Rolla)*—he gives the reader the illusion of a completely artificial and premature decrepitude in the Russian poetic language. Kuzmin's poetry is the premature senile smile of the Russian lyric. Khodasevich cultivated the theme of Baratynsky, "My gift is poor and my voice quiet" *(Moi dar ubog i golos moi negromok)*, and worked every possible variation on the theme of the prematurely born child. His younger line is that of the secondary poets of the Pushkin and post-Pushkin periods, the domestic amateur poets like Countess Rostopchina, Vyazemsky, and so on. Coming from the best period of Russian poetic dilettantism—that of the home album, the friendly epistle in verse, the casual epigram—Khodasevich carried right into the twentieth century the intricacy and the gentle crudeness of the common Moscow idiom, used in the literary circles of the nobility of the last century. His poetry is very much of the people, very literary, and very elegant.

An intense interest in the entire range of Russian poetry—all the way from the powerfully clumsy Derzhavin and reaching to that Aeschylus of the Russian iambic line, Tyutchev—preceded the rise of Futurism. At that time, roughly just before the beginning of the World War, all the old poets abruptly began to seem new. Everyone was seized by a fever of revaluation and hasty correction of historical injustice and short memory. Essentially, what happened then was that all Russian poetry struck the new curiosity and the renovated hearing of the reader as transsense. The revolutionary revaluation of the past had preceded the creative revolution. To assert and justify the real values of the past is just as revolutionary an act as creating new values. Most unfortunately, however, memory and deed quickly parted and did not go hand in hand. Those directed toward the future *(budushchniki)* and those toward the past *(passeisty)* very quickly awoke to find themselves in two warring camps. The futuremen indiscriminately rejected the past, though their rejection was nothing more than a diet. For reasons of hygiene, they denied themselves the reading of the old poets, or they read them on the sly without admitting it publicly. The pastmen prescribed exactly the same sort of diet for themselves. I will go so far as to say that many respected men of letters refrained from reading their contemporaries—up to recent times, when they had to do so. It would seem that the history of literature has never known such implacable enmity and misunderstanding. The quarrel, say, of the classicists and the romantics was child's play as compared to the abyss that opened up in Russia. But very soon there appeared a criterion by means of which one could understand this impassioned literary litigation between two generations: whoever does not understand the new has no comprehension of the past, and whoever comprehends the past must also understand the new. The whole tragedy arises when, instead of the real past with its deep roots, we get "yesterday." This "yesterday" is easily understood poetry, a hen-house with a fence, a cosy little corner where domestic fowl cluck and peck about. This is not work done upon the word but rather respite from the word. The frontiers of this world, this comfortable repose from active poetry, are at the moment defined approximately by Akhmatova and Blok, and not because Akhmatova or Blok, after the necessary deletions have been made from their works, prove to be bad in themselves—Akhmatova and Blok, to be sure, were never meant for people with a moribund consciousness of language. If the linguistic consciousness of the age was dying in them, it was dying a glorious death. It was "what in a rational being we call / the lofty diffidence of suffering," and certainly not the inveterate stupidity, bordering on malicious ignorance, of their sworn critics and admirers. Akhmatova, writing in the purest literary language of her time, used with extraordinary obstinacy the devices of the Russian folksong—and not only of the Russian folksong but of all folksongs in general. What we find in her poetry is by no means psychological discontinuity but the typical parallelism of the folksong with its acute asymmetry of two adjacent theses, on the pattern of: "The elder tree is in the garden, but Uncle is in Kiev." Hence her twofold stanza with the sudden thrust at the end. Her poetry is close to the folksong not only in structure but in essence, for it consists always and exclusively of lamentation. Considering the poet's purely literary vocabulary, filtered through clenched teeth, these qualities make her especially interesting and permit one to divine in this literary lady of the twentieth century an old peasant woman.

Blok is the most complex phenomenon of literary eclecticism—he is a gatherer of the Russian poetry that was scattered and lost by the historically shattered nineteenth century. The great work of collecting Russian poetry carried on by Blok is still not clear to his contemporaries and is felt by them only instinctively as a kind of melodic force. The acquisitive nature of Blok, his striving to centralize poetry and language, recalls the governmental instinct of the historic figures of Moscow. His is a powerful, stern hand as regards anything provincial: everything for Moscow, i.e., in the present case, for the historically formed poetry of the traditional language of the man of government.

Futurism is all in provincialism, in the tumultuous conflict of the medieval principalities, in folkloric and ethnographic dissonance. Try looking for that in Blok! His work proceeded at right angles with history and serves to prove the fact that the government of language lives its own special life.

Actually, Futurism ought not to have aimed its blade against the paper fortress of Symbolism but against Blok, alive and really dangerous. And if it failed to do this, it was only thanks to its native inner piety and its literary decorum.

Futurism confronted Blok with Khlebnikov. What were they to say to each other? Their battle is going on in our own time, when neither the one nor the other is still alive. Like Blok, Khlebnikov conceived of language as a state, only not spatial, not geographical, but temporal. Blok is contemporary to the marrow of his bones; his time will crumble and be forgotten, but he will still remain in the consciousness of generations as a contemporary of his own time. Khlebnikov does not know the meaning of contemporary. He is a citizen of all history, of the whole system of language and poetry. A kind of idiotic Einstein, incapable of distinguishing which is closer—a a railroad bridge or the *Igor Tale*. Khlebnikov's poetry is idiotic in the genuine Greek,inoffensive meaning of that word. His contemporaries could not and cannot forgive him the absence in his work of the least trace of his epoch's temporary insanity. How horrible it must have been when this man, completely oblivious of his audience, making no distinction between his own time and other millenia, proved on top of everything to be extraordinarily sociable and supremely gifted with the purely Pushkinian gift of poetic small talk. Khlebnikov makes jokes—and no one laughs. Khlebnikov makes light, elegant allusions—and no one catches them. A huge part of what Khlebnikov wrote is nothing other than what he took to be poetic small talk, corresponding to the digressions in *Eugene Onegin* or to Pushkin's "Order yourself some macaroni with Parmesan in Tver, and make an omelette" *(Zakazhi sebe v Tveri / S parmazanom makaroni, / Da iaishnitsu svari)*. He wrote jocular dramas—*The World Hind Part Before (Mir s kontsa)*— and tragic buffonades—*Miss Death (Baryshnia Smert')*. He left examples of marvelous prose, virginal and incomprehensible as a story told by a child because of the onrush of images and ideas, each driving the other from one's consciousness. Each line that he wrote is the beginning of a new long poem. Every tenth line is an aphorism seeking some stone or bronze plaque upon which to rest. Khlebnikov did not even write poems or epics but a huge all-Russian book of prayers and icons upon which, for centuries and centureis, everyone who has the energy may draw.

Alongside Khlebnikov, as if for contrast, the mocking genius of fate placed Mayakovsky, with his poetry of common sense. There is common sense in all poetry. But specific common sense is nothing other than a pedagogic device. The teaching in schools, instilling already evident truths into the heads of children, makes use of visual aids, i.e., of a poetic tool. The emotion of common sense is a part of school pedagogy. Mayakovsky's merit is in the poetic perfection of school pedagogy—in applying to the enlightenment of the masses the powerful techniques of visual education. Like a school teacher, Mayakovsky walks about with a globe of the world and with the other emblems of the visual method. He has replaced the repulsive newspaper of recent times, in which no one understood anything, with a simple wholesome school. A great reformer of the newspaper, he has left a deep imprint on the poetic language, simplifying the syntax to the limits of the possible and directing the noun to the honored place of priority in the sentence. The strength and precision of his language make Mayakovsky akin to the traditional farcical sideshow man. Both Khlebnikov and Mayakovsky are so much of the people that populism, i.e., folklore with a crude sugar coating, would seem to have no place beside them. It continues, though, to exist in the poetry of Esenin and partially in that of Klyuev. The significance of these poets is in their rich provincialisms, which link them to one of the basic tendencies of the age.

Aseev stands completely aside from Mayakovsky. He has created the vocabulary of a qualified technician. He is a poet-engineer, specialist, work-organizer. In the West such people—engineers, radio technicians, inventors of machines—are poetically mute, or they read Francois Coppée. It is characteristic of Aseev that he puts the machine like some practical contrivance at the basis of a poetry that says nothing about the machine at all. The coupling and breaking of the lyrical current gives the impression of a rapid fusing and strong emotional discharge. Aseev is extraordinarily lyrical and sober in his relation to the word. He never poeticizes but simply installs the lyrical current like a good electrician, using the required material.

The dams which artifically restrained the development of the poetic language have now already collapsed, and all foppish or dress-uniform innovation is unnecessary and even reactionary.

In poetry the truly creative is not the epoch of invention but the epoch of imitation. When the prayerbooks have been written—that is the time to perform the service. The last Poetic Prayerbook to be issued for the general use and practice of all Russians was Pasternak's *My Sister Life (Sestra moia zhizn')*. Not since Batyushkov has such a new and mature harmony sounded in Russian poetry. Pasternak is neither a falsifier nor a magician, but the founder of a new mode, a new system of Russian poetry, corresponding to the maturity and manhood achieved by the language. With this new harmony it is possible to say whatever one likes. Everyone, whether he wishes it or not, will use it, since from now on it is the general property of all Russian poets. Up to this time the logical structure of the sentence came to an end at the same time as the poem itself, i.e., it was only the briefest means of expressing the poetic thought. Owing to its frequent use in poetry the customary logical process has become effaced and imperceptible as such. Syntax, i.e., the circulatory system of poetry, is stricken with sclerosis.

Then there arrives a poet who resurrects the virginal strength of logical structure in the sentence. It was just this in Batyushkov that astonished Pushkin, and Pasternak awaits his Pushkin.

Translated by Clarence Brown

---

[1]The Russian title *"Buria i natisk"* is the normal equivalent of the German *"Sturm und Drang."* This essay first appeared in the journal *Russian Art (Russkoe iskusstvo),* 1 (1923), 75-82.

[2]"Transsense" is the usual English translation for the Russian *zaum,* an artificially concocted "language" made up of nonsense words and briefly affected by certain of the Futurist poets. There are other terms for it. Vladimir Nabokov's is "sub-mental grunt."

POETRY

Alexander Blok

NIGHTINGALE GARDEN

Translated by
Rodney L. Patterson

I

At ebbtide on the silty beach
I shatter these rippled shells
And my burro hauls the pieces
On his strong and shaggy back.

And we'll take them up to the railway,
Pile them up and return to the sea.
We follow the furry legs to the sea
And the burro begins to bray.

And he trumpets and brays in his gladness
For the joy of returning unladen.
And hard by the road, deeply shaded,
Is the garden, in a pool of coolness.

Superfluous rosebuds abundantly fall,
Trail down from the high, long wall.
Incessant, the nightingale's songs resound
Within the whispers of brooks and leaves.

And each time, as we pass the garden wall,
My burro stops to send within his call
And someone quietly laughs within,
Then, retreating, begins to sing.

I would sink in the song's disturbing deeps,
And, as I urge my burro on, I watch
The murk descending, blue and deep,
On the scorched and scalloped rocks.

II

The searing day fades out without a trace,
Twilight creeps through the leaves,
And the burro, poor thing, is amazed
At his master's *aboulie.*

Or am I deep in twilight dreams?
Or has the heat disturbed my mind?
Yet ever more relentlessly I dream
Of another life—mine, not mine.

Dispossessed and hapless, what do I await
In this close, dilapidated shack,
All the while repeating strange refrains
That ring within the garden of nightingales?

The curses of life cannot transgress
The sentinel, fragrant wall around the garden.
In the twilight blue within, a white dress
Gleams beyond the fretted trellis.

As I go by these portals
In the evenings, in the mists of sunsets,
She gracefully entices me
With songs and pirouettes.

And I apprehend what I've unlearned
In her alluring whirls and melodies,
And I come to love my languor
And walls' impenetrabilities.

III

The pickax lies discarded by a rock
And my exhausted burro rests
While his enamored master walks
Beyond the night, beyond the burning haze.

The rocky, empty trail I knew so well
Is now a most mysterious route
Returning to the shadowed wall
Receding deep in murky blues.

And this endless languor deepens,
And monotonous hours the hours ensue,
And today the thorny roses grew
Nutant under lavish dew.

Will I find reward or retribution
If I stray from the road by the garden?
What would happen if I dared intrusion,
If I rapped at the gate of the garden?

Now even the past has grown foreign
And the hand refuses its burdens,
But the heart prepares for its welcome,
Its welcome in nightingale garden.

IV

And my heart spoke the truth—
The wall concealed no terrors.
I didn't even need to knock.
It was she who threw open the redoubtable doors.

By the cool, lily-strewn trail
The brook ran sweet with song.
And, stunned by the rush of its song,
My soul was stolen by the nightingale.

Her embraces now opened to me
A mysterious realm of astonishing bliss—
And the ring of her falling jewelry
Rang louder than in my poor dreams.

While drunk with gold-hued Ai
And scorched by golden-veined flames,
I forgot the rock-strewn trail to the sea
And I even forgot my hapless friend.

V

Let the wall, sunk in roses deep,
Be a shelter from earthly grief
And muffle the murmuring sea—
The nightingale's song is not free!

In its song I hear an anxious note,
Merged deep in combers' roar it comes to me...
All at once—a vision: a wide road
And the tired perambulation of my donkey.

While in the dark and fragrant heat,
Entwined by her burning hands,
I listen as she anxiously repeats:
"Beloved, what troubles you?"

But staring lonely in the darkness,
Athirst to inhale this bliss
My listening soul cannot miss
The incoming tide's distant thunder.

VI

I awoke in the fog-shrouded gloaming,
In the dawning—who knows of what day.
She slept like an infant, smiling,
And I was the dream that she had.

What beauty when twilight, enchanted at dusk
Transfigures such faces made limpid from lust!
By the distant, even breakers' roar
I knew the tide was on the rise.

I pushed apart the azure panes
And thought I heard, it seemed,
Far beyond the distant, bickering surf
A plaintive, beckoning scream.

Though I quietly drew the canopy
To prolong the bewitching dream,
My burro's long and longing scream
Sank in my soul like a keen.

And I broke the blossoms' oblivion
As I scaled the sentinel stones.
Sharp thorns, like hands from the garden,
Reached after me, caught at my coat.

VII

The familiar path, once easy,
This morning was rocky and hard.
I step out on the beach, now empty,
Where I left my burro and home.

Or am I the butt of a joke?
Or was I astray in the haze?
No, I know these shapes of rocks,
The gaunt bushes, boulder over the waves...

I stumble against the discarded ax
With slipping feet...But where's the shack?
Rusted, heavy, beneath the black boulder,
Covered with sea-dampened sand...

Stretching with a familiar motion
(Or am I dreaming still?)
I shatter foliated shells on the ocean's
Floor with the rusting pick.

And from the place where the gray octopi
Have swayed in chinks as blue as the sky
A crab began to clamber out,
Shaken and cowed on the sandy shoal.

I moved a bit—He reared
With widely opening claws...
But immediately met another—
They fought and disappeared.

At the place where my cabin once stood,
On the path that I had furrowed,
A worker began to descend with an ax,
Driving before him another burro.

The Unknown Lady

The restaurants on hot spring evenings
Lie under a dense and savage air.
Foul drafts and hoots from drunken revelers
Contaminate the thoroughfare.

Above the dusty lanes of suburbia
Above the tedium of bungalows
A pretzel sign begilds a bakery
And children screech fortissimo.

And every evening beyond the barriers
Gentlemen of practiced wit and charm
Go strolling beside the drainage ditches—
A tilted derby and a lady at the arm.

The squeak of oarlocks comes over the lake water
A woman's shriek assaults the ear
While above, in the sky, inured to everything,
The moon looks on with a mindless leer.

And every evening my one companion
Sits here, reflected in my glass.
Like me, he has drunk of bitter mysteries.
Like me, he is broken, dulled, downcast.

The sleepy lackeys stand beside tables
Waiting for the night to pass
And tipplers with the eyes of rabbits
Cry out: "In vino veritas!"

And every evening (or am I imagining?)
Exactly at the appointed time
A girl's slim figure, silk raimented,
Glides past the window's mist and grime.

And slowly, passing through the revelers,
Unaccompanied, always alone,
Exuding mists and secret fragrances,
She sits at the table that is her own.

Something ancient, something legendary
Surrounds her presence in the room,
Her narrow hand, her silk, her bracelets,
Her hat, the rings, the ostrich plume.

Entranced by her presence, near and enigmatic,
I gaze through the dark of her lowered veil
And I behold an enchanted shoreline
And enchanted distances, far and pale.

I am made a guardian of the higher mysteries,
Someone's sun is entrusted to my control.
Tart wine has pierced the last convolution
of my labyrinthine soul.

And now the drooping plumes of ostriches
Asway in my brain droop slowly lower
And two eyes, limpid, blue, and fathomless
Are blooming on a distant shore.

Inside my soul a treasure is buried.
The key is mine and only mine.
How right you are, you drunken monster!
I know: the truth is in the wine.

1906   *Translated by George M. Young, Jr.*

Today I don't remember what happened yesterday,
And every morning all my evenings go away.
In broad day I forget the light,
And I forget the day at night.

But all the nights and days flow in to us
At the solemn hour of death.
And then—the closeness chokes our breath,
Too painful is the sight
Of beauty past
You cannot see,
You want to rise at last
And it is night.

Feb. 3, 1909   *Translated by Barbara Heldt Monter*

I pass away this life of mine,
This life so mad, so dark and dull;
Today I soberly exult,
Tomorrow I shall sing and whine.

But if perdition does impend?
But if right there behind my back
That one—whose hand, immense and black
Has veiled the mirror—does attend?

The mirror's light sparks in the eyes,
And horrified, my lids drawn tight,
I step back to that realm of night
Where not a single exit lies...

Sept. 27, 1910   *Translated by Gary Kern*

For Anna Akhmatova

"Beauty is frightening," they will tell you—
Lazily you will arrange
A Spanish shawl on your shoulders,
A red rose in your hair.

"Beauty is simple," they will tell you—
Clumsily with a motley shawl
You will cover a child up,
A red rose on the floor.

But, distractedly heeding
All the words sounding around you,
Sadly lost in thought
You will say about yourself:

"I am neither frightening nor simple;
I am not so frightening, that I would simply
Kill; I am not so simple
That I do not know how frightening life is."

December 10, 1913   *Translated by Barbara Heldt Monter*

'Twas there a man burned out.
                    Fet

How burdensome to walk among the people
And to pretend you have not died,
And of the play, so tragical, of passions
To tell to ones not yet alive.

And, peering deep into your private nightmare,
To find a shape in feeling's shapeless swirl,
So from the livid scarlet glows of art
They will perceive a deathly lifetime's flare!

May 10, 1910   *Translated by Gary Kern*

From sunset she appeared,
Her cloak pierced by a bloom
Of unfamiliar climes.

She summoned me somewhere
Into the northern gloom
And aimless winter ice.

And bonfire burned 'mid night,
And with its tongues the blaze
Did lick the very skies.

The eyes flashed fiery light,
And falling as black snakes
The tresses were released.

And then the snakes encircled
My mind and lofty spirit
Lay spread upon the cross.

And in the snowdust's swirl
To black eyes I am true,
To beauty of the coils.

November 8, 1907

Translated by Gary Kern

The Twelve

Translated by Arthur Clifford

1
Black evening,
white snow.
Wind! Wind! Wind!
Men up-ended; legs, feet unpinned.
Wind! Wind! Wind!
sweeps through God's vast land.

Winds, whirling, cleaving,
powder the snow.
Under the powder — ice.
Heavy, slipping, slow,
each walker tries
somehow — ah, poor fellow!

From corner to corner
they hang out grimly
a disconsolate banner:
"All power to the Constituent Assembly!"
A whimpering old woman asks humbly,
But what can it mean, this banner?
From such a splendid streamer
how many rags could be got?
Excellent foot-wrappings for her family,
and all — unclothed, unshod . . .

The Twelve

Translated by Natasha Templeton

1

Black evening.
White snow.
Wind, wind!
Man can't stand it.
Wind, wind —
All over God's world.

The wind whirls
The white snowflakes.
Under the coat of snow, there's ice.
It's slippery, it's hard going,
Everyone skidding —
Oops! — Oh, poor soul!

They've stretched a rope
Across the street,
And on it's a banner:
"All Power to the Constituent Assembly!"
The old woman's crying her heart out,
Can't think what it's all about,
What such a banner's for,
Such a huge piece of stuff?
So many foot-rags there for the boys,
All of them wanting clothes, and boots!

She shakes her head, incredulous;
hen-like, scurries through snowdrifts, darts and weaves.
    — Oh, Mother, intercede for us!
    — The Bolsheviks will drive us to our graves!

        The frost grows no warmer,
        the wind's bite no duller.
        A bourgeois on the corner
        hides his nose in his collar.

And who's this? A long-haired one
rasps in an undertone:
        — Traitors!
        — Russia is cursed!
One of those writers —
        of verse . . .

Here also, long-skirted —
a ghost at the feast . . .
Why today so downhearted,
        comrade priest?

Can't recall how you'd pass,
paunch well advanced,
and the paunch with its cross
held the people entranced?

Ah! Milady in fur
saw a friend, runs to her:
— But my dear, but how awful . . .
        Oops! A fateful
slip — bang! — a pratfall.

        Oh! Oh!
        Pull, heave ho!

        And the wind in spurts,
        now rogue, now clown,
        peeps under skirts,
        mows people down;

Like a hen, any-old-how,
She's scrambled up and over the snowbank.
　　　— Och, Mother of God, pray for us!
　　　— These bolsheviks, they'll drive us to the grave!

　　　　　The wind's like a whip,
　　　　　And there's frost to follow up!
　　　　　The bourgeois at the cross-roads
　　　　　Tucks his nose into his coat.

And who's that? — with the long hair,
Muttering beneath his breath:
　　　　　— Traitors! he says,
　　　　　— Russia's done for!
Must be a writer —
　　　　　An orator . . .

And there's that fellow in the cassock —
Behind the snowbank, sneaking past . . .
Hey, what's eating you today,
　　　　　Comrade priest?

Remember how it used to be,
How you sailed about, all belly,
With your cross, and how it shone,
Your belly, on the people? . .

And over there, in her astrakhan,
Madame swept up to a friend:
— Oh how we cried and cried . . . But then
　　　　　She slipped
And — bam! — went sprawling!

　　　　　My, my!
　　　Up she comes — heave!

　　　The gay wind's
　　　Both glad and angry,
　　　Twists skirts,
　　　Cuts people down

93

rips, ruffles, nimbly
plays with the bunting:
"All Power to the Constituent Assembly!" . . .
and sends phrases floating:

. . . Yes, we organized a union . . .
. . . reached certain conclusions . . .
. . . after serious discussion —
passed resolutions:
Our price for one, we said, is ten;
the night-rate, twenty-five a head . . .
. . . Coming to bed? . . .

Late night.
Empty street.
One, ill-dressed,
still on his feet.
How the winds bite! . . .

Distressed?
Come with me —
charity . . .

Bread!
What's the world coming to?
Off with you!

Black, black skies.

Fury, bitter fury
seethes in the breast . . .
Black fury, holy fury . . .

Comrade! Keep your eyes open .
Be wary!

2
In flying snow, in playing wind —
and bonfires, bonfires all around —

And tears and crumples and drags about
The enormous banner:
"All Power to the Constituent Assembly!" . . .
And whispers these words:

. . . We too had a meeting . . .
. . . In this very building . . .
. . . We've discussed,
And we've decided:
A short time, ten; twenty-five for the night . . .
. . . And nothing less from anyone. . .
. . . Let's get some sleep . . .

Late evening.
The street's soon empty.
Only a tramp,
Hunched up,
And the wind whistling . . .

Hey you, you poor bugger!
Come over here —
Come and give us a hug . . .

Bread! Yes —
But what's ahead for us?
Go on, get off with you!

Black, black sky.

Hatred, sad hatred
Boils in the breast . . .
Black hatred, holy hatred . . .

Comrade!
Watch out!

2
The wind whirls off, the snow dances down,
And twelve men go marching out.

walk twelve red guardsmen through the streets,
chewing on newsprint cigarettes.

Black rifle straps, crushed caps — perhaps
the ace of diamonds on their backs!

> Liberty, liberty!
> But not the cross? A pity!

> Tra-ta-tee!

It's a cold night, comrades, a cold, cold city!

— Look, Vanka and Katya are on a spree . . .
— He's tucked some cash behind her knee!

— Oh, Vanka's a trooper now. He's rich . . .
— Vanka was ours once. He's gone higher!

— Well, Vanka, big shot, son of a bitch,
that's my girl, damn you. Kiss her! Try her!

> Freedom, freedom, free-ee-dom.
> Alas, without the cross!
> Katya and Vanka are passing time,
> but — how do they make it pass?

> Tum-ti-tum!

Fires, fires, fires, all around . . .
A shoulder-strap to hold the gun . . .

Keep to the revolution's step!
The tireless enemy never sleeps!

Comrade, take courage, let nothing crush you!
We'll just put a slug through holy Russia —

> Through her wooden hide,
> through her huttish heart,
> into her fat ass!

> Alas, without the cross!

Black slings to their rifles,
Lights, and lights, and lights . . . all round them . . .

Fags in their teeth, and crumpled caps,
They want broad-arrows on their backs!

> Liberty, liberty,
> ay! Ay, and without the Cross!

> Tra-ta-ta!

It's cold, comrades — it's cold!

— Vanya's with Katya there in the pub . . .
— 'Er stockings are stuffed with Kerensky roubles!

— He's rich himself now, is old Vanya . . .
— He was one of us, and now he's a soldier!

— C'mon Vanya, you sonofabitch, you bourgeois,
You try and kiss my girl, I dare you!

> Liberty, liberty,
> ay! Ay, and without the Cross!
> Katya's busy with Vanya. — How,
> How's she busy?

> Tra-ta-ta!

Around them, lights, and lights, and lights . . .
Over their shoulders, rifle-slings . . .

For the Revolution, keep in step!
The tireless enemy's never asleep!

Come on, get a grip on your rifle, comrade!
Let's shoot off a bullet into Holy Russia —

> Good, sound
> Peasant stock,
> With her fat backside!

> Ay, ay, and without the Cross!

3

How our heedless headstrong lads
ran to join the young red guard —
ran to join the young red guard —
rushed to lose their precious heads!

You, poor little life, too bitter —
sweet to play at war!
Overcoat in tatters,
gun from Austria!

Watch us play! Let every master
watch! We fan the world fire faster,
stoke the world fire with our blood —
Cross yourself, by God!

4

The blizzard howls, a cabman bawls,
crazily a carriage rolls.
Shaft-lamps show up fleeing Vanka
and Katya in their glare . . .
Take aim — fire! . . .

Handsome in his military
coat and idiotic stare, he
twirls and twirls a black mustache.
Now he mopes a little,
Now he jokes a little . . .

Oh that Vanka — he's a gent!
Oh that Vanka — eloquent!
Hugs fool Katya still more tightly,
chatters on so brightly.

Laughing through a mass of curls,
Katya's teeth glisten like pearls . . .
Ah, my Katya, silly miss,
fair and fat of face . . .

3

That's the way the boys went off,
Off to serve in the Red Guard —
Off to serve in the Red Guard —
Mad-keen to get their heads shot off!

Ach, and a sorry life it is,
The only life we've got!
With an Austrian rifle
And a torn old coat!

Won't we make the bourgeois sorry
When we fan the world to fire,
Fan the world afire with blood —
    Bless us Thou the work O Lord!

4

Whirling snow, the driver yelling,
Vanya, Katya, off and racing —
There's the elecstetric lantern
    Twinkling on the shafts . . .
    Ready, steady — go! . .

With his military greatcoat
And his dopey-looking mug,
Keeps on twirling his moustache,
    Twisting it, and twirling it,
    Cracking jokes, cracking jokes . . .

Look at Vanya — look at those shoulders!
Look at him — he's full of blarney!
    Hugs that dummy Katya now,
        Chats her up a treat . . .

Back she lies, she smiles at him.
Her pretty teeth like shining pearls,
    That's my Katya, that's my own
    Wee cuddlesome Katya . . .

5

On your lovely neck, my Katya,
an ugly wound still needs a stitch.
Just below your breast, sweet Katya,
surely not a fresh scratch?

Ah, ah, she dances!
Pretty legs reward glances!

Lacy lingerie caressed you —
lift your arms, dear, show your charms!
Dashing officers undressed you —
Stole your charms, close in their arms!

Ah, ah, go straying!
A tender heart was your undoing!

Katya, what was your connection
with that poor young officer
knifed to death? . . No recollection? . .
You've forgotten the affair?

Ah, ah, relive it!
Go to bed now with it!

Once you had cadets to love you,
kiss the dainty shoes you wore,
buy you sweets, escort you — have you
now become a soldier's whore?

Ah, ah, so cosy!
Let your conscience rest easy!

6

. . . Again at a gallop the cabman tears,
screams . . . yells . . . roars . . . swears . . .

Halt! I'll fire! Andrushka, here,
help me! Run, Petrushka! The rear! . .

5
The knife-scar on your neck
Hasn't healed yet, Katya.
That scratch beneath your breast,
That's fresh too, Katya!

    Hey, hey, do a dance for us!
    Let's see those pretty legs of yours!

Once you had lace underwear —
So wear it, keep wearing it!
You whored around with officers —
So whore away, get on with it!

    Hey, hey, get on with it!
    My heart leaps when I think of it!

The officer, Katya — remember him?
He didn't escape the knife . . .
Or don't you think of him now, you bitch?
Isn't that memory fresh?

    Hey, hey don't you forget!
    Put me down for a night of it!

Once you'd fancy spats to wear,
Liqueur creams to guzzle on,
Once you went with the officers —
Now you've got around to men?

    Hey, hey, screw away!
    It doesn't matter a damn to me!

6
The cabby gallops back again,
Screeching, yelling out to them . . .

Stop, stop! Andryukha, give us a hand!
Petrukha, you get round behind! . .

T-r-rahk — tarar-r-rahk — tahk-tahk — tahk-tahk!
Snow-puffs mark the bullets' track . . .

The cab careens. Vanka holds on . . .
They're still in range! Cock your gun!

Trahk — tararahk! You won't be so quick
.   .   .   .
to steal a man's chick behind his back! . .

We've lost the bastard! Let him go.
I'll settle accounts with him tomorrow.

But where's Katya got to? — Dead, dead!
Here on the street. Shot through the head!

What, Katya, the merry one? — Sh! No one's to know . . .
Lie there, carrion, in the snow!

March to the revolution's step!
The tireless enemy never sleeps!

7
And again the twelve go marching,
shouldered rifles strapped in place,
footsteps crunching, faces searching
for the poor murderer's face . . .

Panic-stricken, now with quickened
steps he draws himself apart,
muffler wrapped around his neck and
desolation in his heart . . .

— Hey there, comrade, what's your hurry?
— Hey, your nose is dragging, friend.
— Hey, Petrushka, feeling sorry
over Katya's sticky end?

— Comrades stop! My heart is breaking.
Oh how close she was, how dear . . .

Trakh-tararakh-takh-takh-takh-takh!
The snow spun up in the air like dust!

The cabby's off — and Vanya with him . . .
Once again now! Pull the trigger! . .

Trakh-tararakh! I'll see you learn
.   .   .   .
To play around with another's man girl! . .

Got away, the rat! You wait, though,
I'll get even with you tomorrow!

But where's Katya? — Dead as dead!
Shot, shot right through the head!

Happy, Katya? — Not a cheep!
Lying on the snow in a heap!

For the Revolution, keep in step!
The tireless enemy's never asleep!

7

And again the twelve march on,
At their shoulders their rifles swing.
Only the poor murderer's face
Looks blank, featureless . . .

Faster now, and faster still.
He goes striding on ahead.
He's wrapped his scarf around his neck —
He just can't snap out of it . . .

— And what's eating you, comrade?
— What's struck you dumb, old man?
— Petrukha, what's made you so sour?
You feeling sorry for Katya now?

— Oh my friends, dear friends,
I did love that girl . . .

Oh, those dark intoxicating
nights I tossed about with her . . .

— Just because her eyes would smoulder,
filled with fire and deviltry,
just because beside her shoulder
there's a crimson strawberry,
so in senseless rage I killed her,
killed her — killer her senselessly. . . Ah!

— Silence, oaf, that tune's been played out.
Shut it off! Give it a rest!
— Want to turn your soul inside out?
Are you some old woman? Yes?
— Stand erect! Show what you're made of!
— Try to be a man at least!

— Please dear comrade, we can't nurse you.
We've got load enough to bear!
While you follow on this course you
make our burden heavier!

Petka bravely wipes a tearful
eye and slows his hasty steps . . .

lifts his head and shows a cheerful
grin that spreads across his lips . . .

It's no sin
to have, tra la, a bit of fun!

Burghers, barricade the floors!
Robbers roam outside your doors!

Leave the cellar latchkeys out —
The poor are thirsty. It's your shout!

8
Ah, how bitter, wearisome!
    Deadly drearisome,
        tiresome!

104

Drunk with our love, we were, those nights
I used to spend with her . . .

— All for the reckless bravery
That flashed in her eyes like fire,
All for the sake of the scarlet mole
By her right shoulder there,
I've killed her now, and in anger — Oh!

— What d'you know, the bastard's whining!
What are you, Petya, a girl, or what?
— So now he wants to turn his soul
Inside out for us? So what!
— Hitch up your dignity!
— Take care to keep yourself in control!

— My dear comrade, don't depend
On us to nurse you now.
In times like these you're going to find
We've bigger jobs to do!

And Petrukha slows
His hasty stride . . .

  Hi-ho!
It's no sin to have fun!

Lock up your flats!
There's looting tonight!

Open the cellars —
The gang's on the town tonight.

8
Now I know what grief is,
    The emptiness,
        Like death, it is!

Listlessly watching
it grow late, it grow late . . .

Restlessly scratching
at my pate, at my pate . . .

Moodily spitting
empty husks, empty husks . . .

Futilely whittling
until dusk, until dusk! . .

Fly away, bourgeois, fly with the starling!
        I'll drink a toast in
        blood to the ghost of
        my black-browed darling . . .

Peace to her soul, dear Lord, and receive thy slave. . .

        Tedium!

                9
A stillness falls on Nevsky Tower;
wine and the city's noise are gone;
No night watch walks to call the hour —
Make merry, boys, as best you can!

A bourgeois stands at a lonely corner,
his collar raised to hide his nose.
A mangy wire-haired fellow-mourner
tucks in its tail and presses close.

The bourgeois stands in silent wonder
like a hungry dog, a question mark;
and, like a dog with its tail tucked under,
the old world lifts a frightened bark.

So, for now,
To pass the time . . .

To pass the time,
I'll scratch my head . . .

Sunflower seeds
I'll crack and spit . . .

And take my knife
And slash, and slit . . .

Yes, bourgeois, you fly away, like a sparrow!
    I'll drink your blood,
    For that girl that I loved,
    Those dark eyes she had . . .

Lord, have mercy on her soul . . .

    The emptiness!

9

Not an echo now of the city's roar,
By the tower on the Neva silence reigns,
And no policeman any more —
So live it up, boys, without your wine!

The bourgeois stands at the cross-roads
And into his collar he's tucked his nose,
And the scabby cur cringing at his side
Tucks in its tail and presses closed.

The bourgeois like a question stands there
Silent, hungry as the dog,
And like a stray the old world stands
Behind him, tail between its legs.

10

Now the snowstorm raged, besotted.
      — trees matted, streets clotted!
Men from other men were blotted
      scarcely four short steps ahead!

Snow in tunnels was boring.
Snow in columns was soaring . . .

— Snow will bury us! Dear Mother!
— Petka, honest! From what other
dangers have you ever been
rescued by the altar screen?
Use your reason, comrade. Steady!
Aren't your hands already bloody? —
Aren't they stained with Katya's blood
just because you lost your head?
— March! The revolution marches!
Watch! The sly enemy approaches!

      On, on, on again,
        workingmen!

11

. . . On into the distance go the marchers
      still without the cross,
        ready for the future,
          heedless of the past . . .

Rifles trained on the remotest
hidden foe, prepared to shoot, . .
into alleys where the snowdust
shows no print of living foot, . .
into drifts that grimly protest
when a man steals back a boot . . .

      Let the red folds
      proudly shake.

10

The blizzard's gone berserk,
  Hey blizzard, blizzard hey!
Can't see the other blokes
  Even four steps away!

The snow spun like a funnel . . .
The snow rose like a pillar . . .

— Och Savior, what a storm it is!
— Hey Petya, steady on with your lies!
Tell me, when's your precious savior
Ever done any good?
You're not being sensible about it,
You stop and think, and get things straight —
Wasn't it Katya's love, that caused
Your hands to be so stained with blood?
— Keep your step, for the Revolution!
The tireless enemy is not far off!

  On, on, on,
   Workers, march on!

11

. . . And on they march, without God's blessing,
  On, and on, all twelve of them.
   Ready for anything,
   Sorry for nothing . . .

Their steel rifles trained
On the invisible foe . . .
Into silent alleyways
Where only the storm whisks up the snow . . .
And into drifts like feather-beds
That won't let your boot go . . .

  Again the red flag
  Strikes the eye.

Measured footfalls
dully creak.

Look! The artful
foe's awake!

And the driving snowdust plays on
eyes for the days and
nights on end.

On, on again,
workingmen!

12

. . . On they stride into the distance . . .
— Halt! Who goes there? Foe or friend?
Just the sibilant resistance
of a red flag in the wind . . .

On they thrust into the driving
snow. — Does anyone respond? . .
Just a miserable starving
dog that hobbles on behind.

— On your way, scabby mongrel.
You'll get teased with my bayonet!
Down, old world, mangy scoundrel.
You've a taste of cat to get!

. . . On behind them trails the friendless
dog, its wolfish teeth laid bare —
tail tucked inward — cold and kinless . . .
— Look here, answer, who goes there?

— There's the red flag but who carries
it? — Open your eyes. What gloom!
— Who among the houses hurries?
— Stop! What are you hiding from?

The measured tread
Resounds, resounds.

Look out! The deadly
Enemy stirs . . .

But the blizzard fills their eyes
Nights and days
Ceaselessly . . .

On, onward,
Workers, on!

12

. . . With sovereign tread they march away.
— Who's that there? You come out!
That's the demented wind there playing
With the red flag out in front. . .

Out in front, there's a cold snowdrift.
— Who's in the snowdrift? Out of there! . .
Only that beggar limping after
At their heels, the hungry cur . . .

— Get out of that, you scabby creature,
I'll tickle you with my bayonet!
Get lost, like the mangy hound you are,
You old world — or I'll beat you up!

It bares its teeth like a hungry wolf,
Tucks in its tail, won't let them go —
The cold, homeless mongrel brute . . .
— Who goes there? Hey, speak up, you!

— Who's there, that's waving the red flag?
— You try and see — how dark it is!
— Who goes there, like a fugitive,
Hiding behind every house?

— Well, it's all the same, I'll get you.
Live or die, it's up to you!
— Comrade, we don't want to shoot you.
Speak up or you'll force us to!

Trahk-tahk-tahk! — But only echoes
stir the houses' sleeping rows . . .
only the snowstorm's laughter cackles,
long, long laughter in the snows . . .

           Trahk-tahk-tahk!
           Trahk-tahk-tahk!

      . . . So, behind a blood-stained standard,
      trailed by a hungry dog, they go
striding onward. In their vanguard
      out of sight above the storm —
      safe, disdainful of the storm
of bullets, haloed in white roses,
with a footstep that diffuses
      just a scatter of pearl-like dust —
      at their head — walks Jesus Christ.

— Wait and see, I'm going to get you,
Better give yourself up alive!
— Hey, comrade, you'll regret it,
Come on out, or we'll open fire!

Trakh-takh-takh! — But only the echo
Answers from the houses now . . .
Only the blizzard with its gigantic
Laughter pealing through the snow . . .

      Trakh-takh-takh!
      Trakh-takh-takh . . .

    . . . So they march with sovereign tread —
      At their heels, the hungry dog,
At their head — with a bloody flag,
      And unseen behind the storm,
      Among the bullets free from harm,
As softly walking upon the blizzard
As snowy pearls roll lightly scattered,
      His brow with white roses wreathed —
      At their head, goes Jesus Christ.

ANDREI BELY

To Friends

The poet trusted
Golden lustres.
But
It was
A solar arrow's thrust
From which he died.
Bridging ages
With his mind
He met his death
With half a life
Still left
Unlived.
Do not deride
The poet.
Bring him laurels
In wintertime
And summertime
My china wreath
Still beats
Against his cross.
The china flowers
Have all worn off,
The ikon faded
In the withering wind.
Someone someday
Will surely cart away
These heavy headstones.

He loved only
The pealing belfry
And sunset.
Then why this pain?
This pain?
I'm not to blame.

Come! Spare me!
I'll rush to meet you
With a garland.
Oh, love me!
Love me!
Perhaps I
Didn't die,
Perhaps again
I'll stir again,
Return again!

Translated by
Rodney Patterson

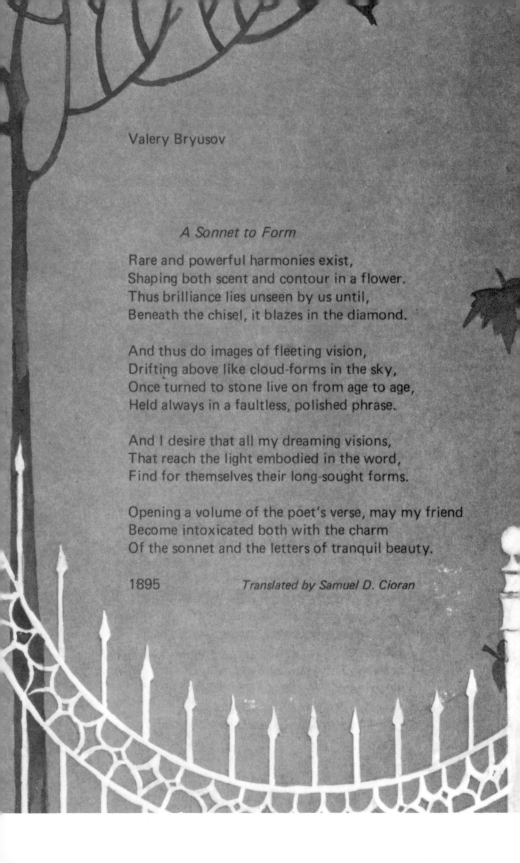

Valery Bryusov

A Sonnet to Form

Rare and powerful harmonies exist,
Shaping both scent and contour in a flower.
Thus brilliance lies unseen by us until,
Beneath the chisel, it blazes in the diamond.

And thus do images of fleeting vision,
Drifting above like cloud-forms in the sky,
Once turned to stone live on from age to age,
Held always in a faultless, polished phrase.

And I desire that all my dreaming visions,
That reach the light embodied in the word,
Find for themselves their long-sought forms.

Opening a volume of the poet's verse, may my friend
Become intoxicated both with the charm
Of the sonnet and the letters of tranquil beauty.

1895   *Translated by Samuel D. Cioran*

POEMS BY KONSTANTIN BALMONT

Translated by Rodney Patterson

She Rests

She rests. Two ivory goblets are her breasts,
And her closed eyes—twin azure skies.
Is she to blame that in the turquoise heights
Her dreams fall still, then glow in dread unrest?

Through her the battling man becomes sublime,
And fairy tales are spun from gray-maned storms;
From moments' tears immortal pearls are formed
And dulcet wonders cradle bloody times.

She rests, and on her supple, tender thigh,
On graceful curves, her tapered fingers lie.
A quiet vision—fated not to change.

Beyond both good and ill, absolved by ages,
She finds among the stars a place of measure,
And, ceaseless, the hexameters of Homer.

The Feast

The sky is heavy with a molten feast—
And flaming streams have come to distant deeps.
The branches laze in veils of haze—so soon!
The days of cracking ice seem barely gone.

The willows deep in sweet-breathed flower-drifts
(For winter burst the clasps of holy writ).
The golden bells of daisies sway at last
In place of leaden grief and wintry blast.

Sweet buttercups are here—but butterless!
Globeflowers and cymbals, knelling bells.
I drink the raptures of the gentle moment.

Before the feast—a solemn stillness.
A bluer blue. From clouds grown stout,
The Flame, on gnarled vines, roars its blossoms out.

Portrait

The stallion, bird, the lightning bolt, gazelle,
Are parts of you, and in your eyes foretell
Tomorrow. Midnight conjures in your raven curls
While in your quickened words the lightning swirls.

Familiar faces come to us in dreams,
And danger lurks in them, in love's delights.
I sink, my monarch Byzantine
In deepening maelstroms of your eyes.

The tapered softness of your hands
That nimbly do the bidding of your lust
I take in mine with courteous love.

As sunset's fires are quenched I take your hand,
Bejeweled with sapphires, rubies, opals of a queen—
And Night commands the constellations of our dreams.

Sonnets of the Sun

The sonnets of the Sun, of Honey and the Moon,
At sunrise all the bees have quit the hive
To navigate the scents of mountain blooms
In languorous conflagrations of Julys.

A humming solar strumming on the peaks,
A mountain ram has fallen with a hind.
A single bullet felled both ram and hind.
I took their blood to daub my gaudy dreams.

I pitilessly fed flesh to beasts—
The meat of beasts that death had preened.
The honey-mead that bees had gleaned

I took. From all the odysseys of bees
I learned to live without timidity—
I learned that life is boundless, bold and sweet.

The Birth of Music

The sea resounded, rushing to its banks,
When all things in the world were young,
And freshly-risen combers' songs were sung,
And horns roared, strings strummed in them.

And everything was music—every glen,
Each forest, flowers' blooms as big as moons—
When strings of mind were finally attuned.
But other sounds came first in dreams' accords:

The wind made melodies of soughing reeds,
The wind-piped reeds made meadows come to life,
And so the first reed-flute was queen

Of wind and will, of sea against the beach.
I made another flute—of bloody strive
And vengeance—carved from bones of enemies.

119

The Reed Pipe

The dawn has made its harmony; it blends
With purling shepherds' pipes of reed.
The lowing herds move far afield.
I doze. So good to be in bed.
On soft corolla-beds of flowers
The dew absorbs the sunrise sapphires.
My eye had sipped these jeweled dews
A day ago—and now they glow anew.

It's cold outside, but in this warm retreat
My languid eyelids slowly close—
Indifferent to past and future—free.

My mind sinks deep. Rows of trees.
A flood, the sparkle of an oar and
The songs of blue birds in a forest.

The Palace

From flashing sparks of horses' hooves,
From leaping flames, vermillion leaves,
From clash of tusks and horns' duels,
From roar of storms, and drone of streets—

From words grown heedless of my call,
From frankincense in blue-veined, fragrant wisps,
I've alchemized the meaning, built these halls
From molten flows of cryptic writ.

This palace, where my visions spin,
Where lines cross lines to weave a hint,
Is honeycombed with countless rooms.

The darkness swells with fire and blooms
Of aloe; the palace vases' thick infusions
Throw fairy tales in drunk confusion.

Through the Ages

The Chinese monarch's drowsing paradise,
The early morning gongs, the flaxen hues,
The etched embrace of silk trees, flights
Of rarest birds, the birth of Moons, the dew—

A harmony of dreams that float with scent
Of opium, the silent tale of faces
Ingraved in jade, all finite, all boundless,
All bright, drunk, gentle, pale and sage.

An ecstasy: to be the humblest slave,
A terror: knowing poles of total sway—
And dawning shame, the snows of impotence—

Millenia in seas of sightless grays;
With eyes grown keen, millenia in blue.
I know it all! But joy—I never knew.

Anchorite

They call me now a dendrite-anchorite.
I left a life that clutched its vice
With iron fists. I found this hollow tree
That serves me as a church and monastery.

This lightning-blasted trunk is home to me—
I stand, contemplative, in ever-silent
Solemnity. And fifty years have passed.
I watch the world as through a darkened glass.

I do not know how I should call this place.
No reason now to learn its name—
This hollow where my moment passes.

A serpent glides within from time to time.
I hear its silken fork among the leaves.
I pray a prayer around it—and it flees.

Translucence

The gloaming fades. Far away
The sunset golds flow molten into night,
While spindles murmur here for me.
In marvels manifest to sight
My window incandesces far away.

The dusk has dimmed—it won't be back.
The blossomed light-drenched world is good.
I go the ways I dreamed I would—
Through days of love. I won't be back.

The Anchorite

I trustingly lived in that oddest of clans
    Known here on this planet as man.
Their boring, false-faced festivals are shams.
    Accept me, your anchorite son, o wasteland!

I've survived my affliction with human affairs.
    The flying fish at sea, the rose-filled summer air,
The vernal storms, the dragonflies on wing
    Are dearer far—and burning amber evenings.

Sound of Sounds

The Moon has splashed the north with light
And rimed the flight of leaping deer.
The snowy wastes are lifeless, bright,
And shadowed wisps of clouds appear.

Moon! Ringed with crystal, frost and ice,
What rainbows do you smelt tonight
As I direct my northern flight
From flickering keys of black and white?

Beneath a Lunar Sign

Beneath this youthful, sickle-Moon
That glows above the emerald Sea,
  You walk beside the waves with me.
I whisper words, we silently dispute.

  This came to me in dreams one night,
As combers roared in you and me.
  I saw with moonlight-flooded sight
That you and I were sinking in the Sea.

  We were, in crespuscule and brine,
Two ocean flowers, entwining blooms
  Of salt and sea—dreaming Moons
And stars of novel lands and strange designs.

Sparks of Mysteries

Planets circumnavigate their seas.
Sudden tails. An undiscovered moon.
Merging currents, waves and dunes:
Numberless flecks of shells at sea.

Days and stormy waters turn them into dust.
Constant tumbling in the currents breaks them.
Time and tides' enamored dances grind them
Into sand. Riptides! Celebrate your victory!

Sandy surge, a vision washed in gold,
Sea-fires flickering out, flashing lines of waves,
Broken seashells, lingering dreams,
Sunken sparks and last remarks of mysteries.

What Has Happened to Me?

All of me sings. What has been done to me?
I twine my thoughts in finely flowing sonnets,
Caressing everything in fine-edged gaze.
I own Eternity entirely.

I forge from black blocks white. The tale
Of feeling is bedecked in light and iron.
Perceiving only summertime, I see
I'm typsied by a warming tide of breezes.

But what has happened? I am happy
Without a cause, though I have also known
What pain is, walking barefoot over glass.

My soul peruses dewdrops, ever seeking
What never will return; within me sun
Songs sing, and I'm in solar beauty sunk.

The Sunbeam

I've gored my brain with solar rays.
I watch the world. I have no memory.
I see a light, a jeweled haze.
My spirit's drunk with love and ecstasy.

Those rays have burned my fingertips!
The touch of fire is sweet to me!
The human is forgotten. All is mixed.
I blend with All, and with eternity.

What joy this glowing fever brings!
I burn the moments with delight!
With lights I speak the tongue of light.
I burn. I reign. I soar and sing.

The Honey of the Ages

At first I saw the world was the singing of songs,
    And so, trembling, I put it into song.
And then I chanted lines of poetry—
    Which was my second boundary.
And then I carved my oath in stone
    And raised an altar, slim and tall,
Allowed the rounded moon within my walls,
    And was a singer, wizard, tsar.
And now, when ages' swarms have flown,
    And the circling course of tribes is closed,
I can recall the days when all were babes
    As clearly as I summon lively dreams to mind.
From stealthy Moons I turned to other charms,
    Betrayed the Moon in sylvan nymphets' arms;
Then, staggered, drunk with colored flames,
    I knew the Sun was god to me.
When condors soar above the rippled hills
    And wastelands are a saffron dream,
Then, son of Sun, I gather countless honeycombs of time—
    And crown the goddesses and gods.
Then came the many triumphs, fetes;
    And leaving Pyramids, long ago I set
My mind to sailing through the mists of sorcery—
    Again the torch of night brings light to me.
But not the Moon, the candle and the lamp
    Above the ancient pages' cerements
Now lead me to the realms wherein I summon up
    A host of shades with one imperious look.
An alchemist of dusty ores, I drew from ancient books
    The ecstasies of transformation,
And ordered lightning bolts to shake away their sleep
    And sealed them up in heavy ploughs of steel.
An ebon hawk, I fly; an albatross, I soar,
    Predicting comets' cause and course.
And I would rise toward lunar peaks
    When I have made the runic omens speak.

* * *
    * *
        *

POEMS BY VLADIMIR SOLOVYOV

Dearest friend, do you not see
All that we perceive—
Only reflects and shadows forth
What our eyes cannot see?

Dearest friend, do you not hear
In the clamour of everyday life—
Only the unstrung echoing fall of
Jubilant harmonies.

Dearest friend, do you not sense
That the essence of the world lies hid—
Only in that which heart to heart
Carries its silent greeting?

1892   *Translated by Samuel Cioran*

Vladimir Solovyov

THREE MEETINGS

Translated by
Ralph Koprince

Triumphing over death in advance,
And conquering the bonds of time with love,
Eternal friend, I shall not name you,
But you will feel my trembling melody.

Not trusting the deceptive world,
Beneath the coarse surface of matter
I touched the imperishable purple
And recognized the radiance of deity...

Didn't you let yourself be clearly seen three times—
Not by an imaginary sign, oh, no!—
Your image was the reply to the plea of my heart
For an omen, or help, or reward.

I

And the first time—oh, how long ago that was!
Thirty-six years have passed
Since a child's soul unexpectedly felt
The agony of troubled dreams.

I was nine, and *She*—she was nine as well.
"It was a May day in Moscow," as Fet exclaimed.
I confessed. Silence. O, Lord!
I have a rival. Ah! he'll give me satisfaction.

A duel, a duel! Mass on Ascension Day.
My soul seethed in a flood of passionate torments.
Let us banish...worldly...cares—
The sound drawled out, faded, and died away.

The altar was open... But where were the priest and the deacon?
And where was the throng of people offering prayers?
The flood of torments suddenly ran dry, not leaving a trace.
There was azure all around, and azure in my soul.

Suffused with the golden azure,
Holding a flower from distant worlds in your hand,
You stood with a radiant smile,
Nodded to me, and vanished in the mist.

And a child's love grew alien to me,
My soul was blind to worldly concerns...
And my German governess repeated sadly:
"Volodenka—ah! he's much too ignorant and foolish!"

II

The years went by. As a docent and instructor
I rushed abroad for the first time.
Berlin, Hanover, Cologne—in rapid succession
Flashed suddenly by and disappeared from sight.

Not the world's capital, Paris, not the Spanish nation,
Not the bright magnificence of Eastern colors—
But the British Museum was my dream,
And my dream it did not betray.

Will I ever forget you, six blissful months?
Not the illusions of transient beauty,
Not the people's way of life, not passions, and not nature—
You alone possessed all of my soul.

Let the human myriad there scurry
Beneath the din of fire-breathing machines;
Let the soulless monsters be created—
Sacred peace, here I am alone.

Well, of course, *cum grano salis:*
Though lonely, I was no misanthrope,
And in my seclusion I came across people,
Of whom which should I now name?

It's a pity in my meter I won't be able
To fit their names, not unknown to fame...
I'll only say: two or three British miracle workers
And two or three docents from Moscow.

More and more I was alone in the reading room;
And whether you believe it or not—God knows
That forces hidden from me selected
Everything I could possibly read about her.

Whenever sinful whims would prompt me
To take up a book on another subject
Such tales would be there
That I would go home in embarrassment.

And then one day—it was toward autumn—
I said to her: O, blossom of a deity!
You're here, I sense it—why haven't you revealed
Yourself to my eyes since childhood years?

And no sooner had I thought this prayer
Than everything was filled with a golden azure,
And before me she shined once more—
But only her face—it alone.

And that moment became a lasting joy;
Again my soul was blind to earthly matters,
And if my words encountered an "attentive" ear
They were inarticulate and *foolish*.

III

I said to her: your face has appeared,
But I want to have a look at all of you.
That which you did not begrudge the child,
You must not refuse the youth!

"Be in Egypt!" a voice within me sounded.
To Paris! And a vapor carried me south.
My feelings didn't even struggle with my reason:
Reason kept silent like an idiot.

To Lyon, Turin, Piacenza, and Ancona,
To Fermo, Bari, Brindisi—and then
A British steamer was already speeding me
Over a trembling blue surface.

Credit and a roof were offered me in Cairo
By the hotel "Abbot"—it is no more, alas!—
Comfortable and modest, the best in the entire world...
There were Russians there, even from Moscow.

A General—the tenth—was entertaining everyone,
He reminisced on old Caucasian days...
To name him is no sin—he died long ago,
And I will always think well of him.

That was the famous Rostislav Faddeev,
In retirement the soldier wielded a skillful pen.
To label a courtesan or estate council
A thousand talents were concealed in him.

At the table of our host we met twice daily:
He used to speak both joyfully and long;
He was at no loss for risque anecdotes
And philosophized to the limit of his strength.

Meanwhile I awaited the cherished meeting;
And then once in a quiet hour of night
There came a breath as fresh as a light breeze:
"I'm in the desert—go there after me."

I had to go on foot (from London to the Sahara
They don't drive young people for free—
There was nothing at all in my pockets
And for many days I'd been living on credit).

God knows where, with neither money nor food supplied,
I started off to one fine time—
Like Uncle Vlas, on whom Nekrasov versified.
(Well, in spite of everything, I found a rhyme.)

You must have laughed when in the middle of the desert,
In a high top hat and an overcoat,
Taken for a devil I provoked
A tremor of fear in a sturdy Bedouin, and for that

I was nearly killed—when noisily, in Arabic,
The sheiks of two tribes took council
On what to do with me, and when later they servilely
Bound my arms and without a wasted word

Led me further off, and most nobly
Untied my hands and went away.
I laugh with you: both gods and people tend
To ridicule misfortunes—once they've passed.

Meanwhile night as still as death descended
Straightaway to earth,without beating about the bush.
All around I only heard the stillness
And saw the black amidst the starry lights.

Lying on the earth I looked and listened...
Quite maliciously a jackal began to howl;
In his imagination he was probably dining on me,
But I didn't take up even a stick against him.

What's a jackal! It's the cold that's terrible...
It must be zero, yet the afternoon was hot...
With ruthless clarity the stars were glaring;
The brilliance and the cold both fought off sleep.

And long I lay in an eerie drowsiness,
And then there wafted: "Sleep, my poor friend!"
And I fell asleep; and when gently I awoke
The earth and vault of heaven breathed of roses.

And in the purple of the heaven's splendor,
With eyes filled with an azure fire,
You looked like the first radiance
Of a universal and creative day.

What is, what was, and what will always be—
A single motionless look encompassed everything here...
The seas and rivers showed dark blue beneath me
As did the distant forest, and the heights of snowy mountains.

I saw everything, and everything was one thing only—
A single image of female beauty...
The infinite fit within its dimensions:
Before me, in me—were you alone.

O, radiant woman! In you I am not deceived:
In the desert I saw all of you...
Those roses will not wither in my soul
Wherever life's wave may speed.

Only an instant! The vision concealed itself—
And the sun's orb rose in the sky.
The desert was silent. My soul was praying,
And the ringing of church bells didn't cease in it.

Vladimir Solovyov

My spirit was cheerful. But still for two days I hadn't eaten
And my higher sight was beginning to grow dim.
Alas! however sensitive of soul you may be,
Hunger's still no lady, as they say.

I made for the Nile by the sun's westward path,
And in the evening arrived home in Cairo.
My soul preserved traces of rosy smile,
But in my boots many holes could be seen.

From a detached point of view everything was quite foolish
(I related the facts concealing the vision).
In the silence the General, having finished his soup,
Began with importance, fixing his gaze on me:

"The mind, of course, permits one to be *foolish,*
But better not abuse your mind:
Human obtuseness, after all, is no expert
At accurately distinguishing types of madness.

"And therefore if it offends you to pass
For a madman or simply a fool—
Speak no more in front of anyone
About this shameful incident."

He made a lot of jokes, but before me
The light blue mist was already shining,
And conquered by the secret splendor
Life's ocean withdrew into the distance.

———————

While still a slave to the vain world,
I thus perceived imperishable purple
Beneath the coarse surface of matter,
And sensed the radiance of a deity.

Triumphing over death by a premonition,
And conquering the bonds of time with a dream,
Eternal friend, I shall not name you,
And you forgive me, for my melody is weak.

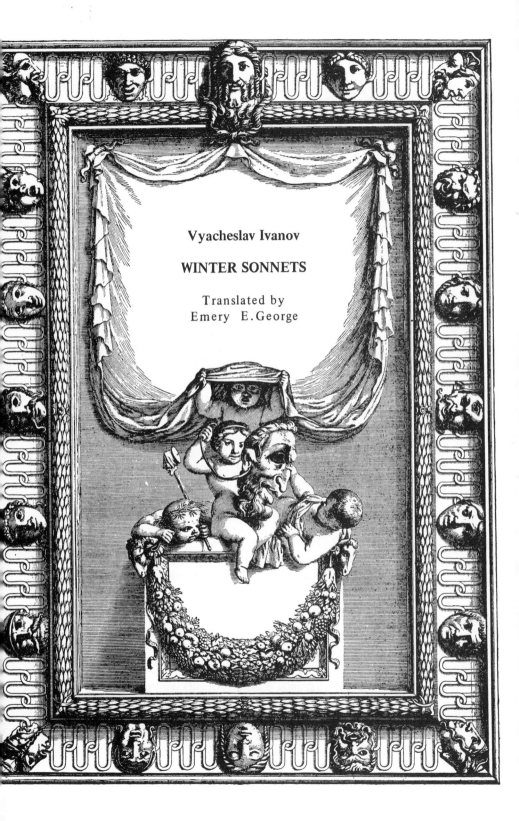

Vyacheslav Ivanov

WINTER SONNETS

Translated by
Emery E. George

I

The sleigh boards creak. That gleaming was dead snow.
The festive woods are magic: snowed-in deep.
Heaven's roof is bedded with swan's down.
Sublunar clouds fly faster than the deer.

Hush! a bell sings about the distant shore....
And the dream of the fields is unknown and immense....
Bedless our journey; of fate we are not yet clear.
Holy night, where will you grant me rest?

And, as if in a fortune teller's mirror,
I see my family nearby, under shelter,
In a honey-rich light of holiday fires.

And my heart, longing with secret nearness,
Waits for little sparks among the pines.
But the sleighs run past, run past in flight.

II

Invisible pilot on my stone-deaf roads:
You have been testing me these years and days
In deep purgatorial fires whose threshold
We name fate: a parting of our ways.

And here is my *summa* of extinguished pride:
To things not dear I am bound with knots,
While to someone I could not grow fond of
I will not go with a forgiving kiss.

I have thus fled winter's severity:
Epicure of the kisses of high noon,
I would keep Nature's eternal holiday.

But the blizzards' burial grounds, the gloom
Of clouds too read their glacial requiem
My wrathful teacher became linked to me.

III

Winter of the soul. With oblique rays
From far-off the living sun gives her heat.
She of course freezes in the deaf-mute drifts,
And the snowstorms sing for her their grief.

Heap an armful of kindling near the hearth;
Cook your millet: your hour is victory.
Then fall asleep as all grows numb and hard...
O, deep is the grave of Eternity!

The tap of life-giving water is frozen over;
Stiff as ice, the fountain of liquid fire.
Do not look for me under that shroud!

My double drags his coffin, humble slave,
I, at least, am real, though changed to flesh.
Far-off, I build me a church no hand can shape.

IV

Dark winter has reached its center days.
The gates of sun, which the women would meet
So eagerly on high, I celebrate
With long vigil. All stupor flees the eyes.

Into a laurel wood the wintry jail cell
Was transformed by the descent of the Muse.
It vacillates between what is and seems.
And inside it stands a heavenly self.

"Faithless one!" I hear an ambrosial whisper.
"Has your cowardly murmur stung your song?
You rustled like a branched-out skeleton

With the remains of dry and black-brown leaves,
As an oak under snow. Wind whistled in the shrubs,
And I sought your downcast glance in stars."

V

Scouring wizard, ferocious thief, gray wolf,
For you I cast the winter mood in glory!
I hear a hungry howl. Next to you, earth
Is a good host, men's words are charity.

We hate you, yes. A house dog knows a slave's
Indebtedness. More magian and more borrowed,
Delphic beast, Polyhymnia's prophets own you
As long as their voices are not silent.

Next to where the skiff moored souls from dark
Coastal waters and I consulted Fates,
There wolfish Colonel Igor mounts his guard.

That, Shaman, was your regiment's drawn howl;
Since childhood I have known the dismal call
Of homeless fire on the frozen steppes.

VI

New moon night. And winter whiskers, she-bears
Fiercely sent the singer of hope the word:
He and the Muse met the frost damage early,
More credulously than lighthearted children.

No faith is ever orphaned but by news.
Our courage shone with unstilled promises.
Hour of night—and hear! a horn proclaims
Spring, lovelier, more holy than all springs.

That very trumpet note I mean, the one
That opens the last locks on winter's gates
Heralds, Usher of dawn, your hoarser hymn,

And, having lived through a midnight of bereavements,
With a secret throbbing the heart hastens
The return of loved ones to the face of earth.

VII

How moonlit and white it is on the highways
Which my double, with a dead shade, paces,
While I, my own true self, a secret pupil,
Marveling, walk the palace rooms of Isis.

And here I feel I am lying on the hearse,
Fixing my dead, sharp glance upon the heavens:
And in the snowed-in foothills the black horses
Are led by our guide through lonely mountains.

And moving alongside, the train of shades
Marches past along the snowthick white.
The lead alone remains untraced in dark,

As if shining straight through him the moon
Fused with the pinkish dawn its every ray.
And the Luminous Lady points the way.

VIII

The wind shakes the worn-out roof: the clanging-
And-moan of iron rumbles in half-dark.
Winter drapes a nearby vacant lot,
And a snow-drift cemetery: an alley.

Midnight is an unseasonable hour
For strolls through town where a soul of pestilence
Has passed (it seems) and for its dreary cells,
Life has interred itself in hidden corners.

I drag my feet to my tiny hut,
Through whose fragile walls the blizzard blows,
But where one nook will cloak me from the frost.

It's warm within the magic circle's bounds;
I have a kettle bubbling on the stove,
And like a friend's smile, Agni shines.

IX

Winter, winter, Orphanhood is your name.
Your mournful music is despondency.
Disgrace of deaf-mute gods your destiny,
And a closed-mouthed widowhood your face.

High up in night there is a feast of glory:
Of fleshless beings, high light-wingedness.
Here we have freezing, dark, forgetfulness....
And in the depths the sun—the Sun is born!

Between her alabaster fingers, Psyche's
Oil lamp (so easily she chills)
Hardly glimmers. The deep blue plays with diamonds.

The crystal mass hangs up there, threatening.
Seek shelter, dark life, where firewood crackles,
Flee from the cold's celestial javelins.

X

House the homeless, God! Give the earth-born
His much-needed burrow, a den as deep.
And wintertime will drive the animal
Into the warmth of his stone-deaf ravine.

This is not proud forces at free play.
For that small rising flame anxiety rules me
And fellow men held dear—such misery
Are life and love. Yet soul spells energy.

A flame on wings will feed a body's fire.
Attired in a soft and shaggy fleece,
Man is happy with his brutish face.

He glides on skis, steers the running deer.
He strikes the spark—and is himself split clean
In flesh and spirit: two worlds of desire.

140

XI

Far-off into the field the night wind echoes,
And with hot gust it flies: is he a guest
From the islands where, west of the sun,
Dwell a congress of the high-elect?

Rages with a spring come premature;
In its breath the jail of winter hides.
And with wakeful hoof the horse tests
Over the narrow ford the river ice.

February Fish swim in the stars,
Pierce the gravelike blocks of ice with rays,
With gravity alarm the realm of souls.

Their law is arbitrariness, their habit play:
Last night grew stiff (ferocious frost, sheer malice)—
By morning, thaw shines blue throughout the valley.

XII

Is this life—or dream before the dawn,
When, the air fresh and my bed turned chill,
Winged shivering comes creeping over the skin,
And in the Realm of Ice a dream is built?

Deluded by phenomena of change—
Where is imagining, where essence, God?
Are not being and vision also one?
Being you are—to you there leads no road.

Love is no lying ghost: I hope, believe it!...
Yet in my dream of dreams I love as well,
Tremble for family: watch, wait to meet them....

On a winter night I hear the Easter bell:
I knock on graves and quicken the dead,
Until at last in a grave I see—myself.

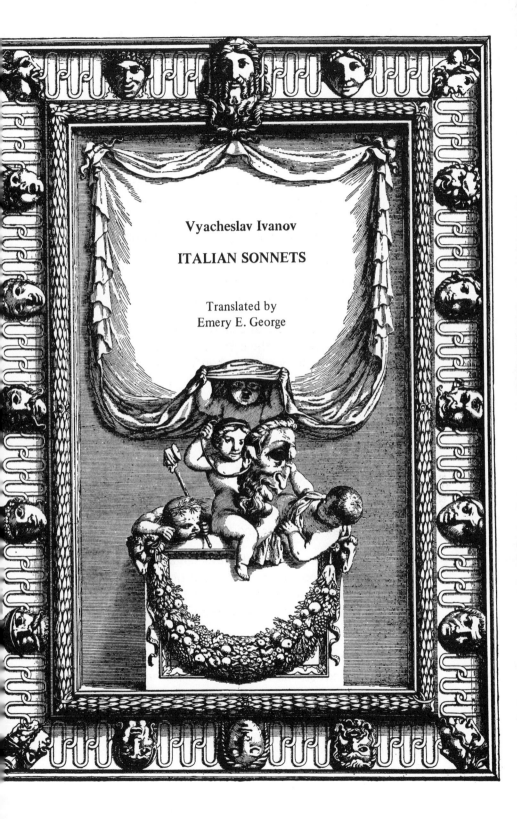

Vyacheslav Ivanov

ITALIAN SONNETS

Translated by
Emery E. George

I

Regina Viarum

Anew: true pilgrim of the ancient arches,
In my late hour, with a Vesper "Ave Roma"
I greet you as the roof of my parents' house,
Refuge of wanderers, eternal Rome.

Troy of our fathers we leave to the flames;
Chariot axles splinter amid the thunder
And the Furies of this world's hippodrome:
You, Queen of Highways, watch—we burn to cinders.

You also burned and rose again from embers,
And retentive of memory, the blue
Of your deep skies did not grow blind.

And in the fondle of a golden dream
Your gatekeeper the cypress will recall
How Troy grew strong when Troy lay low: consumed.

II

Monte Cavallo

Holding their obstinate horses by the tether,
Blazing with sun-drenched power, resolute
And Naked as Olympians in the nude,
The pair—brothers and twins—stepped front and center.

Heralds—to Quirites, brothers-in-arms—
Of field and victory, near Juturnian water,
Appeared incognito (the myths record)
On the Fora of Rome. Newcomer gods.

And there they stayed until the world's end.
And the twin idols of colossal youths
Have not stirred from there for millennia.

Where they have stood since founding days they stand,
For six hills ranging dark blue all around,
To shine like stars from high on Quirinal.

III

L'acqua felice

Pindar, as swan, sang: "No gift under the sun
Sweeter than water." Rome runs along the veins,
The bends of aqueducts chased out of mountains,
Moisture of happy springs since ancient days.

Into the hollow of a sarcophagus
She splashes, ringing in the blue, a column
Drumming far. She ripples the cold, uncurbed.
Carves rivulets out of the marble rim.

For her purling there is but a narrow lane
Magically animated; and surrounding,
Gods of the sea lead their choric dances:

One chisel gathered them. The dreamlike chambers
Sound deserted as the waters play
Delightfully in mist, their voices rumbling.

IV

La Barcaccia

Turned to stone under the spell of murmurs
From rivulets spilling over the full
Brims, here lies a boat half under water.
The Campagna sends it girls with flowers.

And the stairway, stepping over the buildings,
Its double path wide and ornate, lifts
The points of two towers into the blue;
Above the Piazza di Spagna, an obelisk.

I love the orange sunburn of the houses,
Old walls with crowded passages between,
Above them in the noon heat, rustling palms—

Then on dark nights, the cavatina's sighs,
The plucking of a roving mandolin
To the chords of velvety guitars.

V

Il Tritone

This dolphin-tangle brought out on their tails
An open bivalve. In it the Triton grows.
He plays on a snail trumpet; no rough tones.
The jet pierces the blue air with sunrays.

Amid hot stones thirsting for clouds of pines,
How the moss green makes a chiton on the creature!
The chisel's age-old dream resembles nature
In its primeval fantasy of lines.

Bernini—ours again!—I always will
Relish your play, walking from the Four Fountains
To Pincio up this memorial hill,

Where Ivanov came to Gogol's cell-like room,
Where Piranesi with his fiery needle
Sang Titan architects and grieving Rome.

VI

La Fontana delle Tartarughe

Laying captive humpbacks into the flat
Shallow basin, tortoises shoulder height,
Where at ease—divers all—the monsters splash
Clumsy, having learned not to be afraid—

Adolescent boys dance on the heads
Of snub-nosed freaks: their prankish games a feast.
Goggle-eyed monsters lie under their heels;
From each round mouth there sprays a watery dust.

Atop dolphins the four of them are prancing.
On these sunbronzed calves, these backs of bronze
The day's green-wavering laughter shines,

And within this bliss, so free and lazy,
I catch echoes of your festive joys,
Lorenzo—and of your melancholy.

VII

Valle Giulia

Asleep, the autumn reservoir is sprinkled
With imperial rags, a beggarly purple.
Amid moss and rocks the man with the snake, Asklepios,
Looks out from under the arch at the red maple.

And the blue vault of heaven, as if by bronze, is framed
By the magnificently somber cloak of leaves
Not stung here and there by chains of killer frosts,
Nor by palls of snow in sparkling sheets.

The blessed gazed on us with a smile as wistful
As the sun's on a plane tree now withered.
Clear, the splashing waters ring like crystal:

The jet flings its shifting silhouette to the sun,
And on the mirror surface, upside-down, are reflected
Asklepios, the maple, the sky, and the fountain.

VIII

Aqua Virgo

News of powerful waters, fresh coolness blowing
May be heard; and in them a bellowing, sheltered.
Come near the din: it is great masses moving.
Trevi, the queen of water cascades, glitters.

Billows pour down silver from the chambers;
Sea chargers play in brilliant vertigo.
Sent from the goddess's rocks, they welcome strangers.
Neptune himself goes out, meets Aqua Virgo.

Rash runaway from Rome, how many times,
With prayer for return in a good hour,
Over my shoulder I would throw you coins!

Each spoken vow has held reality:
Just as today, you have, magic fountain,
Restored a happy pilgrim to things holy.

IX

La Cupola

Slowly I drink the sun's melliferous rays,
Thickening like the valley's parting bell;
There shone the spirit to unmournful sorrow,
A plenitude, of which no name will tell.

The honey of full resurrected years,
The Day's wedding cup: do we not drink this light?
Did not Eternity offer the Day his bridal
Ring, beyond our throw, our earthly sight?

Such is the glory of the fiery welding
Of heaven to the mirror-level sea
Where the disk hides and the giant drowns.

Sunrays: fingers groped blind above the crowns
Of the pines; our eyes went out. Alone,
The blue Dome revolves in golden light.

POEMS FROM INNOKENTY ANNENSKY'S *A CYPRESS CHEST*

Translated by R. H. Morrison

Twilight Trefoil

Lilac Dusk

Our street is covered in snow; over the
Snow runs the lilac dusk. Passing by, it
Merely glanced in the window and I knew I
Had loved it for a long time. I implored
The lilac dusk: "Visit me a while, stay
With me in my nook, do not dispel my
Old, old grief, share your own with me,
My longed-for one!" But only from afar
I heard its reply: "If you love me, then
Seek out my tracks yourself; my flight
Ended, I will stay a brief hour where
The thin ice over the pool shows blue
And no one has seen us by the stove....
Only those are mine who are free and daring!"

Anguish of Transitoriness

Without trace day has sunk. Turning yellow, the
Moon's hazy disk, still shadowless, looks on the
Balcony, and in the despair of windows flung
Open are drearily white walls, already unseeing.

This moment night begins. The clouds are so black...
I pity the evening's last instant: all that is
Spent is there—longing and anguish; all that
Approaches is there—despondence and oblivion....

Here evening is like a dream, both timid and fleeting,
But to the heart there are neither strings nor tears
Nor perfumes, and where so many clouds are rent
And merged, it is somehow closer than the rosy sunsets.

A Candle Is Brought In

Does it not seem to you at times, when
Twilight walks through the house, that
Right here alongside us is another element,
In which we live quite differently?

So softly there has shadow merged with
Shadow, and there such moments can occur,
That it is as though we penetrated
Each other by eyes' invisible rays.

And we fear to frighten this instant away
With a movement, or disturb it with a word,
As if someone alongside pressed an ear to us,
Compelling us to listen to what is distant.

But the candle has hardly burst into flame, when
That delicate world yields without fighting;
Only along the inclines of a ray from the eyes
The shadows flow down into the blue flame.

Trefoil of Allurement

Poppies

The joyful day blazes.... Amid the languid grass,
Everywhere are poppies in patches—like eager
Impotence, like lips filled with temptation and
Poison, like outspread wings of scarlet butterflies.

The joyful day blazes.... But the garden is both empty
And overgrown. It has long since finished with temptations
And feasting, and the withered poppies, like old women's
Heads, are blessed from the skies with a radiant chalice.

Variant

Poppies at Midday

Scentlessly and flowerily someone's
Delicate enfolding is opened—
Wings of scarlet cambric have
Unrolled and will not quiver....
       Offending with their bloodstained spot
       All that cherishes—distance and
       Nearness—the poppies have spread avidly
       Through the languid, succulent grass.
But not even day makes them rejoice;
The poppies' spots are dark in the
Sky, and their bright destiny is
Wearied by a heavy autumn dream.
       By the dream that the garden will be
       Empty and overgrown, and that in it,
       As in church, the old women's heavy
       Heads are blessed by the Sacrament.

The Bow and The Strings

What heavy, dark delirium! How turbid
And moonlit these heights are! To have
Touched the violin for so many years and
Not recognize the strings in the light!

Who needs us? Who has kindled
The two yellow, dismal faces?...
And suddenly the bow felt someone
Take them up and mingle them.

"Oh, how long ago! Through this darkness
Tell me only, are you the one, the one?"
And the strings caressed the bow ringingly,
But trembled as they caressed.

"Is it not true, we will never part
Again? That is enough..."
And the violin answered *yes,*
But the violin's heart was aching.

The bow understood everything
And fell silent, but in the violin
The echo held on... and what seemed
Music to people was agony to them.

But the man did not extinguish his
Candles till morning... and the
Strings sang.... Only the sun found them,
Devoid of strength on the bed's black velvet.

In March

Forget the nightingale in the fragrant flowers,
Only do not forget love's *morning...*
And the bright-black breast of revivified earth
    In the unrevived leaves!

Among the tatters of its snowy shirt
Only once did the earth desire too—
Only once was it intoxicated by fiery March,
    Headier than wine!

Only once could we not tear our envious
Eyes from the moisture-swollen earth....
Only once we clasped cold hands and,
Shivering, left the garden hurriedly....
    Only once... this time....

Sentimental Trefoil

Dandelions

The little girl with the
Green belt is bustling
About planting two poor
Yellow seedlings in the sand.

They don't stand up—and why on
Earth! Isn't the sand glad of
Them? But the sun is already in the
West and the garden turns golden.

The child shakes one small
White hand after another:
"As soon as I make a little
Hole it fills in...

Nasty, stubborn things!"—
Hush! little daughter, if
They find the holes unpleasant
We will take away their stems.

There, see? All's for the
Best, cheer up, child! On
That shifting hillock two
Small stars have caught fire.

Shaggy, saffron little stars,
Made out of flowers...
There, my precious, your
Little garden is ready.

Her small feet skip and
Laughter breaks out, but
When night comes, God has
Beds for everybody....

You will fall asleep, little
Angel-girl, in down, on your
Elbow... and the two yellow
Seedlings will lie flat in the sand.

The Old Barrel Organ

The sky has driven us quite out of our minds:
It has blinded us, now with fire, now with
Snow, and stubborn winter, baring its teeth
Like a wild beast, has retreated behind April.

Scarcely for a moment does it sink into forgetfulness,
When again the helmet is pulled over its brows, and
The streams that have departed under the snow's crust,
Without singing on to the end, will fall silent and freeze.

153

But the past is long since forgotten, the
Garden filled with sounds, and the stone white
And resonant, and the opened window sees
How the grass has clothed the secluded nook.

Only the old barrel organ shivers with
Cold, and in May's sunset swoon it can
In no way mince its deadly insults,
Turning and pressing the tenacious barrel.

And in no way will this clutching barrel
Understand that there is no reason in this
Work, that the insult of old age will grow
On the thorns from the torments of the turning.

But if the old barrel did understand what
Was its and the barrel organ's destiny,
Would it not cease then to sing while turning,
Because it could not sing without agony?...

Palm Week

To Valia Khmara-Barshchevsky

Having taken leave of the starry
Wastes, Palm Week was sailing on the
Last ruinous piece of frozen snow
Into defunct April's yellow dusk.

It was sailing in fragrant smoke, in
The fainting of death knells, from
Icons with profound eyes and from
Lazaruses forgotten in the black pit.

The white moon on the wane rose high, and
For all whose life was irretrievable,
Ardent tears swam along the palm
Branch on to a cherub's rosy cheeks.

Autumn Trefoil

Again You Are With Me

Again you are with me, my friend autumn,
But your bluish color never froze paler
Through your bare braches' net,
And I do not recall more lifeless snow.

I have never seen your tatters
Sadder and your waters blacker;
The yellow clouds' pattern in
Your faded old sky wearies me.

To the end to see everything growing
Torpid... Oh, how strangely new this
Air is!... You know... I thought it was
More painful to see words' secrets empty....

August

The rays still burn under the roads' arches,
But there among the branches it is ever darker and
More silent: thus a gambler smiles, turning pale,
Already not daring to reckon the blows of fate.

Day is already behind shades. Dismal summonings
Are slowly trailed over earth with the fog, and with
Them, ever more suffocatingly, yesterday's splendor still
Crumbles in the crystal, and only the asters are alive....

Or is this a procession showing white through the leaves?
And fires are trembling there beneath a dull crown,
Trembling and asking: "And you? When will you?"
In the bronze language of funereal weariness....

The game may have ended and the tomb have glided away,
But the impressions on the heart are growing brighter;
Oh, how I understand you: both the warmth's insinuation and
The splendor of flowerbeds where decay is showing through....

It Happened at Vallen-Koski

It happened at Vallen-Koski.
Rain was falling from hazy
Clouds, and wet, yellow planks
Flowed down the dismal slopes.

Since the cold night we had been
Yawning, and tears came into our
Eyes; for fun they threw a doll in
For the fourth time that morning.

The sodden doll dived obediently
Into the gray waterfall, and at first
It whirled round for a long time, for
All as though it longed to go back.

But in vain the foam licked at the
Joints of its arms pressed to its
Sides—its salvation was predestined
For new and yet newer torments.

See how the turbulent current is
Already yellowing, submissive
And drowsy; the Finn was honest,
And took half a rouble for the job.

And there—the doll is already
On a stone, and the river is
Flowing on.... This comedy was
Distressing to me on that gray morning.

There can be such a sky, and such
A play of rays, that our heart feels
An insult to a doll is more
Piteous than an insult to oneself.

Like the leaves then, we are sensitive:
Given life, the gray stone has become
Our friend, but this friend's voice,
Like a child's violin, is out of tune.

And in our heart is a deep consciousness
That with it was born only fear,
That it is lonely in the world,
Like the old doll in the waves....

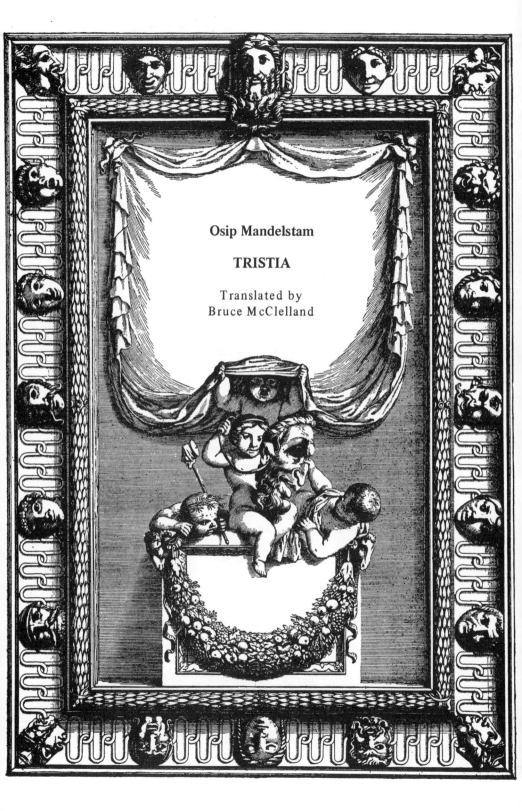

Osip Mandelstam

TRISTIA

Translated by
Bruce McClelland

— No matter how I concealed them, even the
splendor of this attire is burdensome amidst my shame. —

— There will be a famous calamity in stony Troezen,
the royal staircase will grow red with disgrace
. . . .
. . . .
and for the mother in love,
the black sun will rise.

— O, if hate would boil in my breast —
but see, the confession itself
has fallen from my lips. —

—Phedre burns in black flames
        in broad white daylight.
The funeral torch fumes
        in broad white daylight.
Dread your mother, Hippolytus:
Phedre — night — lies in wait for you
        in broad, white day.[1]

— I have stained the sun with blackened love. . .
. . . .
— We are afraid, we do not dare
to help in the king's time of need.
Wounded by Theseus, night
fell upon him. But we,
who with funeral songs bring home the dead
will possess the black sun
in wild and sleepless passion.

THE MENAGERIE

1

The rejected word "peace"
At the beginning of an outraged era;
A church lamp in a deep catacomb
And the air of celestial regions like ether;
And ether we did not want,
Or know how, to breathe.

Again, with a goat-voice,
The shaggy reed-pipes sing.

2

While sheep and oxen lived
On fertile pastures,
And friendly eagles perched
On the shoulders of sleepy cliffs, —
A German raised an eagle,
And a lion submitted to a Briton
And a Gallic comb appeared
From a rooster's crest.

3

But now the savage has captured
The sacred mace of Heracles,
And the black earth has dried up,
Ungrateful, as before.
I will take away the dry staff
And extract fire from it;
Let the frightened beast go away
With me into the deaf night.

4

The cock, the lion, the dark brown
Eagle, and the affectionate bear —
We shall build a chamber for war,
And warm the wild beasts' hides.
But I sing the wine of the times —
The source of Italian speech —
And in a Great-Aryan cradle,
Slavonic and Germanic flax!

5

Italy, is it not indolence for you
To disturb the chariots of Rome,
With the clucking of a domestic bird
Flying across your fence?
And you, neighbor, do not collect;
The eagle spreads and grows angry.
What if for your sling
A heavy stone is of no use?

6

While the beasts are in the menagerie,

We are content for awhile,
And the Volga stays at high tide,
The Rhine's current grows brighter —
And a wise man will unwillingly honor
A foreigner as a demi-god
With the exhuberance of a dance
On the shores of great rivers.

Every church sings its own soft part
In the polyphony of a girl's choir,
And in the stone arches of the Cathedral of Assumption
I see high, arched brows.

And from the ramparts, fortified with archangels,
I surveyed the city from a marvelous height.
Within the walls of this acropolis, I was
consumed with sorrow for the Russian name,
for Russian beauty.

Isn't it strange and wonderful, that we dream
of an orchard, where pigeons soar in the hot blue sky,
and that a nun is singing the litany:
the tender Assumption: Florence in Moscow.

The five-domed cathedrals of Moscow,
with their Italian and Russian souls
remind me of Aurora, but with a
Russian name, and in a coat of fur.

On a sleigh, padded with straw,
barely covered with a mat,
from the Vorobievy hills to the familiar chapel
we rode towards enormous Muscovy.

But in Uglich, the children play knucklebones
and it smells of bread still in the oven.
They carry me along the street without a hat,
and three candles burn in the oratory.[2]

Not three candles glowing, but three meetings.[3]
One consecrated by God himself.
A fourth would never be, but Rome is far, —
And He was never fond of Rome.

The sled dashed through black ruts,
and the people jumped back from the street.
The wretched peasants and their angry wives
were knocked over at the gates.

The damp distance grew black with
flocks of birds, and the bound hands[4] swelled.
They are carrying the Tsarevich,
his body grows terribly numb,
they set fire to the reddened straw.

Solominka[5]

I

When you are not sleeping, Solominka,
In your enormous bedroom, and are waiting,
Dreamless, for the high and heavy ceiling to come down
With quiet sorrow on your keen eyes,

Sonorous Solomka, or seasoned Solominka,
You've drunk down all death, grown tender and
Been broken, my dear Solomka, no more alive —
Not Salome, no, it is Solominka.

In hours of sleeplessness, objects are heavier
As if fewer of them — such a stillness —
The cushions glitter in the mirror, grow almost white,
And the bed is reflected in the round pool.

No, it is not Solomka in her solemn silk
In a huge room above the black Neva.
For twelve months they sing of the final hour,
And the pale blue ice waves in the air.

Solemn December sends out its breath
As if the great Neva were in the room.

No, not Solominka — Ligeia, departed —
I have found you, glorious words.

II

I have found you, blessed words:
— Lenore, Solominka, Ligeia, Seraphita —
In the enormous room, the great Neva,
And from the granite flows the blue blood.

Solemn December shines above the Neva.
For twelve months they sing of the final hour.
No, not Solominka in her silks
enjoying a slow, oppressive rest.

In my blood lives Decembrish Ligeia,
Whose blissful love sleeps in a sarcophagus,
But that Solominka, perhaps Solome,
Was crushed with pity, and shall never return.

"I've lost a delicate cameo,
I don't know where, on the
shore of the Neva.
I pity the beautiful Roman girl,"
You said to me, almost in tears.

But why, fair Georgienne,
stir up the dust on a sacred tomb?
One more downy snowflake
melted away on the eyelid's fan.

And you bowed your gentle neck.
Alas, no cameo, no Roman girl.
I pity the tawny Tinotine — virgin
Rome on the shore of the Neva.

I

I am cold. Clear Spring dresses
Petropolis in verdant down.
But like a medusa,[6] the Neva's wave

stirs up in me a slight aversion.
Along the northern bank,
the headlights speed away.
The steel dragonflies and beetles are flying,
the golden pinpoints of starlight glimmer,
but not one of those stars surpasses
the massive emerald of the water's wave.

II

We shall die in transparent Petropolis
Where Persephone reigns over us.
We drink with every breath the deadly air
and every hour is our last.

Terrible Athena, goddess of the sea,
take off your mighty helmet of stone.
We shall die in transparent Petropolis,
where Persephone rules, not you.

1

Not believing in the Resurrection,
we strolled to the cemetery.
— You know, the earth everywhere
reminds me of those hills

. . . .
. . . .

where Russia breaks off
above the black, deaf sea.

2

The broad meadow runs away
from the monastery's slopes.
I really didn't want to be
south of Vladimir's expanse,
but to stay in this wooded, dark,
and crazy freedom with such a dizzy nun
means to be in misery.

3

I kiss the sunburned elbow
and a waxy patch of forehead.
I know it is still white
under the tawny golden locks.

I kiss the wrist where a bracelet
has left a white band.
The flaming summer of the Taurides[7]
causes such marvels.

4

How quickly you browned,
and approached the poor Saviour,
embraced him, unrebuked —
but in Moscow, you were proud.
Only the name is left for us —
A marvellous sound for a long day.
Take this sand being poured
with my hands.

This night is beyond recall,
but your house is still bright.
At the gates of Jerusalem,
the black sun has risen.

The yellow sun is more fearful —
Baiu, baiushki, baiu. . .[8]
In a bright temple, the Jews
have hidden my mother.

Not having Grace,
and deprived of priesthood,
the Jews, in a bright temple,
chanted over the dust of the woman.

And the voices of the Israelites
rose over the mother.
I awoke in a cradle, shined upon
by a black sun.

The Decembrist

To this the pagan senate testifies:
— THESE DEEDS SHALL NEVER DIE! —

He lit his pipe and wrapt his cloak around
while they play chess about him.

He bartered his ambitious dream
for a godforsaken Siberian plot
and an elegant pipe at the venomous lips
which uttered truth in a tortured world.

When the German oaks first rustled,
Europe wept in their shade.
Black horses in *quadrigae*[9] reared
on each triumphant turn.

Once, the azure punch glowed in our glasses.
With the broad noises of the samovar,
A friend from across the Rhine spoke
in muted tones, a freedom-loving guitar.

The lively voices murmur still
about the sweet liberty of citizenship;
but the martyrs don't want blind skies,
Toil and Consistency are truer.

Everything's confused and no one can tell
that, as things grow colder,
everything's confused, nor sweetly repeat:
Russia, Lethe, Lorelei. . . .

Meganom'

1

Still far the asphodels,
gray-transparent Spring.
Meanwhile, the sand rustles,
the wave foams.
But here, like Persephone,
my soul joins the gentle circle,
and in the realm of the dead,
seductive, sunburnt arms
do not exist.

2

Why do we trust the boat
the heaviness of the funerary urn,
and end the festival of black roses
over amethystine water?
My soul rushes there,
to the cloudy cape of Meganom',
and from there the black sail returns
after the funeral.

3

How quickly clouds pass
in sunless layers and
petals of black roses drift
under this windy moon.
There is a bird of death and weeping,
and the enormous flag of remembrance
is dragged along the mournful border
behind a cypress stern.

4

The sorrowful fan of past years
unfolds with a riffle.
My soul rushes there,
to the cloudy cape of Meganom',
where with dark trembling, an amulet
is buried in the sand, and from there
after the funeral
the black sail returns.

When on the squares and in our private silence
We slowly go out of our minds,
Rigorous winter will offer a toast
Of cold and clear Rhine wine.

The frost offers us in a silver pail
The white wine of Valhalla,
And for us it recalls
A clear picture of a northern man.

But northern skalds are rude,
Don't know the joy of the game,
And the only loves of northern troops
Are amber, feasts, and flames.

They only dream of the southern air,
the magic of a foreign sky,
— and nevertheless the stubborn friend
still refuses to try.

The young Levite among the priests
stayed long on morning vigil.
Jewish night grew thick around him,
and the ruined temple was solemnly raised.

He said: the yellowing of the skies is alarming.
Run, priests, for night is already over the Euphrates!
But the elders thought: this is not our fault;
Behold the black and yellow light, the joy of the Jews.

He was with us when, on the river's shore,
we enveloped the Sabbath in precious linen
and with a heavy Menorah lit the night of Jerusalem
and the smoke of non-existence.

1
The thick golden stream of honey flowed
from the jar so long that the hostess had time to say:
"Here in the sorrowful Taurides, where fate has brought us,
we are not bored at all" — and she looked over her shoulder.

2
The services of Bacchus everywhere, as if on earth
were only guards and dogs. You go along, you notice no one—
like heavy barrels, the peaceful days roll by:
Far off. Voices in a hut: you do not apprehend, nor reply.

3

After tea, we went out into the huge brown garden,
the dark blinds were lowered like eyelashes.
Past white columns, we walked to see the vineyard,
where the drowsy mountains are glazed with airy glass.

4

I said: a vineyard is like an ancient battle
where curly-headed horseman fight in twisted order.
The science of Hellas in the stony Taurides — and here
there are the noble, rusty layers of golden acres.

5

In the white room, silence stands like a spinning wheel.
From the cellar, smells of paint, vinegar, fresh wine.
Do you recall, in the Greek house; the woman courted
by everyone — not Helen — another — how long she wove?

6

Golden fleece, where are you, golden fleece?
The sea's heavy waves roared the whole way.
The ship abandoned, the sail worn out,
Odysseus returned, satiated with space and time.

That evening the forest of organ pipes did not resound.
Schubert was sung for us — a native cradle.
The mill grinds, and the blue-eyed drunkeness
Of the music laughed in the songs of the hurricane.

The world of old song is brown, green,
But only eternally young
Where the Forest-king shakes
The rumbling crowns of nightingaled
Linden trees in senseless rage.

And the awesome strength of night's return
Is that wild song, like black wine:
This is a double, an empty ghost
Absurdly peers into the cold window!

Your marvelous pronunciation —
the parched whistle of birds of prey;
Or should I say: a living impression
of some silken summer lighting.

Shto? — your head grew heavy.
Tso?[10] — I am calling you.
And far away, a whisper:
I, too, live on earth.

Let them talk: love has wings,
death, a hundred more;
my soul is filled with strife,
but our lips fly to it.

So much air and silk and
wind in your whisper,
and like blind men, the long night
we drink a sunless mixture.

Tristia

1

I've learned the science of parting
In the laments of night, her hair let down.
Oxen graze, and the waiting's drawn out.
The town's last hour of vigil, and I
Revere the ritual of the night when
The cock crowed and exhausted eyes
Raised their load of wandering sorrow,
Gazed into the distance, and a woman's weep
And muse's song combined.

2

Who knows, at the mention of "farewell,"
What separation awaits us,
What the cockscrow augurs
When flames glow in the acropolis,
And on the dawn of some new life,
While an ox chews lazily in his shed,

Why the cock, herald of new life,
Beats his wings on the town's walls?

3

And I love the practice of spinning:
Shuttle weaves, spindle buzzes,
Look how barefooted Delia flies
To meet you, like swansdown.
Oh, the meager warp of our life,
Like the thin language of joy!
All things were in ancient times,
All will be again and only the instant
Of recognition is sweet to us.

4

So be it: a transparent figure
Lies on a clean earthen dish,
Like the spread pelt of a squirrel,
And the girl stares, bowing over the wax.[11]
We cannot tell the fortunes of Grecian Erebus,
Wax is for women what bronze is for men.
Our fate slips out only in battle,
But they die telling fortunes.

Tortoise

1

On the stony spurs of Pierius[12]
the Muses conducted the first khoros
so blind lyrics, like bees, might give us
Ionic honey.
And with a great chill, it began to blow
from a virgin's prominent forehead
so the tender graves of the Archipelago
might be uncovered for distant grandsons.

2

Spring rushes to trample the meadows of Hellas,
Sappho put on a dappled boot, and
cicadas click like hammers forging out a ring,
as in the little song.[13]
A stout carpenter built a tall house,

they strangled all the hens at a wedding,
and an inept cobbler stretched
all five ox-hides for shoes.

3

The slow tortoise-lyre
barely creeps along,
sets herself down in the sun of Epirus,[14]
quietly warming her golden belly.
Who will caress her so,
who will turn her over, sleeping —
She awaits Terpander in her sleep,
foreseeing the sudden sweep of dry fingers.

4

A cold sprinkler waters the oaks,
the untrimmed grasses murmur,
the honeysuckle smells, to the joy of the bees.
O where are you, sacred islands,
where they do not eat wretched bread,
where there is only wine, milk and honey,
creaking toil does not darken the sky, and
the wheel turns easily.

1

Let us go there, where there are varied sciences
And business — Shashlik and cherebuki,
Where a sign, showing trousers, gives us
An idea of a man.
A man's frock coat — desire without a head.
The flying fiddle of a barber, and a mesmerizing iron,
The appearance of celestial washer-women —
The smile of heaviness.

2

Here, the girls, growing gray in the forelocks,
Comtemplate the strange dresses,
And admirals in firm three-cornered hats
Recall the dream of Scheherezade.
The clear distance. A few vineyards.
And always a fresh wind blowing.
Not far from Smyrna and Baghdad,

But difficult to navigate,
For the stars are everywhere the same.[15]

1

In a crystal pool, such steepness!
Behind us, the sienna mountains protect,
and the jagged cathedrals of raving mad cliffs
are suspended in the air, where
there is wool and silence.

2

From the hanging staircase of prophets and kings,
descends an organ, the fortress of the Holy Ghost,
the brave barking and gentle ferocity of sheepdogs,
the sheepskins of shepherds, and the staffs of judges.

3

Here is unmovable ground, and along with it
I drink the cold mountain air of Christianity,
the twisted Credo and the psalmist's lull,
the keys and rags of apostolic churches.

4

Such a line could deliver
the crystal of high notes in the invigorating ether,
and from the Christian mountains in the astounding space,
a blessing descends, like a song of Palestine.

Go back to the tainted lap, Leah,
Whence you came,
Since you preferred the yellow twilight
to the sun of Ilion.

Go, no one will touch you,
Let the incestuous daughter
drop her head on her father's breast
in the dead of night.

But the fatal change
must be fulfilled in you;
You shall be Leia — not Helen, —
and thus not chosen,

for it is harder for royal blood
to flow in the veins —
No, you are in love with a Jew,
You will vanish in him, and
God will be with you.

O this air, intoxicated with unrest,
on the black square of the Kremlin.
The agitators rock the teetering world.[16]
Restlessly the poplars sway.

The waxen facade of the cathedral,
the thick forest of bells,
as if a tongueless bandit
could vanish in the stony rafters.

But in the sealed up cathedrals,
where it is cool and dark,
as in delicate clay amphoras,
the Russian wine plays.

The Assumption, surprisingly rounded,
all the marvel of the arches of Paradise,
and the Annunciation is green, and it seems
it suddenly begins to crow.

The Archangel and Resurrection[17]
shine like a sheet of glass,
everywhere the secret burning, —
and in the wine jugs a hidden flame. . .

1
In Petersburg we'll meet again,
As though we'd buried the sun there,

And for the first time utter
The blessed, senseless word.
In the black velvet of Soviet night,
In the velvet of world-wide emptiness,
The kind eyes of blessed women still sing,
The immortal flowers still bloom.

2

The capital arches like a savage cat,
A patrol is standing on the bridge,
A single angry car speeds by in the dark,
And cries out like a cuckoo.
This evening I do not need a pass,
I am not afraid of the sentries:
I will pray in the Soviet night
For the blessed and senseless word.

3

I hear a light rustling in the theater
and a young girl's "oh" —
In Kypris' arms, a huge bunch
Of immortal roses.
Out of boredom, we warm ourselves
By a bonfire. Perhaps centuries will pass,
And the kind hands of blessed women
Will gather up the light ashes.

4

Somewhere are the red rows of the gallery,
The sumptuous chiffon of the boxes;
The clockwork-puppet officer;
Not for black souls or vile hypocrites. . . .
Yes. Extinguish, please, our tapers
In the black velvet of world-wide emptiness,
The sloped shoulders of blessed women still sing,
But you don't notice the night sun.

From the clock, grasshoppers sing,
and fever whispers
and dry stove crackles:
It is red silk burning.

The mice grind with their teeth
the very thin ground of life,
a swallow and her daughter
have loosened my shuttle.

Rain murmurs on the roof —
It is black silk burning,
but the alder tree hears,
and on the bottom of the sea: forgive.

Because death is guiltless, and
there is no cure for anything,
in a nightingale's fever,
there is still a warm heart.

I dream of hunchbacked Tiflis,
Where a *Sazandar's*[18] groan resounds
The people cluster on the bridge,
The whole capital is carpeted,
And below, the Kura murmurs.

Above the Kura are *dukhans*[19]
With their wine and good pilaf,
And a ruddy *dukhanshik*
Gives glasses to the guests,
And is ready to serve you.

The dense, cachectic drinking
Is good in the cellar, —
There in the coolness, in peace,
You drink your fill, drink two,
Or you don't have to drink at all.

In the same, small *dukhan,*
You will find a friend
If you ask for Teliani.
Tiflis is swimming in a fog,
Your head is swimming at the inn.

A man grows old,
But a lamb, young,
And under the narrow moon,
With the vapor of rosé wine,
Flies a *shashlik* thought.

Sisters — Heaviness, Tenderness — your signs are identical.
Bees and wasps suck the heavy rose.
A man dies, the heated sand grows cool, and
yesterday's sun is carried away on a black stretcher.

Oh! heavy honeycombs, tender meshed,
easier to raise a stone than say your name!
I have one purpose left on earth, it is
a golden one: to throw off time's yoke.

I drink the turbid air as if it were muddy water.
Time is ploughed up, and the rose was the earth.
In a slow vortex, love has twined the heavy,
tender roses, the roses Heaviness and Tenderness,
into double wreaths.

1

I want to serve you
On an equal footing with others;
From jealousy, to tell your fortune
With dry lips.
The word does not slake
My parched mouth,
And without you, again
The dense air is empty.

2

I am not jealous anymore,
But I want you,
And will suffer by myself
Like a hangman's victim.
I will call you
Neither joy, nor love;

Something wild and strange
Was substituted for my blood.

3

One more moment,
And I will say to you:
It is not joy, but torment
I find in you.
And, like some transgression,
It drags me to you,
The bitten, confused,
Tender cherry mouth.

4

Return to me sooner:
It is awful to be without you,
I have never felt
More strongly about you.
And all that I want
I see in waking.
I am not jealous anymore,
But I will call you.

1

A phantom scene barely glimmers,
the soft choruses of shades,
Melpomene[20] lashed the windows of her room with silk.
The wagon stand in the black gypsy-camp.
The frost crackles in the courtyard.
Everything is disshevelled — people and things,
and the burning snow crunches.

2

Piece by piece, the servants take down
the piles of bear skin coats.
In the rummage a butterfly,
a rose muffled in the fur.
Moths and money boxes of colorful linen,
a light theatrical fire.
But on the street the lamps flicker,
and the heavy steam gathers.

3

The coachmen are weary from shouting,
and the darkness heaves and snorts.
No matter, my dove Eurydike,
that it is winter for us.
For me, my native tongue is sweeter
than the music of Italian speech,
for in it, the fount of foreign harps
will mysteriously stammer.

4

The pitiful sheepskin smells of smoke,
from a snow drift the street is black.
Out of the glorious melodic stream
immortal Spring flies to us, so that
the aria eternally resounds:
— You will return to the green meadows,
and the living swallow fell back
on the burning snow.

Venetian Life 21

1

The meaning of somber and sterile
Venetian life is clear to me: here
she looks into a deep decrepit glass
with a cool smile.

2

Thin leather air. Blue veins.
White snow. Green brocade.
They are all placed on cypress stretchers,
taken warm and drowsy from a cloak.

3

And the candles burn, burn in baskets,
as if a pigeon had flown into the shrine.
At the theater and the solemn concil,
A person is dying.

4

Because there is no salvation from love and fear:
Saturn's rings are heavier than platinum!
The chopping block is covered with black velvet,
and on it, a beautiful face.

5

Your jewels are heavy, Venetia,
in the cypress mirror-frame.
Your air is faceted. In the bedroom,
the blue mountains of decrepit glass dissolve.

6

Only in her hands are the rose and the hourglass —
Green Adriatic, forgive me.
Why are you silent, Venetienne,
tell me how to escape this solemn death.

7

Black Hesper glimmers in the mirror.
Everything passes, the truth is vague.
A man is born, a pearl dies.
And Susannah has to wait for old men.

I am sorry it is winter now,
and you can't hear gnats in the house.
But you remind yourself
Of the light-headed straw.

The dragonflies hover in the blue sky,
And fashion turns around like a swallow;
A basket on the head,
Or a bombastic ode?

I won't endeavor to give advice
and useless excuses,
but the taste of whipped cream
and orange peel lasts forever.

You define everything without thinking,
and by doing no worse,

the most sensitive mind
is put wholly outside.

And you attempt to beat the yolk
with an angry spoon.
It grew white, it succumbed.
But there's still a little more.

Justice, it is not your fault,
why the appraisals and reverses?
You are so purposely created
for comical mutual quarrel.

In you everything provokes, everything sings
like an Italian trill,
and a small cherry mouth
demands a dry vineyard.

Do not take such pains to be wise,
In you everything is whimsy,
and the shadow from your cap —
a Venetian *bautta*.[22]

The chalice was suspended in the air
like the golden sun for a golden moment.
Here it is proper for only Greek to be heard:
To take in its hands the whole world, like a simple apple.

The triumphal zenith of the divine service,
Light in a round room under a cupola in July,
That we could sigh about that meadow beyond time,
Where time does not run, with a full chest.

And the Eucharist drags on like an eternal midday —
Everyone takes the Sacrament, performs, and sings,
And the sacred vessel, to everyone's favor
pours out with inexhaustible rejoicing.

As Psyche-Life goes down to the shades
in a translucent forest in Persephone's tracks,
A blind swallow falls at her feet
with Stygian tenderness and a green branch.

The shades flock to meet the fugitive,
welcome their new visitor with weeping,
wring their feeble hands before her
bewildered and in timid hope.

One holds a mirror, another a phial of perfume —
the soul is a woman, fond of trifles
(and the leafless forest is sprinkled with fine rain of
laments, dry transparent voices.)

And in the gentle confusion,
not knowing where to start,
she does not recognise the spectral wood,
and breathes on the mirror, holds the
copper coin for the misty crossing.

Just for joy, take from my palms
A little sun, a little honey,
As Persephone's bees have commanded.

An unfastened boat cannot be untied.
A spirit in shoes walking through furs cannot be heard.
In the thick forest of life fear cannot be overcome.

Only kisses are left for us.
Furry, like small bees
that die, having left the hive.

They buzz in transparent thickets of night,
their habitat is the dense Taiga woods;
their food — time, honeysuckle, mint.

So take for joy my passionate gift,
A dry, unsightly necklace
Of dead bees, who changed honey into sun.

The Twilight of Freedom

1

Let us glorify, brothers, the twilight of freedom —
the great setting year.
A weighty forest of nets is lowered
into the bubbling waters of night.
You are rising into barren years,
O sun, judge, people.

2

Let us glorify the burden of fate,
which in time of tears takes the nation's helm.
Let us glorify the dark burden of power,
her unbearable oppression.
Whoever has the heart should learn, time,
how your ship is sinking.

3

We tied the swallows into battle legions
and so, the sun's obscured? the whole element
warbles, whirls, lives;
Thru the nets — a dense twilight —
the sun's obscured, and the land sets sail.

4

But still, let us try: an enormous, awkward
screeching turn of the wheel.
The land is sailing. Take courage, men!
Dividing the water, like a plow,
we will recall even in Lethe's frost,
that our land was worth ten heavens.

1

At a dreadful height, a wandering fire —
But does a star really flicker like that?
Transparent star, wandering fire,
Your brother, Petropolis, is dying.

2

At a dreadful height, earthly dreams are burning,
A green star is twinkling

O if you, star, are water and sky's brother,
Your brother, Petropolis, is dying.

3

A monstrous ship flies at a dreadful height,
Spreading its wings —
Green star, in beautiful poverty
Your brother, Petropolis, is dying.

4

Above the black Neva, transparent Spring
Is smashed, the wax of immortality is melting.
O if you, star, are Petropolis, your city,
Your brother, Petropolis, is dying.

Swallow

1

I have forgotten the word that I wanted to say.
On clipped wings the blind swallow returns
To the hall of shadows, to play with the transparencies.
A night song is sung in forgetfulness.

2

The bird cannot be heard. The *imortelle* does not bloom.
A herd of night mares with transparent manes.
An empty canoe glides on a waterless river.
Among the grasshoppers the word becomes forgotten.

3

And it grows slowly, as if it were a temple or tent,
And suddenly, like crazed Antigone, falls on its side,
Lands at the feet, like a dead swallow,
With Stygian tenderness and a green branch.

4

O, if I could give back the disgrace of
Fingers that see and the joy of recognition.
I am so afraid of the Aonides' weeping,
Of mist, ringing, the abyss.

5

Yet the power to love and perceive is given to mortals,
For them even the sound spreads to their fingers,

But I forgot what I want to say, and
The intangible thought returns to the hall of shadows.

6

The transparency always repeats the word,
Always: swallow, friend, Antigone. . .
But on the lips, like black ice, burns
The remembrance of a Stygian sound.

If I am to know how to restrain your hands,
If I am to relinquish the tender, salty lips,
I must wait for daybreak in the dense acropolis.
How I hate those ancient weeping willows.

Achaian men equip their steeds in darkness.
With jagged saws they rip firmly into the walls.
The dry noise of blood does not subside at all,
And for you there is no sound, no name, no mold.

How daring it was to think you would return!
For what were we separated so prematurely!
The gloom has still not dispersed,
The cock has not finished his song,
The glowing axe has still not entered the wood.

The resin came forth like a transparent tear,
And the city feels its wooden ribs,
But the blood rushed out to the stairs, went on the attack,
And thrice the men dreamed of the tempting figure.

Where is pleasant Troy, where is the king's, the maiden's home?
Priam's great starling coop will be destroyed,
And the arrows will fall in a dry forest rain,
And more will spring up like a hickory grove.

The last star's sting will be extinguished painlessly,
And morning will knock on the window like a gray swallow,
Slow day will begin to stir, like an ox in the haystack
Just awakened from a long dream.

I love the gray silences of *Te Deum*
Under the arches, the wandering of the requiem,
And the moving ceremony, which everyone should see —
The funeral of Isaac.

I love the unhurried step of the priest,
The grand bearing of the shroud
And in a worn-out seine, the Janissarian[23] gloom
Of the Lenten Week.

The Old Testament smoke on warm altars,
And the final, orphaned cry[24] of the priest,
A regal, humble man: clean snow on his shoulders,
And the savage purple mantles.

The eternal cathedrals of Sofia and Peter,
Storehouses of air and light, the possessions
Of the ecumenical granary
And the barn of the New Testament.

The spirit is not drawn to you in sorely troubled times,
Here drags the wolf's track of unhappiness
Along the cloudy steps;
We will never change it:

For the slave is free, fear is overcome,
And preserved beyond measures
In the cool granaries, in deep combines,
Is the kernel of deep, full belief.

Translated by Bruce McClelland

NOTES

Editor's note. These poems have been arranged according to the order in which they appeared in Osip Mandelstam's *Tristia*, assembled and edited by Mikhail Kuzmin and published in Petersburg in 1921. But a small number of the poems have not been translated here. Additional poems listed under the heading *Tristia* in Gleb Struve's edition have not been included.

     1. The scene here is most likely taken from Racine's *Phedre,* and not from Euripides' *Hippolytos.* See *Phedre,* Scene III.

     2. Most likely an allusion to the Time of Troubles (1598 - 1613) in Russia, from the rule of Boris Godunov to that of Vladislav of Poland, tsar elect. Basically, this poem concerns Theodore's half brother, Dmitri Tsarevich, who in 1591 was found in the courtyard of his estate in Uglich, a small town outside of Moscow, with his throat mysteriously slashed, thus paving the way for a dynastic crisis.

     3. *three meetings:* The Metropolitan of Moscow was consecrated as the third Rome in 1589, under Theodor I. It is conjectured that the reason for this was that "those who formulated [the doctrine] believed the end of the world was approaching and the Last Judgement. They were merely trying to keep Orthodox Christianity alive as a last refuge to the end." For more on this, see George Vernadsky's *A History of Russia.*

     4. *bound hands:* It is believed that Dmitry was an epileptic.

     5. *Solominka:* Princess Salomeia Nikolaevna Andronikova, or, as she was better known in Western Europe, Lou-Andreas Salomé.

     6. *medusa:* Here, since it is not capitalized, can mean either a generalized Medusa, snakes and all, or a sea-nettle or type of jellyfish.

     7. *Taurides:* A mountain range in Turkey near the Black Sea. See also "The thick golden stream of honey flowed...".

     8. "Baiu, baiushki, baiu...": The beginning of a well-known Russian lullaby.

     9. *Quadrigae:* Latin, "four-horsed chariots."

     10. "Shto...tso:" Different pronunciations of the word for *what* in Russian and Polish (or Ukranian), respectively.

     11. *wax:* A Slavic method of divination was the spilling of molten wax or lead into cold water. Its final, cooled-off shape would then be interpreted.

     12. *Pierius:* Mountain in Northeast Greece, said to be the first place known where the Muses were worshipped.

     13. *little song:* "In the Blacksmith's Shop."

     14. *Epirus:* A region in western Greece.

15. In the Struve edition of Mandelstam's works these stanzas are included as the concluding lines (25-40) of the poem printed below:

[111]

Theodosia *

Surrounded by high hills, you
Run down from the mountain with a herd of sheep,
And you sparkle in the dry, clear air
Like rosy, white stones.
The pirate *feluccas* flounder, the poppies
Of Turkish flags seem to burn in the port,
And the reeds of masts, the elastic crystal of the wave,
And skiff-hammocks hanging on the ropes.

And in all ways, from morning till night
and cried over by everyone, "Yablochko" is sung.
The wind carries away the golden seed —
It was lost, never to return.
But in the alleys, just become dark,
the incapable musicians, huddled in twos and threes,
Begin to sing their improbable variations.

O figures of hook-nosed travellers,
This joyous Mediterranean menagery!
The Turks in their towels wander about
Like chickens at a little inn.
They transport dogs in prison-like wagons,
The dry dust on the streets flies up,
And indifferent among the bazaar fury
Is a monumental cook from a battle ship.

* A resort in the Crimea, where Mandelstam
   lived in 1919.

16. *world:* The Russian word for *world* is the same as the word for *peace: mir.*

17. *Assumption, Archangel, Resurrection:* Cathedrals in Moscow.

18. *Sazandar:* A musician; a member of the National ensembles of Azerbaijan, Armenia, Georgia, Iran.

19. *Dukhan:* A Caucasian Inn. A *dukhanshik* is apparently a waiter at one of these inns.

20. *Melpomene:* The "Muse of Tragedy."

21. This poem most likely is derivative of one, if not many, of the paintings of Susannah in the Bath or with the Elders done by Renaissance artists. The story is in the Apocrypha.

22. *bautta:* Italian, "a black cape with a hood or mask; a cowl."

23. *Janissarian:* Pertaining to *Janissaries,* orig. "One of a former body of Turkish infantry, constituting the Sultan's guard and the main part

main part of the standing army. The body was first organized in the 14th century, and was composed mainly of tributary children of Christians; after a large number of them had been massacred in 1826, the organization was finally abolished." — O.E.D. As to Mandelstam's usage, this is unclear.

24. *cry* (Russian *vozglas*): I know of no English word or phrase which will translate this word, which means, roughly, "the final notes of a prayer which are sung (chanted) in a loud voice." An alternate translation of this line might be: "And the orphaned final notes of the priest."

Hagia Sophia

Hagia Sophia—God has ordained
That nations and rulers halt themselves here;
Thus does your dome, as an eyewitness said,
Suspend as on chains from the heavenly sphere.

When Justinian stole for alien gods,
With the Ephesian Diana's permission,
One hundred and seven green marble columns,
For all ages to follow a model was given.

But in his soul and intellect exalted,
What was your generous architect's thought
When he disposed obliquely west and east
The exedrae and apses beside the vault?

The temple is beautiful, bathing in its peace,
And triumphant the light, the forty windows' rays,
But the finest of all on pendentive sails
Are the four archangels at the cupola's base.

And before the edifice, spherical and sage,
Nations and ages will first disappear,
And never will seraphims' resonant plaints
Warp the dark leaves of its gilded veneer.

1912   *Translated by Struven Fehsenfeld*

Notre Dame

Where an alien race was judged by Roman courts,
There a basilica stands; as blithe as Adam's
Primitive gladness, the delicate, cross-shaped vault
Lets its muscles play, its nerves outstretched and taut.

But from without the secret scheme betrays itself:
Here the saddle-girth arches' strength was wary,
That walls not be crushed under massive loads
Nor the brazen vault's battering ram thrust past stone.

Elemental labyrinth, impenetrable forest,
The reasoned abyss of the Gothic spirit,
Egyptian might with timid Christianity,
The oak by the reed, and the plumb—caesar of gravity.

But the more observantly, stronghold Notre Dame,
I studied your structure's monstrous ribs,
The more often I thought: one day I as well shall create
A kind of beauty out of unkind weight.

1912   *Translated by Struven Fehsenfeld*

Given my body—how shall I use it,
So much a part of me, yet so unique?

For the quiet joys of breathing and living
Tell me, who shall I praise in thanksgiving?

Both as gardener and flower grown,
In the world's dungeon I am not alone.

Already my breath and my body heat
Becloud the lenses of eternity.

The design whose imprint it has borne
Appears of late in unfamiliar form.

May the mist of the moment dissipate
And not obliterate that lovely shape.

1909   *Translated by Jane Gary Harris*

Orioles in the trees, and the length of vowels
Determines the measure of a classical line.
But on one day each year quantity overflows,
Spills from nature's bosom, like Homeric meter.

And like a caesura that day opens with a yawn:
Dawn brings tranquility and almost painful peace;
Oxen in the pasture, and golden indolence
Thwarts me from extracting rich, round notes from my reed.

1914   *Translated by Jane Gary Harris*

Insomnia

Insomnia. Homer. Taut canvas sails.
I scanned the catalogue of ships half-way:
Like a long line of birds, a train of cranes,
That long ago soared high over Hellas.

Like a wedge of cranes crossing an alien line
(The foam of the gods showers crowned heads),
Where are you sailing? If not for Helen,
O great Achaeans, what would Troy signify?

The sea and Homer—all is moved by love's will.
Whom shall I heed? Homer lies silently,
But the black sea resounds eloquently
And rumbles gravely toward my pillow.

1915   *Translated by Jane Gary Harris*

I was washing outside in the darkness,
the sky burning with rough stars,
and the starlight, salt on an axe-blade.
The cold overflows the barrel.

The gate's locked,
the land's grim as its conscience.
I don't think they'll find the new weaving,
finer than truth, anywhere.

Star-salt is melting in the barrel,
icy water is blackening,
death's growing purer, misfortune saltier,
the earth's moving nearer to truth and to dread.

1921   *Translated by*
                 W. S. Merwin and Clarence Brown

The Age

My age, my beast, to whom will it be given
To behold the pupils of your eyes,
To cement two centuries together,
Giving of his blood to glue their spines?
Out of earthly things the blood for building
Pours along the throat and gushes forth,
While the hanger-on can only tremble,
Standing at the new day's door.

To the end of life a creature
Has to bear his backbone's ridge,
While the playful wave keeps cresting,
Unseen vertebrae across its edge.
Like a baby's tender cartilage
Is the age of childish earth;
Now life's cranium's brought forth again
To be offered like a lamb and burnt.

So that a new world can take its place
And imprisoned life be broken loose,
Elbow-joints of knotted days
Must be bound together with a flute.
It's the age that rocks the wave
To the tune of man's lament,
And the golden measures of the age
There in the grass, on the viper's breath.

Still the buds will swell, and swollen
Shoots still burst, spreading their verdant spray,
But your backbone is already broken,
My beautiful, wretched age.
And behind your mindless smile,
Ruthless, of your strength bereft,
You look back now, like a beast once lithe,
On the tracks your paws have left

1923   *Translated by Struven Fehsenfeld*

January 1, 1924

He who has kissed the wizened crown of time
Shall recall with filial tenderness
The moment time settled down to sleep
On a sheaf of wheat beneath his window.
He who has faced the age with lifted eyelids
(Those two enormous sleeping apples)
Shall know the voice of the river of time—
The eternal roar beguiling and certain!

The sovereign age has two sleeping apples
And an exquisite fragile clay mouth,
But the fingers of his aging son grow numb
As they grip him falling over, dying.
Life's breath grows weaker each passing day,
I know, little remains. My simple song
Of fragile clay wrongs shall never be sung,
And my lips shall be molded in tin.

O life, fragile as clay! O dying age!
How I fear you shall be apprehended
By a stranger flaunting the bloodless smile
Of a man forced to forfeit his soul.
What agony to search out a lost word,
What torture to lift my ailing eyelids
And, with quicklime congealing in my blood,
To gather herbs for an alien tribe.

The age. Quicklime congeals in the sick son's blood.
Moscow sleeps, like a wooden coffer;
There is nowhere to run from the sovereign age...
Snow smells of apples as in the olden days.
I want to run, to run far, far away.
But where? It is pitch black outside,
Though my conscience grows white before my eyes
As if someone were sprinkling the road with salt.

Past alleys, starling boxes, drooping eaves,
I finally set out, just a short way off;
A common man clad in a flimsy coat,
I need all my strength to fasten my laprobe.

One street flashes past, then another,
The hard sled resounds like a crunchy apple,
The narrow buttonhole just won't hold,
The button keeps slipping through my fingers.

Wintry night thunders through Moscow streets
Gliding along on frozen runners.
Now someone knocks offering fresh fish,
Now steam gushes from rose-colored taverns.
Moscow, Moscow. How warmly I greet her:
"Don't judge too harshly, the worst is over;
With time I've come to respect the brotherhood
Of severe cold and the pike's justice."

Raspberry drops ablaze in the snow,
And somewhere the clicking of an Underwood;
The driver's back, and snow half a yard deep:
What more can you ask? No one can touch you, kill you.
Winter's beauty, and the stars of Capricorn
Scattering goat's milk and sparkling;
Like a horse's mane rubbing frozen runners
My laprobe rustles and rings.

But the alleyways smoking from oil stoves
Gulped down the raspberries, ice and snow,
And devoured all that they came to know
Like a Soviet sonatina of the famine years.
Must I really condemn to shameful scandal
(Again the cold has the fragrance of apples)
That wonderful oath to the fourth estate
And those fierce vows confirmed only through tears?

Who else shall you kill? Who else shall you praise?
What other lies shall you invent?
There's gristle caught in the Underwood: quick,
Pull out the key—you'll find a pike's bones;
The quicklime congealed in the sick son's blood
Thaws and splashes his blissful smile...
But the typewriters' simple sonatina
Is but a shadow of the sonatas of old.

1924   *Translated by Jane Gary Harris*

Anna Akhmatova

A POEM WITHOUT A HERO

A Triptych

1940-62

Di rider finirai
Pria dell' aurora
Don Giovanni

Leningrad-Tashkent-Moscow

Deus conservat omnia
Motto on the seal of the House on the Fontanka

IN PLACE OF A FOREWORD

Some are no more, others are distant.

It came to me for the first time in the House on the Fontanka on the night of December 27, 1940, after previously sending a small fragment as a herald that fall.

I did not call for it. I was not even expecting it that cold and dark day during my last Leningrad winter.

Its appearance was preceded by several petty and insignificant facts which I cannot resolve to call events.

That night I wrote two sections of the first part ("1913" and the "Dedication"). In the beginning of January, almost unexpectedly for myself, I wrote "Tails," and in Tashkent (in two sittings)—the "Epilogue," which became the third part of the poem, and I made several basic interpolations in both of the first two parts.

I dedicate this poem to its first listeners—my friends and countrymen who perished in Leningrad during the siege.

I hear their voices and I remember them when I read the poem aloud, and for me this secret chorus has become a permanent justification of the work.

April 8, 1943
Tashkent

FIRST DEDICATION
December 27, 1940

In memory of Vs. K.

. . . .
. . . and because I ran out of paper,
I am writing this on your rough draft.
And there, an alien word shows through,
And just as *then,* a snowflake on my hand
Melts trustingly, with no reproach.
And the dusky lashes of Antinous
Abruptly rose, and inside—green smoke
And a familiar wind began to blow...
Is it the sea?
　　　　　No, only the pine needles
On a grave, the foaming waves
Ever nearer, ever nearer...
　　　　　　　　Marche funèbre...
　　　　　　　　　　　　Chopin...

Night
The House on the Fontanka

SECOND DEDICATION

O. A. G.-S.

Is it you, Confusion-Psyche,
Fluttering a fan of black and white,
Are you bending down to me;
Do you want to tell me in secret
That Lethe you've already passed
And you breathe of a different Spring.
No dictation—I can hear it myself:
　　　　A warm shower has shattered on the roof,
　　　　　　I hear the wispy whisper in the ivy.
Someone tiny, in his intention to live,
　　　　Turned green, got fluffy, tried
　　　　　　To sparkle in a new cloak tomorrow,
I sleep—
　　　　she alone is over me—
The one people call Spring

I call loneliness.
I sleep—I dream of our youth,
    That cup which passed *him* by;
In waking reality I will, if you wish,
    Give it to you as a momento,
    Like a pure flame in clay
    Or a snowdrop in a grave.

May 25, 1945
The House on the Fontanka

THIRD AND LAST

Once on Christmas Eve...

I'm tired of freezing from fear,
    better I'll call for Bach's Chaconne,
      and a man will enter behind it.
He will not become my dear husband,
    but he and I will deserve such things
      that the Twentieth Century will be embarrassed.
I accidentally took him for the one
    who is offered by the mystery,
      with whom the most bitter times are ordained.
He is late to see me
    in the Fontanka Palace on a foggy night,
      to drink the New Year's wine.
And he will remember Christmas Eve,
    the maple in the window, the wedding candles
      and the mortal flight of the poem...
But he will bring me not the first sprig of lilac,
    not a ring, not the sweetness of entreaties—
      he will bring me doom.

January 5, 1956 (Le Jour des Rois)

INTRODUCTION

FROM THE YEAR NINETEEN-FORTY
  AS FROM A TOWER I LOOK OVER ALL,
    AS IF I AM PARTING AGAIN
      WITH WHAT I LONG AGO SAID FAREWELL TO,
        AS IF I HAD CROSSED MYSELF
          AND AM WALKING UNDER DARK VAULTS.

August 25, 1941
Leningrad under siege.

PART ONE

THE YEAR NINETEEN-THIRTEEN

A Petersburg Tale

Chapter One

> New Year's Eve opulently lingers
> Moist are the stems of New Year's roses.
> *Beads*

> We're not to conjure with Tatyana...

> In my hot youth—when George the Third was king.
> *Don Juan*

New Year's Eve. The House on the Fontanka. Instead of the one whom the author has been awaiting, the shades of the year nineteen-thirteen come to me as mummers. A white mirrored hall. A lyrical digression—"Guest from the Future." A masquerade. A poet. A phantom.

> I have lit the cherished candles,
> To make the evening shine,
> And with you, who have not come to me,
>   I meet nineteen-forty-one.
>   But...
>   The Lord's power be with us!
>   In crystal drowned the flame
>   "And the wine burns like poison."
> Those are splashes of harsh conversation,
>   When all the deliriums are resurrected,
>   And the clock still has not struck...
> My anxiety knows no measure,
>   Like a shade on the threshold
>   I myself guard the final cozy refuge.
> And I hear a protracted ring at the door,

And I feel a clammy cold,
    I turn to stone, I freeze, I burn...
And as if recalling something,
      Turning half-way around,
      I say in a soft voice:
"You've made a mistake: Venice of the Doges—
That's nearby... But today
You will have to leave your masks
      In the hall—and your cloaks, and crowns, and staffs.
Today I've decided to cover you with glory,
      You New Year's madcaps!"
      Here's one as Faust, there's one as Don Juan,
      As Dapertutto, as Jokanaan;
The most modest—as the Northern Glahn,
Or as Dorian the murderer,
And all are whispering to their Dianas
Speeches learned by heart.
      And someone with a timbrel
      Brought a satyr-legged bacchante.
And the walls moved apart for them,
Lights flared on, sirens wailed,
      And the ceiling bulged like a cupola.
It is not that I fear publicity...
What are Hamlet's suspenders to me!
What is the whirlwind of Salome's dance to me,
      What are the footsteps of the Iron Mask to me!
      I myself am more iron than all of them...
And whose turn is it to be frightened,
To flinch, recoil, surrender,
      And pray forgiveness for an ancient sin?..
It's all clear:
            if not to me, to whom then!
Not for them was this supper prepared,
And it's not for them to walk my path with me.
His tail he has hidden under the flaps of his frock...
      How lame and elegant he is...
      However...
I hope you did not dare
To bring the King of Darkness here?..
Whether it is a mask, a skull, or face—
      The expression of malicious pain is one
      That only Goya dared convey.
Everyone's pet and mocker of all—
Next to him the vilest sinner

Is virtue personified...
If I'm to make merry—then let me make merry!—
But how could it happen
    That of all of them only I am alive?
Tomorrow morning will wake me up,
    And no one will condemn me,
    And the blue outside the window
        Will smile into my face.
But I am terrified: I will enter,
    Without removing my lacy shawl,
    I'll smile to everyone and be silent.
Before the Valley of Jehoshaphat,
    I have no wish to meet again
        Myself as I once was,
            Wearing a necklace of black agates...
            Are not the final deadlines near?..
I have forgotten your lessons,
    Rhetoricians and false prophets,
        But you have not forgotten me.
            As in the past the future ripens,
                So in the future the past decays—
                Terrible festival of lifeless foliage.

W   *The steps of those who are not here,*
H   *Across the resplendent parquet,*
I   *And the bluish smoke of cigars.*
T   *And all the mirrors reflect*
E   *A man who has not come*
      And could not penetrate this hall.
H   *He's no better than others, nor worse,*
A   *But he breathes not of Lethe's chill,*
L   *And in his hand is warmth.*
L   *Guest from the Future! Can it be*
      He will really come to me,
      Turning from the bridge to the left?

...Mummers I have feared since childhood,
    For reasons unknown, it always seemed to me
      That a certain superfluous shade,
Among them "without face or name,"
    Interloped...
            Let us open the meeting
            On this solemn New Year's Day!
This midnight Hoffmanniana

I will not proclaim all over the world,
And I would request others...
Wait,
You seem not to be on the list of guests,
Among the Cagliostros, magicians, Liziskas,
Dressed like a striped milestone—
Painted motley and coarsely—
You...
are as old as the oak of Mamre,
Ancient interlocutor of the moon.
Feigned moans will not deceive me,
You write cast-iron laws;
The Hammurabis, Lycurguses, and Solons
Should take lessons from you.
A creature of peculiar character,
He does not wait for gout and glory
To hastily seat him
In plush anniversary armchairs,
But bears his triumph
Across blossoming heather and desert.
And is guilty of nothing: not of the first thing,
Nor the second, nor the third...
Sins
In general do not suit poets.
Dance before the Ark of the Covenant
Or perish!.. But why discuss it! Of this
Their poetry told better.
We just dream of a crowing cock,
Beyond the window smokes the Neva,
Unfathomable is the night, and on and on goes
The Petersburg diaboliad...
Through the slender windows the stars are unseen,
Doom lurks here somewhere, it would seem,
But the babble of the masquerade
Is carefree, frothy, and shameless...
A cry:
"Hero to the center stage!"
Don't worry: now he will
Certainly take the hulk's place
And sing of sacred vengeance...
Why are you all running away together,
As if each had found a fiancée,
Leaving me in the dusk,
Face to face with the black frame

Out of which this hour stares,
    An hour become a bitter drama,
        And unlamented still.

This does not surface all at once,
Like a single musical phrase,
I hear a whisper: "Farewell! It's time!
I am leaving you alive,
But you will be my widow,
You are a dove, a sun, and sister!"
On the landing two contiguous shadows...
Then—the flat steps of the staircase,
A scream: "Don't!" and in the distance
A clear voice:
        "I am ready to die."

The torches go out, the ceiling descends. The white (mirrored) hall becomes the author's room again. Words out of the darkness:

There is no death—everyone knows that,
    It is insipid to repeat;
        But what is there—let them tell me that.
Who's knocking?
        Everyone has been admitted.
    Is it a guest from inside the mirrors? Or
        That which suddenly flashed past the window...
A jest of the new moon,
    Or is someone really standing there
        Between the stove and chest again?
A pale brow, and eyes agape...
    So gravestones are brittle,
        So granite is softer than wax...
Drivel, drivel, drivel! —From drivel like this
    I will soon grow gray
        Or be completely changed.
Why are you beckoning to me?
    For one minute of peace
    I will give up posthumous peace.

ACROSS THE LANDING
(Intermezzo)

"I assure you that's not new...
    You are a child, senor Casanova..."
        "On St. Isaac's Square at six o'clock sharp..."
"Somehow we'll still manage to get
    Through the dark from here to *The Dog.*"
        "Where are you going from here?"—
                "God knows!"

The Sancho Panzas and Don Quixotes
    And, alas, the Lots of Sodom
        Sample the fatal   juice,
The Aphrodites have risen from the foam,
    The Helens shimmered in the glass,
        And near moves the hour of madness.
And again from the Fontanka Grotto,
    Where love's drowsiness grows cold,
    Through spectral gates
    Someone, shaggy and red-haired,
    Brought the satyr-legged bacchante.
Best-dressed and tallest of all,
    Though she doesn't hear and doesn't see,
    Nor does she curse, nor beg, nor breathe,
        Is the head of Madame de Lamballe,
And you, a cut-up and beauty,
    Dancing the satyr's tap-dance,
        Again you purr meekly and tenderly:
            "Que me veut mon Prince Carnaval?"

And simultaneously in the depths of the hall, stage, Hell—or on top of
Goethe's Brocken, *She* appears   (or maybe her shade).

    Like hoovlets click her boots,
        Like cymbals cling her earrings,
           With wicked hornlets in pale locks,
                Intoxicated by a cursed dance,—
As if off a black-emblazoned vase
    She ran to the azure wave,
        So ostentatiously décolleté.
And behind her in greatcoat and helmet,
    You who came in here without a mask,
        Ivanushka of the ancient fairytale,
           What torments you today?

How much bitterness in every word,
　　How much darkness in your love,
　　　　And why does that rivulet of blood
　　　　　　Irritate the petal of your cheeks?

CHAPTER TWO

Or is he whom you see at your knees
The one who left your thralldom for white death?
　　　　　　　The Voice of Memory, 1913

The heroine's bedroom. A wax candle is burning. Over the bed are three portraits of the mistress of the house in her roles. On the right she is the Bacchante, in the center—Psyche, the portrait on the left is in the shadows. To some it seems that this is Columbine, to others Donna Anna (from "The Steps of the Commendatore"). Outside the mansard window slave boys are throwing snowballs. A snowstorm. New Year's Night. Psyche comes to life, steps down from the portrait, and she imagines a voice which is reading:

The satin coat has been thrown open!
Don't be angry with me, my Dove,
　　For touching this goblet too:
　　　　I'm punishing myself, not you.
No matter what, retribution draws near—
　　Do you see—there through the big-flaked blizzard
　　　　Meyerhold's little slave boys
　　　　　　Are kicking up a fuss again.
　　　　And all around is old "Peter" City,
　　　　　　Which chisled off people's hides
　　　　(As the people said at the time),—
In manes, in harnesses, in carts of flour,
In tinted tea roses,
And under the clouds of raven wings.
But you, our ineffable swan,
Fly on, smiling fleetingly,
Prima of the Marinsky Theater,
And a late-arriving snob plies his wit.
The sound of an orchestra as if from the next world—
(The shadow of something flashed by somewhere),
Didn't the chill ripple across the rows of seats
Like a premonition of the dawn?
And again that familiar voice

Like an echo of mountain thunder,—
Our glory and victory!
It fills the heart with trepidation
And sweeps over roadless spaces,
Across the country which nurtured it.
Branches in blue-white snow...
The corridor of the Petrovsky collegia
Is endless, resonant, and straight
(Anything can happen here,
But it will be the stubborn dream
Of anyone who walks through it today).
The denouement is ridiculously close;
From behind the screen Petrushka's mask,
A coachman's dance around the bonfires,
Over the palace a blackish-yellow standard.
All who are necessary are in their places;
The Summer Garden smells of
Act Five... The phantom of the hell of Tsushima
Is here too. —A drunken sailor sings.
How gaily the sled-runners zing
And the goat-fur lap robe drags along...
Pass by, shades! —He's there alone.
His steely profile is on the wall.
Is your Paladin, o beauty,
Gabriel or Mephistopheles?
The Demon himself with the smile of Tamara,
But such charms lie hidden
In his terrible dusky face:
Flesh which has almost become spirit,
And an antique lock of hair over his ear—
Everything about this visitor is mystery.
Was it he in that overcrowded hall
Who sent the black rose in the wine glass,
Or was all that a dream?..
With lifeless heart and lifeless eyes,
Was it he who met the commendatore,
Having penetrated into that cursed house?
And has it been told in his words
How you were in a new space,
How you were outside of time—
And in what polar crystals
And in what amber gleamings
There, at the mouth of the Lethe-Neva.
You came down here from the painting,

And the empty frame on the wall
     Will wait for you till dawn.
Thus you're to dance without a partner.
I agree to take on myself
     The role of a fatal chorus.

    On your cheeks there are scarlet spots;
    You should return to the canvas,
    For tonight is the kind of a night
    When one must pay one's accounts...
    And it is more difficult than death
    For me to overcome this benumbing somnolence.

. . . To Russia you came out of nowhere,
O my flaxen-haired miracle,
     Columbine of the nineteen-tens:
Why do you stare so sadly and sharply,
You actress, you Petersburg doll—
     You are one of my doubles.
To the others this title too
Must be added. O companion of poets,
     I am heir of the fame that was yours.
Here to the music of the marvelous meter
Of the wild Leningrad wind,
And in the shadow of a sacred cedar,
     I see a dance of courtly bones. . .
The wedding candles gutter,
Under veils there are kissable shoulders,
     The cathedral resounds: "Come, O Virgin!"
Mountains of Parma violets in April—
And a rendezvous in the Malta bell-tower,
     Like a curse in your breast.
Is it a vision of the Golden Age,
Or a black crime
     In the menacing chaos of distant days?
At least answer me now. Can it be
That you really did live once,
And tapped the bricks of public squares
With your bedazzling foot?...

A house more motley than a circus wagon,
Amours which are peeling off
       Protect the altar of Venus.
You did not put songbirds in cages,

You bedecked your bedroom like a gazebo,
    The merry man of Pskov
        Will not recognize his country-girl neighbor.
Concealed in the walls is a crooked stairway,
    And on the azure walls—there are saints,
        These riches have half been stolen...
All decked in flowers like Botticelli's "Spring,"
    You received your friends in bed,
        And torment was suffered by dragoon Pierrot,—
Most superstitious of all who have been in love with you
    Is he, with his smile of evening sacrifice;
        You are to him as a magnet is to steel.
Turning pale, he watches through his tears
    As others bring you roses,
        And how renowned his enemy is.
I did not see your husband,
    I, cold pressed close against the glass...
        There it is, the striking of the fortress clock...
Don't be afraid—I don't mark houses with crosses—
    Come boldly out to meet me—
        Your horoscope has long been ready.

CHAPTER THREE

And under the archway on Gallery Street
A. Akh.

In Petersburg we'll meet again,
As if we buried the sun there.
O. M.

It was the last year...
M. Lozinsky

Petersburg, 1913. Lyrical digression: Last Reminiscence of Tsarskoe Selo.
The wind grumbles, as if reminiscing, or perhaps prophesying:

Christmas was warmed by yuletide fires,
And carriages fell off the bridges,
    And the whole funereal city swam
Toward some enigmatic goal,
Along the Neva's current or against it—

Anything to head away from its graves.
On Gallery Street stood the black archway,
A tenor coat-of-arms sang in the Summer Garden,
And a moon of vivid silver
    Froze over the Silver Age.
Because on every road,
Because to every threshold
    A shade was slowly drawing near—
The wind was tearing posters from the walls,
Smoke was dancing on the roof
And the lilac smelled of the cemetery.
And cursed by Tsaritsa Avdotya,
Dostoevskian and possessed,
The City disappeared into its mist.
And again it peered out of the darkness—
Old Petersburger and drunkard...
A drum rolled as if before an execution...
And always the incomprehensible rumble lurked
In the atmosphere of frozen suffocation,
    The pre-war, prodigal, menacing air...
But then it was hollowly audible,
It scarcely touched one's ears at all,
    And drowned in Nevsky's snowdrifts.
As if in the mirror of a terrible night
Man rages and does not wish
    To recognize himself—
While along the legendary quay
Approached not the calendar,
    But the real Twentieth Century.

But now—homeward as quickly as possible
By way of the Cameron Gallery,
To the icy mysterious garden,
Where the waterfalls are silent,
Where all nine will be glad to see me,
As you were one time glad.
There, beyond the island, there, beyond the garden,
Won't our glances meet again
With the unclouded eyes of youth?
Won't you say to me again
    The word which conquered death
        And the answer to the riddle of my life?

FOURTH AND LAST CHAPTER

> Love passed, and the mortal features
> Became lucid and dear.
>   *Vs. K.*

A corner of Mars field. The building built at the beginning of the XIXth century by the brothers Adamini. In 1942 it will suffer a direct hit from a bomb. A huge bonfire is burning. The tolling bell of Our Savior on the Blood Cathedral is heard. On the field, through the snowstorm, the phantom of a palace ball. In the interval between these two sounds Silence herself speaks:

Who froze by the darkened windows,
> On whose heart is the "pale-yellow lock,"
>> Who has blackness before his eyes?
"Help, it's still not too late!
> Night, you have never been
>> So frosty and alien!"
A wind, full of Baltic salt,
> A dance of snowstorms across Mars field,
>> And the clop of invisible hooves...
And there is a measureless anxiety in the one
> Who has only a short time to live,
>> Who is just asking God for death,
>>> And who will be forgotten forever.
He wanders outside the windows at midnight,
> The dun ray of the corner streetlight
>> Is mercilessly beamed at him—
And he finds what he waited for. The shapely masker
> On the return "Journey from Damascus"
>> Returned home. . . not alone!
With her is someone "without face or name". . .
> Through the slanting flame of the bonfire he saw
>> Their unambiguous parting.
The buildings collapsed... And in answer
> A snatch of sobbing:
>> "You, my Dove, my sun, my sister!
I will leave you alive,
> But you will be *my* widow,
>> And now...
>>> It's time to say goodbye!"
It smells of perfume on the landing,
> And a dragoon cornet with poetry
>> And senseless death in his breast

Will ring, if he is brave enough...
He will spend his last moment
In order to glorify you.
Look:
He is not in the accursed Mazur swamps,
He is not on the blue Carpathian heights...
He is on your threshold!
Across it.
May God forgive you!

How many deaths the poet faced,
The stupid boy: he chose this one—
He could not bear the first affronts,
He did not know whose threshold
He was standing on, and what road
Was opening up before him...

It is I—your olden conscience—
Who sought out the burned story,
And on the edge of the windowsill
In the home of the deceased
I left it—
and on tiptoes walked away...

AFTERWORD

ALL IS IN ORDER: THERE LIES THE POEM,
AND, AS IS CHARACTERISTIC OF IT, IS SILENT.
BUT WHAT IF SUDDENLY A THEME BREAKS LOOSE,
KNOCKS ON THE WINDOW WITH ITS FIST;
AND, FROM AFAR, IN ANSWER TO THIS CHALLENGE,
A TERRIBLE SOUND RESOUNDS—
GURGLING, AND MOANING, AND SCREAMING,
AND A VISION OF CROSSED ARMS...

216

PART TWO

Intermezzo

TAILS

My future is my past.

I drink the waters of Lethe.
My doctor forbade me to be depressed.
Pushkin

Setting: the House on the Fontanka. Time: January 5, 1941. In the window the phantom of a snow-covered maple tree. The hellish harlequinade of the year nineteen-thirteen has just passed, disturbing the silence of the great silent epoch and leaving behind it the kind of disorder which is characteristic of every holiday or funeral procession—the smoke of torches, flowers on the floor, sacred souvenirs lost forever... Wind is howling in the stovepipe, and it is in this howling that one can divine the following stanzas. It is better not to think about what seems to appear in the mirrors.

... a jasmine bush
where Dante walked, and the air is empty.
N. K.

I

My editor was unhappy,
He swore to me he was busy and sick,
Concealed his telephone number,
and grumbled: "There are three themes at once!
When you finish reading,
You don't know who loves whom.

II

Who met whom, or where, or why,
Who perished, and who was left alive,
Or who's the author, and who the hero,—
And what need we have today
Of these ruminations about the poet
And a swarm of some sort of phantoms?"

217

III

I replied: "There were three of them—
The main one was garbed as a milestone,
But the other was dressed as a demon—
Their poetry insured
That they would reach through centuries...
The third lived only twenty years.

IV

And I felt sorry for him." And out
Fell word after word again,
The music box played loudly,
And over the fractured flagon
In a crooked angry tongue of flame
An enigmatic poison burned.

V

In my dream it kept seeming to me that
I was writing a libretto for someone,
And there was no relief from the music,
And of course a dream is a material thing too,
Soft embalmer, Blue Bird,
Parapet of Castle Elsinore.

VI

And I myself was not glad
To hear in the distance
The howl of the hellish harlequinade.
I kept hoping that pine needles
Would float past the white hall
Like puffs of smoke in the dusk.

VII

There's no escaping this motley stuff.
Old Cagliostro is fooling around—
That most elegant Satan
Who does not weep for the dead with me,
Who does not know what conscience means,
And why it exists.

VIII

And it does not seem to be
A Roman midnight carnival. The tune of a prayer
Trembles near Empire-style churches.
No one knocks at my door,

Mirrors just dream of mirrors,
Silence is sentinel for silence.

IX

And I have with me my "Seventh,"
Half-dead and mute,
Her mouth is agape in grimace,
Like the mouth of a tragedian's mask,
But it's smeared with black paint
And stuffed with dry earth.

X

. . . .
. . . .
. . . .

And the decades pass:
Wars, deaths, births—
Don't you see, I cannot sing.

XI

. . . .
. . . .
. . . .
. . . .
. . . .
. . . .

XII

. . . .
. . . .
. . . .
. . . .
. . . .
. . . .

XIII

Will I melt in an official hymn?
Give me not, give me not, give me not
A diadem from the brow of a corpse.
Soon I will need a lyre,
But of Sophocles, not of Shakespeare.
Fate stands at the threshold.

XIV

And for me that theme
Was like a crushed chrysanthemum
On the floor as a coffin is being carried out.
Between "remember" and "recall," friends,
The distance is like that from Luga
To the country of satin masks.

XV

The devil made me dig around in my trunk...
Well, how could it happen
That I am guilty of everything?
I am a most quiet woman, I am simple,
The Plantain, White Flock...
Make excuses...but how, my friends?

XVI

You may be sure of this: there'll be charges of plagiarism...
Am I really more guilty than others?
However, I don't care about that,
I agree to failure,
I do not hide my embarrassment...
The box has a triple bottom.

XVII

But I confess that I used
Sympathetic inks,
That I am writing in mirror handwriting,
And there is no other road for me—
I wandered onto this one by a miracle,
And I am in no hurry to part with it.

XVIII

So that emissary from a long-past age,
From El Greco's cherished dream,
Would explain to me without words,
But just with a summer smile,
How I was more forbidden for him
Than all the seven mortal sins.

XIX

And then let the eyes
Of this unknown man from the future age
Stare at me brazenly,

So he can give the departing shade
An armful of wet lilacs
At the hour when this storm passes.

XX

But the hundred-year-old enchantress
Suddenly awoke and wanted
To have some fun. I have nothing to do with it.
She drops a lace handkerchief,
She seems to blink languidly from behind the lines,
And she entices with a Bryulovian shoulder.

XXI

In every drop I drank her in,
And seized by a devilish black thirst,
I did not know how I was
To rid myself of this possessed one:
I threatened her with the Star Chamber
And drove her to her natal attic—

XXII

Into the darkness, under Manfred's pines,
And to the shore where lifeless Shelley
Lay, looking straight into the sky—
And all the skylarks of all the world
Were cleaving the ethereal abyss,
And Lord George was holding a torch.

XXIII

But she repeated firmly:
"I am not that English lady,
And not at all Clara Gazoul,
I have absolutely no genealogy
Except a sunny and fantastic one,
And July itself brought me here.

XXIV

But I will serve even better
Your ambiguous fame
Which has lain in a ditch for twenty years.
You and I will still have this feast,
And with my royal kiss
I will reward your evil midnight."

January 3-5, 1941
The House on the Fontanka, and in Tashkent, and after.

PART THREE

EPILOGUE

I love thee, creation of Peter!
The Bronze Horseman

And the deserts of mute city squares
Where people were executed till dawn.
Annensky

The white night of June 24, 1942. The city is in ruins. From the Harbor to Smolny everything is flattened and visible. Here and there old fires are burning themselves out. Lindens are blooming and a nightingale is singing in the Sheremetiev Gardens. One third-floor window (in front of which there is an injured maple) is broken out, and beyond it yawns black emptiness.

Thus 'neath the roof of the House on Fontanka
Where the evening langour wandered
With a lamp and ring of keys—
I hallooed with a distant echo
Disturbing with my inappropriate laughter
The impenetrable sleep of things;
Where, witness of everything on earth,
At dusk and at dawn,
The old maple looks into the window.
And foreseeing our parting,
It extends its black and withered hand
To me as if to help.
The earth rumbled underfoot,
And O, what a star stared
Into my still unabandoned house,
And waited for the password...
It's somewhere there—near Tobruk,
It's somewhere here—around the corner.
You are not the first and not the last
Dark listener of bright nonsense,
What kind of revenge do you plan for me?
You won't drink up, you'll just take a sip
Of this grief from the very depths—
The news of this our parting.

222

Don't put your hand on my head—
Let time stop forever
On the watch you gave to me.
Misfortune will not pass us by,
And the cuckoo will not cuckoo
In our scorched forests...
But behind the barbed wire,
In the very heart of the dense taiga—
I don't know how many years it's been—
Turned into a handful of prison-camp dust,
Turned into a fairytale from a true and terrifying tale,
My double goes to the interrogation,
And then he goes back from the interrogation;
Two emissaries of the Noseless Wench
Are fated to guard him.
And even from here I can hear—
Isn't this a miracle!—
The sounds of my own voice:
I paid for you
                    In cash,
For exactly ten years I walked
                    Under threat of a Nagan pistol,
Neither to the left nor the right
                    Did I look,
And behind me ill fame
                    Rustled.
And without becoming my grave,
You, granite, hellish, beloved,
You grew pale, moribund, and quiet.
Our separation is transient:
I am inseparable from you,
My shadow is on your walls,
My reflection in your canals,
The sound of my footsteps in the Hermitage halls,
Where my friend wandered with me,
And on old Volkov Field
Where I can sob at will
Over the noiselessness of fraternal graves.
All that was said in Part One
About love, betrayal, and passion,
Free verse cast from its wings,
And my City stands mended...
Heavy are the gravestones
On your sleepless eyes.

It seemed to me that you were chasing me,
You who stayed there to perish
In the gleam of spires and reflection of waters.
Your desired lovely heralds didn't come...
Only the series of your charmers,
The white nights pass over you.
But the happy words "at home"
Are not known to anyone now,
Everyone is looking in someone else's window.
Some in Tashkent, some in New York,
And the bitter air of exile
Is like a poisoned wine.
All of you could have admired   me
When I was saved from the evil pursuit
In the belly of a flying fish,
Soaring over the forests full of the foe,
As *she*, possessed by the devil,
Soared over the Brocken at night...
And already, directly in front of me,
Was the icy, the frozen Kama,
And someone said, *"Quo vadis?"*
But gave me no time to move my lips
Before the mad Urals
Resounded with their tunnels and bridges.
And then the road opened before me
Along which so many had gone away,
Along which they took away my son,
And long was the funeral path
Amid the solemn and crystal
Silence of Siberia.
Seized by mortal terror
From what had turned to dust,
And knowing the time of vengeance,
Her dry eyes lowered,
And wringing her hands, Russia
Went before me to the East.

Finished in Tashkent
August 18, 1942

224

Carl R. Proffer

A POEM WITHOUT A HERO: NOTES AND COMMENTARY

The English reader will have to accept Akhmatova's mastery of rhythm and rhyme largely on faith, since the translation itself is not a poetic transformation. Akhmatova uses a variety of rhyme schemes and meters (mostly ternary), all of them accepted classical forms, but combined freely and uniquely.

Without some explanation of allusions and background, Akhmatova's poem will seem more opaque than it really is. These notes are for both the general reader who knows no Russian and for the Russian reader who does not know Akhmatova's work intimately. The findings of previous commentators (Zhirmunsky, Dobin, Pavlovsky, Struve, Filippov, and Haight) have been synthesized. The conclusions of new research and previously unpublished facts have also been used. Akhmatova also wrote a ballet scenario for the "Poem"; it is reportedly accompanied by many notes on the historical background and conception of the poem.

One reasonable school of critics will reject the biographical or "prototypical" criticism found below. It is obvious that Akhmatova's attitude toward her youth and the doomed generation she portrays in *A Poem without a Hero* is ambiguous. Therefore, it is important to know as much as possible about that generation and those personalities, just as one must know such details about Pushkin or Lermontov and their friends if one is to interpret their works and lives as fully and truthfully as a historian should.

The problem of the text of the poem is complicated, perhaps ultimately insoluble. The renowned scholar V. Zhirmunsky had access to Akhmatova's papers (now in the Central Archive in Moscow and the Saltykov-Shchedrin Library in Leningrad) when preparing the edition of her works for the Library of Poets series. Though long ready, this volume has not yet been published, so his solution to the textual problem remains to be seen. Many variants are covered by Gleb Struve and Boris Filippov in: Anna Akhmatova, *Sochineniia* (New York, 1968), II, pp. 357-89. Because Amanda Haight says Akhmatova herself checked over a copy of the MS and pronounced it final (while visiting Oxford), this text was used for the translation [it is printed in the *Slavonic and East European Review*, XLV, 105 (July, 1967), 474-96]. Except for layout, it is basically the same text as that in Struve's edition (pp. 95-133), to which a few concessions are also made in the translation. (Where line numbers are quoted below, they can be checked most easily in the Struve edition.) However, Akhmatova's friends testify that she was somewhat careless about her manuscripts, and that many times the "Poem" possessed her involuntarily after she had pronounced it finished. Furthermore, at least one eminent Akhmatova scholar has privately disputed

Amanda Haight's claim, noting, for example, that "From a Letter to N." (which Miss Haight does not use) is definitely part of the final text (see below) and should be printed with the poem. Another scholar and critic mentions that the use of parentheses for sections interpolated by Akhmatova was abandoned in the final versions (but Miss Haight uses these). [See V. Zhirmunskii, "O tvorchestve Anny Akhmatovoi," *Novyi mir*, No. 6 (1969), p. 250.]

Originally intended for the notes following the text, the following letter written by Akhmatova was also a kind of mystification—a conscious literary device which Akhmatova used to make certain explanations.

FROM A LETTER TO N.

...Knowing the circumstances of my life then you can judge this better than others.

In the fall of 1940 while going through my old papers (which subsequently perished during the siege), I ran across some letters and verses which I had had for a long time, which I had not read before ("The Devil prompted me to rifle through the chest"). They related to the tragic event of 1913 which is told about in *A Poem without a Hero.*

Then I wrote the verse fragment "You came to Russia out of nowhere" in connection with the poem "A Contemporary Woman." Perhaps you even remember my reading both of these poems to you in the House on the Fontanka, in the presence of that ancient Sheremetev maple ("and the witness of everything on earth...").

On the sleepless night of December 26-27 this verse fragment unexpectedly began to grow and be transformed into the first sketch of *A Poem without a Hero.* The history of the subsequent growth of the poem is set forth after a fashion in the mumbling under the title "In Place of a Foreword."

You cannot imagine how many wild, absurd, and ridiculous interpretations this "Petersburg Tale" has engendered.

It was judged most severely by my contemporaries, however strange that may seem, and their indictments were formulated in Tashkent by K., when he said that I was settling some sort of old accounts with an epoch (the 1910s) and people who either were no longer around, or who could not answer me. For those who do not know certain "Petersburg circumstances," the poem will be incomprehensible and uninteresting.

Others, especially women, considered that *A Poem without a Hero* is a betrayal of some sort of former "ideal," and what is even worse, an expose of my old poems in *Beads* which they "love so much."

Thus for the first time in my life, instead of a tide of treacle, I encountered sincere indignation from my readers, and this, of course, inspired me. Then, as every literate person well knows . . . . and I completely stopped writing poetry, and still for fifteen years this poem kept catching me unexpectedly, over and over, like fits of some incurable disease (it could happen anywhere—at concerts to the music, on the street, even in my dreams), and I could not tear loose from it, as I kept adding to and correcting an apparently completed work.

> ("But for me that theme was
> Like a crushed chrysanthemum
> On the floor when they carry out the coffin."
>
> "I drank in every drop,
> And possessed by a demonically
> Black thirst, I did not know how
> To get rid of the devilish thing.")

And it is not surprising that K., as you know, said to me, "Well, you're done for, it will never let you go."

But...I notice that my letter is longer than it should be, and I still have to...

May 27, 1955. Moscow.

TITLE PAGE AND DEDICATIONS

Di rider finirai... "You will stop laughing / Before the dawn." From Mozart's *Don Giovanni*. In Lorenzo da Ponte's libretto the words are addressed to the hero. Further allusions to Don Juan are found in Part I, Chapter 1, line 27; Chapter 2, Argument; Chapter 4, lines 425-27, 437. For the Russian reader these references also have associations with Pushkin's *The Stone Guest* (on which Akhmatova wrote an essay) and Blok's "The Steps of the Commendatore" (1910-12). Meyerhold's production of Molière's *Don Juan* (1910) was also much discussed in those days, along with Blok's play *The Puppet Theater* and A. Schnitzler's *Columbine's Scarf*.

Motto...House on the Fontanka. "God takes care of everything." For several years Akhmatova lived in one of the wings of the "House on the Fontanka" (or "building" as *dom* could be translated). It was the former St. Petersburg palace of the Sheremetevs, built on the Fontanka Canal in mid-18th century.

Some are no more... The line is originally from the Persian poet Saadi. Pushkin uses in it his *Fountain of Bakhchisarai,* but this is from the last stanza of *Eugene Onegin.* Pushkin bids farewell to his poem, and notes that many of his first readers are no longer around—including those hanged and exiled for their part in the Decembrist Uprising. Presumably, the political associations are important.

It came to me... In Russian "It" is the feminine "She" (the word *poema* is feminine). Akhmatova uses this personification of the poem all through her introductory letter.

December 27, 1940. Amanda Haight quotes Nadezhda Mandelstam as saying

Akhmatova changed this date to December 27 when it was learned that Osip Mandelstam probably died December 27, 1938. A few other connections of Akhmatova's poem to Mandelstam are mentioned in N. Mandelstam, *Hope Against Hope* (New York, 1970), pp. 70, 202.

Vs. K. Vsevolod Knyazev, variously referred to as a "dragoon Pierrot" and "Ivanushka of the ancient fairytale," was a cornet with whom Akhmatova was in love. Knyazev was in love with Olga Glebova-Sudeikina (see notes below), and committed suicide after being rejected by her—and seeing her with Alexander Blok. A book of his poetry (*Poems*, St. Petersburg, 1914) was published the year after his death. Akhmatova kept at least one picture of him until her death [it is described in E. Dobin, *Poeziia Anny Akhmatovoi* (L. 1968)].

Antinous. One of Penelope' suitors, killed by Odysseus.

O. A. G.-S. Olga Afanasievna Glebova-Sudeikina was a famous ballet dancer, singer, and actress (the Alexandrinsky Theater), wife of the eminent artist and designer Sergei Sudeikin. She was a good friend of Akhmatova, and at one time in the 1920s they lived in the same apartment [see Iurii Annenkov, *Dnevnik moikh vstrech* (New York, 1967), II, 125-27]. Akhmatova wrote two poems dedicated to Olga: "The Voice of Memory" (in *Beads*, 1913, translated below) and "O. A. G.-S" (*Anno Domini,* 1921). On several occasions they had the same love interest.

In this poem Olga is referred to as Psyche, Columbine, the "satyr-legged bacchante," "friend of poets," "the Dove," "Petersburg doll," and one of Akhmatova's doubles.

She seems to have been a free spirit, but a creature very much of the flesh as well. (The only detailed memoir is an effusive eulogy by A. Lurie in *Vozdushnye puti,* V, 1967, pp. 139-46. This deals also with her later years in emigration.) She was also a close friend of Kuzmin and his set, given to performing in public and private theatricals such as Kuzmin's "Venetian Madness." She was also one of the first actresses to work as a fashion model in Petersburg fashion houses. Balzac's *Splendeurs et misères des courtisans* was one of her favorite novels.

Confusion-Psyche. "*Putanitsa-Psikheia*" was the name of a character in Yury Belyaev's play (of the same title) in which Olga performed. Her husband painted her portrait in this role—and the painting is mentioned in the text of the poem. The *commedia dell'arte* was one of her passions.

Third and Last. The last dedication is to Sir Isaiah Berlin. He is also the "Guest from the Future" in Part I, Chapter 1.

Once on Christmas Eve... The opening line of Vasily Zhukovsky's ballad *Svetlana* (1808-1812). To learn of her lover's fate, Svetlana uses one Russian method of fortune-telling: she sits before a mirror, with a candle burning, at midnight. In the mirror she sees a messenger enter the door; he takes her to her fiancé, who turns out to be dead—at which point she wakes up and the whole vision is said to be only a dream. Her beloved returns the next day, and the moral is we should have faith in Providence. "Unhappiness here is a fickle dream / Happiness is—awakening." The first two lines of the last stanza of *Svetlana* ("Never know these frightful dreams...") were used by Pushkin as the epigraph to Chapter V of *Eugene Onegin;* this ties in with Akhmatova's second epigraph to Chapter 1 here.

Chaconne. A majestic solo piece, theme and thirty-one variations, for violin. It is in the last movement of Bach's *Partita, No. 2,* in D minor.

Maple in the window... The maple tree outside her window at the House on the Fontanka is called the "witness of everything on earth" in the Epilogue.

PART ONE

THE YEAR NINETEEN-THIRTEEN. The last year before World War I and Revolution, the year of Vsevolod Knyazev's suicide.

A Petersburg Tale. This genre indication was used by Pushkin for *The Bronze Horseman,* a romantic narrative poem in which the tragic fate of an individual hero is treated along with historical events—notably the founding of St. Petersburg by Peter the Great

CHAPTER ONE

First epigraph. From "After the wind and frost...", a poem written in January 1914 not long after Knyazev's suicide:

> After the wind and the frost
> I love to warm up by the fire.
> There I failed to keep track of my heart
> And it was stolen from me.
>
> The New Year's holiday moves on luxuriously,
> Moist are the stems of the New Year's roses,
> And in my heart no longer audible
> The quivering of dragonflies.
>
> Oh! It's not hard for me to guess the thief,
> I recognized him by his eyes.
> Only it's so terrible that soon, so soon,
> He will return his booty himself.

Second epigraph. From *Eugene Onegin,* V, X. In stanza ten,Tatyana, like Svetlana in Zhukovsky's poem, wants to conjure up her lover. She goes outside with a mirror, but her lover does not appear in the mirror—only the sad moon trembles in the dark glass. In stanza ten, she has a table set for two (like Svetlana):

> But suddenly Tatyana is afraid...
> And I —at the thought of Svetlana—
> I am afraid; so let it be....
> We're not to conjure with Tatyana.

After this, Tatyana has her famous premonitory dream of Onegin as commander of beasts and murderer of Lensky.

Third epigraph. The quote comes from Byron's *Don Juan,* I, CCXII, and involves a play on a quote from Horace *(calida juventa).* The poet would not have avoided certain literary battles when he was younger:

> I was most ready to return a blow
> And would not brook at all this sort of thing
> In my hot youth—when George the Third was king.

This stanza is part of the long digression on the subject of the poet's youth which ends Canto I. The freshness of youth is gone, beautiful emotions have passed:

> No more—no more—Oh! never more, my heart,
>   Canst thou be my soul world, my universe!
> Once all in all, but now a thing apart,
>   Thou canst not be my blessing or my curse... (CCXV)
>
> My days of love are over... (CCCXVI)
>
>   "Time is, Time was, Time's past:"—a chymic treasure
> Is glittering youth, which I have spent   betimes—
> My heart in passion, and my head on rhymes. (CCXVII)

This is followed by a section on "What is the end of fame?" which concludes poets have a dark future and that "All things that have been born were born to die" (CCXX). It ends with the famous lines sending off his book ("Go, little book, from this my solitude! / I cast thee on the waters") which Pushkin paraphrases in the last stanza of the first chapter of *Eugene Onegin.* The relevance of all these themes (youth, past love, the poet's fame, death) for Akhmatova's poem is clear. The constant return to and resonance of Pushkin is symptomatic.

Argument. The use of a synopsis or "argument" is not typical of the Russian nineteenth-century romantic poem, but rather, echoes Keats, Shelley, and Byron, all of whom are alluded to later. None of the prose introductions or remarks was in the poem originally, but over the years Akhmatova gradually added them.

White mirrored hall... The theme of mirrors is tied to the conjuring suggested in the epigraphs.

Guest from the Future. Sir Isaiah Berlin. Akhmatova returned to Leningrad in May 1944 and first spoke of him to Moscow friends in April 1946, so apparently they met in the winter of 1945.

Masquerade. Lermontov has a romantic drama in verse entitled *Masquerade* (written in 1835), which is perhaps among the works whose associations penetrate *A Poem without a Hero* (Petersburg, the theme of life as masquerade, tragic passion and death).

I have lit...the candles. Byron's *Manfred*, which Akhmatova alludes to later, begins in a Gothic Gallery at midnight: "The lamp must be replenished..." Whereupon seven Spirits come and visit Manfred.

And the wine burns... A quote from "A New Year's Ballad," the last poem in the collection *Anno Domini* (1921). See translation above. The missing person, the one with whom she meets 1941, is presumably Knyazev.

Dapertutto. This was the pseudonym used by Vsevolod Meyerhold in *The Love for Three Oranges,* a theatrical journal (1914-16) in which he propagandized his ideas, strongly influenced by the *commedia dell'arte.* Akhmatova was a contributor to the journal.

Jokanaan. John the Baptist. This probably alludes to the Richard Strauss opera which outraged morals in that generation—Salome's sensual love for John leading to his decapitation and her Dance of Seven Veils before the head—and her execution. Oscar Wilde's play *Salomé* was also part of the "popular" culture of the time.

Northern Glahn. A character in Knut Hamsun's novels *Pan* and *Victoria* (his complete works were published in Russian translation in St. Petersburg in 1910). Hamsun's characters have tortured love relations. In this period of his work love is a fatal battle between the sexes, a source of evil.

Dorian. Dorian Gray. In Wilde's novel, Gray has murdered the painter of his portrait—and in the end murders himself by slashing the picture with the same knife.

Satyr-legged bacchante. Literally, "the goat-legged female" *(kozlonogaia).* The heroine is called this, partly because she was a dancer. (There is some doubt whether these two lines even belong in the final text.)

Salome's dances. In Michel Fokine's ballet (Glazunov's music) which premiered in Petersburg in 1909, Ida Rubenstein as Salome.

Iron Mask. A mysterious prisoner of Louis XIV, famed from Dumas' romance of that title, and, for educated Russians, from a note by Pushkin on him.

Lace shawl. Akhmatova was famous for wearing shawls, though she objected that in the following poem Blok was inventing things, because of his infatuation with *Carmen* and things Spanish. Thus, in his "To Anna Akhmatova," written December 16, 1913:

> "Your beauty is terrifying," they'll say to you,
> You lazily throw
> The Spanish shawl across your shoulders,
> There's a red rose in your hair.
> "Your beauty is simple," they'll say to you...
> . . . .
> You fall sadly pensive
> And murmur to yourself:
> "I am not terrifying and I am not simple;
> I am not so terrifying as to simply
> kill; I am not so simple
> as not to know that life is terrifying."

Valley of Jehoshaphat. "The presumed place of the Last Judgment." Akhmatova's note.

As in the past the future ripens. See the epigraph to Part II.

Guest from the Future. These lines refer to Sir Isaiah Berlin.

"Without face or name." An allusion to Blok. Akhmatova reportedly said the "rival" who accompanies the heroine home was Blok. And it is known that Sudeikina did once go with Blok.

Cagliostros...Liziskas. Cagliostro is the first allusion to the poet M. Kuzmin.
  In one text Akhmatova's own note says Liziska was the pseudonym of the Empress Messalina in the Roman dives. Third wife of Emperor Claudius (who had her executed), Messalina was notorious for her promiscuity.

Like a striped milestone. The costume seems to resemble the striped markers used to mark distances on Russian roads.

Oak of Mamre. Presumably this means as old as Genesis and the story of Abraham on the plains of Mamre. However, there was also a famous oak on Chekhov's estate Melikhovo called the "oak of Mamre" (*Mamvriiskii dub*). A picture of him standing under it can be found in his *Complete Collected Works,* volume 15 (Moscow, 1949), p. 400.

Hammurabis, Lycurguses, Solons. King Hammurabi (c. 1955-1913 B.C.), Lycurgus (9th c. B. C.), and Solon (638?-559 B. C.?), one of the Wise Men of Greece, are all famous as lawgivers.

Ark of the Covenant. Apart from Noah's Ark, the Ark of the Covenant was the chest, symbolizing the presence of the Deity, carried by the Israelites during the Exodus, the most sacred object in the temple of Jerusalem.

Face to face with the black frame. Around the picture of Olga as Psyche.

"I am ready to die." Mandelstam's words to Akhmatova in 1937. See. N. Mandelstam, p. 202.

Guest from inside the mirrors. (Gost' zazerkal'nyi.) That is, like the beloved one can see in a mirror when conjuring, as Zhukovsky's Svetlana does and Pushkin's Tatyana tries to do in the moonlight (as here, line 168).

Or is someone really standing... An allusion to the scene where pale, wide-eyed Kirillov kills himself in Dostoevsky's *The Devils.*

St. Isaac's Square. Massive St. Isaac's Cathedral, which stands opposite Falconet's statue of Peter the Great, is one of the landmarks of Petersburg.

The Dog. "The Stray Dog" was a bohemian Petersburg cafe decorated partly by Olga Sudeikina's husband, habituated by most of the major writers and artists of the period (1912-15). Before the Revolution it was renamed the "Cellar of Comedians" (i.e. actors). Akhmatova was a regular visitor; Olga performed there, as did Kuzmin. Blok's diary shows his disapproval of his wife's being there: "Dead people performed there: Kuzmin and Olechka Glebova..." (August 21, 1917). Akhmatova's somewhat decadent poem *"Cabaret artistique"* (1913) was originally entitled "The Vagabond Dog."

Madame de Lamballe. Maximilian Voloshin's poem "Madame de Lamballe's Head" (1906) made this victim of the guillotine (during the French Revolution) famous in Russia. Note the echo with *Salome.* —The poem is translated in V. Markov (ed.), *Modern Russian Poetry* (Indianapolis, 1967), pp. 499-501.

Ivanushka of the ancient... Here, Knyazev. The allusion is to "Ivanushka the Fool" of many Russian fairytales. He usually has two intelligent brothers who get married and work hard while he lies on the stove and catches flies.

CHAPTER TWO

Epigraph. From Akhmatova's poem, dedicated to Olga, "The Voice of Memory":

> What do you see, staring wanly at the wall,
> At the hour of heaven's latest light?
>
> A seagull on the tablecloth of the water
> Or Florentine gardens?
>
> Or the vast park at Tsarskoe Selo,
> Where anxiety cut across your path?
>
> Or is he whom you see at your knees the one
> Who left your thralldom for white death?
>
> No, I see only the wall—and on it
> The reflections of heaven's dying fires.
>
> June 1913

Columbine. This stock character from the *commedia dell'arte* appears in Blok's play *The Puppet Theater.* Pierrot loves her, but she is portrayed possibly as death (feminine in Russian), and in the end Pierrot (played by Meyerhold) says she is cardboard (as the artificiality of all the characters is intentionally stressed). Olga's husband did the decorations for the first production. —In early drafts Columbine-Olga is called "Traviata."

Donna Anna. Blok's poem "The Steps of the Commendatore" (1910-12), like Pushkin's *The Stone Guest,* is on the Don Juan theme. As Donna Anna sleeps, her features reflected in mirrors, the stone commendatore enters the house at dawn (recall the epigraph to *A Poem without a Hero*):

> It's eerie and cold at the hour of dawn,
> At the hour of dawn—the night is murky,
> Maid of Light! Where are you, Donna Anna?
> Anna! Anna! Silence.

Donna Anna will rise at the mortal hour of Don Juan.

Meyerhold's...slave boys. His 1910 production of Molière's *Don Juan* opened with slave boys *(arapy)* running onto stage, lighting candles, ringing bells dressing the actors, etc. [Yu. Elagin, *Temnyi genii* (New York, 1955), p. 164.] They were also used in his production of Lermontov's *Masquerade.*

Steps down from the portrait. In the production of Belyaev's *Psyche,* Olga did enter the stage from the portrait of her as Psyche.

"Peter" City. Piter was the colloquial name for St. Petersburg, which was built on a swamp at the expense of the common people's hides and lives.

Prima. Anna Pavlova, dying to Saint-Saens *The Swan* (1907). Like the allusions to Chaliapin, Stravinsky's *Petrushka,* old Petersburg, and some of the material on Blok, this was an interpolation in the basic text. According to Zhirmunsky, Akhmatova tended not to cut, but to add lines and make minor revisions in existing ones.

And again that familiar voice. The voice of Fyodor Ivanovich Chaliapin.

The corridor of the Petrovsky Collegia. A corridor some 1500 feet long in the present building of Leningrad University—originally begun by Peter the Great for his twelve ministries (i.e. "colleges").

Petrushka's mask. Stravinsky's ballet *Petrushka* is also based on the Pierrot-Columbine-Harlequin plot.

Black and yellow. The Imperial standard was a black eagle on a saffron-yellow field.

Summer Gardens. Famous Petersburg gardens along the Neva, the city's central park and meeting place for lovers.

Hell of Tsushima. Tsushima was one of the bloodiest battles of the Russo-Japanese War. The Russian fleet was destroyed.

Demon...Tamara. Alludes to the dusky-faced Demon in Lermontov's romantic poem *Demon.* He attempts to find salvation from total negation in pure love for a Circassian maiden named Tamara. She is destroyed by the Demon's kiss, but her soul is taken to Heaven by an angel. It was a popular opera, and

234

Vrubel's celebrated paintings on the theme were relatively new in 1913.
Here the Demon is Blok.

Who sent the black rose. Alludes to Blok's short poem "In the Restaurant"
("V restorane"), written in 1910. Stanza two has the lines: "I sent you a
black rose in a glass / Of Ay as gold as the heavens."
 This allusion was Akhmatova's way of making it clear that Blok is one
of the heroes in *A Poem without a Hero.* In Blok's lyric the girl to whom he
sends the rose rejects him haughtily, but as she walks out, he sees her face in
a mirror and her face tells him to pursue her. It is important that in his poem
he casts doubt on the reality of the events, suggesting that the whole thing
may be a dream.

Commendatore. This again alludes to the Don Juan theme (Molière, Mozart,
Pushkin, Blok), the stone ghost of the commendatore returning to Donna
Anna's house to do away with Juan.

You came down here... Again, Confusion-Psyche (played by Olga) entering
the play from the frame of her portrait.

Sacred cedar. A tree in the garden of the "House of Creation" (run by the
Union of Soviet Writers)in Komarov.

Malta bell-tower. It was built in 1798-1800 by order of Pavel I in the former
palace of the Vorontsovs in Petersburg.

Songbirds in cages. Olga Sudeikina's passion for keeping birds is described in
Lurie's memoirs.

Man of Pskov. Akhmatova uses the word *skobar',* noting that it is "an
insulting nickname for Pskovians."

Botticelli's "Spring." In Botticelli's painting, queenly, long-limbed Primavera
is strewing handfuls of roses gathered from the folds of her dress. Her loose
hair, her neck and waist are bound in flowers. The painting also has sexual
motifs—Venus in the center, Cupid with a flaming arrow, and Zephyr grabbing Flora, who is clad in a transparent robe.

Dragoon Pierrot. Knyazev again. In Italian comedy and pantomime Pierrot is
usually a tall, thin man, his face and hair covered with white powder, clad in
a white gown. Gradually Pierrot has become more romantic, an artist lover of
fiery emotion who hides his real passions behind a comic mask. —In Blok's
The Puppet Theater, Pierrot(like the "hero" here) sees another man (Harlequin) kiss his Columbine and take her home—but she turns out to be
cardboard.

And how renowned his enemy. Alexander Blok.

Don't be afraid...crosses. As crosses on doors saved Catholics from slaughter on St. Bartholomew's Day, 1572.

CHAPTER THREE

First epigraph. With the first word changed to "and," from Akhmatova's *"Verses* on Petersburg" (1913). The Arch is the one which joins the Senate and Synod buildings. Gallery Street begins there. It was a favorite spot for rendezvous (see Mandelstam's "The Egyptian Stamp").

Second epigraph. The first two lines of a grim lyric by Mandelstam, written on November 25, 1920. The Revolution has come, and the poet stands in the black velvet of the Soviet night, the velvet of universal emptiness. (For a translation see *Russian Literature Triquarterly,* No. 1 (1971), p. 6.

Third epigraph. That is, 1913 was the last year before the War and the Revolution. The line is apparently taken from an unpublished poem by Mikhail Lozinsky (1886-1953). He is best known now as a translator, but he was an Acmeist, one of the regular members of the Guild of Poets. Akhmatova's memoirs of him can be found in her "Speech on Lozinsky" [Akhmatova, II, 188-91] and her memoirs of Mandelstam [Akhmatova, II, 166-88]. A sympathetic portrait of him as friend of Akhmatova and Mandelstam can be found in Nadezhda Mandelstam's *Hope Against Hope.*

Last Reminiscences in Tsarskoe Selo. This is the title of two famous poems by Pushkin. The later (December 14, 1829) and less chauvinistic is probably the one Akhmatova has in mind. The poet recalls his youth and quick passions, comparing himself to the prodigal son. Russia on the eve of war with Napoleon is also recalled (thus the parallel with Chapter III—Russia on the eve of war again). Tsarskoe Selo is just outside Petersburg.

Tsaritsa Avdotya. Evdokiya Lopukhina, the first wife of Peter the Great (who founded the city of Petersburg); he abandoned her in Moscow and married again.

Dostoevskian. "Dostoevskii" is used as an adjective modifying "city," as is *"besnovatyi"* (meaning "devilish" and containing the word *"bes"* from Dostoevsky's novel *Besy (The Devils, The Possessed).*

Real Twentieth Century. From 1914 on.

But now—homeward... The section in italics is addressed to N. V. Nedobrovo, author of a study of Akhmatova which she praised very highly (Akhmatova, II, 328). In *The Noise of Time* Mandelstam describes him as "a mordantly polite Petersburger, loquacious frequenter of the salons of late Symbolism, impenetrable as a young clerk guarding a state secret." [See Clarence Brown (ed.), *The Prose of Osip Mandelstam* (Princeton, 1965), pp. 129-30.] He was also Akhmatova's first love.

Cameron Gallery. This structure is at Tsarskoe Selo.

CHAPTER FOUR

Where all nine... Nine muses. (Akhmatova's note.)

Vs. K. Vsevolod Knyazev.

Mars field. A large open area between the Summer Gardens, the Mikhailovsky Gardens, and the Neva, used for military parades.

Adamini. Akhmatova lived in this building from 1924-1926.

Our Savior on the Blood. A church built on the spot where Tsar Alexander II was assassinated in 1881. It is surrounded on three sides by the Mikhailovsky Gardens.

"Journey from Damascus." As noted by Filippov and Struve: "The Journey from Damascus" was the title of one of the miniature miracle plays put on at "The Stray Dog." Saul meets Christ on the way back from Damascus, and becomes the apostle Paul. Thus the "return" can be either the re-transformation of Paul into Saul, or Olga's (the "mask's") return home from the Vagabond Dog.

You will be my widow. This appears to be a play on the words of the commendatore to his widow Donna Anna.

PART TWO

TAILS. This is used in the sense "heads and tails" on a coin.

First epigraph. Amanda Haight says that these words of Mary, Queen of Scots, were marked in Akhmatova's manuscript as: "T. S. Eliot." They recall, "Time future is contained in Time past" ("Burnt Norton") and "In my beginning is my end" ("East Coker").

Second epigraph. Klyuev. In Akhmatova's memoirs of Mandelstam she writes: "Osip recited from memory some excerpts from N. Klyuev's poem 'The Blasphemers of Art'—which was the reason for the doom of poor Nikolai Alekseevich. At Varvara Klychkova's I personally saw Klyuev's petition (for mercy, from the camps): 'Condemned for my poem *The Blasphemers of Art* and some insane lines in my rough drafts.' I took two lines from it for my epigraph to my *Tails.*"

I replied: "There were three..." The prototype of the main one is Olga, the demon Blok, the "third" Knyazev.

Soft embalmer. In English in Akhmatova's text. She notes that this is from Keats' sonnet "To Sleep": "O soft embalmer of the still midnight!"

Blue Bird. Maeterlinck's "symbolic" play *L'Oiseau bleu* (1909).

Elsinore. Alludes to *Hamlet*, III, 1 ("To sleep! Perchance to dream...").

Cagliostro. Satanic Cagliostro is Mikhail Kuzmin (1875-1936), poet and prose writer, organizer of "Stray Dog" productions, apologist for homosexuality, theoretician of Acmeism, compiler and entitler of Mandelstam's famous book *Tristia*, author of *The Marvelous Life of Joseph Balsamo, Count Cagliostro* (1919).

The summary of a talk by R. Timenchik at Tartu University suggests that *A Poem without a Hero* may be a polemic with Kuzmin's cycle of poems *Trout Breaks the Ice (Forel' razbivaet led)*. Knyazev seems to be the model for Kuzmin's hero, and a few motifs from his poems are echoed in Akhmatova. [*Materialy XXII nauchnoi studencheskoi konferentsii* (Tartu, 1967), pp. 121-23.] See also Akhmatova, II, 604-605.

However, Cagliostro seems not to have been identified as Kuzmin until now. Her description of Cagliostro-Kuzmin suggests he played some role in Knyazev's suicide, or at least that his attitude toward the suicide is one which Akhmatova finds intolerable. Some further information about the prototypes perhaps sheds some light on this matter. In Kuzmin's book *Clay Pigeons (Glinianye golubki,* Berlin, 1923) there are several poems which show one aspect of the decadence of the doomed generation. Three of them are homosexual expressions of love from the poet to another young man—and two of these are dedicated to "V. K." ["The hands I kissed" *("Tselovannye mnoi ruki");* "I'd like to set off around the world" *("Pustit'sia by po belu svetu")*]. Both of these poems were written in 1912, the year before Knyazev's suicide. The first one also has a two-line epigraph taken from the poetry of "V. K." The third poem ("In sad and pale make-up"—*"V grustnom i blednom grime")* is addressed to a "blond Pierrot" whom the poet wishes to kiss endlessly (this poem is dated 1912-13).

My "Seventh." Akhmatova's "seventh book" of poetry included the cycles "In 1940" and "The Secrets of Craft" which were evacuated from Leningrad with her. The book did not appear. (B. Filippov notes that there are seven masked guests in Chapter 1, and Shostakovich's *Seventh Symphony* is alluded to in some versions of the poem. I doubt any of this leads to numerological conclusions. —Akhmatova was evacuated from Leningrad on the same plane as Shostakovich.)

Stanzas X-XII. Akhmatova's note to the missing stanzas reads: "The omitted stanzas are an imitation of Pushkin." See *Eugene Onegin.* "I also humbly admit that there are two omitted stanzas in *Don Juan*" (wrote Pushkin). The few lines which are known to have been in stanzas X-XII (X, 4-6) suggest that Akhmatova, like Pushkin in some cases, omitted the stanzas because of political considerations.

Luga...satin masks. Luga is a town near Petersburg. Akhmatova's note explains that the satin masks come from Venice (like Petersburg a city of canals).

The Plantain...White Flock. Two of Akhmatova's early books of verse.

Triple bottom. The box with the triple bottom has been explained in various ways. Probably the "triplets" which occur in the poem should be considered in whatever interpretation one makes: the triangle of characters based on the Knyazev-Olga-Blok affair; the reflection of Olga as three different characters and the three portraits; the triplicity of Time—past (the year 1913), present (the siege), future (the ending, implicitly looking ahead).

Hundred-year-old enchantress. In one of the variants of the prose "argument" to Part II: "The author speaks of her poem *1913* and many other things, in particular the romantic poem of the beginning of the nineteenth century (the 'century-old charmer'). The author mistakenly supposed that the spirit of this poem came to life in her Petersburg tale." Note that most of the examples given here (especially stanza XXII) are English romantic poems.

I have nothing to do with it. "It" in Russian is the feminine "she" and refers to the "enchantress," the romantic poem which speaks to Akhmatova in XXIII and XXIV.

Bryulovian shoulder. The Russian artist Karl Bryulov (1799-1852). His women's shoulders are round, plump, sloping, and sensual. (In Kuzmin's *Trout Breaks the Ice* he also refers to "Bryulovian beauties.")

Manfred. In Byron's dramatic poem *Manfred* (1817) the hero (who sells himself to the Prince of Darkness) lives in solitude in the Alps. He views the pines from a cliff at the beginning of Scene II.

Shore...Shelley. A reference to Shelley's death—by drowning in the Bay of Lerici.

Skylark. Akhmatova's own note quotes the first three lines of Shelley's "To a Skylark."

George. Byron was present as Shelley's body was burned on the beach.

Gazoul. Alludes to Merimée's hoax, the *Théâtre de Clara Gazoul* (1825).

Your ambiguous fame. That is, Akhmatova's fame had been unacknowledged and her poetry (with few exceptions) unpublished in the Soviet Union between the early twenties and 1941.

PART THREE

First epigraph. A famous line from the "Introduction" to Pushkin's *The Bronze Horseman.* The sonorous ode to the city of Peter's creation which opens the poem is tempered by the tragic story of an individual which follows.

Second epigraph. From Innokenty Annensky's (1859-1909) "Petersburg," a seven-quatrain poem published in *Apollo* in 1910. Annensky was head of the Tsarskoe Selo Lycée and Gumilev's teacher. "Petersburg" condemns the city rather than praising it. The poet says Petersburg gave us only "stones" and the "deserts of mute squares / Where men were executed before dawn." Tsar Peter was unable to trample the snake of evil (which is represented on the Falconet statue called "The Bronze Horseman"). All one is left with is "consciousness of a cursed mistake" and "the poison of fruitless desires." It is translated in Markov, pp. 125-27.

Smolny. The Smolny Monastery and Institute, away from the city center.

Sheremetev Gardens. Outside the Sheremetev Palace, otherwise known as the House on the Fontanka.

And O, what a star. "Mars in the summer of 1941." (Akhmatova's note.)

You are not the first... These lines (19-30) are addressed to Akhmatova's last husband, Vladimir Georgievich Garshin—a pathologist, nephew of the well-known nineteenth-century short story writer.

But behind the barbed wire... Akhmatova's son by Gumilev, Lev Nikolaevich, was arrested and imprisoned in 1935 and 1938. The allusions to barbed wire mean the Siberian prison camps. Akhmatova spent ten years trying to get her son freed; her cycle of poems *Requiem* deals with this.

Noseless Slut. Death.

Hermitage halls. The former Winter Palace, now the Hermitage Museum of Art.

You who remained. Garshin remained in Leningrad.

In the belly of a flying fish. The airplane in which Akhmatova was evacuated.

Kama. A large navigable river which flows south through the middle Urals and empties into the Volga.

POEMS BY ANNA AKHMATOVA

Delusion II

Sultry breezes wander, parching,
By the sun one's arms are seared,
Over me a bluely arching
Cupola of glass is reared.

Immortelles are drily fragrant
In my half unbraided hair.
Of the rugged fir-stump, vagrant
Ants have made a thoroughfare.

There the pond is silvered slowly,
Living now is freshly light...
Whom today will slumber show me
In my hammock netting bright?

1910, Kiev   *Translated by Walter Arndt*

In Tsarskoe Selo III

Down the tree-rows a swarthy youngster
Roamed the banks of the lake and pined,
And a century now amongst us
Have his whispering steps been enshrined.

The pines have spikily nested
In needlework each low tree...
Here his three-cornered hat once rested,
And a dog-eared tome of Parny.

Tsarsk. S. 1911   *Translated by Walter Arndt*

My dreams could frequent you more rarely,
As much as we meet in the day;
But only in night's dim aerie
Are you wistful, or tender, or gay.
More sweetly than elf-song befuddle
Your lips with their flattery dear...
No getting my first name muddled,
Or heaving the sighs you do here.

1914   *Translated by Walter Arndt*

The incense of world and country
It wasn't what I sought.
To my lovers, all and sundry,
The best of luck I brought.
One is still around and responds
Like mad to his lady fair,
The other has turned to bronze
In a snowed-up public square.

1914   *Translated by Walter Arndt*

The immortelles are dry and pink. The clouds
Upon the laundered sky are roughly molded,
The leaves still blossomless and half unfolded
Upon the single oaktree hereabouts.

Midnight, and sunset rays still here to see.
How snug it is, my tightly jointed carvel!
About all kind of loveliness and marvel
The birds of the Almighty speak to me.

I'm happy here. But dearest to my heart
I hold the sloping forest trail, the brittle
Untidy bridge that seems to sag a little,
And that from which I'm only days apart.

1916   *Translated by Walter Arndt*

I know that you are my reward
For years of suffering and dearth,
For never having grubbed a hoard
Of the amenities of earth,
For my unwillingness to call
"I love you" to each love-possessed,
For my forgiving all to all,
You're come to be my Angel blest.

1916   *Translated by Walter Arndt*

All things were pledge to me of him:
The rim of heaven, obscurely golden,
At Christmas time a friendly dream,
The wind of Easter, bell-beholden.

The waterfalls of garden size,
The purple saplings of the thicket,
The pair of mighty dragonflies
Perched on a rusty iron wicket.

I never merely nourished hope
That he would come and be my own,
As I would walk the mountain slope
Along the flaming path of stone.

1916   *Translated by Walter Arndt*

In Memoriam, July 19, 1914

We grew a hundred years in age, and all
Within a single hour, it seemed:
Brief summer merged already into fall,
The open flanks of ploughed-up acres steamed.

And of a sudden bloomed the quiet road,
A sobbing went, as with a silvery crack.
I covered up my face, imploring God
To strike me dead before the first attack.

Swept out, as trappings out of place and flighty,
Were shades of song and passion—and instead
The mind was reordained by the Almighty
For thunderous tidings as an archive dread.

1916   *Translated by Walter Arndt*

Blessing of the Lord, the morning's beam
Glided down my lover's face; the sleeper
Looked a little paler in his dream,
But his slumber presently grew deeper.

Warmly wandering, that ray of heaven
Must have felt to him like lover's nips;
Just so with my mouth I used to travel
Down his tawny shoulders and dear lips.

Now, more disembodied than a dream,
In my grief no wandering can allay,
Only as a song I fly to see him,
And caress him as a morning ray.

1916   *Translated by Walter Arndt*

The river dawdles, valley waters gathering;
Half up the slope a many-windowed hall.
We might be living in the reign of Catherine,
We hold devotions and await the fall.
A gulf of two days' absence bridged, a caller
Comes riding up through where the barley burns:
He kisses Granny's hand in the front parlor,
And me in private where the staircase turns.

Summer, 1917   *Translated by Walter Arndt*

Beyond the lake the waning moon has slowed,
And stands there like a window open wide
Into a hushed and brightly lit abode
Where something dreadful has occurred inside.

The master has been carried home for dead,
The mistress has absconded with a lover,
Or a small girl is lost, and they discover
A little slipper by the river-bed...

From earth you cannot tell. But some appalling
Misfortune sensing, we had fallen quiet.
Placatingly the eagle owls were calling,
And in the park a sultry wind ran riot.

1922   *Translated by Walter Arndt*

To fall sick now, delirium blazing, what fun—
To be meeting them all again,
In the park by the sea, full of wind and sun,
Taking this and the other broad lane.

Then the very departed consent to throng,
And the exiles, my no-man's land.
Won't you lead up the little one by the hand,
I have missed him so much, so long?

I will eat blue grapes from my lover's hands,
I will drink with him icy wine,
And look on as the hoar-maned waterfalls' strands
Into brimming shingle-beds twine.

1922 (?)   *Translated by Walter Arndt*

Here's the shore, then, of the northern ocean,
Here's the bar our griefs and glories meet—
Is it bliss or sorrow, that emotion
That has flung you weeping to my feet?

I don't fancy any more condemned men,
Convicts, hostages, or slaves—instead
Only with my lover, one unbending,
Will I share both roof and daily bread.

1922   *Translated by Walter Arndt*

It is fine here: all rustle and creak,
With each morning the frost only grows,
Flaming white hangs a bush, frozen sleek,
In a dazzle of rose upon rose.
Down this holiday glory of snow
Runs a ski-track, as if it would try
To recall that dim ages ago
We went walking this way, you and I.

1922   *Translated by Walter Arndt*

In a White Night

I left the door unfastened,
I did not strike a light,
I never, though exhausted,
Lay down, you know, that night.

To watch the pine-fronds blurring
The sunset's glimmering spoors,
Gasp at some voice's burring
In passing just like yours,

And know this is the curtain,
And life, the scourge and rack!
Oh, I had known for certain
That you were coming back.

Ts. Selo, 1911   *Translated by Walter Arndt*

In the Wood

Diamonds four—two pairs of eyes blending,
The owl has two, and two have I,
Dreadful, dread is the story's ending
How my bridegroom came to die.

The grass where I lie is dense and lovely,
My words make a disconnected din,
How gravely the owl peers from above me,
Intently takes it all in.

By spruces we are hemmed in and girded,
Above us the sky, an inky square,
You know, you know it, that he was murdered,
My eldest brother, he slew him there.

It was not done in single combat,
Not in a war, in the battle's tide,
But as in the wood on a lonesome log-track
Love sent him striding to my side.

1911   *Translated by Walter Arndt*

There's the flag, on the customshouse flashing,
Over town hangs a yellowish stain,
More alertly my heart now is thrashing,
And to draw each breath is a strain.

Be again a young seaside slattern,
Slip sandals over bare toes,
Braid my hair in a coronet pattern,
And sing as my free voice chose!

And be seeing, bronze-peaked, from the porch
All the Chersonese temple-ridge roll,
And not know fame and fortune scorch
So pitilessly the soul.

1913   *Translated by Walter Arndt*

The evenings feverish, the mornings drooping,
The taste of lips chapped raw, aroma gory.
So this is how it feels, the final stooping,
So this is it, the anteroom of glory.
All day I look through this tight window-socket:
White shines—a little warmer—the enclosure,
Slick goosefoot has the path all sprouted over,
It would be such a joy for me to walk it.
The sand should crackle, and the paws of spruce
Should whip and swoosh, the sere, the full of juice,
And I should see the moon's amorphous shell
Once more reflected in the blue canal.

December 1913   *Translated by Walter Arndt*

Hark, kind wanderer, though distant,
What I speak to you about,
In the sky new candles glisten,
Sky that sees the sunset out.

Quick, dear wanderer, I am guiding
Your bright gazes hither—see
Here a crafty dragon biding
Who has long been lord of me.

And within the dragon's cavern
Neither law nor mercy govern,
And a lash hangs on a ring
For the songs I must not sing.

Winged dragon racks the body,
Humbleness he has me study,
So, my brazen laugh suppressed,
I'll be better than the rest.

Wanderer mine, to our far city
Carry these my words and give
What should stab the one with pity
But for whom I would not live.

June 1921   *Translated by Walter Arndt*

For V. K. Shileiko

Had you forgotten, free and firm one,
To those caressing knees a prey,
That the primeval sin will earn one
Annihilation and decay?

Why give her for a bedside story
The code to wonderworking days—
Her, who will dissipate your glory
With her expropriating ways?

For shame—the fruitful sadness never
Through earthly woman seek to wake.
Such have been shut in cloisters ever
Or burnt to cinders at the stake.

1922   *Translated by Walter Arndt*

Love

Now by the heart, furled still
Like a snakelet, its magic brewing,
Now on the white of the sill
Whole days as a dovelet cooing,

Now a glint in the hoarfrost's glaring,
Now an edge to the stock's slow scent,
But surely and secretly bearing
Away from delight and content.

So sweetly it melts its distresses
In the violin's suppliant moan,
And it frightens one when one guesses
Its lurk in the smile yet unknown.

Translated by Walter Arndt

—"I have come to take your place, sister,
At the wooded, at the tall fire.

Your hair has turned gray. A tear
Has dimmed, misted your eyes.

You no longer understand what the birds sing,
You notice neither the stars nor the glow of distant
lightning.

And the tambourine beat has stopped long ago,
Though I know you are afraid of quiet.

I have come to take your place, sister,
At the wooded, at the tall fire..."

—"You have come to bury me.
Then where is your pick, where is your spade?
You have only a flute in your hands.
I will not blame you,
For is it a pity that long ago, at some time,
Forever my voice fell silent.

Wear my clothes,
Forget my alarm,
Let the wind play with your curls.
You smell like lilacs,
Though you have come by a difficult road
To stand here, dawn-lit."

And one went away, yielding,
Yielding her place to the other,
And wandered unsure, as if blind,
By an alien, narrow path.

And it always seemed that the flame
Was near...the hand holds the tamborine...
And she is like a white standard,
And she is like a lighthouse beam.

1912   *Translated by*
                Barbara Heldt Monter

The Guest

All as before: against the dining-room windows
Beats the scattered windswept snow,
And I have not changed either,
But a man came to me.

I asked: "What do you want?"
He replied: "To be with you in Hell."
I laughed: "Oh, you'll foredoom
Us both to disaster."

But lifting his dry hand
He lightly touched the flowers:
"Tell me how men kiss you,
Tell me how you kiss men."

And his lusterless eyes
Did not move from my ring.
Not a single muscle quivered
On his radiantly evil face.

Oh, I know: his delight
Is the tense and passionate knowledge
That he needs nothing,
That I can refuse him nothing.

January 1, 1914   *Translated by*
                      Carl R. Proffer

A New Year's Ballad

And the moon, bored in its cloudy darkness,
Cast a wan glance at the room.
There stand six glasses on the table
And only one glass is empty.

It's my husband, and I, and my friends
Meeting the New Year.
Why do my fingers seem to be bloody,
And the wine burn like poison?

The host, lifting a full glass,
Was grave and motionless:
"I drink to the land of our native plains
In which we all lie!"

And a friend, glancing at my face,
And recalling God knows what,
Exclaimed: "And I drink to her songs
In which we all live!"

But the third, who knew nothing
When he left this world,
Uttered in answer to my
Thoughts: "We should drink to the one
Who is not yet with us."

Translated by
Carl R. Proffer

Memory

Only snakes cast off the skins they're wearing,
So that souls may grow as skin is shed.
But, alas, there can be no comparing
Us and snakes. We change our souls instead.

Memory, with your huge hand you lead me
Like a bridled horse my whole life through
And describe those you have seen precede me
In this body—souls known just to you.

Thin and unattractive was the very
First. A child of magic, he preferred
Gloomy woods and fallen leaves strewn there; he
Often stopped the raindrops with a word.

'Twas a tree and red-haired dog he took for
Friends. O, Memory, as years go by,
You will never find the sign you look for,
Nor convince the world that this was I.

And the second loved the south wind's sighing,
In each sound he heard a lyre play.
And the world was like a carpet lying
Under foot. Life was his friend, he'd say.

Toward this one I can no fondness show; it
Seemed he saw himself as godlike or
As a tsar. He hung the sign of poet
In my silent house above the door.

Him I love who valued freedom dearly,
Rifleman and swimmer in the sea.
Ah, to him the waters sang so clearly,
As the clouds themselves watched jealously.

253

Straight into the sky arose his lofty
Tent, and strong mules frolicked on their own,
Here he drank, like wine, the sweet air wafting
Gently o'er a land to him unknown.

Memory, your powers now have faded;
As the years have passed, you've grown less bright.
Which of these two souls was it who traded
Your gay freedom for a holy fight?

With both thirst and hunger well acquainted,
He knew endless paths, nights without rest,
But the holy bullet of the sainted
George twice entered his yet untouched breast.

I, a sternly structured temple, tower,
Breaking through the mist, immovable.
I was jealous of the Father's power,
Glory of which heav'n and earth are full.

In my heart a fire will burn, not ending
Till the day when I can clearly see
On my native plains the walls ascending
Of the New Jerusalem to be.

And it's then a strange wind will start blowing—
And the sky be filled with awesome light,
Suddenly the Milky Way is glowing,
Lit by dazzling planets in the night.

Then a traveler will appear; I'll find him
Standing there before me, face concealed,
Eagle overhead, lion behind him,
And to me will all things be revealed.

I'll cry out . . . that my soul may not perish,
On whom can I count to give me aid?
Only snakes cast off the skins they're wearing,
But it's in our souls that change is made.

1921   *Translated by Jamie Fuller*

254

The Sixth Sense

Beautiful is wine in love with us,
And good bread put into the oven for us,
And the woman who, after tortuous resistance,
Gives herself for our pleasure.

But what are we to do with the rosy sunset
Over skies which grow cold,
Where there is silence and unearthly peace,
What are we to do with immortal verses?

Not eat them, nor drink them, nor kiss them.
Inexorably the moment rushes,
And we wring our hands, but again
We're condemned to keep on, keep on moving past.

As a young boy who forgets his games
Sometimes spies on bathing girls,
And ignorant in every way of love,
Is still tormented by mysterious desire,

As once upon a time 'mid tangled ferns
A slimy creature, of his impotence aware,
Roared when sensing on his shoulders
Wings which had not yet appeared,

So age after age—will it be soon, O Lord?—
Beneath the scalpel of nature and art,
Our spirit screams, our flesh depletes itself,
Giving birth to an organ for the sixth sense.

1921   *Translated by*
                              Carl R. Proffer

A Baby Elephant

Right now my love for you is a baby elephant
Born in Berlin or in Paris,
And treading with its cushioned feet
Around the zoo director's house.

Do not offer it French pastries,
Do not offer it cabbage heads,
It can eat only sections of tangerine,
Or lumps of sugar and pieces of candy.

Don't cry, my sweet, because it will be put
Into a narrow cage, become a joke for mobs,
When salesmen blow cigar smoke into its trunk
To the cackles of their girl-friends.

Don't imagine, my dear, that the day will come
When, infuriated, it will snap its chains
And rush along the streets,
Crushing howling people like a bus.

No, may you dream of it at dawn,
Clad in bronze and brocade and ostrich feathers,
Like that Magnificent beast which once
Bore Hannibal to trembling Rome.

Translated by
Carl R. Proffer

256

The Streetcar Gone Astray

I was walking along an unfamiliar street,
And suddenly heard a cawing of crows,
And resonant lutes, and distant rumbling,
—Before me a streetcar flew.

How I leapt to its platform
Was a riddle to me,
Even in the light of day
It left a fiery trail in the air.

Rushing ahead like a dark-winged storm,
It went astray in the abyss of Time...
"Stop, conductor,
Stop the car right now!"

Too late. We had already passed the wall,
We leapt through the grove of palms,
Across the Neva, the Nile, the Seine,
We boomed across three bridges.

And flashing past the window's frame,
Casting a searching glance after us was
An old man—of course, the same one
Who died in Beirut a year ago.

Where am I? So languid and anxious,
My heart hammers in answer:
"Do you see the station where one
Can buy a ticket to the India of the Spirit?"

A sign... letters poured from blood
Announce—"Vegetables." I know this is where,
Instead of cabbages, instead of rutabagas,
Corpses' heads are being sold.

Clad in red shirt, with a face like an udder,
The executioner cleaves my head too,
It was lying here with the others,
On the very bottom in a slippery box.

And in an alley—a board fence,
A three-windowed house with gray grass.
"Stop, conductor,
Stop the car right now!"

Mashenka, here you lived, and here you sang,
You wove a rug for me, your love,
Where are your voice and body now,
Can it be that you are dead!

How you sobbed in your chamber,
But I with powdered queue
Was going to present myself to the Empress,
And never again did we meet.

Now I understood: our freedom
Is only light which strikes from there,
Humans and shades are standing at the gate
To the zoological garden of the planets.

And suddenly a sweet, familiar wind
And across the bridge, flying toward me—
The iron-gloved hand of the Horseman
And the two hooves of his steed.

That faithful bulwark of Orthodoxy,
St. Isaac's is chisled into the sky,
There I'll have some prayers for Mashenka's
Health, and a requiem mass for myself.

And still my heart is dark forever,
And it's hard to breathe, and pain to live...
Mashenka, I never believed
It possible to love and grieve like this.

1921   *Translated by*
                        Carl R. Proffer

PROSE

Fyodor Sologub

THE POISON GARDEN

Translated by
Samuel Cioran

"Oh handsome Youth, why are you so deeply sunk in thought?" asked the Old Woman who was renting a room to him.

One evening she quietly entered his gloomy room, and her soft slippers rustling almost inaudibly along the uneven floor by the red painted bureau, she came up to the Youth and stood by his side. He shuddered in surprise—he had been standing by the only window of his cramped quarters in the uppermost lodgings of an old house for half an hour, staring fixedly at the beautiful Garden before him where a great multitude of plants were blooming with a tender, sweet and strange fragrance.

Answering the Old Woman the Youth said, "No, Old Woman, I am not thinking about anything. I am just standing, gazing and waiting."

The Old Woman shook her gray head reproachfully and the knots on her dark kerchief bounced up and down like two attentive ears pointing sharply inward. Her wrinkled face, more yellow and withered than those of the other old women living on that street on the outskirts of the Old City, now expressed concern and anxiety. The Old Woman said softly and sadly, "I feel sorry for you, dear Youth."

Her voice, although already hoarse from age, rang so sadly and with such genuine compassion, and her eyes, already colorless from age, peered so mournfully that for one brief moment it suddenly seemed to the Youth in the dusk of his room that all these external signs of age were only a successfully assumed mask concealing a young and beautiful Woman who had just felt that heart-piercing grief of a mother who has wept for her dying son. But this strange moment passed and the Youth smiled at his fantasy.

He asked her, "Why do you feel sorry for me, Old Woman?"

The Old Woman stood beside him and looked out the window at the Garden, so beautiful, flowering and everywhere illuminated by the rays of the setting sun, and said, "I feel sorry for you, dear Youth, because I know where you are gazing and what you are waiting for. I feel sorry for you and your mother."

Perhaps because of these words, or perhaps because of something else, there was a change in the Youth's mood. The Garden, flowering behind the high fence below his window, and exuding a wonderful fragrance, suddenly seemed somehow strange to him; and an ominous sensation, a sudden fear, gripped his heart with a violent palpitation, like heady and languid fragrances rising from brilliant flowers.

"What is happening?" he wondered in confusion.

He did not want to give in to this gloomy enchantment of evening melancholy—he made a concerted effort, smiled cheerfully and with a swift movement of a powerful hand tossed back a lock of black hair from his forehead and asked, "What then, Old Woman, is so terrible and wrong with what I am gazing at or waiting for?"

And at this moment he was cheerful and unafraid, beautiful, and his dark eyes flashed and his rosy cheeks reddened and his crimson and striking lips seemed as if they had just been kissed, and from behind them flashed strong white teeth, exuberant, sinister.

The Old Woman asked, "Here you are, dear Youth, you are looking at the Garden and do not know that it is an evil Garden. Here you are waiting for the Beautiful Woman and do not know that her beauty is destructive. You have been living in my room for two years and never before have you become so engrossed as you have today. Apparently your turn has come too. Go away from the window before it is too late, do not breathe the evil fragrance of these deceitful flowers and do not wait for the Beautiful Woman to appear below your window and enchant you. She will come, she will enchant you, and you will follow her against your will."

Speaking thus, the Old Woman lit two candles on the table where some books were lying, banged the window shut and drew the curtain tightly across the window. The curtain rings scraped lightly along the bronze curtain rod, and the yellow linen of the curtain fluttered and once again lay motionless— and the room became cheerful, comfortable and peaceful. And it seemed that there was no longer any garden beyond the window, nor was there any sorcery in the world, and everything was simple, ordinary, and would remain so once and for all.

"But it is true," said the Youth, "I never paid any attention to this Garden, and today for the first time I saw the Beautiful Woman."

"He has already seen Her," the Old Woman thought sadly. "The evil seed of fascination has already fallen into your soul."

But the Youth was neither talking to the Old Woman nor even reasoning with himself. "It was never so earlier. During the day—at the lectures in the university, during the evening—at my books or with cheerful comrades and sweet girls at a party or the theater, somewhere up in the gallery or even in the parterre on a student pass when there was not much paying public: the producers loved us, we applauded heartily, shouted and called for the performer before all the lights were turned off. In the summer you went off to your parents. And so I had only heard that the magnificent Garden of our professor, the renowed Botanik, was next door."

"He is famous because he sold his soul to the devil," the Old Woman said angrily.

The student burst out laughing.

"Well, nonetheless," he said, "it seems strange to me that I had never seen his daughter until this evening, although I had heard a great deal about her fascinating beauty and about how many of the distinguished youths of the Old City as well as from other places far and near sought her love and hoped and deceived themselves, while others even died, unable to bear her coldness."

"She is cunning," said the Old Woman. "She knows the price of her charms and does not display herself to all. It would be difficult for a lowly student to make her acquaintance. Her father has instructed her in a great deal that not even scholars know, but she will not attend your gatherings. She spends more time with rich people from whom she can expect many gifts.

"Old Woman, today I had a good look at her," objected the Youth, "and I think that a girl with such a beautiful face, with such virtuously bright eyes, such exquisitely graceful movements and dressed so beautifully, cannot possibly be cunning and mercenary and chase after gifts. I have firmly resolved to meet her. This very day I shall go to Botanik."

"Botanik will not let you past the doorstep. His servant will not even go to announce your presence when he sees your wretched clothing."

"What does he care about my clothing!" the Youth replied with annoyance.

"Well, if you came riding up on a winged serpent, then they would let you in without looking at your patches."

The Youth laughed and exclaimed merrily, "Well then, Old Woman, I will saddle a winged serpent if there is no other way of getting in there!"

The Old Woman grumbled, "There is no longer anything good to be expected from the students' strikes. If you all studied peacefully, everything would be fine. And there would not be any grief in store for you in this sly Beauty and the terrible Garden."

"What is there so terrible in her garden?" asked the Youth. "And there was no alternative for us but to strike: all our rights and the rights of the university have been destroyed—do you really believe that we should debase ourselves without a struggle?"

"Youths should study," grumbled the Old Woman, "and not take the laws apart. And you, dear Youth, before you become acquainted with the Beautiful Woman, take a good look into her Garden through the window tomorrow morning, when everything is clearly and genuinely visible in the light of the sun. You will see that in the Garden there are no flowers which are familiar to anyone here, and only such flowers as none of us in the City know. Just think about this carefully, after all, there is something strange about it. The devil is cunning; is this not his creation for the damnation of people?"

"These foreign plants," replied the Youth, "have been brought from tropical lands where everything is different."

But the Old Woman no longer wanted to talk. She waved her hand in annoyance and shuffling her slippers she muttered unkind words in an angry, indistinct voice, and she left the room.

The Youth's first impulse was to go up to the window, turn back the yellow linen of the curtain and take another look into the enchanting Garden and wait. But he was prevented from this: a Comrade came, a noisy, clumsy young fellow, and he invited the Youth to go to a place where they often gathered to talk a great deal, argue, make noise and laugh.

Along the way the Comrade, laughing, indignantly waving his arms somewhat more than necessary, told the Youth about what had happened that morning in the lecture halls and university corridors when all the lectures had been halted and how the opponents of the strike had been disgraced, what beautiful words the popular and good professors had spoken, and how ridiculously the unpopular professors, that is to say, the bad ones, had behaved.

264

The Youth spent an interesting evening. He spoke just as excitedly as the rest. He listened to sincere and passionate speeches. He looked at his comrades whose faces expressed both the carefree bravado of youth and its fiery indignation. He saw girls that were dear, intelligent, modest, and dreamed of choosing himself a companion out of their cheerful circle. And he had almost forgotten about the Beautiful Woman in the enchanting Garden.

He returned home late at night and fell soundly asleep.

In the morning when he opened his eyes and when his glance fell upon the yellow linen of the curtain by the window, it seemed to him that its yellowness was suffused with the crimson of dark desire and that there was some strange and eerie tenseness in it. It seemed that the sun was insistently and fervently concentrating its burning and bitter rays towards this linen pierced by a golden color and summoning and demanding, and disturbing. And in reply to this fascinating external tension of gold and crimson the veins of the Youth were filled with a fiery agitation. His muscles were suffused with a resilient strength and his heart became like a spring of ardent fires. Sweetly pierced by millions of exciting, burning and arousing needles he leapt up from the bed and with a childlike gleeful laugh he began to leap and dance around the room without dressing.

Attracted by the unusual noise, the Old Landlady looked in at the door. She shook her head reproachfully and said, grumbling, "Dear Youth, you are dancing and rejoicing and disturbing everyone, and you yourself do not even know why you are happy, nor do you know who is standing beneath your window and what she is preparing for you.

The Youth was embarrassed and became quiet and modest as before, such as befitted his character and the fine upbringing which he had received at home. He washed up more carefully than ordinarily, perhaps because he did not have to hurry to lectures today, or perhaps from some other reason; and with the same care he dressed, and for a long time he cleaned his thoroughly frayed clothing: he did not have any new clothes since his parents were poor and could not send him very much money.

Then he went up to the window. His heart began pounding excitedly when he turned back the yellow linen of the curtain.

An enchantingly beautiful spectacle was revealed before him—although today he immediately noticed that there was something strange in the entire aspect of this extensive and excellently arranged Garden. Precisely what amazed him he was still unable to say right away, and he began to examine the Garden attentively.

What was there so unpleasant in its beauty? Why was the Youth's heart trembling so painfully?

Was it that everything in the enchanted Garden was too exact. All the paths were laid out geometrically, and all were of the same width, and all were covered with precisely the same amount of yellow sand; the plants were all arranged with exaggerated orderliness; the trees were trimmed in the form of

265

spheres, cones and cylinders; the flowers were arranged according to the various shades so that their composition was pleasing to the eye, but for some reason or other this wounded the soul.

But giving it careful thought, what was there unpleasant in that orderliness which merely bore witness to the careful attention which someone paid to the Garden?

Of course there was no reason for this to cause the strange apprehension which oppressed the Youth. But it was in something else as yet incomprehensible to the Youth.

One thing was for certain, though, that this Garden did not resemble any other garden which the Youth had happened to see in his time. Here he saw giant flowers of an almost too brilliant color—at times it seemed that many-colored fires were burning in the midst of the luxuriant greenery—brown and black stalks of creeping growths, thick like tropical serpents; leaves of a strange shape and immeasurable size, whose greeness seemed to be unnaturally brilliant.

Heady and languid fragrances wafted through the window in gentle waves, breaths of vanilla, frankincense and bitter almond, sweet and bitter, ecstatic and sad, like some joyous funereal mysterium.

The Youth felt the tender yet lively touches of the gentle wind. But in the Garden it seemed as if the wind had no strength and lay exhausted on the tranquil   green grass and in the shadows beneath the bushes of the strange growths. And because the trees and grass of the strange Garden were breathlessly quiet and could not hear the softly blowing wind above them and did not reply to it, they seemed to be inanimate. And thus they were deceitful, evil and hostile to man.

However, one of the growths moved. But looking closer the Youth began to laugh. What he had taken for the leafless trunk of a strange plant was a person small in size, gaunt and dressed all in black. He was standing before a bush with bright purple flowers, and then he slowly walked along the path, leaning on a thick cane and drawing near that very window out of which the Youth was looking.

Not so much from the face which was hidden by the broad brim of a black hat and only partially visible from above, but rather from the movements and walk, the Youth recognized Botanik. Not wishing to appear immodest, the Youth retreated somewhat from the window into the depth of the room. But suddenly he saw the Beauty, his beautiful daughter, approaching Botanik. Her bare arms were raised towards the black braids gathered on her head, for she was just putting a bright crimson flower in her hair. Her short, filmy and open dress was fastened over one shoulder with a golden clasp. Her graceful white feet were adorned with gilded sandals and entwined with broad pink ribbons.

The Youth's heart began to pound, and forgetting all caution and modesty, he rushed to the window once again and stared greedily at this sweet vision.

The Beauty cast a fleeting and ardent glance in his direction—blue eyes gleamed from beneath black, even eyebrows—and she smiled tenderly and slyly.

If there exist fortunate people, if from time to time the wild sun of joy soars towards foreign lands in a sweet whirling of ecstasy—then where are the words which might tell of this? And if in the world there exists a beauty for enchantment, then how might one describe it?

But now the Beauty stopped, fastened her eyes on the Youth and began to laugh cheerfully and merrily—and amid the indescribable whirling of ecstasy the Youth forgot everything on earth, leaned impetuously out of the window and cried in a voice ringing with excitement, "Dearest! Beautiful one! Heavenly one! Come to me! Love me!"

The Beauty drew near and the Youth heard her softly ringing, clear voice, every sound of which rent his heart with a sweet pain, "Dear Youth, do you know the price of my love?"

"Let it be the price of life!" exclaimed the Youth, "Let it lead even to the dark gates of death."

Her face was pale, her cheeks rosy, her eyes blue, her lips crimson—like some flaming and laughing sunset she stood before the Youth, stretching out her slender, naked arms to him. And she spoke, and there wafted from her words a fragrance both seductive and languid, like the sighs of a lily, "O dear Youth, so wise and passionate, you know, you see. you wait. Many have loved me, many have lusted to possess me, beautiful, youthful strong people, many have I smiled at with a fascinating smile, the smile of the ultimate consoler, but never before you have I spoken to anyone the sweet and terrible words: I love you. And now I desire you and await you."

Her voice quivered with passion and desire. From her waist she unfastened a black silk string with a brass key on it and was about to throw it to the Youth, but not in time. The father had already rushed up to her when he noticed from afar that she was talking to a strange Youth. He seized her roughly by the hand, took the key from her and began to cry in a hoarse, senile voice which was as repulsive as the belabored cawing of some old crow in a graveyard, "You fool, what are you trying to do? There is nothing for you to talk about with him. This Youth is not from that sort for whom we have cultivated our Garden, where the juices of these plants have been mixed with the poisonous pitch of the upas tree. It was not for such as this beggar that our ancestor perished after inhaling the pernicious scent of the horrible pitch. Go home and do not dare to speak with him."

The old man dragged his daughter back to the house which was visible in the depths of the Garden, her hands both tightly grasped in one of his. The Beauty followed her father obediently as she laughed. And her laughter was bright, clear, sweet, and stung the raging heart of the Youth with thousands of agonizing stings.

He stood for a long time at the window and stared intensely for a long time into the neat and orderly expanses of the enchanted garden. But already the Beauty was out of sight. All was calm and motionless in the wondrous

Garden, and the marvellously brilliant flowers seemed breathless; and they suffused the Youth with a scent which made the head whirl and oppressed the heart with a sinister languor—a scent which was reminiscent of the obscure, rushing, thirsting sighs of vanilla, cyclamen, datura and lily, of evil and fateful flowers which in dying themselves destroy, bewitching with a mysterious death.

The Youth resolutely decided to make his way into the wondrous Garden, to inhale the mysterious fragrances which the Beauty inhaled, and gain her love even though the price might be life itself, even though the road to it might be a fatal road, a road of no return. But who could help him make his way into the home of the elderly Botanik?

The Youth left the house. For a long while he wandered around the City, enquiring of all his acquaintances concerning the Beauty, the daughter of Botanik. Some could not, others would not take him into the home of the elderly Botanik, and all spoke of the Beauty with hostility.

One comrade said to him, "All the young Aristocrats of the City are in love with her and praise her delicate and exquisite beauty. But for us, the Plebians, her beauty is hateful and undesirable: her lifeless smile chafes us, and the chaos lurking in the azure of her eyes repulses us."

Supporting him a girl said, "Her beauty, about which many idle and rich youths talk, is really no beauty at all in our eyes. It is the lifeless beauty of decay and ruin. I even believe that she rouges and powders her face. She exudes an odor almost like that of a poisonous flower; even her breath is fragrant, and this is repulsive."

A popular Professor said, "My colleague, Botanik, is a man of renown and learning; but he has no desire to subjugate his science to the lofty interests of humanity. They say that his daughter is bewitching; some speak of the uniqueness of her garments and manners, but I have not had the opportunity of speaking with her in more or less thorough fashion; moreover, in our circle one seldom has the opportunity of seeing her. I believe, though, that her charms contain something which is pernicious to well-being—I have heard strange rumors the veracity of which, of course, I cannot vouch for, rumors which say that the rate of mortality among the young Aristocrats visiting this house is higher than normal."

The abbot, with a pointed smile on his pale, shaved face, said, "When the Beauty comes to me in the church she prays too zealously. This could lead one to believe that she is seeking forgiveness for very serious sins. But I am certain that our eyes would never behold her in the woolen mantle of the repentent sinner."

Sending out of the room all of her daughters, one mother said, "I do not understand what people see in her. People are destroyed through her; she is a coquette who breaks the hearts of youths, steals grooms from the brides, and yet loves no one herself. I do not allow my dear daughters, Minochka, Linochka, Ninochka, Rinochka, Tinochka, and Zinochka, to be acquainted with her. Mine are such modest, dear, sweet, cheerful, friendly, diligent daughters, such wonderful housekeepers and so clever with a needle. And how sorry I would be to part with them, but nonetheless I would give the eldest one in marriage to a fine and modest youth such as you.

* * * * * * *

Old Botanik brought his daughter home. His wrath had subsided, but in spite of the fact that he had not released her folded hands from his large bony fingers he no longer squeezed his cheerfully smiling daughter so painfully, nor did he push her so roughly. His face was sad. He released his daughter's hands, and of her own accord she obediently followed him into his study, a huge, gloomy room whose walls were weighed down by shelves with a multitude of colossal and dusty books.

Botanik sat down in an upholstered chair of dark leather by his heavy oak desk. He seemed to be tired. He covered his still youthfully flashing eyes with a trembling hand, yellow like parchment, and stared reproachfully at his daughter from under his hand.

The Beauty knelt down at his feet and looked up into the face of the elderly Botanik and smiled tenderly and submissively. She sat there straight, with her arms at her side, and in her pose there was a modest submissiveness, and in the smile of her seductive lips a tender insistence. Her face appeared to have grown paler, and it seemed as if there were a mocking insanity flaring up almost imperceptibly on her lips and in the azure of her eyes there lurked the insanity of grief. She was silent, and she waited for what her father would say.

And he spoke slowly, finding words almost with difficulty, "Dearest, what did I hear? I did not expect this of you. Why did you do it?"

The Beauty bowed her head and said softly and sadly, "Father, sooner or later all this will come to pass anyway."

"Sonner or later?" asked the father as if in surprise. And he continued, "Better late than sooner."

"I am all aflame," said the Beauty softly.

And the smile on her lips was like the reflection of some searing flame, and in her eyes there gleamed blue lightning, and her naked arms and shoulders were like some delicate vessel of alabaster, filled to the brim with a molten metal. Her firm breasts rose and fell impetuously, and two white waves strained forth from the tight confines of her dress, the delicate color of which was reminiscent of the yellowish rosiness of a peach. From beneath the folds of her short dress were visible against the dark green velvet of the rug and entwined by the pink ribbons of her gilded sandals her white and trembling legs.

Her father shook his head silently and said in a sad and severe voice, "You, dear daughter, so experienced and so clever in the wondrous art of bewitching and yet remaining chaste yourself, you should know that it is still too soon for you to leave me and abandon my uncompleted project."

"But will there ever be an end to it," protested the Beauty. "They keep coming again and again."

"No one knows," said Botanik, "there will be an end to all this and we shall see the completion of our project, or we shall pass it on to other generations. But we will do what we can. Remember that a young Count is supposed to come to you. You will kiss him—but nothing more—and you will give him a poisonous flower of his choice. And he will leave, full of sweet hopes and trembling expectations—and the inescapable will happen to him too."

An expression of submissiveness and melancholy was visible on the Beauty's face.

"Go," said the father.

He bent forward, kissed her on the forehead. The Beauty applied her crimson-hot lips to his wrinkled and yellow hand, pressing her white, half-naked bosom against his hard knees, sighed deeply and arose. And her sigh was like a fluting moan.

In half an hour the Beauty, smiling tenderly, was speaking to a young, handsome, arrogant Count, standing before him in the middle of the Garden by a circular bed of large brilliant flowers which gave forth a stupefying scent.

"Dear Count, you want a great deal. Your desires are too inflamed and impatient."

Her smile was so tender and devilish, and her chaste, pure eyes slid along the well-proportioned physique of the Count with caressing admiration, along his rich attire, which was handsomely and stylishly tailored from the most expensive fabrics and trimmed with gold and semi-precious stones.

"Dearest bewitcher," the Count began, "I know that you have been cold towards many who sought your favor. But to me you will be more tender. I will know how to win your love. I promise you on my honor that I will force the cold azure of your eyes to darken with passion."

"By what means will you gain my love?" asked the Beauty.

The expression on her beautiful face was unaffected and her voice did not betray that agitation which so easily overcomes maidens when they hear the searing voice which inspires passion in them. But the self-confident, arrogant Count was not dismayed. He replied, "Through my forebears I have gathered no small treasure and with gold and valor I have increased it. I possess many precious stones, valuable rings, necklaces, bracelets, oriental silks and perfumes, Arabian steeds, silk and velvet garments, rare weapons and much more than I can even mention at once, nor even remember. I shall scatter all at your feet, my bewitching one, I shall reimburse your smiles with rubies, your tears with pearls, your fragrant sighs with gold, your kisses with diamonds and your cunning infidelity with the blow of a swift dagger."

The Beauty began to laugh. She replied, "I am not yours yet, and already you fear my infidelity and threaten me. After all, I could get angry at that."

The Count quickly bowed down on his knees before the Beauty and covered her hands with kisses, hands so soft and slender, and whose flesh exuded a delicate, exotic fragrance.

270

"Forgive my madness, fascinating Beauty," he begged, suddenly forgetting all his arrogance, "my love for you has deprived me of all calmness and prompts me to wild actions and strange words. But what am I to do! I love you more than my own soul, and to possess you I am ready to pay not only with my treasures, not only with my life, but even with that which is dearer to me than life or the salvation of my soul—with my honor!"

The Beauty replied in a bewitchingly tender voice, "Your words have touched me, dear Count. Arise. I will not take from you an excessively large payment for my love—it cannot be bought, nor can it be sold. But he who loves must know how to bide his time. Genuine and faithful love will always find a path to the heart of the beloved."

The Count arose. With a delicate motion he straightened the lace cuffs of his green velvet cloak and fastened a lingering, ecstatic look on the Beauty. Their eyes met, and as before the expression of the Beauty's chastely clear eyes was unchanged.

Seized with that feeling of vague apprehension which overcomes even the arrogant and self-confident in moments of mortal danger, the Count went away from the Beauty. On the bench close by there lay a beautifully adorned casket made of oak. The Count opened it, and with a respectful bow he presented it to the Beauty.

The rays of the sun quivered like cheerful laughter on the diamonds and rubies of a diadem. And it seemed to the arrogant Count that the brilliance and laughter fell on the priceless stones from the glowing lips of the Beauty. But her smile was unchanged from what it had been before, and she admired the present as if it were of little value, although a pleasant sign of esteem. And then in a flash she was saddened and said, "My ancestors were slaves and you present me with a diadem which not even a queen would refuse."

"O, bewitching one!" exclaimed the Count, "You are worthy of an even more brilliant diadem."

The Beauty smiled at him in a friendly way, and again became somewhat melancholy and said softly, "The fate of my ancestors was the burning flow of blood beneath the lashes of cruel men, whereas I receive magnificent rubies and am crowned with joy."

And quite, quite softly she whispered, "But I shall not forget."

"Why think about what is long since forgotten?" exclaimed the Count. "Joyous are the days of bright youth, and let us abandon the grief of memories to old age."

The Beauty began to laugh and with this laughter she chased away a grief as fleeting as a puff of smoke melting in the summer sun.

She said to the Count, "In exchange for your beautiful gift, dear Count, I shall give you a single flower of your choice today, and one kiss. But only one."

The young Count was in such ecstasy and expressed himself in such an impetuous and outspoken manner that the Beauty repeated tenderly but severely, "Only one, no more."

And she inquired of the Count, "Which flower, dear Count, do you wish to receive from me?"

The Count replied, "Beautiful enchantress, whatever you may give me I shall be thankful to you beyond words."

The Beauty smiled and said, "All the flowers which you see here, dear Count, have been gathered from afar. They have been collected with great difficulty and even with danger. With painstaking care my father has improved their form, color and scent. For a long time he has studied their properties, replanted them, crossed them, introduced new qualities into them, and finally managed to produce out of miserable, wild and ugly flowers of the field and forest these enchanting and fragrant flowers."

"And the most enchanting flower is you, my dear Beauty!" exclaimed the Count.

The Beauty quietly sighed and continued, "Many consider their scent to be too powerful and overwhelming. And I notice that you, dear Count, are growing pale, you and I have spent too much time in the midst of these intense fragrances. But I have become accustomed to inhaling them, since childhood, and my very blood is drunk with their sweet fumes. But it is not good for you to stand here for a long time. Choose quickly whichever flower you wish to take from me."

But the young Count insisted on the Beauty selecting a flower for him. He was waiting impatiently for her second present, the promised kiss—her first kiss.

The Beauty looked at the flowers. Once again her face was darkened by a delicate shade of sadness. Suddenly, as if prompted by some strange will, she quickly stretched out a hand, so exquisite in its naked whiteness, and plucked a many-petalled flower. Her hand hesitated, and she bowed her head, and finally with an expression of shy indecision she approached the Count and placed the flower in a buttonhole of his cloak.

The powerful and pungent scent wafted into the young Count's face, which grew pale as his head reeled in languid impotence. Indifference and tedium overcame him. He was scarcely aware of himself, he hardly noticed that the Beauty took him by the arm and led him into the house, away from the fragrances of the wondrous Garden.

In one of the rooms of the house where all was bright, white and rosy, the Count came to himself. A youthful vitality returned to his face, his black eyes were aflame with passion once again, and he felt the joy of life and the surge of desire anew. But already the inescapable lay in wait for him. A white hand, bare, slender, lay on his neck; and the fragrant kiss of the Beauty was tender, sweet, long. The two blue lightnings of her eyes flashed close to his eyes and were masked with the subtle mystery of her long eyelashes. The sinister fires of some sweet pain swirled like a whirlwind about the heart of the young Count. He raised his arms to embrace the Beauty—but with a soft cry she stepped away and softly, quietly, ran away, leaving him alone.

The Count was about to rush after her. But in the doorway of the pink chamber he was met by the elderly Botanik. Poisonous was the smile on his thin lips, which slit the yellowish parchment of his face like a crimson line. The Count was embarrassed. With a sense of confusion uncharacteristic of him, and sensing a strange weakness through his entire body, he said goodbye to the elderly Botanik and left.

Strange whirlwinds of sweet pain kept whirling faster and faster about the heart of the young Count as he rode home on his raven-black Arabian charger, and the rhythmic pounding of its hooves against the roadway was barely audible. His face grew paler and paler. Suddenly his eyes closed, his hand released the reins, and he slumped over heavily as he fell out of the saddle. The frightened horse reared up on its hind legs, cast off its rider and galloped away.

They found the Count already dead, his head smashed against the cobblestones. And they did not know what he died of. They were amazed—for he was such an accomplished horseman!

* * * * * * * * *

Night fell. The full moon shone sweetly and tremulously, bewitching and foreboding with rays which were cold and funereally silent. The heart of the Youth was filled with an apprehensive fear as he went up to his window. His hand, clutching the edge of the yellow curtain, hesitated and vacillated for a long time before he resolved to draw the curtain slowly aside. The yellow linen rustled as it slowly gathered, and its rustle was like the barely audible hissing of a serpent in the forest's undergrowth; and the thin brass rings jingled and scraped against the brass curtain rod.

The Beauty stood beneath the window and looked at the window and waited. And the heart of the Youth shuddered, and he could not make out whether his heart was seized by ecstasy or terror.

The black braids of the Beauty were undone and fell on her naked shoulders. A sharply outlined shadow lay on the ground beside her. Illuminated from the side by the moon, she stood like some distinct and well-defined spectre. That half of her face which was illuminated by the moon,as well as her shoulders and her arms, were deathly white, as white as her robe. The folds of her white robe were severe and dark. Dark was the azure of her eyes, mysterious her frozen smile. A smooth, burnished clasp, fastened at the shoulder, gleamed dully against the strange tranquility of her body and garments. She began to speak softly, and her words, ringing like the fine silver chains of a lighted censer, gave forth a fragrance of ambergris, musk and lily.

"Dear Youth, I love you. Obedient to your summons I went against the will of my father and came to tell you: beware of me and my charms, flee from this Old City far away and leave me to my gloomy fate, I who have become intoxicated with the evil breath of the upas tree."

"O, Beautiful One!" replied the Youth to her, "you whom I have hardly known and who for me are already dearer than my own life and soul—why do you speak such cruel words to me? Or do you not believe in my love which has burst into flame so suddenly and still burns unextinguished?"

"I love you," repeated the Beauty, "I do not want to destroy you. My breath is full of poison, and my beautiful Garden is poisoned. You are the first one whom I have told of this because I love you. Do not linger in this City, flee from this Garden of pernicious beauty, run far away and forget all about me."

Intoxicated with an ecstasy and a grief sweeter than all earthly joys, the Youth exclaimed, "My beloved! What do I ask of you? My soul only thirsts for a single instant! To be consumed in the blissful flame of ecstasy and love, and to die at your most exquisite feet!"

A gentle shiver ran through the Beauty's body, and she became like the bright joy of the sunset behind the white cloud. With a solemn, expansive motion she raised her white, bare arms and reached towards the Youth, saying, "O my beloved! Let it be as you wish, and it shall be sweet for me to die with you. Come to me, into my frightful Garden, and I will tell you my gloomy tale."

Again, as in the morning, there gleamed in her hand a brass key on a pink ribbon. She began to laugh, shrilly, like a child, and she ran backwards, the whiteness of her slender legs flashing on the yellow sand of the pathway. She raised her arm quickly and adroitly hurled the key through the window. The Youth reached out his hands and caught the key in the air.

"My dear, I am waiting, I am waiting!" repeated the Beauty.

* * * * * * *

There in the poisoned Garden, beneath the canopy of mysterious growths, where the lifeless moon mixed the bane of its melancholy with the poisonous breath of the evil flowers of earth, they stood, the Youth and the Beauty, intoxicated with ecstasy and grief. They looked into each other's eyes; and the Beauty, in a voice ringing like the fragile voice of the clavecin, said, "My ancestors were slaves—but even slaves long for freedom. Obedient to the command of the ruler one of my ancestors made an exhaustingly long journey to reach the desert where the upas tree grows. He gathered the poisonous pitch of the upas tree and brought it to his ruler. The poisonous arrows won many a victory for the ruler. But my ancestor, having inhaled the evil scent, died. His widow thought she could have revenge on the evil race of rulers. She stole the poisonous arrows, soaked them in water and hid these infusions in deep caves like some precious wine. She poured one drop of this compound into a barrel of water and with this water she irrigated the wasteland on the edge of the Old City where our house and garden now stand. Then she took a drop of water from the bottom of this barrel, mixed it into bread and fed her son. And the soil of this Garden became poisonous and she accustomed her son to this poison. And from that time our entire line, from generation to generation, has been raised on poison. And today there flows in our veins blood aflame with poison, and our breath is aromatic but pernicious, and whoever kisses us will

274

die. And the power of our poison does not weaken as long as we live in this poisonous Garden, as long as we breathe the scents of these fantastic flowers. Their seeds have been brought from afar, my grandfather and father traveled wherever it was possible to procure growths evil and harmful to people—and here in this soil, so long poisonous, these evil, pernicious flowers displayed all their wrathful power, exuding such a sweet, such a joyful fragrance, and they cunningly converted even the dew falling from heaven into a fatal poison."

Thus spoke the Beauty and her voice had a cheerful ring, and her face was aflame with a great rejoicing. She finished her story and began to laugh quietly, but not cheerfully. The Youth bowed down before her and silently kissed her hands, inhaling the languid fragrance of myrrh, aloe and musk which wafted from her body and her fine robes. The Beauty began to speak again.

"There came to me streams of oppressors, because my evil, poisonous beauty bewitches them. I smile at them, they who are doomed to death, and I feel pity for each of them, and some I almost loved, but I gave myself to no one. Each one I gave but one single kiss—and my kisses were innocent as the kisses of a tender sister. And whomsoever I kissed, died."

The soul of the troubled Youth was caught in agony, between two quite irresolvable passions, the terror of death and an inexpressible ecstasy. But love, conquering all, overcoming even the anguish of death's grief, was triumphant once again today. Solemnly stretching out his trembling hands to the tender and terrifying Beauty, the Youth exclaimed, "If death is in your kiss, o beloved, let me revel in the infinity of death. Cling to me, kiss me, love me, envelop me with the sweet fragrance of your poisonous breath, death after death pour into my body and into my soul before you destroy everything that once was me!"

"You want to! You are not afraid!" exclaimed the Beauty.

The face of the Beauty was pale in the rays of the lifeless moon, like a guttering candle, and the lightning in her sad and joyful eyes was trembling and blue. With a trusting movement, tender and passionate, she clung to the Youth and her naked, slender arms were entwined about his neck.

"We shall die together!" she whispered. "We shall die together. All the poison of my heart is afire and flaming streams are rushing through my veins, and I am all envelopped in some great holocaust."

"I am aflame!" whispered the Youth, "I am being consumed in your embraces and you and I are two flaming fires, burning with the immense ecstasy of a poisonous love."

The sad and lifeless moon grew dim and fell in the sky—and the black night came and stood watch. It concealed the secret of love and kisses, fragrant and poisonous, with gloom and solitude. And it listened to the harmonious beating of two hearts growing quieter, and in the frail silence it watched over the final delicate sighs.

And so, in the poisonous Garden, having breathed the fragrances which the Beauty breathed, and having drunk the sweetness of her love so tenderly and fatally compassionate, the beautiful Youth died. And on his breast the Beauty died, having delivered her poisonous but fragrant soul up to sweet ecstasies.

Andrei Bely

ADAM

Translated by Charlotte Douglas

*Notes**

*Notes found in an insane asylum. According to our inquiries, one of
the mental patients in Doctor Haldin's hospital, having some inclination
toward literary activity, wrote down and worked into literary form the
confession of his late friend, who was completely insane.

In the Coach

The train plunges on. But where is it going? Why ask? Away it runs, away forever it runs, for the last day has begun.

He shook hands. With greening faces, with eyes full of sparks, his two friends leaned upon their canes. One had on a crushed bowler (why?)... Both were weary. Both knew that what was approaching was *the end.* Both had spent the day in their offices and when they interrupted their work with an indiscreet nod, when they turned the conversation toward *that end,* both broke in "Lord, we have strayed from our business." And ever deeper sunk their eyes, a deathly shadow was descending. The words of his friends had been bought with blood, but they were stolen. Someone, listening, recorded them on a phonograph and thousands of cylinders began to twang. A new enterprise opened, on sale a bronze throat, a screaming cavity; an experienced mechanic installed the throat phonograph. The purchased throat squealed day and night and his friends grew exhausted and one day he said to them both "Lord, I am going." He grinned. And they grinned: they understood everything. Now they stood on the platform, stood with him and saw him off. Someone long and dark with the face of an ox, shoulders crooked as a sorrowful cemetery cross and wrapped up in a frockcoat, swept into the coach. And then the bell rang, and then they waved their bowlers; three wooden arms swung in the air.

"Tahtahta-ha-ha" clattered the wheels. A lamp outside the window nodded to him. Another. A third. The lamps ceased to wink. Night without winking clung to the windows.

Everything was finished. Somewhere a dark passenger went up obliquely to the rack and stretched out his arms and stiffened and it seemed that pain nailed him, crucified, to the wall. There were only the two of them in the compartment, he and the passenger. "The passenger is being crucified, too," he thought. Rising from his seat and pretending to look for the conductor he moved closer to the crucified man. But the passenger, turning away his stuporous face, lay down on the seat where the shadows poured down on him so profusely, so profusely. A coat with protruding sleeves and a widebrimmed hat hung on the rack. He returned to his seat and sat down; the road is so long, so long; he had to get through these spaces where stations clustered about the track amidst the black night like some black coffin set with candles. He thought that minute was flying after minute, mile after mile, everything was moving—even he was moving—but to *where?*

He wanted to approach his sleeping companion who for only a moment had stretched his arms at the rack as if crucified but had not been hung, he had hung his coat and settled down to snort and snore in torment—

"You are going? So am I."

"Where?"

"Over the border, beyond the pale; the border is no defense, the *end* is breaking through; they are all undefended at the coming, but they say it is the coming of happiness. They don't suspect so they aren't crossing over, they're not coming out of the pale to meet the invasion from beyond the border. *There, there am I going."*

"You must be a philosopher who goes in for politics. I am also a patriot and not reconciled to a foreign invasion but, forgive me, I don't understand the philosophical aspect of your words."

The passenger turned his back and he could soon hear him snoring again. Oh how he longed to shout at him "Do you really know *where* I am going? Do you know *what* this journey is called? Not long ago we cried to you, wake up, see the signs. But you just swore and didn't wake up. There used to be days and what sunsets what sunsets we dreamed of—no, but what kind, what kind? But we sinned when we told you what sunsets we dreamed of. We knew that through our powers we spoke unto you and that our words were the signs. Who are we? A secret society? Oh no... But now we are such pedants, such pedants. Listen!"

The passenger tossed, turned over, but didn't come to.

"Awake and weep, we have resolved to take from you everything that was given. You muddied those hands, clean, like lilies, which brought you a nugget of golden fortune. And our fortune turned to misfortune. And so we retract the signs. We passed by your windows and as we peeked in gave hope to whomever we saw. We made hope of your mud. And we passed on and you thought that *our* luck was with you. And then you invited us to your feast of hope—that was not your feast, but ours. There we sat with arms crossed and kept silent as you devoured *our daily bread.* And so we retract the signs; wake up, *for you* there are no more signs."

Here he approached the sleeping man—who jumped up in fear, grabbing for his wallet. He thought it was a thief. But the one whom friends had seen off inclined his pallid face above him, put on his pince-nez, put it on over his weary weaksighted eyes and softly remarked, "Could I smoke please, I don't have any matches."

Did the sleepy traveler know that at that moment they were taking everything from him, they were taking the signs?

The train sped on and on, to where? A lamp flashed, and another and another. Everything came to a stop; a black stranger clung to the window. It was the conductor. Beneath the coach a little man ran tapping his hammer "thorn-thong" beating the broken heart, beating and stopping. The sleeping passenger sprang from the couch and clutched his heart with insane hands and his mouth flew open and the black maw gaped (but did you get it sweetie?) sweetly he yawned and fell into a sound sleep. And the coach started off. A lamp flashed. Again. And again. Then the lamps flashed no longer.

Adam Antonovich Koreish was sitting at the window completely at ease. His blond graying beard lay fluffed out on his white shirt front, his eyes were fastened on a treatise of finance law. But it only seemed that way, he was watching sharply as the passenger squirmed on his bed (but did you get it, did you get it, we are flying at dizzying speed!).

The train flew thundering onto an iron bridge. White fog swaddled the river. The bridge began but the bridge could not come to an end, and neither could the iron din cease. Adam Antonovich's eyes reached the line "The budgetary commission petitioned..." "Petition? That din will kill them..." Terrified the passenger tossed and turned, evidently his torture was exceeding the bounds of human suffering. Adam Antonovich glanced out of the window, the train hadn't returned to firm ground, it flew through the clouds. Adam Antonovich said "I petition." The iron rumbling ceased. A station appeared. The long coat of fat-father clung to the window "There he is, he's come. We've been waiting for you, old man." Adam Antonovich gathered his strength. He had crossed the border. He caught up his traveling bag and got down from the coach. Fat-fogey the father who had been lying for his son in the country kissed him. A troika appeared.

At Father's

Son. Father, you are my father. You sired me. I have sired no one because I left the primordial. I left you, I studied, I suffered, and my visions were pure. Before me, my father, new horizons were opened.

Father. Yes, I am your father. I sired you and nowhere did I go. Where I was in the beginning, there I remained. I dwell in the old home, my estate is as it was. I spawned, I lived with your mother. Then I lived with peasant women and girls, spawning. I surrounded myself with chickens, roosters, turkeys. My poultry lay dozens of eggs a day. But I studied nothing, never did I suffer. My horizons remain the same, oh just the same. These spaces, ancient, veritably Russian, assembled around us are all—all just the same.

Son. But you are taking up ever more room in these spaces, father, you've gotten fat; it's about time to tie up a wheelbarrow to your belly. You used to be my enemy. You wanted to keep me in my native place; you tried to keep me from knowing the truth so I ran away. But now I have returned to you to be cured. I want your health.

Father. Yes, son, I am swelling, soon the whole world will fit in me and I shall become father to my world and you will be the son. But I will not give out information about my wealth, although the estate books are in order. And you won't have my health. My health comes from a proper life; I have a liaison with the cook and she is a sweet soul, the soul of everything I have. But why did you return to me?

Son. There beyond the borders of your domain in the great world, in that other, I was word of a new life, but I did not give them life, they spoiled everything I tried. And I took my hopes from them. A hopeless dark world of nonexistence is now beyond the borders of your realm, I can no longer see it. Now I have no other world but my native one, the primordial, the world of the village, your estate.

Father. My son, live quietly in this quiet asylum, drink up, be fruitful and multiply, and in everything serve your father.

Son. Not for that did I come. I came to begin with something small. I will quit your world but only when I have made reforms in our affairs. The new life shall be established here. Then will I return whence I came.

Father. My son, my tired one, my sick one; I will give you your childhood annex, I will send for the doctor and we will return your health.

Son. Father, I am not ill; your intrigues have begun but we will prevail.

*

And they went out into the garden. The old gentleman put his arm solicitously about his son. Clusters of lilacs bowed before them. Birds sang. No one could have told that what had been spoken there had been spoken. The housekeeper ran by crying "The little turkeys have begun to die." The stout old man glanced suspiciously at his son. At supper everyone was dead drunk.

The Annex

Fat father's ashgray dressing gown threw an uneasy shadow on Adam Antonovich; they were in the secluded annex, truly a secluded world. Adam Antonovich knew where he was and what he was doing. The old man shuffled about in his slippers and the cook, the sweet soul, washed plates; the old man puffed contentedly on his pipe. When he caught by the feeler a cockroach running across the table thunder and voices fairly flew from his mouth "Be fruitful, be fruitful, you little rascals, he-he!"

He gazed at the healthy ruddy goldplaited cook and said "This is not life, it's heaven." When he went out pleased with himself, the cook also quite pleased with herself, burst out laughing and bent her plump waist over Adam Antonovich. "Now we are alone, take me, I can't make it with that old man." Together they climbed onto the bed above the stove in the kitchen. Adam Antonovich knew what he was doing, he was saving humanity. But the deathly sinister visage of his father stuck out from behind the door "That Adam, that son of ours, is falling, falling... Aaaa!" And he nailed Adam Antonovich painfully.

There was a burning haze in the closet and Adam sat rolling bread into balls, working by the sweat of his brow. He knew what he was doing, he was saving humanity—to the laughter and racket of the old man who was romping with the cook on the other side of the partition. Afterwards the old man crushed cockroaches "twenty-one, twenty-two, twenty-three, enough; the cockroaches I will drown." And turning on the water he flung a tin tub at Adam Antonovich "Get in and swim." And a sleepy muttering of streams sounded 'Shaaa...'' Adam Antonovich got in the bath and swam; he knew what he was doing, he was saving humanity.

Adam Antonovich's father was a tubby tyrant with a triple chin and chinks where his eyes should have been. All his life he had amassed money. In old age he exchanged it for space; his estates grew, grew and swelled. Since then he had acquired the cook and often he used to say to her "You, my soul, are the soul of everything I have, the soul of my world." Evil tongues rumored that the son would beat his father out of his soul and begin a new relationship. The old man himself realized the horror of his position and often used to say "My son is growing up, Adam the blockhead. He will beat me out of everything." Already the peasantry looked with dignified disapproval at the old man, saying to one another "We're getting a new master, the son." And the good news about Adam Antonovich spread.

Adam Antonovich sitting in the annex understood dimly, he knew *what he was doing,* he was helping the peasantry. Now he stared stupidly at the cook's palegray skirt speckled with stains. "Ah well now, my soul, wash my feet, here I sit, now I know I'm your master." The cook stared at him, concentrating stupidly, and began to wash his feet. "You've got your papa running, running right down to his grave," she smirked. And Adam Antonovich, the new master, solemnly pronounced his new testaments. He knew what he was doing, he was establishing order, saving something small and thus also the great because only he had crossed the border, only he knew that the time had come, the final time.

A dog trailed in, a large watch-dog which had wet in the courtyard and Adam mounted astride him. And the dog hauled him outside. And there in the courtyard Adam Antonovich sat establishing his justice, he knew *what he was doing.*

The local police seized him and brought him to his old father. And the father said "It's an epidemic, my son is stirring up the village, a plague, we're all in God's hands. Gavryuka, Filya, you asses, flog my son, I tell you. Filial duties must be performed everywhere." And they flogged him with lashes "Ash, shash; five, six... Ash, shash; ten, twenty." Afterwards they laid him in a bed as in a grave; they piled him with quilts like stones colorless deathly still. At the head of Adam Antonovich's bed keened the cook, crooken, looking old, her frightened orphaned silhouette drawn close to him; and he squinted as if he were drunk; but throwing back the quilts and stretching out his hands to the cook, he stood up swaying in his drawers and shirt "I have risen from my pallet, my soul, don't be blind."

The cook nudged Adam Antonovich now hiccoughing drunkenly "Master, wake up."

Moaning and groaning down he sat on the bed; yes, it was only a dream and he hadn't yet let out the secret of why he had come. Last night he had arrived at his father's house and right away his father had made him drunk. Oh, just to hide it, if only it doesn't get out! He knew what he was doing, he was saving humanity. Over the night-table Adam Antonovich Koreish inclined his pallid, pallid, pallid face with its weary weaksighted blue eyes and deftly flipping his pince-nez onto his nose he bent over the tract on finance law. "Master, may I open the shutter?" He did not respond, he was reading. But that's only the way

282

it seemed, he was watching the cook carefully to see if she had discovered his secret.

So he has arrived. Here he will be about his business, already he has broken with the old and from here he will begin his coming into the world. But for now, silence! Yesterday he drank, ate and drank and drank. As he was raising the glass of vodka he still remembered he had to be secretive but lowering it he no longer remembered. He had embraced his father; both, drunk, had staggered through the garden in the morning at daybreak and something had been said.

He was dressing. A herd of cows trailed in to dinner. The herdsman blew a tune on his horn and 'pplakh' his whip cracked. He inclined his weary, pallid, pallid, pallid face and deftly flipped on his pince-nez; he knew what he was doing, he was saving humanity.

He knew that his dream was not a dream, but the prototype of the future. He had turned the symbols into substance, he had created in the world of existence a world of values.

At Home—On Vacation!

Adam Antonovich went out of the annex which as a child he had called the "world." Through the glass he shouted jokingly to his servant "You are still in the 'world' but I'm not in the world, I'm in Russia."

The hunchbacked plains spread out on every side, Russian plains, eaten away by ravines, ancient, native, all—all just the same. "With the mind, Russia cannot be embraced; she is a special case, one can only believe in Russia," he thought, "The Slavophiles were right, they believed in my coming. I go forth to meet the bridegroom." And he went to his father's to have tea. As they were drinking their tea women's voices came from the next room "These turkeys of yours are dying?"

"Yes, they're dying."

"A-a-a."

And silence ensued.

The father stared suspiciously at his son "When you were drunk, my friend, you said something absurd." And Adam Antonovich, thinking up a counterattack, tossed back his pallid, pallid, pallid face, screwed up his blue weaksighted eyes and stroking his gray beard answered "And I dreamt that I rode on a dog." Both sighed deeply. His father asked "What do you intend to do?" "At one time I did a bit of writing and reading but now I don't write anything, I don't read anything." His father clapped him on the shoulder "Stay here quietly in your own home, in the old days." And pointing out the window he added "This is our native land, this space. Here people have lived quietly from time immemorial. And we too shall be native unchanging." And from the next room came a soft muttering "You should have wet the turkey's head with vodka."

"Yes, we had been wetting them."

"A-a-a!"

And silence ensued.

The father looked suspiciously at his son "What was that dreadful thing you said when you were drunk?" Adam Antonovich tried to remember. He remembered nothing. His hands hung down indifferently over his knees, he stared out the window at a pale gray clod of dust speckled with rubycolored insects. He was thinking about his father. His father used to say "Time is money" and on this basis he saved up time; he had exchanged time for space and the estates grew, grew and swelled. From then on he dragged around a miserable existence and a gigantic stomach, directly proportional to his space and inversely proportional to his eloquence. Evil tongues joked that they would tie a wheelbarrow under his stomach to ease his lot and that he used to claim "When they approach suddenly I will vanish, for I am old, then you can cart away my carcass left in legacy," and with this he would keep repeating "As is the stomach, so also is the legacy." Adam Antonovich knew that the end of time was at hand and that the spaces of his earths must return back to time to save and deliver the soul from time, his soul, that is, the soul of humanity.

The cook passed by, the sweet little soul, looking suspiciously at Adam Antonovich with her skyblue eyes.

"My son, why so thoughtful? My son, I am afraid for your health." Adam Antonovich tossed back his pallid, pallid face but gave it up, tired, when a muzhik, bridle in hand and concentrating fiercely, ran by in the window, in front of him galloped a horse. "He is swelling, he is swelling into his grave; the days are fulfilled, it will begin, soon it will begin." Drops began to fall, dusty rainy aromas drifted into the room. A storm cloud trailed through without bringing forth rain and the dry haze embraced it. "My son, say something. You are doing me in, my heart pounds, I am short of breath. What does it all mean?" But Adam Antonovich sprang up and ran out into the garden; quickly he sauntered to the village pursued by the shouts of his old father "Open your eyes, you are in the dark..."

"Father, father! I shall wring your power from you, I shall set free my soul, I shall save my mother land. It grieves me to kill you but the prophecy shall be fulfilled."

So Adam Antonovich walked on, lifting up his hands in the fields. He knew what he was doing, he was saving humanity.

People who had been burnt out sat on the smouldering ruins, black tearless faces stared into darkness. The lone chimney of a charred fireplace stuck up in the distance. To one side a bugridden old man with a protruding lip sat on a scorched log talking to some whining old women "What we know we don't forget, oh-ho-ho.... It used to be just like this in the days of persecution. But the *end* comes. And so let's sit here and whisper about the coming." The sun went down, sanguine, in flames, and immediately it grew dark but it didn't affect the haze. Sheep were stirring up the ashes. Somewhere far off they sang "Russia, Russia, Russia mine, remember January nine!" And the old man continued "It's not our mother, our country." But Adam Antonovich drew near, lifted up his hand and touched him with a reed of grass. "I am the alpha and omega, the beginning and the end, upon you I bestow my world." "Just

284

so, your grace, lands be piddling" grunted the muzhik, but Adam Antonovich, after whispering something to the muzhik, moved on. "How's that?" asked an old woman. "He says, see, soon we won't see him, he is shoving off, see, for Lisichensk; but later, see, he'll come again; mayhaps, he says, they won't get him away from us." "Democrat!" someone sneered and began to sing "Russia, Russia, Russia mine, remember January nine!"

"Father, I will dress in a purple pall, a wreath of wheat henceforth will I wear. Fortune you went from me but I have returned to my native land. I will not depart from you, my land, my mother, leaving I will not leave, forsaking, I will abide. Yes I will abide." A scarecrow flapped before Adam Antonovich. The bast, dispersing in shreds in the sunset whispered "Time has begun." The son, Adam, stripped naked, descended into the Old Testament of his native land and arrayed himself in bast; a wreath of roadside field grass he placed upon his brow, a staff, not a switch, he pulled from the ground, flourishing the birch branch like a sacred palm. On the road he stood like a guard. The dustgray road ran into the sunset. And a crow perched there, perched and croaked, there where the celestial fire consumed the earth.

There were blind men along the dustgray road running into the twilight. Antique, crooken, they trailed along, lonely and sinister silhouettes, holding to one another and to their leader's cane. They were raising dust. One was beardless, he kept squinting. Another, a little old man with a protruding lip, was whispering and praying. A third, covered with red hair, frowned. Their backs were bent, their heads bowed low, their arms extended to the staff. Strange it was to see this mute procession in the terrible twilight. They made their way immutable, primordial, blind. Oh, if only they could open their eyes, oh if only they were not blind! Russian Land, awake!

And Adam, rude image of the returned king, lowered the birch branch to their white pupils. And on them he laid his hands, as, groaning and moaning they seated themselves in the dust and with trembling hands pushed chunks of black bread into their mouths. Their faces were ashen and menacing, lit with the pale light of deadly clouds. Lightning blazed, their blinded faces blazed. Oh, if only they opened their eyes, oh, if only they saw the light!

Adam, Adam, you stand illumined by lightnings. Now you lay the gentle branch upon their faces. Adam, Adam, say, see, see! And he restores their sight.

But the blind men turning their ashen faces and opening their white eyes did not see. And the wind whispered "Thou art behind the hill." From the clouds a fiery veil began to shimmer and died out. A little birch murmured, beseeching, and fell asleep. The dusk dispersed at the horizon and a bloody stump of the sunset stuck up. And spotted with brilliant coals glowing red, the bast streamed out from the sunset like a striped cloak. On the waxen image of Adam the field grass wreaths sighed fearfully giving a soft whistle and the green dewy clusters sprinkled forth fiery tears on the blind faces of the blind. He knew what he was doing, he was restoring their sight. And it was not the bloody lace of tears which was burning his wreathed radiant image; the kingdom of the father burned, wreathed with fire.

"Father, I shall not return to you for you are no more; you are burning, you are going up in smoke, you are returning unto dust." He was returning to the city, he knew what he was doing. He was passing from the small to the great in order to return to everyone.

Below, the plain spread out and in the distance, in Lisichensk, sparkled a gold cross.

Meanwhile the cook was serving father his pudding. He choked on a greasy piece of it as a plate slipped from the hands of the goldplaited cook and the room was filled with a soft mellow chime; the women appeared to grow younger, to turn transparent and—oh!—off she floated, a soft cloud. There she was already at the window smoking like a wisp of incense in the night dark, but that is no puff of smoke, it is the pungent silk of a flame, silk which runs along the walls of a house. The house was catching fire, the soul was sailing off, and now the fire was impossible to extinguish.

Lisichensk

Who was sitting down at the counter there in the station, somber silent but still in control of himself? In a wicker clothes basket covered with a blue calico cloth the kingly regalia was kept, the bast and the wreath of real copper and a lot of other things—about which one shouldn't ask. Pallid, pallid, pallid Adam Antonovich bowed his head; he knew what he was doing, he was returning to the capital, charged with his terrible secret. Who had set fire to his father's house? Or did no one set it? Why ask—the train will plunge onward, ever onward, to where?

He was bowed over a beer. Next to him a fat man mopped his brow. (There was one less fat man now.) The fat man next to him was saying "I had agreed to sell the rye standing. All day I fooled around with that kike, I fed the dirty gypsy, stood him drinks." His companion yawned "Aaa." And silence ensued.

The red skirt of a young lady with a turned up nose fluttered by and flew away onto the platform. In the window the telegrapher sniggered, tchicked his tongue and settled back into his apparatus. The young lady eyed an SR (the SR had on a black shirt) as he went by with a girl friend in a tight tidy hat. The young SR removed his cap as he walked past "My compliments to Adam Antonovich." Gloomily a fur-bearer stood there, what for, the devil knows, but he had a saber and a high Caucasian hat. Somewhere the engine was complaining about the distance and at the buffet the flyspecked pies were drying up.

Adam Antonovich stood up "I shall teach, I shall enlighten, for I am the light and the hope; our sorrowful earth I shall not abandon but with my garment shall I cover it, mine own garment."

Going up to the basket, he raised the calico cloth slightly, holding his pince-nez at his nose: everything was intact.

The train was a long time in coming. He stepped out of the station; his

286

native Lisichensk baked in a scorching heat, its shacks casting dreary shadows, and in the distance the village watch tower stuck up stupidly. A gig glided smoothly by. Only a cab danced on the broken cobblestones and inside the constable danced, his cap slipping down. People sat on a bench nibbling sunflower seeds; a fat lady in a kerchief was spitting out the husks with a protruding lip and whispering with another lady "Koreish, Adam Antonovich, he laid away his father this summer past, his estate burned up completely and the old man burned up too. He was living there alone, he rented an annex from Zuchika." Her neighbor gaped "A-a-a-a." And silence ensued. An evening ray fell upon a sign and the boldface gold letters turned sanguine on the black: **Grane — Bouht and Sold.**

Russian Land, the enemy is not sleeping. Everything has changed, the end is approaching for everyone. Russian Land!

Adam Antonovich Koreish boarded the train. The engine complained of the distance, sad and senselessly.

King Adam

One. The city. Heat. Look, the dull haze of night has replaced the dull haze of day. Already it is three months since he was no more, he has gone— forever. Here are his trousers and here is his hat. Could you make out the manuscripts? They would make a good book. But he is gone. The sun's dull circle has gone down, let us close the windows the roads are steaming.

The Other. We lost news of him when he vanished into the middle stripe. There he fell like some bright spark and since then everything has begun to smoke, forest fires are coming from that region. And here is his knife.

One. The trains are stopping because dense smoke and dense flames are pouring down on us and surrounding the city with a fiery ring. The trains are stopping.

The Other. That doesn't mean anything... And here is his cigar case; how he used to love to turn it over and over aimlessly as he had a smoke. Today, I think, there was a yellow sunset.

One. His favorite sunset but yellow-yellow and a bit terrible. We didn't understand Adam then, but now...

The Other. Let us gather the things together in one place and light the candles; over a glass of red wine, *his wine,* we shall partake until dawn, until exhaustion. And in the morning there will be a yellow dawn.

A light tap at the door, a light tap at the door. Listen, a light tap at the door. Yes, yes, without a doubt. They had gathered all the things; the sunset's yellow flame so vividly reminded them of everything and the yellow candles, the yellow candles—it wasn't possible that all this did not bring back the master. And the master had returned.

And the door opened: unkingly kindly king, king of hope, Adam, who descended upon the dilapidated ancestral home of his own, his native land—

yes, there among them...he stands—

—in a cloak of bast covered with the
brilliant coal of dead worlds (and in their
hands dance yellow candles). How the
striped cloak intensifies in the night dark!
Wreaths of field grass lay on his waxen
brow (sway, the yellow candles sway) and
his birch sceptre's leafy fringe laden with
succulent dew strews golden tears. "Henceforth, I shall not go from you, my brothers."

The night is dark. Droshkys are creaking. A stifling black cloud is heaped
up in the window. A line of lantern fires reaches far away.

—Henceforth you won't leave us brother?
"Well, speak up, speak up! Hey, why don't
you say something? Come on, come! Share
our meal! A glass of dark wine, your own
wine. Dead tired but before us, Adam, king,
unkingly king." The three of them were
there and they smiled in the candles.

Dull tears of night knocked at the windows. In the morning yellow,
yellow it was, a yellow sunrise. The candles were extinguished, the things were
stashed away; no, he will not return. When they go, they don't come back.
Where are you? Where are you?

Valery Bryusov

THE REPUBLIC OF THE SOUTHERN CROSS

Translated by
Pierre Hart

ALBERTO • MARTINI

Recently, a whole series of articles has appeared describing the terrible catastrophe which has befallen the Republic of the Southern Cross. They differ markedly and report numerous events which are clearly fantastic and improbable. Apparently, those compiling the descriptions relied excessively upon testimony by surviving residents of Star City. They, as we know, were *all stricken by a psychic disorder.* Therefore, we consider it opportune to gather all the reliable information presently available concerning the tragedy that has occurred in the Southern Hemisphere.

The Republic of the Southern Cross developed forty years ago from the steel mill trust situated in the south polar regions. In a note circulated to the world's governments, the new state laid claim to all lands, both continental and insular, contained within the limits of the Antarctic Circle, as well as to all portions of these lands extending beyond the limits indicated. The state declared its willingness to purchase these lands from governments which regarded them as being under their protectorate. There were no objections to the new republic's claims by the fifteen great powers of the world. Dispute over several islands lying completely beyond the Antarctic Circle, but immediately adjacent to the south polar territories, required separate treaties. With the completion of the various formalities, the Republic of the Southern Cross was accepted into the family of nations and her representatives accredited by its governments.

The Republic's major city, named Star City, was situated right at the pole. At the imaginary point through which the earth's axis passes and all the meridia converge, the city hall stood. The tip of its spire, rising above the city's roofs, was pointed toward the nadir. The city's streets diverged from the city hall along the meridia and were intersected by other streets arranged in concentric circles. In both height and exterior construction, all buildings were identical. The walls were without windows since the buildings had interior electric lighting. The streets were similarly lit. Due to the climate, a roof, impenetrable to light, was built over the city with powerful ventilators for continual circulation. These regions of the earth have but one six month day and an equally long night during the year, but the streets of Star City were constantly bathed in a bright, even light. Similarly, the outside temperature was artificially maintained at an even level through all the seasons.

According to the latest census, the residents in Star City numbered 2,500,000. All the remaining population of the Republic, some 50,000,000, was concentrated around the ports and factories. Externally, these other settlements resembled Star City. Through the intelligent use of electric power, the entrances to the local ports remained open all year. Elevated electric railroads connected the populated areas of the Republic; tens of thousands of people and millions of kilograms of goods were transported daily. The country's interior remained uninhabited. Through the train window, a traveller saw only monotonous waste lands, completely white during the winter and covered by sparse grass for the three summer months. Wild animals had long since been killed off and there was nothing to sustain human life. The tempo of life in the port cities and factory centers was so much the more striking by contrast. The fact that, in recent years, approximately seven-tenths of the metal mined on Earth has been processed in the Republic's state factories, provides some indication of the nature of life there.

To judge by appearances, the Republic's Constitution seemed the epitome of populism. Workers in the metal factories, who constituted about sixty percent of the total population, were considered the only fully enfranchised citizens. These factories were state property. The worker's life at the factories was not merely comfortable but luxurious. In addition to beautiful quarters and superb cuisine, various educational institutions and amusements were provided for them—libraries, museums, theaters, halls for all varieties of sports, etc. The number of working hours per day was extremely low. Child rearing and education, medical and legal aid, the direction of religious services for the various sects—all were concerns of the state. Workers in the state factories, virtually guaranteed the satisfaction of all their needs, demands and even whims, did not receive wages, but the families of citizens who had served in the factories for twenty years, as well as of those who had died or been disabled while in service, received large life pensions, providing that they did not leave the Republic. From among these workers, representatives were selected for the Republic's Legislative Chamber in a general election. The Chamber had charge of all questions concerning the country's political life but lacked the authority to change basic laws.

This democratic exterior, however, concealed a totally autocratic tyranny by member institutions of the former steel trust. While granting the deputies' positions in the Chamber to others, they unfailingly installed their own candidates in the factory directorships. The factories' economic life was controlled by the Council of these directors. They received all the orders and distributed them among the factories; they acquired the materials and machines for the work; they ran the factories' affairs. Huge sums of money, amounting to billions, passed through their hands. At the Council's direction, the Legislative Chamber merely approved the statements of expenses and income presented to it, although the total of these statements greatly exceeded the total Republic's budget. In foreign affairs, the Council of Directors' influence was enormous. Its decisions could destroy entire nations. Prices which it set determined the wages for millions of workers throughout the world. At the same time, the Council's influence on the Republic's internal affairs, although indirect, was always decisive. The Legislative Chamber was, in essence, merely the obedient executor of the Council's will.

To retain power, the Council was obliged, first of all, to maintain merciless regimentation over the life of the nation. Seemingly free, the citizens' lives were controlled down to the most inconspicuous of details. Buildings in all the Republic's cities were built from the same model, prescribed by law. The furnishings of all the workers' quarters, however luxurious, were strictly uniform. Everyone received the same food at exactly the same time. The dress, issued from government stores, had been unchanged for decades and was of the same style. After a specified hour, indicated by a signal from the City Hall, a curfew was in effect. The entire nation's press was subject to strict censorship. No articles opposed to the Council's dictatorship were permitted. Everyone was so fully convinced of this dictatorship's beneficence that the compositor's refused to set type for lines critical of the Council. Factories were filled with the Council's agents. At the slightest indication of dissatisfaction with the Council, agents hurried to hastily called meetings to inspire doubters with passionate speeches. There was, of course, the most disarming fact that the life of the Republic's workers was a source of envy throughout the world. It has been claimed that in isolated cases of persistent agitation, the Council did not refrain from political murder. In any event, during the whole of the Republic's existence, there was never a single director elected by popular vote who was hostile to the member institutions.

For the most part, Star City's population consisted of workers who had completed their employment. They were, so to speak, rentiers. Their government allowance permitted them to live in wealth. Thus, it is not surprising that Star City was considered one of the gayest cities in the world. Various entrepreneurs and business men found it to be a gold mine. Celebrities of the entire world brought their talents here. The best operas, concerts and art exhibits were here; the most informative newspapers were publiched. Stores in Star City were noted for the great variety in their selection, the restaurants—for their luxury and attentive service. Every form of vice devised by ancient and modern civilization beckoned. The government's regimentation was, however, maintained in Star City as well. To be sure, the furnishings in the apartments and the styles of dress were not restricted but a curfew remained in effect, strict censorship of the press was preserved, and an extensive network of spies retained by the Council. Officially, the People's Guard maintained order but, in addition, the omniscient Council had its secret police.

Such was the general pattern of life in the Republic of the Southern Cross and its capital. The task remains for some future historian to determine how much it contributed to the appearance and spread of the fatal epidemic which led to the destruction of Star City, and perhaps, of the entire young nation.

The first cases of infection with "contradiction" were noted in the Republic twenty years ago. At that time, the disease had the character of an accidental, sporadic infection. Local psychiatrists and neuropathologists, however, became interested in it, described it in detail and at an international medical congress in Lhassa, several papers on it were given. Later it was somehow forgotten although in the psychiatric hospitals of Star City there were always infected persons. The disease was so named because those infected constantly contradicted their own wishes, wanting one thing but speaking and

acting otherwise. (The scientific name for the disease is *mania contradicens.*)
At first its symptoms are rather weakly expressed, primarily as a characteristic
aphasia. Instead of saying "yes" the afflicted says "no," wishing to say some
tender words, he assails his companion with curses, etc. At the same time, the
afflicted generally begins to contradict himself in his actions, turning to the
right when intending to go left, pressing his hat down over his eyes while
thinking to lift it so that he might see better, etc. As the illness progresses,
theses "contradictions" fill the whole of the afflicted's corporal and spiritual
life in an infinite variety of forms corresponding to the idiosyncracies of each
individual. In general, the afflicted's speech becomes incomprehensible, his
behavior absurd. The proper physiological functioning of the organism is also
destroyed. Recognizing the irrationality of his behavior, the patient becomes
extremely agitated, frequently to the point of frenzy. A great many commit
suicide, sometimes during an attack of insanity but sometimes, on the contrary,
at a moment of spiritual enlightenment. Others die of cerebral hemorrhages.
The disease almost always leads to a quick death, cases of recovery being
extremely rare. *Mania contradicens* became epidemic in Star City midway
through this year. Prior to that time, the number of afflicted with "contradiction"
had never exceeded two percent of the total number of persons ill. But this
figure suddenly grew to twenty five percent during May (an autumn month in
the Republic) and continued to increase during the months following, while the
absolute number of persons ill grew at the same rapid rate. In the middle of June
about two percent of the entire population, that is, about 50,000 persons, had
already been officially diagonosed as afflicted with "contradiction." There is no
statistical data for periods later than this. Hospitals were filled to overflowing.
The number of doctors quickly proved completely inadequate. In addition, the
doctors themselves, as well as the hospital staffs, began to fall victim to the same
illness. Very soon, the ill had no one to turn to for medical aid and an accurate
count of the afflicted became impossible. According to testimony given by all
the eye witnesses, however, it was impossible to find unaffected families by July.
Thus, the healthy consistently declined in number so that a mass emigration from
the city began, as from a place infected with the plague, while the number of
those ill soared. As some have maintained, it would probably not be far from
truth to say that by August, all those remaining in Star City were stricken with
psychic derangement.

The first appearance of the epidemic can be followed in the local newspapers,
which reported it under the increasingly larger headline "Mania contradicens." Since
diagnosis of the disease in its early stages is very difficult, the chronicle of the first
days of the epidemic is filled with comic episodes. An afflicted subway conductor
paid the passengers instead of collecting money from them. A street patrolman
responsible for the regulation of traffic, snarled it up all day long. A museum visitor,
while walking through the halls, took all the pictures and turned them to face the
wall. A newspaper which had been checked by an afflicted proofreader turned out
to be absolutely filled with amusing nonsense. During a concert, a sick violinist
suddenly disrupted an orchestral piece with the most frightful dissonances, and so
forth. A great series of such incidents provided fuel for the witticisms of the local
columnists. But several incidents of another sort quickly stilled the flow of jokes.

293

The first concerned a doctor who had fallen ill with "contradiction" and prescribed a totally fatal remedy for one girl and his patient died. The newspapers were filled with accounts of this incident for several days. In addition, two nurses from the municipal nursery, in an attack of "contradiction," cut the throats of forty-one children. News of this shook the entire city. And on the evening of that same day two sick policemen rolled out a Gatling gun from the building which housed their headquarters and sprayed a peacefully strolling crowd with shot. The dead and wounded totalled some five hundred.

After that all the newspapers and the whole of society demanded that measures be taken against the epidemic. A special joint session of the City Council and the Legislative Chamber decided to immediately invite doctors from other cities and from abroad, in order to expand the existing hospitals, and to open new ones. They further resolved to construct rest homes for the isolation of those stricken with "contradiction," to print and distribute 500,000 copies of a brochure about the new illness, with descriptions of its symptoms and methods of treatment, and to organize a special watch involving both doctors and their aides on each street, for visits to private apartments to administer first aid, etc. It was also decided to send trains daily to all the other cities which would be exclusively for those ill, since the doctors considered a change of locale the best remedy for the disease. Similar measures were taken simultaneously by various private associations, unions, and clubs. A special "Society for Combating the Epidemic" was even organized and its members quickly proved themselves through truly selfless work. But despite the fact that these and other measures were carried out with unfailing energy, the epidemic did not subside but rather increased with each day, striking the aged and the young, men and women, those at work and at rest, the temperate and the dissolute, without distinction. And soon the whole society was gripped by an overpowering primordial fear in the face of the unprecedented disaster.

The flight from Star City began. At first a few individuals, particularly from among the leading dignitaries, directors, members of the Legislative Chamber and City Council, hurriedly sent their families to the southern cities of Australia and Patagonia. Behind them trailed the transient population of newly arrived foreigners who had willingly congregated in this "gayest city of the Southern Hemisphere," artists of every profession, con men of various sorts, women of easy virtue. Later, with the epidemic's new advances, the merchants fled. They quickly sold out their merchandise or left their stores to the whims of fate. The bankers, theater and restaurant owners, and the book and newspaper publishers left with them. Finally, the population at large was affected. By law, former workers were forbidden exit from the Republic without special permission from the government, under threat of losing their pension. But this threat made no difference to those concerned with self preservation. The exodus began. Municipal employees fled, members of the people's militia fled, nurses from the hospitals, pharmacists and doctors fled. The urge to flee subsequently became a mania. Everyone fled who was able.

The electric railroad's stations were besieged by enormous crowds. Train tickets were purchased for enormous sums and obtained by struggle. At the moment of departure, strangers would burst into the cars and refuse to yield the spaces they had captured. Crowds halted those trains that had been provided exclusively for the sick; they dragged them from the cars, occupied their berths and forced the engineers to proceed. The entire rolling stock of the Republic's railroads operated solely on the lines connecting the capital with the port cities after the end of May. The overloaded trains left Star City; passengers stood in all the aisles and even ventured to stand outside the cars, although with the speed of modern electric trains, death by suffocation threatened. Steamship companies in Australia, South America and South Africa made exorbitant profits by transporting emigrants from the Republic to other countries. Trains heading for Star City, by contrast, were almost completely empty. No salary was sufficient to attract persons to work in the capital. Rarely, some eccentric tourists went to the plague-ridden city, those who loved strong sensations. An estimated million and a half persons, that is, almost two thirds of the entire population, left Star City by all six electric railroad lines between the beginning of the emigration and the twenty-second of June, when regular rail service was interrupted.

Horace DeVille, the chairman of the City Council, gained lasting distinc-tion during this period with his enterprise, strength of will, and courage. At the City Council's special session of June 5, by agreement between the Council of Directors and the Legislature, DeVille was granted dictatorial power over the city with the title of Commander. Control of municipal funds, the people's militia, and city enterprises was transferred to him. Subsequently, the govern-ment agencies and archives were removed from Star City to North Port. Among mankind's noblest names, that of Horace DeVille should be inscribed in gold. During the next month and a half he battled growing anarchy within the city. He succeeded in gathering about himself a group of equally selfless aides. For a long time he was able to maintain discipline and obedience among the people's militia and the municipal employees, who were seized with fear in the face of the general disaster and constantly decimated in numbers by the epidemic. Hundreds of thousands owed their salvation to Horace DeVille, for it was thanks to his energy and capable management that they succeeded in escaping. For additional thousands he made the last days more bearable, providing them with the opportunity to die in the hospital, under good care, rather than under the blows of the maddened crowd. In addition, DeVille preserved a chronicle of the entire catastrophe for mankind, because it is impossible to describe in any other terms the brief but concise telegrams which he sent as many as several times daily from Star City to the temporary seat of government in North Port.

DeVille's first act after assuming his position as Commander of the city was to attempt to calm the disturbed population. Manifestos were issued stressing the fact that the psychic infection was most easily transmitted to those who were excited and the healthy and cool-headed were urged to exert their authority over the weak and nervous. At the same time DeVille entered into an alliance with the Society for Combating the Epidemic and assigned its members to all public places, theaters, meetings, squares and streets. During this period scarcely an hour passed without the discovery of the disease in some place or other. First here and then there, individuals or whole groups were noticed who were clearly abnormal in their behavior. For the most part those who understood their own condition immediately desired help. But influenced by a deranged psyche, this desire was expressed in all sorts of hostile actions against those in the immediate vicinity. The ill should have like to hurry home or to the hospital, but instead they began running fearfully toward the city's outskirts. They realized that they should ask others for help, but instead they seized passers-by by the throat, choking and beating them, and sometimes even wounding them with knives and sticks. And so, as soon as a person stricken with "contradiction" approached, the crowds turned and ran. At such moments members of the Society would come to help. Some of them overpowered the afflicted, calmed him and sent him to the nearest hospital; others attempted to bring the crowd to its senses, explaining that there was absolutely no danger and that everyone had to combat this new misfortune with all available means.

In theaters and at gatherings unexpected seizures very often led to tragic consequences. At the opera several hundred spectators who had been stricken by mass insanity, rather than expressing their enthusiasm for the singers, rushed to the stage and showered them with blows. At the Great Dramatic Theater an actor who was to commit suicide in his role was suddenly seized and fired several times into the hall. Of course the revolver was loaded with blanks, but under nervous tension many members of the audience suddenly exhibited signs of the illness that had been previously unexpressed. During the subsequent confusion the natural panic was compounded by the "contradictory" acts of the insane and several score of people were killed. But an incident in the Fireworks Theater proved the most terrible of all. A detail of the city militia which had been ordered there to guard against fire, ignited the stage and curtains behind which the fireworks were stored. No less than two hundred persons died in the flames and crush. After that Horace DeVille ordered the curtailment of all theatrical and musical performances in the city.

The breakdown of society left the way open for pillagers and thieves, who posed a great threat to the residents. We have been led to believe that a number of them came into Star City during this period from abroad. Some affected insanity to escape punishment. Others did not even consider it necessary to conceal their obvious thefts through such sham. Gangs of robbers boldly entered the abandoned stores and carried off the more valuable items, broke into private apartments and demanded gold, or stopped pedestrians and took their valuables, watches, rings and bracelets. In addition to the thefts there was violence of every sort and women suffered especially. The city's Commander dispatched whole detachments of militia against the criminals, but the latter refused to engage in open warfare. Terrible cases of unexpected seizure with "contradiction" occurred, both among the thieves and the militia, with the afflicted turning their weapons against their comrades. At first, the Commander expelled the arrested thieves from the city. But the citizens freed them from prison cars and took their places. The Commander was then forced to sentence street thieves and rapists to death. Thus, after an interval of almost three centuries, open capital punishment was reintroduced in the world.

During June, the city began to feel the lack of basic supplies. Neither provisions nor medication could be obtained. Supplies by rail began to decline and almost all production ceased within the city. DeVille organized a municipal bakery and arranged a distribution of bread and meat to all resident. Public dining halls were constructed on the model of those which had existed in the factories. But it was impossible to find sufficient workers for them. Volunteer laborers worked until exhausted but their numbers continued to decline. The municipal crematoria blazed for days on end but the number of bodies in the mortuaries grew rather than dwindling. Corpses began to be found on the streets and in private homes. Fewer and fewer people serviced the municipality's central functions, including the telegraph, telephone, power, water and sanitation departments. It was astonishing how DeVille managed to be everywhere. He looked after everything. From his communiques, one would think he never rested. And all of those saved were unanimous in their testimony after the catastrophe that his activity deserved the highest praise.

In the middle of June, the shortage of workers on the railway began to be felt. There were no engineers or conductors to operate the trains. On June 17, the first crash occurred on the Southwestern Line, the reason being the engineer's attack of "contradiction." During his seizure, the engineer crashed his train onto an ice field from a height of over thirty feet. Almost all the travellers were either killed or maimed. The news, which was brought into the city with the next train, struck like a bolt of lightning. A hospital train was immediately dispatched. It returned with the corpses and the mutilated, half-dead survivors. But toward evening of the same day, news spread of a similar catastrophe which had occurred on the First Line. Two railroad lines connecting Star City with the world had been ruined. Units were sent from both Star City and North Port to repair the tracks but work in those regions is nearly impossible during the winter months. These two catastrophes simply set the pattern for what followed. The greater the engineers' concern for their duties, the more likely they were to repeat the acts of their predecessors during an attack of the illness. It was precisely because they feared wrecking the trains that they wrecked them. In five days, from the 18th through the 22nd of June, seven trains, all jammed with people, were thrown from the tracks into the void. Thousands of people died from injuries and hunger on the snow-covered plains. Only a very few had sufficient strength to get back to the city. As a consequence, all six of the main lines linking Star City with the world were destroyed. The city's population, now reduced to 600,000, was cut off from all humanity. For a while, only the telegraph wire connected them.

On June 24, the municipal subways stopped running because of a shortage of employees. On June 26, the city's telephone service was interrupted. On June 27, all the pharmacies with the exception of a single central location were closed. On July 1, the Commander issued an order for all residents to move into the city's Central Quarter and to completely abandon the outskirts in order to facilitate the maintenance of order, the distribution of supplies and of medical aid. People left their own apartments and settled in those abandoned by their owners. The sense of ownership disappeared. No one regretted having left what was his, no one felt strange about using someone else's. To be sure, there were still marauders and robbers who might more accurately have been called psychopaths. They continued to steal and their half-rotted corpses can now be found lying alongside veritable treasures of gold and other valuables in the empty chambers of the deserted homes.

It is, however, remarkable that, despite the general destruction, life still kept its previous forms. There were still merchants who kept shop and sold the remaining goods, including flowers, books, weapons, and delicacies at incredible prices. The customers rid themselves of their useless money without regret and the miserly merchants hid it away for some unknown reason. Secret dens for cards, wine, and debauchery still existed and the distressed people hastened to them to forget the terrible reality. The sick mingled there with the healthy and no one has recorded the terrible scenes which occurred. Two or three newspapers still appeared whose editors tried to maintain the meaning of the literary word in the midst of the general rout. Issues of these newspapers, are already selling for ten to twenty times their original price, should become the greatest of bibliographic rarities. Written during a time of insanity and set by half-mad compositors, their columns contain a vivid and frightening account of everything endured by the unhappy city. There were reporters who presented the "news of the city," writers who heatedly discussed the state of affairs, and even columnists who attempted to entertain during those tragic days. But the telegrams which arrived from other countries, describing real, healthy life, must have filled those readers, destined to die, with despair.

People frantically tried to save themselves. At the beginning of July, a huge crowd of men, women, and children led by a John Dew, decided to walk from the city to a nearby settlement, Londontown. DeVille realized the insanity of their effort but was unable to stop them and personally provided warm clothing and supplies of food. The entire crowd, numbering some two thousand, lost its way and perished in the snow covered fields of the polar country during the dark six month's night. A certain Whiting began to preach another, more heroic means. He proposed killing all of of the ill, assuming that the epidemic would subsequently cease. He had more than a few followers but, for that matter, the most insane and inhumane proposition which promised salvation would have found supporters in those dark days. Whiting and his friends searched through the whole city, broke into all the houses, and exterminated the sick. In the hospitals, they committed mass murder. In the course of events,

298

even those were killed who might only have been suspect because they were not completely well. The pillagers and the insane united with these ideological killers. The entire city became a battle ground. During this difficult period, Horace DeVille collected his co-workers into a brigade, inspired them and personally led them into battle against Whiting's forces. For several days the chase continued. Hundreds of persons fell on both sides. Finally Whiting himself was captured. He turned out to be in the final stages of *mania contradicens* and he had to be taken to the hospital rather than executed, and he subsequently died there.

On July 8, the city suffered one of its most terrible blows. Persons supervising the operation of the central electrical station smashed all of the machines during an attack of the disease. The electricity failed and the entire city, its streets, and all its private residences were plunged into absolute darkness. Since no other source of illumination or heating was used in the city, the residents all found themselves completely defenseless. DeVille had anticipated such a danger. He had prepared stores of pitch torches and firewood. Bonfires were lit on the streets. But these feeble lights were insufficient to illuminate the enormous vistas of Star City which stretched in straight lines for tens of kilometers. Nor did they light the imposing heights of the thirty story buildings. With the onset of darkness, the remaining discipline in the city was lost. Terror and madness gripped people's hearts permanently. The healthy could no longer be distinguished from the sick. A fearful orgy of desperate people began.

An astonishingly rapid loss of moral feeling became apparent in everyone. Culture, like a thin crust which had accumulated over the milennia, was sloughed off to expose the savage animal-man such as had once roamed the primordial world. All sense of morality was lost and only force recognized. The lust for pleasure became woman's single standard. The most modest of mothers conducted themselves like prostitutes passing willfully from hand to hand and using the obscene language of the brothel. Girls ran about the streets, provoking those who wished to take advantage of their virginity. They led their chosen mates to the nearest door and surrendered themselves on strangers' beds. Drunks arranged parties in ruined cellars, oblivious to the uncollected bodies lying about them. Everything was increasingly complicated by attacks of the prevailing illness. Those children who had been abandoned to the whims of fate by their parents were in a pitiful situation. Some were raped by corrupt debauchers, others subjected to torture by persons inclined to sadism, who suddenly appeared in significant numbers. Children died from hunger in their nurseries and from the shame and suffering of being raped. They were killed intentionally and by accident. It is asserted that there were monsters who caught children in order to satisfy their aroused cannibalistic instincts.

In this final period of tragedy, Horace DeVille was naturally not able to help the entire population. But in the City Hall, he provided a refuge for everyone who had kept his reason. The entrances were barracaded and continually guarded. Within, a forty days' supply of food and water sufficient for 3000 persons had been prepared. But there were only 1800 men and women with

DeVille. Still others remained in the city with unaffected minds but they did not know of DeVille's shelter and hid themselves in their homes. Many decided not to go out onto the streets and the bodies of those who died of hunger in the solitude of their rooms are now being discovered. It is remarkable that, among those locked in the City Hall, there were very few cases of infection with "contradiction." DeVille knew how to maintain discipline in his small community. Up to the final day, he kept a journal of everything that happened and this journal, together with DeVille's telegrams, provides the best source of information about the catastrophe. This journal was discovered in a secret cabinet in the City Hall, where particularly valuable documents were kept. The last entry dates from the 20th of July. DeVille reports that a maddened crowd had begun to storm the City Hall and that he was forced to repulse the attack with volleys of revolver fire. "What I have to hope for," writes DeVille, "I do not know: It is impossible to expect help before spring. To live until spring with the stores at my disposal is impossible. But I shall carry on my duties until the end." These were DeVille's last words. Noble words!

We must assume that the crowd took City Hall by storm, killing or scattering its defenders. DeVille's body has not yet been found. We have no reliable reports of what took place in the city after the 21st of July. From the evidence now being found while clearing the city, it must be assumed that anarchy reached its extreme at that time. One can imagine the half-darkened streets, lit by the glow of the bonfires built from furniture and books. Flint and steel were used to ignite the fires. Crowds of maddened and drunken people whirled wildly about them. A common cup made the rounds. Men and women drank. Acts of bestial debauchery were committed. Some sort of dark, atavistic feelings arose in the hearts of these urban dwellers. Half-naked, unwashed, and unkempt, they danced the circle dances of their remote ancestors who had lived at the time of the cave bears and they sang the wild songs of the hordes who had attacked mammoths with stone axes. The wild cries of the ill, who were no longer able to express their fevered visions in words, mingled with the groans of the dying who writhed among the decomposing corpses. Sometimes, the dances were replaced by fights—over a barrel of wine, a pretty woman, or simply without cause—in a fit of madness which provoked senseless, contradictory acts. There was no refuge; the same terrible scenes occurred everywhere; orgies, fights, animal merriment and malice. Otherwise there was only the absolute darkness which seemed even more terrifying and unbearable to the shocked imagination.

During these days, Star City was an enormous black box containing several thousand human-like beings who still lived, pressed into the mire of a hundred thousand decomposing corpses. Among the living, not a single person realized his position. It was a city of the insane, a gigantic lunatic asylum, the greatest and most repulsive Bedlam which the world has ever known. And the mad annihilated each other with daggers, slit throats, died from madness, terror, hunger, and all the illnesses which filled the infected air.

Of course, the Republic's government did not remain indifferent to the calamity suffered by the capital. But every hope of providing aid had to be quickly abandoned. Doctors, nurses, military units, and employees of every variety absolutely refused to go to Star City. After travel on the electric railroads halted, direct contact with the city was lost since the severity of the climate there did not permit other means of transportation.In addition, the government's attention soon turned to cases of infection with "contradiction" which became apparent in other cities of the Republic. In some of them, the illness also threatened to assume epidemic proportions and a general panic began, reminiscent of events in Star City. This led to an emigration of residents from all the centers of habitation within the Republic. Work in all the factories was halted and the nation's total industrial life came to a standstill. Prompt action in the other cities made it possible to halt the epidemic, however, and it did not attain the proportions elsewhere that it had in the capital.

We well know of the uneasy concern with which the entire world followed the young Republic's misfortunes. At first the prevailing attitude was one of curiosity, for no one anticipated the incredible magnitude which the disaster would assume. Leading newspapers in all the nations (including our *Northern European Evening News*) sent special correspondents to Star City to report on the course of the epidemic. Many of these brave warriors of the pen fell victim in their professional duty. When news of a threatening nature began arriving, however, the governments of various nations and private organizations offered their services to the government of the Republic. Some sent troops, others organized groups of doctors, still others made donations of money, but events proceeded so rapidly that the majority of these projects could not be completed. After rail connection with Star City halted, the only information about life there was provided by the Commander's telegrams. These telegrams were immediately dispatched to every corner of the earth and sold millions of copies. After the destruction of the electrical generating machinery, the telegraph continued to work for a few days, since there were charged batteries at the station. The exact reason for the complete interruption of telegraph communication is unknown; perhaps the apparatus was destroyed. Horace DeVille's last telegram was dated June 27. For almost a month and a half after this date, humanity was left without news from the Republic's capital.

During the last few days of August a pilot, Thomas Billy, reached Star City by airplane. He picked up two people from the city's roofs who had long since gone mad and were half dead from cold and hunger. Through the ventilators Billy saw that the streets were immersed in absolute darkness, and he heard wild cries which indicated that there were still living beings in the city. Billy decided not to descend into the city itself. By the beginning of September one line on the electric railroad had been reopened as far as Lissis station which is sixty miles from the city. A detachment of well-armed men, equipped with supplies for rendering first aid, entered the city through the Northwest Gate. This detachment, however, was unable to go beyond the first few blocks because of the terrible stench in the air. They had to advance step by step, clearing the street of corpses and disinfecting the air artificially. All the people whom they found to be still alive in the city were out of their senses. They resembled wild animals in their ferocity and they had to be captured by force. Finally, by the middle of September, regular communication with Star City was organized and systematic reconstruction of the city began.

At present the greater portion of the city has already been cleared of corpses. Electric heating and lighting have been reestablished. Only the American sectors remain unoccupied, but it is assumed that there are no living beings there. In all some 10,000 persons were saved, but the greater portion of them have incurable psychic disorders. Those who are more or less recovered are very reluctant to talk about their experiences during the disaster. In addition, their stories are full of contradictions and quite often are not supported by documented facts. In various places issues of newspapers have been found which were issued in the city up until the end of July. The most recent which has been discovered so far is dated July 22, and it contains a report of Horace DeVille's death and an appeal to reestablish the refuge in City Hall. It is true that a sheet has been found dated in August, but its contents are such that its author must be regarded as having been clearly out of his senses. (He had probably personally set the type for his delirious report.) In City Hall Horace DeVille's diary has been discovered, and it provides an ordered chronicle of events for the three weeks from June 28 until July 20. From the terrible discoveries which have been made in the streets and houses, a vivid picture can be constructed of the violence committed in the city during the final days. Everywhere there are mutilated corpses, people who had died of hunger, people who had been choked and tortured, people killed by the insane in a state of frenzy, and finally, half-eaten bodies. Corpses were found in the most unexpected places: subway tunnels, sewer pipes, various storerooms, boilers. Those residents who had lost their minds had sought refuge from the encircling terror everywhere. The interiors of almost all the houses were in shambles, and the goods which the plunderers could not use had been cached in secret rooms and underground chambers.

No doubt several months will pass before Star City is once again inhabited. Now, however, it is almost empty. In a city which can accomodate as many as three million residents, about 30,000 workers now live, engaged in cleaning the streets and houses. Incidentally, a few of the former residents have come to find the bodies of relatives and collect the remnants of their ruined and plundered possessions. A few tourists have also come, attracted by the singular sight of the deserted city. Two businessmen have already opened hotels which are doing a fairly brisk trade. In the near future a small nightclub is being opened, for which entertainers have already been gathered.

The *Northern European Evening News,* in its turn, has sent a new reporter, Mr. Andrew Ewald, to the city and intends to acquaint its readers, through detailed reports, with all the new discoveries which have yet to be made in the unhappy capital of the Republic of the Southern Cross.

valery bryusov / NOW WHEN I HAVE AWAKENED
(The Notes of a Psychopath)

As a matter of course I was considered perverted from childhood. As a matter of course I was assured that no one shared my feelings. And I became accustomed to lying to people's faces. I became accustomed to making cliched speeches about compassion and love, about the joy of loving others. But in the depths of my soul I was convinced, and am convinced even now, that by his very nature man is criminal. It seems to me that amid all the sensations called enjoyment there is only one which is worthy of the name—that which possesses one during the contemplation of the sufferings of another. I dare say that a human being in his primitive condition can thirst for only one thing—to torture others like himself. Our culture has placed its bridle on this natural proclivity. Centuries of slavery have brought the human soul to the belief that the sufferings of others are painful to it. And today people weep for others and have compassion for them with complete sincerity. But this is merely a mirage, a deception of the feelings.

It is possible to prepare a mixture of water and spirits so that any olive oil added to it will remain in equilibrium under all circumstances, neither rising to the surface nor sinking to the bottom. In other words, the earth's gravitation will cease to affect it. In the physics textbooks it is said that then, submitting solely to the stress inherent in its particles, the oil will gather into the form of a sphere. Similar to this are those moments when the human soul liberates itself from the power of its gravity, from all goals which are implanted in it through heredity and upbringing, from all external influences usually conditioning our will: from fear of judgment, from the sickness of social opinion and so on. These are not hours of simple sleep when the consciousness of daytime, although having been extinguished, still continues to control our slumbering "ego"; these are not those days of insanity, mental derangement, when in place of ordinary influences there come others even more absolute. These are moments of that strange condition when the body rests in sleep, but the mind suddenly realizes this and says to its spectre who wanders in the world of fantasies: you are free! Understand that your actions will exist only for yourself and you will voluntarily surrender to your own proclivities arising out of the murky depths. In such moments I have never experienced the desire to perform any act of virtue. On the contrary, knowing that I shall remain entirely—to the furthest limit—unpunished, I hasten to commit some wild, evil, and sinful act.

I always loved dreams. I consider in no way lost the time spent in dreams. Dreaming fills the soul with reality and arouses it to such a degree, giving joy and sorrow, that it must be acknowledged as an equal of our waking life. Strictly speaking, dreams are also reality, but a different form of it. Which one prefers—depends on one's personal inclination. From childhood dreams have always been more pleasing to me. Even as a young boy I got used to considering a night without dreams a burdensome deprivation. If I happened to wake up without remembering my dreams, I felt unhappy. The whole day, at home and at school, I would torturously strain my memory until suddenly, in its obscurest corner, I discovered a fragment of forgotten pictures and, with a new effort, suddenly uncovered in all its brilliance this latest dream life. Then I would greedily immerse myself in this resurrected world and reinstate all of its minute details. With this cultivation of my memory I reached the point where I never forgot my dreams. I waited for the night and dreams as though for the hour of a desired rendez-vous.

I especially loved nightmares, because of the shuddering power of their impressions. I developed in myself the ability to summon them forth artificially. I had only to fall asleep, with my head lower than my body, for the nightmare to clutch me almost immediately in its sweetly tormenting claws. I would wake up from an indescribable languor, gasping, but no sooner had I breathed in some fresh air than I hastened once again to plunge there, to the black bottom, to terror and panic. From the earliest years I loved even more those conditions in dreams when you knew that you were dreaming. I comprehended then what great freedom of the spirit they provided. Incidentally, I did not know how to summon them forth at will. In a dream it was as though I suddenly received an electrical shock and suddenly realized that the world was now in my power. I proceeded along the roads of dream, through its palaces and valleys wherever I wished. With concentrated desire I could envisage myself in that circumstance which pleased me, I could introduce into my dream that person whom I expected. In earliest childhood I used these moments to play the fool with people, to perform all manner of tricks. But with the years I moved to other more sacred joys: I seduced women, I committed murders and became an executioner. And only then did I realize that ecstasy and intoxication were not empty words.

The years passed. The days of school and subjugation passed. I was alone. I had no family, I did not have to earn the right to life by labor. Mine was the possibility of dedicating myself undividedly to my joy. I spent the greater part of the day in dream and slumber. I took advantage of various narcotics: not strictly for the sake of the promised enjoyments, but in order to prolong and deepen the dream. Experience and habit offered me the possibility of more and more frequently intoxicating myself with the most unconditional of freedoms that a person could dare dream of. Gradually my nocturnal consciousness in these dreams approached in strength and clarity my daytime consciousness and, to be sure, even began to exceed the latter. I knew how to live in my fantasies and contemplate this life from all sides. It was as though I observed my spectre performing in the dream, directed him, and at the same time experienced with all passion every one of his sensations.

I created a more appropriate setting for my dreams. It was a large room somewhere deep underground. It was illuminated by the red fire of two huge ovens. The walls,to the eye,were iron. The floor stone. Here were all the usual appurtenances of torture: the rack, the stake, chairs with nails, an apparatus for stretching the muscles and for crushing the abdomen, foot tongs, whips, cutting instruments, red-hot pokers and rakes. When joyous fate oppressed my freedom, I immediately, resolutely, entered again into my secret retreat. With a concentrated effort of desire I introduced into this subterranean chamber whomsoever I wished, at times people with whom I was familiar, more often figments of my imagination, usually girls and youths, pregnant women, children. For me there had emerged certain favorite types of sacrifice. I knew them by name. In some I found exquisite the beauty of their bodies, in others their courage in bearing the most extreme tortures, their scorn for all my contrivances, in the third, on the contrary, their weakness, their lack of will, their moans and vain pleadings. Sometimes, and not infrequently at that, I forced those whom I had tortured to be resurrected so that once again I might enjoy their suffering death. At first I alone was both executioner and spectator. Then I created for myself, as helpers, a pack of misshapen dwarfs. Their number grew according to my desire. They presented me with the instruments of torture and carried out my commands, laughing and sneering. In their midst I celebrated my orgies of blood and fire, cries and curses.

Probably I would have remained insane, solitary and happy. But the few friends I had, finding me sick and close to mental derangement, wanted to save me. Almost by force they made me go out, to spent time in theaters and in society. I suspect that they contrived to present in the most attractive light the girl who thereupon became my wife. Incidentally, there hardly could have been a man who would have considered her unworthy of adulation. All the charms of woman and human beings in general were united in the one whom I loved, whom I called so often my own and whom I shall never cease to bewail the rest of my life. And they depicted me to her as a sufferer, as an unhappy person who had to be saved. She began with curiosity and then turned to the fullest and most unselfish passion.

For a long time I could not make up my mind and contemplate marriage. However powerful the feeling was which captivated my heart for the first time, I was terrified by the thought of losing my solitude which had revealed such horizons to me that I could in complete freedom drink my fill of the visions in my dreams. However, the correct life towards which I was driven gradually obscured my consciousness. I sincerely believed that in my soul there could be some transfiguration, that it could renounce a truth unrecognized by people other than myself.

My friends congratulated me on the day of the wedding as if I had emerged from the grave to the sun. After the honeymoon my wife and I settled in a bright and cheerful new home. I convinced myself that the events of the world and the news of the city interested me; I read newspapers, kept up acquaintances. Once again I learned to stay awake during the day. At night after the frenzied embraces of two lovers I was customarily overcome by a dead, senseless sleep without other dimensions and without images. In this temporary blindness I was prepared to rejoice at my cure, my resurrection from insanity into everyday life.

But, of course, never, oh never! The desire for other ecstasies did not die completely. It was only muffled by an overly sensible reality. And in the days of the honeymoon, of the first month after the wedding, I felt somewhere in the secret recesses of my soul an unsated thirst for more blinding and staggering impressions. With each new week this thirst tormented me more and more relentlessly. And together with it another relentless desire grew, which at first I could not make up my mind to acknowledge to myself: the desire to take her, my wife, whom I loved, to my nocturnal celebrations, and to see her face distorted from the agonies of her body. I struggled, I struggled for a long time, attempting to maintain my sobriety. I convinced myself with all the conclusions of logic, but I myself could not believe in them. In vain I sought distractions, not allowing myself to remain alone—the temptation was within me, there was nowhere to escape from it.

And finally I yielded. I pretended that I had undertaken a large work on the history of religions. I placed some wide couches in my library and began to lock myself in there for the night. A little later I began to spend entire days there. In every possible fashion I concealed my secret from my wife; I trembled lest she discover what I hid so jealously. She was as dear to me as before. Her caresses gave me no less pleasure than during the first days of our life together. But I was more attracted by a powerful sensuality. I could not explain my behavior to her. I preferred even that she think that I had ceased to love her and that I was avoiding relations with her. And in fact she thought so, languished and suffered. I saw that she was growing pale and withering, that grief would lead her to the grave. But whenever I submitted to a burst of passion and spoke the usual words of love to her, she would revive only for an instant: she could not believe me, because my actions, so it appeared, were in too great a contradiction with my words.

Although I spent in dreams, as formerly, almost entire days on end, surrendering myself to my visions even more undividedly than before marriage— for some reason or other I lost my former ability to assert my complete freedom. For weeks on end I remained on my couches, awakening only in order to strengthen myself with wine or broth, to take a fresh dose of some soporific— but the desired moment did not come. I experienced the sweet torments of the nightmare, its extravagance and mercilessness, I could not recall and thread together a long series of multiple-imaged dreams, at first logical and terrifying because of this triumphant logic, and then wildly disconnected, exquisite and majestic in the insanity of their combinations—but my consciousness continued to remain enveloped in some manner of obscurity. I did not possess the power to manipulate my dream, I had to listen and contemplate what was presented to me from somewhere below, by someone. I sought recourse in all the devices

and means known to me, in all the available poisons: I artificially destroyed
my blood circulation, hypnotized myself, took opium and hashish, and all
manner of stimulating drugs, but they afforded me only their own spells.
Coming to myself I recalled the sensual visions in which I was impotently
plunged with rage, as if I were the plaything of someone else's will which I
was unable to control. I was exhausted from fury and desire, but impotent.

As I recall, more than six months passed, counting from the time when
I returned to my interrupted delight in fantasies, until that day when my most
sacred happiness was first returned to me. In sleep I suddenly felt that electrical
shock so well known to me and suddenly I understood that once again I was
free, that I was dreaming but able to control my dream, that I was able to perform everything that I desired, and that all this would merely remain a dream!
A wave of indescribable ecstasy flooded my soul. I could not resist my old temptation then. No, I did not wish for my subterranean chamber. I preferred to
appear in whatever situation to which I was drawn, which had been arranged
for me. This was a more refined enjoyment. And suddenly, with my second
dream-world consciousness, I saw myself standing behind the doors of my
library.

"Let's go," I said to my spectre, "Let's go, she is sleeping now, and take
with you a slender dagger, whose handle is worked in fine ivroy."

Submitting, I proceeded along the familiar path, through unlighted rooms.
It seemed to me that I was not walking, not moving my feet, but drifting, as it
often happens in a dream. Passing through the salon I saw in the windows the
rooftops of the city and thought: "All this is in my power." The night was
moonless, but the sky glistened with stars. From behind chairs my dwarfs were
about to emerge, but I made the sign to them to disappear. Soundlessly I
opened the door of the bedroom a crack. A small lamp illuminated the room
sufficiently. I approached the bed where my wife slept. She lay as though
weak, small and emaciated; her hair, braided for the night into two strands,
hung down from the bed. By the pillow lay a handkerchief: she had been
crying, as she lay there, crying that once again I had not come to her. A feeling
of remorse gripped my heart. At this moment I was ready to believe in compassion. There flashed within me a desire to fall on my knees before her bed
and kiss her chilled feet. But at once I reminded myself that all this was
a dream.

A wonderously strange feeling assailed me. I could satisfy my secret
longing—to do all that I desired with this woman. And all this would remain
unknown to her. And in the waking world I could surround her with all the
ecstasy of caresses, comfort her, love and cherish her... Bending over the body
of my wife I seized her throat with a strong hand so that she could not scream.
She woke up immediately, opened her eyes and began to struggle beneath my
hand. But it was as though I had nailed her to the bed, and she writhed, trying
to push me away, bursting to say something to me, looking at me with terrified
eyes. For several moments I gazed at her, filled with an indescribable excitement, then I suddenly struck her with my dagger, in the side, under the

307

blanket. I watched her shudder all over, strain, still unable to scream, but her eyes filled with despair and tears welled out of them. And along the hand holding the dagger flowed sticky, warm blood; I slowly began to deal her more blows, I tore off the blanket and struck her naked body as she strove to protect herself, stand up and crawl. Then I seized her by the head and plunged the dagger into her neck, sideways, behind the jugular vein. I concentrated all my strength and tore through the throat. The blood began to spurt because, dying, she was trying to breathe, her hands wildly wanted to seize something or wave about. Then she was motionless.

Then such a shattering despair gripped my soul that I at once tore myself away in order to wake up, and could not. I exerted all the effort of my will, expecting that the walls of the bedroom would fall away suddenly, depart and melt away, that I would see myself on my couch in the library. But the nightmare did not pass. The bloodied and deformed body of my wife was before me on the bed, covered with blood. And in the doorway crowds of people with candles swarmed around, having rushed there after hearing the sound of the struggle—and their faces were distorted with horror. They did not say a word, but just looked at me, and I at them.

Then suddenly I realized that this time everything that had happened was not a dream.

Translated by Samuel Cioran

boris sadovskoy / LAMIA

For the past month, sitting alone at evening tea, I have been finishing a new article. It has been a long while now since I have written anything. I have not been feeling well. On that day I had felt an unpleasant, cold heaviness in my head since morning; I felt sick at heart; life seemed boring and useless. The wearisome shadow of evening spleen oppressed me ever more tediously and malevolently, and I was already preparing to retire so as to chase away my headache until morning with dull oblivion—when all at once my brain suddenly and unexpectedly returned to its former keeness. I felt fresh and healthy. The feverish melancholy disappeared; the murky gloom in my head, like a snow-storm in a field at night, was illuminated by a transparent moonlight. It seemed that never before had my mind reached such clear, silver heights.

Then suddenly complete silence descended and I froze with uplifted pen. A gentle trembling spread sweetly and sickeningly down my spine—it seemed to me that someone had entered my lonely apartment. For several moments I strove to distinguish the fluttering sounds of the night, and could not tell whether these were footsteps, or the measured fall of drops from the wash-basin. It was neither a mouse gnawing behind the clothes-closet nor my dog Jack lounging in the front hallway and clinking his collar on the rug. Finally, the door into the dining room softly creaked twice, and it was no longer possible to doubt that someone, standing by the threshold of the darkened living room, was uncertainly shuffling his feet in one spot and could not make up his mind to enter. I was seized by an even more violent trembling but I did not move and waited, peering at the doors.

She appeared on the threshold.

The same gray school dress with the regulation pinafore; the same crumpled red ribbon in her black braid. Her hands, as usual, hung limply along her hips. On Zina's fresh cheeks lurked a gentle flush; she smiled. With their customary sly tenderness her sweet eyes gazed at me.

I was not so much upset as surprised. Silently we gazed at each other.

Jack rattled his collar; tapping lightly with his claws, he ran into the dining room and burrowed in my knees. I was still leaning forward expectantly, peering into the black maw of the living room; there was no longer anyone at the door. After Zina there remained in the air only the barely perceptible scent of her beloved violets. Silently I sat stroking Jack, feeling no anxiety whatsoever. Only the earlier murky weariness returned instantly to me and finally resulted in a distressing weakness and sleep.

The following day I spent walking aimlessly. For a long while I wandered along the frozen strees and snowy boulevards with a feeling of unconquerable boredom, sitting down for a while on the benches which were covered over with snow and listening to the frosty cawing of crows. At night I could not sleep. Mice scratched tirelessly, drops fell into the water-basin with wearying monotony, Jack lounged about on the floor, constantly rustling his tail. Seeing that I would never manage to fall asleep, I arose, lit a candle, and after dressing went outside.

Beneath the dull glow of the winter moon the snow glowed like pale blue china. The sidewalks sparkled weakly beneath the rays of the flickering street lamps; the benumbed streets slumbered forlornly. I walked, passing one corner after the other, and suddenly found myself on the edge of town. Further, beyond the square, an endless expanse began to glisten with a somber silverness.

I stopped just before the gates. My intent gaze could distinguish nothing in the distant white expanse. Before me rose the imposing bank of the Volga like a gigantic snowdrift. So barren and uninviting was this deserted view resembling eternity that my heart contracted.

I turned to the right and approached quite close to the monastery enclosure. From behind the bronze gates, glimmered a dense net of crosses and grave stones. The ancient eyes of the church gazed forbiddingly down on me, and with an eerie feeling I thought of the monks sleeping at this moment in tomb-like cells together with corpses. Were any of them thinking of the hour of death on this night?

Pressing my face against the icy grating, I saw Zina's grave clearly in the distance. Above it a large marble cross gleamed white. I imagined Zina in her grave, wearing a muslin dress with white roses on her breast. Her blue fingers clutched an ikon.

Are you comfortable, maiden,
So deep beneath the earth?

. . . .

Weary and resigned I rode home in a carriage and dreamed about how nice it would be to fall asleep now in a warm bed. However, hardly had I opened the door and entered the dark hallway when my heart contracted and began to ache. I was struck above all by the strange, eerie silence in the rooms. It was strange that I had not noticed this silence outside. It was so silent that I felt uncomfortable. The silence permeated the air, rang, shouted in my ears. Taking off my fur coat, I coughed loudly and dropped my walking stick, but these sounds did not disperse the frozen silence of the grave. I quickly passed into the bedroom and immediately lit the candles. Should I call the servant from downstairs? But thinking it over I rejected this idea: it was already three o'clock. I took up my notebook and began to reread what I had written on the previous evening.

I placed one more candle on the table before a small mirror. Then, closing the notebook, I cast a despairing glance into the mirror; in the glass a dark figure was reflected behind me. I recognized Zina immediately. She was standing motionless behind me as before, with her arms hanging at her sides, and looking at me mockingly. This time her face was dark as though poured of lead; in her eyes there glimmered somber hatred, and in the grimace of her bared teeth I seemed to perceive a secret malicious joy. It was all the more frightening because our

310

eyes met in the mirror. This was so terrifying that my knees began to tremble and I almost lost consciousness. With a great effort of will, I cast the candle on the floor and hurled myself into the bed without undressing, burying my head. All night I could not sleep from terror, and I languished in melancholy grief until finally the white wintery day grew light in the room.

In the morning I set about taking all the mirrors out of my apartment and did not leave the house before dinner. With dessert I drank some wine and gradually fell asleep on the couch in the dining room. The boundless evening silence roused me. I awoke in the dusk, alone, and I looked about anxiously. No one was there. I rang and ordered tea prepared. Jack ran in, rubbed against me, and then lay down at my feet.

Until midnight I sat by the samovar reading *Hamlet,* engrossed in my favorite poet. But then gradually and imperceptibly the familiar tedious mournfulness which little by little distracted me from the book began to stir once again in my heart. Something prevented me from concentrating—I listened carefully: the drops were falling regularly; a mouse was scratching diligently.

The door into the living room creaked, swung slightly ajar and then closed again. I hid my face in the worn volume of Shakespeare; the pleasant smell of the printed pages, as it were, calmed me, but my temples were pounding with all their might. Groping without looking, I stretched out my hand to the bell; no one came. I rang once, then again—and suddenly I realized that I was shaking with a petty, faint-hearted trembling. The door creaked once again; this time someone walked resolutely towards me from the living room: the parquet floor creaked beneath the heavy steps. Intermingling with the odor of the book was another one, heavy, unpleasant, yet familiar, which gradually became more and more offensive to my sense of smell. Finally I clearly heard that the person standing at the door had moved into the dining room; at this point was standing by the door itself and, of course, staring fixedly at me. The unbearable silence lacerated my hearing. I threw the book on the table and opened my eyes.

She was standing in the doorway, her feet planted wide apart, and slowly swaying in place, her hands leaning against the door frame. Her face was black like coal. There were no lips at all—only dazzling horse-like teeth illuminated her dark sunken cheeks with a horrible gleam. She crossed the threshold with effort. Her violet-black clenched hands fell soundlessly along her bony hips; dampness and death were exuded by her semi-decomposed clothing.

I wanted to leap up, call for help—and I could not. Dimly I saw the trembling, ruffled Jack, his fur standing on end, crawl beneath the table, but I did not have the strength to take my eyes away from the terrifying corpse who was slowly approaching me. I remember the bony arms were extended and then everything disappeared.

In the morning I awoke calm and gay in my armchair. Fear and grief had left me for good. Changing my clothes, I noticed blood on my nightshirt; on the left of my chest there was a small wound.

311

And from that time on Zina came to me every night. At first she seemed dead, terrifying, like a corpse, but gradually coming to life she was transformed at last back into the flowering bride I had once known. How beautiful she was the last time. I lay naked on the bed—and thirstily seizing me, she clung with her rosy lips to my weary breast with such passion! I smelled the scent of violets from her curly head; a black strand of hair tickled my shoulder sweetly.

But when she was leaving me Zina looked into my eyes with such mournfulness! Her crimson lips, still flushed with hot blood, timidly and tenderly touched my dried out lips. For the first time I heard her voice. Good-bye, my love!—the silvery sounds rang in the silence.

Three nights have passed since that time. She has not come to me and will not come. Now it is my turn to go to her. The hour of meeting is near. Zina, I love you!

Translated by Samuel Cioran

zinaida gippius / HE HAS DESCENDED

There was a meeting.

A snowstorm was howling; it was pitch dark in the street. People were coming in the gate to Vasil Silantich's. They stamped their feet at the threshold, and they stamped them on the porch. They came alone, in pairs, and in threes.

The night was dark, stormy, but even if it were not—fear was only for the faint-hearted; all of the village of Efremovka was there—all of its own, the faithful. But the village Krutoe was six versts away. But there were many of His followers there too. Semyon Dorofeich himself lived in Krutoe. He traveled to Efremovka because Vasil Silantich's cottage was well suited for their purposes.

He had a large room added on which faced entirely on the back yard and was without windows.

It was there that they gathered.

Daryushka arrived with her husband Ivan Fedotych. They met with others in the back yard. All came, muffled, carrying bundles.

There was already a crowd on the front porch of Vasil Silantich's cottage. Beside the host, up front sat the leader himself, Semyon Dorofeich, a mature man, not old, but not young, his beard all gray.

Someone came—they bowed low and exchanged greetings.

Daryushka sat down on the bench too, in the row where the women were sitting. She pulled her dark kerchief lower.

They were silent. And the door kept banging: more and more new brethern and sisters kept arriving, bowing, exchanging greetings and sitting a ways off.

Then the door ceased banging. Ivanushka, Vasil Silantich's son, went out into the yard to see if anyone else was coming and to lock the gates.

A latecomer entered with him. But no one else came—everyone was there.

"Is that everyone?" Semyon Dorofeich asked again.

Then he stood up, the men stood up after him, holding their bundles; and they passed through the porch into the far door.

There were other side-rooms, warm ones, and a small bedroom where they got dressed.

Everyone knew the rules well; each knew the situation, and therefore there was no bustle, no disorder. The sisters remained quietly seated, and when the men had changed, they also went into the spare bedroom to dress.

There was no frivolous conversation. They hastened to change and were silent.

Daryushka nimbly removed all her clothing: stockings, slippers, and she even removed her chemise—and with practiced agility threw over herself another one taken from the bundle, one with wide long sleeves that reached down to her ankles. Over the top she tied yet another white skirt. Everything was in the

313

bundle—a kerchief and a scarf as well. Old Afinushka did not take her stockings off because she had sore feet, but all the other sisters were barefoot.

They lit the candles, one from the other, and silently passed through the doorway into the altar room.

None of the faces, neither the old nor the young, were as solemn and melancholy now as they had been in the hut beneath dark kerchiefs. To be sure, they had brightened and warmed up from the burning candles.

But it was ever so much warmer and brighter in the altar room. Brighter than a church on Easter Morning. Along the windowless wooden walls clusters of candles burned, and up above, hanging from the ceiling, was a candleholder with candles in it. On the floor they had tightly stretched clean sacking.

The brethren sat on benches along the walls. Semyon Dorofeich was on a bench in the corner, by the table covered with folded tablecloths on which a brass cross lay.

Daryushka knew that not all ships of the spirit held such well laid out, expansive altar rooms—and she was happy. She firmly believed that she came sincerely and loved the services. However, even when she whirled about in a circle a great deal, both by herself and in the general ecstasy, both in a single file along the wall and in the circles their processions took, even though she sometimes experienced joyfulness and languid release—she herself had never before been transformed in spirit, nor had she ever made prophecies. "It befits my unworthiness," she would usually say. Within Daryushka, no matter how she whirled, or how intoxicated she became, everything remained somehow stable, unperturbed, dulled.

Even her face was precisely like that: clear, passive, as round as an egg, youthful-looking for her age. But she had already passed twenty-eight.

When the "celebrants were successful," when many took part in the services, when many made prophecies, became intoxicated from the holy "draught"—they also conducted the "destruction of sin by sin": Daryushka, with all the others, exhausted, would fall on the floor, and when the lights were extinguished she would take as her groom "whomever the spirit designated." She would take him simply, simply believing that one had to do so. But in the end even this "holy sin" had never aroused her imperturbable calmness; and as for the unholy sin of the flesh, of worldliness—there was nothing to be said about that. Daryushka had married the elderly Ivan Fedotych when she was still a young girl. At the time he had only been sizing up the true faith. Well, at first they had lived as all people live. But very soon Ivan Fedotych recognized the truth and "having taken a wife—he put her away": and Daryushka understood, and it seemed to her that there was no better place to turn to! Daryushka had a secret worldly sin: a fellow who had come to Krutoe had pleased her. So he had taken her in a small copse. But even if the fellow had pleased her— and she had broken off the whole business with him—the sin tormented her. Daryushka had not confessed her sin to the ship of the spirit, but she burnt her own hands with brimstone; and this fellow became worse than bad for her, he became more repulsive than an enemy. And after that she was even more intimately attracted to the services.

Daryushka caught sight of the bright room—and for some reason this time she recalled her earthly sin; and she was ashamed and terrified. And she was happy that it had been long ago, and now it was bright and radiant here once again.

They began to draw near, bow deeply to one another and exchange kisses.

Everyone sat down with their kerchiefs on their knees. They were silent. The candles burned, flickered; on the other side of the windowless walls the snowstorm groaned and rumbled; and all in white they sat there silent, waiting, and it was as if something were growing in the soul of each one.

Semyon Dorofeich arose, bowed to the host.

"Now then, give us leave, our most gracious host, to rejoice with His majesty the Father, to enjoy the heavenly drink, to take possession of the divinity of brilliance—to take Him for a turn in the holy circle..."

Vasily Silantich replied to him with a long speech, and everyone crossed himself and thereupon began to sing, all at once, harmoniously, long and drawn-out tones, hollowly in the high empty room. They sang a prayer to Jesus:

> Give us, Lord,
> Give us Jesus Christ.
> Give us Your Son,
> Lord God, have mercy on us!

And the verses followed one after the other without interruption. Daryushka had a fine voice, and she knew almost all the verses and always loved to sing. And today for some reason or other she sang especially well. And Varvarushka, standing beside her, sang resonantly. The plaintive singing was slow, slow and then imperceptibly began to pick up.

> Oh love, love,
> You, the most sweet,
> You, the power of the mightiest!
> You, the martyr of all who are saved,
> Oh love, love,
> Pure love!...

Daryushka did not think of anything when she sang of love, but in her eyes there were tears.

> You flow, love,
> In the heart of God,
> Sing forth, love,
> All listen to me!

The candle flames flickered, warming the room; the warm blue smoke from the censer filled one's eyes. Rhythmically, like the waves of song, the white figures moved up and down. And suddenly, all at once, just as if a high-pitched wail were breaking loose more and more often:

> Give heed to God,
> Do not deny the flesh,
> Do not deny Martha,
> Serve God...

Someone leapt into the circle. It was Domnushka; she was always the first. Dressed all in white she whirled and circled; the long white sleeves flew about, a warm wind wafted from the stirred flames.

Now it was no longer only Domnushka, there were already four wings turning red, not four, but six, eight...

As though not by her own will, but seized by the hot air, Daryushka rushed into the circle too. She had never felt like this before. But then it was as if no one were himself. The celebration had succeeded very well.

> To whom is meet—be attired
> To whom is not—be retired...

The verses flowed; in the circle someone was already prophesying. Daryushka, suffocating, flying as though downward on her white sailes, was speaking, shouting something, without herself hearing what. Then she heard, but it was as if the voice were not her own:

"Come with us, Christ, descend from the heavens, Almighty Holy Ghost... He has descended, He has descended! I, the Holy Spirit, will speak unto you, I will show everyone love, I will set you on the path, I will praise the Christians! Confess your sins to me, the Holy Spirit, surrender yourselves to me. I will release you in sin, I will show all the truth!

Many listened to Daryushka in fear. Then when she began to whirl once again—everyone began to circle and dance without ceasing their singing, growing exhausted and melting like hot wax:

> Let us recall the Apostles' time,
> When the Holy Spirit descended
> And from the mighty breath
> The thunderous voice did spread...

A whistling echoed through the room from the flying robes. One, another, a third candle was extinguished. And suddenly each one began to go out, quickly, one after the other, as if someone were putting them out, as if there had been too much light and fire in the room and they were no longer necessary:

> Love, love...
> All live by me,
> All worlds of worlds.
> With beauty
> The heavens are filled.

Daryushka came to herself. She remembered that she had gently fallen in the middle of the circle, lowered herself to the floor just as a bird alights on a branch. The verses still continued, but they were dissipating, dying away. Rustling, whispering, sighs sounded among them. At first Daryushka felt a crowd around her, but then suddenly—one person embraced her, firmly possessively, as no one had ever done before. And she immediately understood and felt that it was he, her first and only groom, he whom the Spirit had designated for her. And everything melted within her, as though from a ray of sunlight, and she gave herself to her groom, thinking of nothing and knowing nothing— to the mysterious, eternal one and the only husband who had long been promised her, according to the Lord's command...

* * * * *

When they began to light the candles again everyone was already standing, sitting or strolling around the room.

They held services for a long time, until dawn.

Semyon Dorofeich prophesied. They sang. Then they sat down to table.

Then they gave thanks and took leave of each other. Quickly they changed clothes in silence, swaying on their feet and smiling. They departed not as they had come, but more in solitude, as if not recognizing each other.

Then snowstorm had grown still, only the drifts swept along. The faint light of dawn tinted the snow blue.

Daryushka arrived at her hut, glanced inside as though into someone else's, then all in smiles for some reason went up to the bed, lay down and immediately fell into a deep sleep. She did not hear her husband come in and lay down too.

In the morning people from every house failed to go to mass in Krutoe, even though it was an important holiday. Not all of them had sufficient strength to get up. The more lively went. But no one in Krutoe was surprised: there was so much snow, the drifts had piled up—the roads were completely covered.

They gathered after mass, sang hymns and read. Everyone had grown even more serene; beneath the sisters' kerchiefs it was as if there were no faces. When they met Daryushka—it was as if they bowed down lower. She was walking in the Spirit.

Daryushka was entirely serene. She was thinking of nothing, had turned within herself, peering inside; and inside her all was smiling ever so gently.

After the storm clear days came, frosty, crackling, clear days. Snow and sky, snow and sky, and the sky was even brighter, whiter, from the snow— and the snow sparkled with blue fires from the sky.

Daryushka went down to the river with buckets, to the ice-hole. She went down to the landing alone... Snow, and sky, and brilliance...

She set the buckets down, looked around although there was nothing to look at. She fancied that it was as though something were wrong. For a long while now she had been thinking about something anxiously.

It was not, in fact, sin—but holiness, illumination, the fullness of the Holy Spirit that enveloped her. The Holy Spirit had revealed her groom to her.

Shown her... But whom? Who was he?

Daryushka did not know herself, and could not guess on the first day who he was. Romanushka? Nikitushka? Or, perhaps, the leader, Semyon Dorofeich? Maybe it was him. Or maybe Nikitushka. Perhaps even Romanushka. She did not know and would never know, and here she felt with a gnawing grief that it was impossible for her not to know, she could not want not to know. It made no difference to her who he turned out to be—even Nikitushka, even Romanushka—as long as he appeared. But it was impossible for him to appear. And every day she would meet with her spiritual mate— and never recognize him; and he would never recognize her, because he did not know who she was.

Daryushka was frightened, she sat down by the ice-hole, sat and gazed at the snow. What a sin it was, Lord! Or was it not a sin? What was it?

Again she fell into gnawing, restless thought: was it Romanushka? Maybe Savelyushka... And what difference did it make to her? Really, never to know. Perhaps Savelyushka... She scooped up the water, and walked away along the path. The buckets were heavy, they pressed downwards; the water dripped and froze into long icicles...

They said there would be another service soon. Once again...

And suddenly Daryushka took such a fright that she could not carry the buckets; she set them on the snow and sat down beside them. The Holy Spirit had designated a groom for her, the one true, genuine groom. He had been designated forever. And she, like one blind, would ask Him, the leader, ask about him once again. Would he turn his gaze upon her unworthiness? But if this is a sin? If the Spirit did not descend this time for her blindness? She would not submit to him, her groom, who had been designated to her in truth, but to someone else, to a stranger, whoever it happened to be...as it had always been before.

Daryushka began to weep from fear. This could go on no longer! A sin, a mighty sin! Here it was, this sin, filthy, terrible! This could not go on any longer, no matter what.

She thought not in words, but tears, tears of lamentation, a woman's tears. And it seemed to her that there was no hope to be expected from any quarter. Where could help possibly come from? What it was—was not to be known; the Spirit had designated him, and she must remain faithful to the Spirit. Inform the ship of the spirit? But of what? She did not know how to do so.

And there was a groom—and yet there was not. She was a bride, and yet he did not know her. The Spirit had descended, and she had not perceived; she had lost him, blind as she was.

What help could she expect from people?

All around her there was sparkling snow and sky, sky and snow.

Once again Daryushka took up the yoke and struggled homeward. She knew only one thing, that now she would not go to the service for anything.

"I'll ask leave of the leader to go wandering" she thought. "He'll let me go. Many go wandering. So I won't go to the services. I can already see that I'm finished! It makes no difference, nothing will change. If I'm to be finished, then finished I must be!"

The silly woman walked and wept; drops of water fell from the buckets and froze; the sun played in the long icicles. But she walked on; and now forgetting about her decision to go wandering, she once again was thinking, listlessly and persistently, senselessly, about only one thing: "Who? Isn't it Romanushka? Maybe Fedoseyushka? Or Nikitushka? Or Mikhailushka?"

Maybe it really was ikhailushka. It was someone, but he was—no one.

Translated by Samuel Cioran

pavel nilus / SUMMER HEAT

I was a youth at that time and a guest on my aunt's estate.

Three cousins and I spent all our time together; we took walks together, read, rode horseback, and apparently it never once entered my mind that they were women.

But once we made our way as usual to the garden beneath the apple trees—our favorite spot.

It was July. The intense heat had sapped all the juices of the grass, the trees, the soil and it seemed that out of the soil's cracks departed its final burning breath.

In a few days the leaves in the garden turned yellow and the pale apples, lusterless and soft like wax, quickly began to ripen amid the azure sky and goldening foliage.

We lay on grass which was dried and crushed to the ground, gazed at the patterns of leaves and fruit in the sky and listened as worm-eaten fruit broke loose and fell with a soft bump, bouncing on the ground.

Near the well at the edge of the garden, in the thicket where it was always cool and green, a cuckoo sang in throaty tones. First it would fall silent and then once again begin its cuckooing and we made riddles, counted and exchanged quips.

My cousins were then in the full bloom of youth. Their bodies were supple and strong. Thick hair hung behind their delicate, pretty heads. They were cheerful, loved pranks and their young neighbors were in love with them. And now we were all in the power of nature, of the earth, an earth overflowing with the joy of fruitfulness: the hay had already been harvested from the fields, in the gardens ripened the pears, apples, and golden melons, and the vineyard was overflowing... We were in the power of the sun which was forcing our own bodies to ripen together with the fruits of the earth. We surrendered to the sweet languor—and some new sensation fogged my head.

A caterpillar was crawling along my neck. I sat up, lazily knocked the soft, downy, writhing little ball to the ground, and kneeling, gazed inadvertantly at Liza.

She lay on her back with her plump white arms crossed behind her head; her cheeks were spread with a mottled flush; her downy eyebrows described an arc curving downwards, disappearing in the fine down of her skin; her long eyelashes trembled; her breast heaved... Everyone said that Liza was a beauty, but I did not believe it. At that time it seemed to me that a beauty was something distant, unreachable.

But this time I was struck by her. With curiosity I examined her—and suddenly I had a desire to kiss her lips thirstily.

We often kissed: we called it "playing telegraph." Usually we would go off to walk in the field in the evening after tea, as far as the vineyard, and there, laughing, we would kiss each other. My kisses, apparently, pleased even my cousins considerably, but for some reason I was completely indifferent to them—at that time I was more captivated by less familiar girls.

Liza opened her eyes, which suddenly turned from gray to blue, looked up for a long while and said, "Do you see over there—the ripe apple? Only don't knock it down, but pick it with your own hands."

"And what will I get for doing it?" I asked.

"Whatever you want."

"I want to kiss you here..." I said softly, looking around at my cousins, pointing at her bare neck at the breast, uncovered by her decolletage.

"Just make sure you pluck it with your hands!"

I quickly climbed up into the first branches, and running the risk of falling, crept higher.

"What is he doing? It's madness!" Olga screamed.

"Let him, let him!" Liza replied, "if he loves me, he must do everything I want."

She stood beneath the tree, and raising her head with its heavy braid, followed my movements.

The apple was quite close, but it was impossible to crawl any further. I tied two branches together with my leather belt, and supporting myself with my right arm, I plucked the waxy-golden apple with my left hand. The sisters who were watching me began to clap, but suddenly the tied branches bent downwards, my belt slipped off them—and I, amid screaming, flew downwards straight into the arms of Liza, who fearlessly grabbed me and tumbled to the ground together with me. The sisters screamed and rushed towards us, but seeing that all had ended fortunately, began to laugh, caress me on the head, kiss me and comfort me just as they had their dolls at one time.

"He's my knight!" said Liza, fastening her kerchief with a pin over her full breast, which had been bared by the fall, and caressing me with her shining eyes.

Then once again we lay down on the down-trodden, slippery grass and tried to fall asleep. Closing their eyes, the sisters breathed more deeply, imbibing the scents of the burning earth and the apples, molten with the heat. But I went on staring at Liza and a sweet sensation which I had never had before engulfed me more and more.

Liza began to seem an extraordinarily strange being to me. It seemed to me that she gave off the delicate fragrance of apples, her golden hair and smooth white forehead—like those of a plaster Juno standing in the middle of a flower garden—transformed her into a divine figure in my eyes, and the feeling which filled my heart was also divine, not at all similar to the feelings of mortals. I gazed at her eyelashes, followed a small spot of light creeping along her flushed lips, along her cheek, down her neck and beginning to burn on her delicate satiny breast, which was only half-concealed by her kerchief, and from joy, from fullness of ecstasy, I closed my eyes.

The sultry wind touched my fiery brow caressingly, rustled the foliage of the apple trees above, letting a ray of sunlight pass through; and I thought that my eyes were being kissed by that very ray which had just touched Liza's lips. I felt my own breathing, leaned my cheek against the earth, felt the closeness of Liza—and my heart was flooded with joy.

"You know," Olga said to her sister, "it feels to me as if someone were kissing me."

"And me too," Liza replied.

"It's the wind," said Zina.

The sultry heat weakened the body, the earth's breathing forced our hearts to beat heavily and dulled our consciousness. The sisters often spoke about love in my presence. They knew about it other than from novels. When spring was approaching they felt the plowed earth's pulsing, the first grass, the first flowers. They slept restlessly during the spring nights—they were awakened by the nightingales, the moonlight... When they saw the love-making of animals their bodies trembled and in fear they ran into the garden, the fields, but even there the voices of birds in love followed after them; they felt that very same mystery of love that the pollinating flowers and flitting butterflies do... They often spoke of men. And once Liza confessed that a neighbor had kissed her on the back of her neck—and from then on she knew that love must be sweet.

Olga too understood this feeling during a waltz—a touch of the strong hand of a man had aroused her... Zina alone, and I, did not yet understand "everything" and only hazily guessed and grew excited when the older sisters talked about it in our presence.

"Why are you looking at me like that?" Liza asked, opening her eyes and suddenly blushing....

I lay right over Liza's face, supported by both my arms.

A sweet mist intoxicated me, I pressed close against her face and softly kissed her on her partly opened lips—a long, ever so long, kiss. She did not resist, only her eyelashes quivered, and she began to breathe more heavily...

"Enough, enough!" she said at last, pushing me away and sitting up; she blushed, her eyes sparkling as she rearranged her hair.

The kerchief, which was barely held by the pin, came unfastened, and I saw before me her virginal breasts, more beautiful than the blossoms of an apple tree, with untouched nipples within delicately rosy circles... But Liza smiled, gazing at me languid-eyed, and it seemed, waited for something...

My head was spinning, and with the irresistible fire of youth I kissed her lusterless, delicately supple, beautiful breasts.

"What are they doing! Oh, the shameless creatures!" screamed Olga, opening her eyes and coming towards us.

And to my surprise she suddenly kissed her sister's breasts...

Liza smiled even more mysteriously, and bowing her head and letting her hands fall, she seemed to freeze, powerless...

Olga lay her head on the naked shoulder and closed her eyes...

Then Zina knelt down beside us, and rushing, beginning to pant, she said, "No, no, her breasts are too large... The breasts should be like those of a goddess... Remember her in Paris...look!.."

And she quickly unfastened her kerchief.

"You show us too, Olga, show us! Let him tell us who has the best..."

And I saw before me the naked, lusterless breasts of Liza, Olga and Zina, and like a madman I began kissing them...

1907   *Translated by Samuel Cioran*

lydia zinovieva-annibal / THIRTY-THREE ABOMINATIONS

December 1

I awoke very early today. A candle was still burning on my bedside table. Vera was kneeling with her head buried in my bed and sobbing. I asked why.

" Everything on earth is unfaithful. Including beauty. You have grown old."

Her face was covered with tears and the tears dripped from everywhere: from her eyes, her nose and from the deep indentations in the corners of her lips which made her mouth seem tragic.

I replied:

"Yes, it is true."

December 6

She is a marvellous actress. There has never been another like her, not today, nor shall there ever be.

I asked her when we had returned from the theater yesterday evening:

"Vera, are you happy?"

Instead of replying, she sat me down on the bed and unbuttoned my dress. Then she said:

"Your bath is ready. Let's go. I have poured your favorite bath oil."

"Vera, the raves and adulation for you!.. You have bestowed such joy on them all. But are you happy?"

"I am used to it. But come, come. The bath will get cold. Come."

"And have you grown accustomed to me as well?"

"No, I never could."

She kissed my eyes and lips and breasts and caressed my body.

Yes, I do have a beautiful body! Does it mean that my joy stems from the fact that I represent beauty?

Don't become accustomed to it! I myself cannot become accustomed to my own beauty.

December 8

Vera ordered silk and woolen fabrics for me in a width that would fit me. From them she cut three lengths. She pinned them on me at the shoulder and along one side from the top to the knee.

These were my chitons.

I am naked except for these. I find it so pleasurable: in them I seem so tall and supple and light, as though I were quite naked. Sandals are on my bare feet.

When strangers visit, Vera casually throws a long piece of fabric down my back, fastens it at the shoulder and, flung over my arms, it hangs down to the floor along both sides of the chiton.

December 15

In the morning she went to the dressmaker's. I remained behind to tie feathers. Then I scattered them all around and laid down with my breasts under me: they are so cosy, small and firm.

There are no chairs or tables in my tiny room. Vera says that only savages sit down. Only a prone position is beautiful and becoming to the body. She has spread carpets on mattresses along the walls and scattered pillows over them...

I lay there, my elbows stretched out in front of me and my head resting on them. It's so conducive for reminiscing. It hasn't been that long since I was still living with them. Grandmother was so sentimental and yet unfeeling. That's what Vera said...

Vera is strange. But I would have submitted to her in everything. And even now I do...

Indeed, this morning, leaning there on my elbows I recalled that night so close to the day arranged for my wedding. Grandmother told me that my mother's husband was neither her husband nor my father. Grandmother thought that I should know this before the wedding and...she wanted me to appreciate her shrewdness. After all, whatever else, she had gotten a groom for me. What's more, she feared that this revelation would shock me. But then she herself would partly find pleasure in the effect. Only she was in for a disappointment and had to calm herself. I was not shocked. After all nothing had changed within me nor around me from the fact that I learned about something which had transpired long ago and which was known to all. At that time I did not even give it any thought or conjecture. It was boring. I simply attempted to recollect mother. Not remember her so much as to imagine her to myself because mother had died in childbirth and grandmother had adopted me. But even this I found impossible: instead of mother I imagined only a younger grandmother, and for me she was of little consequence.

Now, on this very morning, I had been thinking about it more than on that night. But I could not comprehend why that enfeebled man had married my mother. Why he had so cleverly perverted her (so my grandmother had told me), had introduced her to someone else in some restaurant, and then sent her pregnant to grandmother and obtained a divorce on the basis of his impotence?

Even Vera does not know. She thinks that he did it either from resentment at this restriction of life or from the inane hope of curing himself by means of an innocent girl, or from the final act of sensuality left open to him. All the same I quickly became bored with thinking about this incomprehensible man. "A vile affair of high society!" Vera said.

Vera detests society and detests men. Vera is really grand. The way she entered our theater loge the evening before my wedding!

Grandmother had only just left somewhere. I was standing alone with him when she burst impetuously through the door, tall and wearing a rain-cape on top of a queen's costume, a forgotten crown on her head.

She directed some rapid words at him. He began to tremble all over and dropped my hand from under his arm. Vera seized me cruelly by the arm and led me off... She led me through murky, dusty expanses, between strange machinery and constructions, through valleys and mountains and past a precarious wood to her dressing-room. And she still held me cruelly by the arm. There she slammed the door shut, rudely chasing away some handsome women with the amorous eyes of worshippers.

I do not recall her words. It was as though she were all aflame. She kissed my hands and I realized then that she had seen only me that evening, that she had performed for only me, that she loved me and that this was all such madness.

She gazed at me with eyes which admitted no alternatives,—and I remembered them throughout the hallucination which filled that entire night—and then she commanded me to come to her on the following morning.

And then she let me go.

But there, beneath the scene of the woods, he was waiting for me and led me back. How indecisive, pale and speechless he was.

Was it for me that she had burst into our theater loge, or for him, my fiance and her former lover?

But she herself had chased him away. And how could I ever think such a thing, even for a moment? Then, on that evening, I could not think such a thing, nor could I ever afterwards.

Vera! She was not at all kind. She...or is she simply blind, a madwoman, and sees no one else? Only it seems to me sometimes as though she were looking right through herself at something else and not herself. And then I would feel uncomfortable.

Why did I go to the rendez-vous with her the morning of my wedding-day, right here, in this room which was formerly her bedroom...?

She received me lying in bed, ill, having cried the whole night through in some kind of madness. Her voice seemed unpleasant here in the room, not like on the stage, hollow, uneven and unattractive:

"You must give them up. You are not one of them. I shall teach you myself. I shall make you beautiful because I am beautiful. With me you shall be a goddess..."

She squeezed my hand painfully and I did not know whether her face, full of suffering and tears and evil passion, was beautiful or not.

Someone knocked. She rudely chased whoever it was away.

The lines of her body were hard beneath the blanket. I knew that she would be harsh. But her eyes, dark like the purple-blue of grapes, were implacable. But I best not describe her eyes to myself.

In the morning, lying on my elbows... (when I lie, stretched out, with my head resting on my elbows, I understand everything clearly and precisely without any need of thought), in the morning I knew that I would never regret having rejected my fiance and I put on my oldest hat and coat (after all at Vera's everything would be quite different, this I could conceive of) and said to grandmother that I was leaving forever. At first grandmother wept over my immaturity, about gratitude towards a pure woman of the older generation, about my adoption...then suddenly, in complete fury she raised both hands and with a broad gesture she cursed me, depriving me of her motherhood and inheritance. Grandmother turned out to be rather proud...

And once again I was striving to recollect my mother, that is I was striving this morning, but instead I could only think of Vera.

Finally she did return from her dressmaker.

I heard her impatient ring, the falling umbrella, and her somehow unsteady and passionate steps, hurrying towards me.

In a moment's time she burst into my room. Tossing back her head she clung with her lips to mine until my head whirled in a sweet and gentle circle.

"Vera, did he kiss you this way? Did you like it? Vera, how do men kiss?"

"I don't know. I can't remember. I have forgotten everything."

"And is it not painful for you that you can remember no one?"

"And for you? You did lose everything on my account."

"No, I like being with you."

Thankful, she embraced me and sat down beside me, taking me on her knees.

"Vera, why did my mother die without telling me who my father was."

"Obviously because he was too high up in society."

"That's what grandmother said too."

"In this case your grandmother was correct. You have royal blood in your veins."

It seemed to me that Vera was playing the actress speaking in this manner. But she had the right, after all, she was such a great actress.

"Vera, but at times I imagine that my father was a jockey or a stablehand and that is why my mother said nothing."

Vera pushed me aside and wept with anger. But my caresses calmed her.

"Vera, why did you fall in love with me? Why did you take me?.. I have no talent."

"No, you have no talent."

"Why did you take me out on the stage then?"

"Just because. They say that a person must work."

Then suddenly with that fire and in that voice which made everyone shudder and the nerves tingle:

"No, this is not what I said. You do not have to work because you are, in truth, beautiful. But because you are truly beautiful I cannot give you up to people. They look. They see beauty. Nothing is left in life. The spark has flared up and then become extinguished. Only pain and insult remain and it is impossible to comprehend to what purpose. And then there is monotony. And yet more monotony. But beauty! Tell me, my love, where does it come from, what is this thing, beauty?"

Once again she covered my hair, my lips and teeth with her kisses... She unbuttoned the clasps holding the chiton about my shoulders and kissed my shoulders and breasts and my slim back which I love to feel so supple and thrilling under caresses...and Vera could not stop. She kept kissing me, weeping and crying with that voice that so excited the theater-goers in the boxes and galleries, like one amazed body, like one frenzied soul.

She kept wailing:

"I must surrender you to the people. Magnanimity! Magnanimity! This is what has made man distinct from beasts!"

December 16

I could not sleep calmly the whole night. From that morning on Vera's words and voice continued to alarm me. While she was sleeping I prayed to the Holy Virgin. This gave me some peace. I prayed that no misfortune would result from Vera's tone of voice.

December 20

There is no performance this evening. Downstairs the servants have been forbidden to accept any callers. Vera often did this so that we might spend a free evening together.

She was reading "Lear in the Desert."

Her room in no way resembled a desert!

Only masks glimmering uneasily on a transparent screen... Behind them in the fireplace restless flames were flickering and causing this effect.

These masks had been made by her friend, a famous artist. But now Vera had become estranged from him.

It seems to me that Vera does not like artists. Even at the time when she had been close to them she never allowed herself to be a model for them.

It was confusing to hear the outbursts of King Lear on unfaithful love and to see her wild and elemental face as she swept across the thick carpet amid the furniture of her mother who had been a nun.

The torrents of rain and the wind in the desert—and when everything stood still, the fireplace went on burning, crackling drily with blue and red flames, and the two ancient oil-lamps...

All the masks suddenly came to life with those red and blue tongues. They began to cry out, the yawning maws began to wail with their curses and mad laughter.

Then suddenly everything was silent.

Ancient Lear, in his shredded clothing and with his crazed eyes was silent. All the masks were hushed. And the wind and the rain were not to be heard. The flames in the fireplace grew quiet. The silence stretched itself out. Unbearably long, it seemed to me.

The silence of the masks proved to be the most frightening and novel thing that I have ever experienced.

I began to cry out:

"Vera, Vera, come back! You can't do this here in the room so close to me."

December 20

I saw the Virgin in my sleep.

She resembled Vera, only calm, fuller and taller.

Like a goddess.

The same murky dark hair, but beneath a green veil. The eyes were like the deep purple of grapes. And the lips were full and moist, very severe like Vera's, but entirely without the trembling and slight curl that so unsettled me in Vera's and which made her mouth seem tragic (together with dimples at the corners of her lips).

She was very tall and in a long green dress. But still I could see her feet under the green hem. She fell to the ground. It seemed as though there was grass there and the earth smelled of roots and grass. I kissed the white feet of this wondrous and perfect beauty until my heart in prayer and worship ceased to beat in my breast.

And I died.

Then a soft, liquid sweetness slowly spread through my veins...and I awoke, exhausted.

December 22

I couldn't sleep. In the morning I saw her feet. Vera's feet are more beautiful than mine. They are even more beautiful than her divine shoulders. She was sleeping. I knelt beside her bed. I kissed her feet prayerfully.

My heart grew faint.

Vera awoke. She looked at me without withdrawing her warm marble-like skin.

Suddenly, as though swept up in a warm whirlwind, I lost my senses...

Mother, goddess, friend!

She knew everything.

Does it mean that this is my beauty?

I am still weeping. I write and weep.

I lay the whole day with my breasts on the pillow.

Vera was away the whole day. She was being feted somewhere. She had been taken away somewhere.

Suddenly I felt terrified.

How strange was my fate! I believe in fate.

I recalled a painting, a copy of some Italian painting, I believe St. Agatha. Her nipples were being torn off with irons and the two torturers were peering into her eyes with a savage curiosity. But Agatha's eyes were beatific, oh so filled with blessedness!

I often prayed to her when I lived with grandmother but I left her behind. I thought that with Vera everything would be different.

Now I languish. She would have comforted me.

I am terrified. This is why I have sat down to record my notes. Vera taught me to do so when she was not at home.

When she comes I shall bare her feet, lay on the floor all faint and cover her feet with kisses.

I must not show her these notes... There, there's her ring...

December 26

I must record the events of yesterday. It was much too strange seeing Vera the way she was. After all, Vera has not always been an actress. This is probably the reason for what happened.

She once had a child and a husband. At sixteen she had been married because her mother had wished it as she left to enter a convent. Vera's love for her mother had been practically idolatrous. She had kept silent and did not question. Moreover, her husband was a fine fellow. When he died two years after the marriage, Vera had wept like any wife. Enough of submission to her idol after two years!

Her daughter survived for about two months and then died shortly thereafter.

One old actress, the same one who had drawn the despondent Vera into the theater (she provided a mask and a frenzy for the insane and inconsolable grief of a mother, so Vera told me) explained to me a few days ago:

"Just wait and see what will happen on the twenty-fifth: you will be convinced that our marvellous Vera is a good mother. And if you could have seen how she carried on when this suckling child of hers died. What is a suckling child after all? A piece of meat as far as I am concerned. But Vera drank from the graveyard well to communicate with the worms."

It was frightening to hear about the worms. Why drink water like that ... unless you want to die?

The twenty-fifth drew nigh. But not unnoticed. Vera and I worked ourselves to exhaustion during our free moments. She was sewing costumes for dolls, all the costumes which she wore and which she fantasized...I made up the hats and coiffures.

When the dolls were ready we set them out in the salon where the Christmas tree was illuminated in the evening. Both of us went around from morning till night as though in a dream. We ate little in our impatience and wore expectant and knowing smiles.

Vera said:

"I don't care for little boys, that is, I like little girls. And I wish only they would come for their dolls. But don't you see, I do try all the same to be fair. I find this so difficult and yet so necessary. I even allow them to bring their brothers along. We'll give them toy horses and drums. You know, if I had had a son and not a daughter, I don't know whether I would have loved him as much or not. Why I loved her so much I really can't say. I am not a good mother at all. I never wanted a child after that...only then—it's madness!

I used to go about all radiant and smiling to myself. My husband would ask me:

'Why are you smiling?' But he himself knew: 'Of course, because of the child. This is simply a miracle what has happened with you, Vera. Everyone used to say to me that I wouldn't be happy with you. That you were neither a wife nor a mother'..."

Standing before the Christmas tree all lit up, the wax candles softly burning (Vera only liked wax candles) and the loud laughter-chatter and movement, I was struck by the amazement in the eyes of the children who had been brought by the guests and who had been summoned from the courtyard and street, and the absence of beards and moustaches on the faces of the men. I had grown accustomed to actors, but their absence in this large company seemed strange in our salon.

Vera laughed at my remark. Vera was radiant, was soft, and moved about in a kind and tender fashion, smiling at everyone. She called the children over and caressed them and kissed them on the lips.

It was her holiday. One could sense the warm waves, redolent with Christmas pitch, spreading through the room.

December 27

Vera was given a present, the "Recumbent Panther." It was a small piece of sculpture. Her friend, Saburov the artist, brought it.

I was not at home then. I had gone to my grandmother for my birth-certificate. Grandmother, of course, could not deprive me of my name. In fact, I have no name and I find this pleasing.

Grandmother wept. This meant she still loves me. I felt sorry for her. She even called me back. But...she had no way of comprehending my happiness.

Then who of these people would know how to love so that all of my being would become more beautiful and pure?

Vera was somewhat distraught today.

But she loved me even more madly.

But this made me feel somehow or other more terrified.

My God! What strange days! Like a golden mist in my eyes.

It seems to me that my golden mist is visible to all. Not only to those who come to visit but at the rehearsals as well. And yesterday at the soiree as well where Vera had been so magnificent.

But my life is so wonderful, so bizarre, and I feel good.

December 28

Vera is refashioning me. It seems to me that I am becoming beautiful because she sees me. This makes me so calm, self-assured and relaxed all at the same time.

Vera said:

"You have such a benevolent look."

Why should I look malevolent? I wish well to all people, even as I do to myself.

Once Vera asked me:

"What would you do if you desired something that would be harmful to another person?"

For a long time I did not know what to answer: at that time people had inflicted little harm on me. Nor had I, so it seemed. Then I replied:

"Perhaps I would cease to desire such a thing."

"Really, by yourself?"

"Of course. How else?"

For a long time she paced back and forth and then she asked, her eyes burning fixedly and uncomfortably:

"But if you desired something that was harmful to yourself?"

"I think that it would be the same thing."

"You would not wish such a thing?"

"No, I would not."

"But if you did, despite yourself?"

"Then it would mean that in doing such a thing there would be more joy than grief in harm. Or is it not true?"

Instead of replying she kissed my hand.

"You are wise!"

Could this really be, in fact, wisdom? I don't know, but it all seems so simple to me.

December 29

Everyone had let me be.

Yesterday grandmother sent me three hundred rubles. How kind she is!

I am going out to buy a ring for Vera now. I've already had my eye on a ruby, and kept thinking: if only I had the money.

And then suddenly came these three hundred rubles.

December 30

Tanya, it turns out, was in the dining room when Saburov brought the "Recumbent Panther." Today at skating she said as we glided hand in hand around the wondrously slippery ice until our heads swam:

"You know what? Saburov asked Vera whether he could paint your portrait."

I knew nothing of this.

Dropping my hand and suddenly describing a curving arc on one skate, she added:

"I quite envy you. He is a celebrity."

And then after the turn:

"This is quite advantageous for an actress... But of course, Vera refused... You know, it seems to me that at times your intimacy with Vera is not at all advantageous."

Tanya is jealous. But then all people are envious. It's quite fruitless to convince oneself of the contrary.

Or is my intimacy with Vera really harmful?

Anyway, what does advantageous mean?

What do I care about the portrait or whatever. After all I am happy.

December 31

Yesterday evening everyone was talking about the "Recumbent Panther" in our apartment. It seems that importance is attached to the elongated line of the body and tongue. There is something epileptic about the tongue. An impossible and convulsive straightness.

Someone said that this had a disturbing effect.

Many reproached Vera for not praising the sculpture.

Vera did not justify herself. She smiled mysteriously, evilly.

January 1

We greeted New Year's, just the two of us. Flowers. Wine. We told fortunes. Our wax flowed out in a distinctness and beauty that was terrifying.

For Vera the wax formed a burial mound and a cross with a crucified figure on it. The figure was twisted with pain into a serpent-like and muscular tension. How frightening it was!

My wax emerged as a flat piece. The wax had splashed about the surface upwards in many fine, transparent and bursting bubbles—roses. It was a rose garden, effulgent, joyful, and in the middle was a figure of a woman. Her arms were outstretched and her position suggested flight.

We interpreted our fortunes for each other.

Vera said:

"See, see you are a queen. Of course your father poured royal blood into you. Kings go through life like that, as though in a garden. Kings do not revolt. They have no need of revolt. Therefore they seem submissive. They do not lust because there is nothing for them to lust after. They already possess all. Therefore they all seem satisfied. They do not even deliberate because people deliberate while they live. But when life grows cold, they fall silent and drink. Kings possess life forever. You will pass through life as though through a garden of roses and you will adore the pricks of thorns and the fragrant languor of the petals."

Could this be true?

Suddenly Vera burst into tears, unexpectedly, so it seemed, even to herself, and brought everything to an end with the incomprehensible words:

"And my crucifixion comes of you passing through a garden of roses. In them are all joys, all sufferings, all sweetness, and you belong to life... And I cry out to you: stop! Look here—my body is all twisted in pain. This is because I must cry out with every pore: stop! The crucified slave rebels."

In the middle of her tears Vera laughed.

This is how our celebration ended, so sadly and horribly.

Once in bed where she had led me, frightened and trembling, she loosened my hair and caressed it with rapid motions of her sensitive and passionate fingers.

Her fingers feel so fragile when I kiss them and this fills me with a sweet pleasure.

She kissed me, her eyes almost prayerful, again with a purple hue like black grapes.

She prayed for a long while.

Vera does not know how to pray. This is very sad. Prayer is so comforting to me.

I wept for a long while, alone, waking from my tears only when Vera had finally fallen asleep. I was terrified. If this burial mound presaged the grave for her, what about me? I could not bear to remain alone when she would no longer be here. No I can't, I can't exist without her. But perhaps the burial mound does not signify the grave? Why am I so superstitious? It's terrible.

If Vera dies, then I will too, of course. I shall kill myself. What else can I do?

Thus our greeting to the New Year ended very unpleasantly.

January 7

Yesterday in the theater dressing-room I saw a small man with a large balding skull and lively, childlike eyes. I was amazed when I heard his name that this was the great artist.

Incidentally I did not care for him because of his childlike eyes.

I am terribly happy today. I am studying a new role, a rather substantial one. Perhaps I do have talent after all.

It's strange that Vera does not like to coach me in the roles. She does not believe in it at all and the other day pronounced:

"Kings have no need of masks. A mask is a release from oneself, a respite."

But I would have been more happy had it been otherwise. I do love the theater very much.

This is why meeting artists excites me so!

But Vera jokingly keeps me at a distance from them.

January 11

Vera has been acting strangely since the time she wept and cried out:

"I must give you up to the people!"

She gazes at me for long periods of time with her terrifying, completely implacable eyes, and remains silent. Often she asks strange questions which are difficult to answer. I believe they are difficult to answer because if one were to reply simply then one might seem stupid.

Often when she could not wait to hear some incomprehensible reply from me she would run stumblingly and pitifully to her room and there in a terrifying voice she would recite her most terrifying roles. Being so close to her then was unpleasant.

And at nights I became lonely; Vera no longer slept in my bed. I think it was because she wept at night.

How beautiful the tragic seems when it is beneath a mask, but when it appears so nakedly before me and... when I am so forcibly implicated... I don't know whether I care for it so much. Somehow or other it is as though I were torturing myself.

Incidentally, I too am prone to tears and I cry often and at the least pretext.

January 13

In my room the entire window is filled with camellias. A whole camellia bush stands in a wooden tub.

I passionately love camellias. The leaves are dark, so dark and glistening and stiff. The flowers are clear, ripe, and wide-spread and fleshy. Only they have no fragrance. It's precisely because of this that I like them.

For essence I love camellias and not roses. It is Vera who attributes her roses to me. Has not my garden of roses been poured forth for her?

Or those waxen bushes of mine, were they camellias in my fortune?

Saburov came today without Vera. He asked me for a single camellia. I gave it to him. When Vera returned and I told her, she suddenly turned pale, her face became contorted and she beat me. This was monstrous. She slapped me on the cheeks and head with her palms, she was powerful, raging, the vein on her forehead swelled up and her mouth was distorted. I felt both pity and disgust for her.

Then she sat through half the night on the floor in a strange pose, looking somewhat comical in her transparent nightgown: her arms around her knees, her head bent over, all in a ball and suddenly she said mysteriously:

"All the same I did promise... You will be theirs."

I wept.

She did not ask forgiveness.

Is she really not afraid that I will leave her?

It's insane! Sometimes it seems as though she were forcing us to part.

Will I really leave?

Let her beat me.

I don't care, I love her.

January 14

Often I remember the past. Incidentally, without any regret. Every minute was wonderful, even the unpleasant ones. After they were over, of course.

With others, things were not bad for me. But then I don't know what boredom is. I was loved and spoiled. Grandmother took pains so that my teachers would educate me to become a society bride. Those around me were quite beautiful, that is, they weren't really, but they seemed so. I knew this and loved it precisely because they seemed so, and I took it quite seriously.

All the same they could not even *seem* to be half of what Vera is.

Naturally. Vera is beautiful and I don't have to pretend.

It seems to me that she fears most of all two things: habit and infidelity. She often reflects this fear in her eyes: have I become bored with her or am I being unfaithful?

But I could never be bored with her. There is a reason for that: Vera is famous, but after all Vera will die. Despite everything.

With her large, powerful and impetuous body she vacillates and vacillates between fear and ecstasy and the string will break.

I often think about this, that is, I imagine to myself that here is Vera, dead, totally motionless, lying on the table, in a coffin... and I too, of course can no longer live. But for some reason this gives me pleasure, a terrible amount of pleasure to imagine so the one I love: earlier I imagined grandmother and then my fiance in this manner, even my favorite animals, Sparky our cat with the fiery bursts of red on his gray-black fur.

January 17

How pleasant it is that Vera has such large mirrors in her room. Vera is beautiful although her body has become a little worn: the lines of the stomach and breasts have softened somewhat... But I like it very much, terribly much, in fact.

We are together... but Vera is insane... She is acting up as she looks into the deep mirrors at the two of us here together and in the morning she cried:

"Let everything stay the same. Let it stay, understand? Not a step forward, nor a step backward. I shall cry out to life: stop here!"

She is so comical and marvelous.

January 18

I am a child: half-boy, half-girl, just beginning to mature in body as I fill out and the lines of my legs and arms grow lean and long. Vera never ceases to repeat this.

Vera is so comical and marvelous.

February 2

At last I realized why two months ago she wept and cried: "I must give you up to the people." In her heart she had already made up her mind then...

The three of them came yesterday. Vera had invited them earlier, in the theater dressing-room. Incidentally, one of them was the one who had brought her the "Recumbent Panther" and to whom she had refused everything.

Yesterday they said that they were the representatives of the society of "Thirty-Three" artists.

In the dressing-room I had not been able to become more closely acquainted. Everything was always in turmoil and one never had a chance to talk seriously.

I had been drawn to them as though by a magnet, but Vera had driven me away with her eyes.

Truly I was weak and subservient. Was this really not weakness? One glance from her could send me to heaven or hell alike.

Servility I found pleasant. It cost me nothing. Particularly as regards Vera.

Yes, of course, this was a terrible sacrifice for her. But she loved sacrifices. She sought them. Her mask demanded sacrifices from her. She told me so.

In short, yesterday Vera acquiesced. Today she made the announcement to me. There they have, the thirty-three, a large common studio, which is, of course, in addition to their private ones, because among them are well-known artists. They will paint me there. Vera herself will take me there.

But she said nothing more than this. Nor did I question her. I listened to her quietly, like water. Once Vera said to me:

"It seems to me you are a stream and flow softly through the glistening moss like malachite under the sun. In my childhood somewhere in the forest I recall such a quiet, radiant stream."

I now surrender to Vera all of my will. This makes me feel better.

And she is so marvelous and all-knowing.

February 7

Poor Vera, all calamities befall her at once. She began to linger with the days. She could not make up her mind. Of course, whosoever loves, finds it difficult to part even a short while from a loved one! And all at once a further mishap.

Yesterday he showed up, my former fiance and her former lover. Then today we learned that he had shot himself. Vera was shocked and said that she was responsible for his death.

But he came to beg her love once again, or... if only out of pity for him... And he wept. He told her that he wanted to forget me... that she, Vera, was his fated, and I was too, although in a reverse sense. There is something unmerciful

338

in me, just as in Vera, although in an opposite way.

I heard everything because Vera had forgotten about me. Her voice was hoarse, almost a whisper:

"No, no, no..."

How terribly she was able to repeat a single word! It was precisely the single word which she was able to pronounce more frighteningly and implacably than all else.

But he was terribly sincere and hapless yesterday. Actually he had always been that way before. I had loved him for that. And with him I always felt kindly, strong and important.

He was so handsome, round-faced and rosy-skinned. But whenever you looked at him his lashes would begin to flutter like butterflies around eyes that were almost too bright. Yet I smiled yesterday as I listened to his completely disconnected and comical speech from inside Vera's bedroom. He was never completely self-possessed. To be sure, this is why grandmother had succeeded in trapping him. All the suitors had amused themselves with me but who of them would ever have decided to marry a girl of such puzzling background.

He had been brave, he had been real, almost like Vera, although not as intelligent as she and without talent.

But then it seemed to me that my time had come to experience the life of a woman...

But now I do not seek another life besides this one. Vera gave me more than I had hoped to receive and I stood in expectation of the future without impatience.

February 10

On the third day Vera said:

"I love your body because it is beautiful. But I do not know your soul. I do not know whether there is a soul. Nor is it necessary for me because your body is beautiful.

But everything is mutable and you will grow old. At first your face will grow old. Your body will live longer. An old face will be a mockery before a youthful body. And then a wasted body will be a mockery to ravenous desires.

This is like the dead light of the setting sun which from the clouds above was reflected in the water... feeble and full of disillusion.

Should I not kill you so that I might always possess you for myself."

And Vera became terrifying.

I found this unpleasant.

But from these words I understood that she had decided upon the day.

She could not prolong it any longer: Lent was approaching. And joy awaited me in Lent. Vera was traveling to Paris with our troupe. I would see Paris. After Paris we would travel with the troupe to America. Vera's fame had become world-wide.

And I, I would see the world. What joy, what riches!

February 17

And lo, it came and then passed, interrupting that string of days filled with torment.

Vera did not go back on her word! But yesterday had been the day of sacrifice for her and the day of joy as well, and of hope, a great day—(all this she told me during the night as we celebrated) because in truth my poor beauty was serving art.

How I flirted at home yesterday morning! For a long while I stood before the mirror and tried one color after another. I pinned the folds with practiced whimsy. At first Vera watched and then she left, suddenly angered and saying:

"You are silly and do not understand that all this is unnecessary."

Something was weighing on her heart, she was withholding something and not telling me...

But now I know. And what of it? It is over and no longer frightening!

But I should tell everything in order. Today my entry will be a long one.

Today my hair was curled seemingly madly and yet at the same time lightly and elegantly. My forehead appeared so high and the skin so fine and opaque. And it rose so gently and tenderly above the large ovals of my distinct, brilliantly light gray eyes.

My mouth was set softly and fully, severe and yet with a hint of a smile. A brilliant pigment glowed forth on my tender lips like the ardor restrained in the refined alabaster of dying coals—on my opaque cheeks.

How glorious and yet tender was the sloping line of my shoulders! My supple breasts were motionless like two soft waves. My tender and strong neck curved modestly, yet severely.

My body was tall and supple like the rising and curving surf.

Yes, I do belong to the watery elements!

Now I have run to fetch Vera's notebook. I will copy down what she has written about me. She herself read it to me yesterday evening after spending the first morning at their studio.

"Her hair is the rosy and luxuriant ashes on the altar.

Her tender forehead is the airy vault over the caves of her gray eyes. How frightening are these radiant deeps! How severe and blazing her piercing gaze.

The fruit of her lips is sumptuous and soft, yet implacable is her caressing smile. And like the crimson juice of a peeled pomegranate does the blood course beneath her exquisite skin.

Life and death abide in the spiritous juice of the rosy fruit of her fresh lips, the sacred phial of my insane love.

Like the concealed flame in the fine alabaster of glimmering coals does

340

her blood radiate through the exquisite petals of her cheeks.

Joyfully, caressingly, run the lines of her curving shoulders.

The supple stem of her neck bends ever so modestly and delicately.

Like bunches of golden grapes with two petals of the pale crimson rose come to rest upon them are her youthful, perfect breasts, upraised with love as though reaching forward to meet the sun.

Her body, so pale, like the heart of the tea-rose suffused with the sun, yet supple and strong like the towering and exquisite surf upwards curving..."

Here I shall stop...

Even though weary, I admire myself, fastening the curls of my hair and the folds of my clothing!

And what feet! Of course they are too gaunt, but this is because I have such fine bones.

Vera has so tended the soles of my feet and the toes that everyone of them has come alive, free and sensuous.

I never would have ceased admiring myself because I had been so daring yesterday. Vera told me herself in the morning, while we were still in bed (we slept together last night, that is, I slept and she neither slept nor cried), she said to me in that voice of hers:

"Today you are not the same as before. You seem to be one who will keep striving to become something, who will long for something that has not been accomplished and who will change and cannot rest for a moment, not for a single moment and so in fact will never arrive at your destination but will be on the go forever, forever.

This journey without end I can feel with every fiber of my body. How unpleasantly, incomprehensibly and yet unavoidably beats your heart: pound, pound, pound! And your blood whirls all around in a mad frenzy...

Today you will be still, motionless, without craving, eternal, eternal on the canvas. Your blood will not be aflame nor overflowing, nor marking off the seconds, one after another. A single instant will be halted. A single moment will be separated from the rest and will come to a complete stop, all by itself, frozen, complete, by itself, eternal.

This is the essence of art.

In thirty-three attentive and appraising pairs of eyes you will be reflected by thirty-three eternal and everlastingly perfect moments of beauty..."

Then Vera jumped up and walked in prolonged silence about the room with steps that suddenly had become firm, rhythmical and tragic. She seemed almost terrifying and not at all comical in her long transparent night-gown.

Then she stopped by the window and facing the street below, said:

"This, this is magnificent! This, you know, is magnificent enough to make one believe in happiness, so that even I, yes, even I could believe in it and forget that all is mutable. Let her grow old: she will be thirty-three times eternal in her thirty-three eternal moments of youthfulness. This, yes, this is magnificent enough to make life worthwhile for all people in the entire world for all times!"

Of course, never before had Vera so become one with her mask that every word seemed so convincing as though on the stage.

And I believed.

Therefore, of course, I was doubly obedient when as early as eleven o'clock (I had been dressed since eight) Vera, excited to a point of complete frenzy, ran into the room, seized me by the shoulders, tore me away from the mirror, flung the long chlamys over me, muffled me up, pushed and shoved me like someone kneading a piece of dough and then led me down the stairs, thrust me into a carriage and drove me off.

She took me to them, the thirty-three painters, in their studio.

Once there I didn't manage to examine anything and did not know how many of them there actually were.

Someone ushered us in. Vera pushed me along. Someone removed my chlamys, then the shawl and undid the clasps on my shoulders...

Was it me they wanted? My heart rebelled.

I remember nothing beyond those moments.

I felt as though I had plunged headfirst into water... My chiton fell to the floor and became tangled up in my feet, when I attempted to flee. Tears burst forth. My face became wet in an instant. Someone wiped it.

I stood tall. I felt both cold and then as though scorched by fire.

But when I had this burning sensation I suddenly saw my body, usually pale and opaque (not pink as is usually the case with blondes, but opaque with the hint of a very pale tea-rose), and it had begun to crimson, that is, to grow pink shamefully and monstrously.

Then I was completely seized by wrath and pride. I arched my body and immediately my limbs were suffused with life, became supple and full, my heart beat evenly, on my lips there settled a barely perceptible smile of pride and my gray eyes blazed victoriously.

I knew this, I knew it. I could see it. And I saw no one, nor did I perceive time. I was aware only of myself, suddenly calm, motionless and triumphant.

I must have grown weary because I suddenly heard voices.

Someone touched me. Once again I was jostled, dressed and led to the fire and set down beside it as all around me a multitude of faces were smiling timidly and thankfully, abashed and joyful...

Then home again.

What has happened with Vera? She is blissful. She loves me as never before. She has strewn my entire room with flowers. She says that her heart is like an enormous bird at the zenith of flight, that now she will act in a different way because everything, everything has been revealed to her, all the souls, all the blessings, all the torments...

She gave me champagne to drink. We celebrated like lovers.

Like lovers! I have no need of a lover. Never, never. Yesterday I became sacred. Yesterday I gave my oath of fidelity to Vera and she, even she did not dare to kiss my breasts...

342

Why did they not show us the portrait? Were they afraid that I would not comprehend my great feat, that I would not comprehend the entire meaning? Fools! How sweet they are!

Well, all the same, tomorrow I shall see it... But now I will finish my entry. After all it is time to get ready!

I could not sleep all night. I was afraid that I would look ugly. But no, today I am even better, even more beautiful.

I am like a sacrifice and a goddess at the same time! Vera once put it that way on that first evening when she had taken me from the theater-box.

But what is she doing with me? It's madness. I am not my own person. When she awakens I shall say to her:

"Vera, what have you done with me?"

But if I have become so high, then it means that I have come to it my-self. Or like water I have flowed, as Vera might have said.

March 10

More than three weeks have passed.

How could it be?

I must catch up with my entries. For some reason or other it seems necessary.

Vera did not go to Paris and America. She broke all her contracts. She was truly ill. Almost disturbed.

Here is the way it was.

I shall finish writing this diary, these fragments of a diary, because such was her will when she was in possession of herself. Moreover we used to read it to each other. She was adamant in this as well.

After the first day in the studio we went there three more times. And I modelled.

Finally, on the fourth day they showed us and I saw it.

Me? Is this me? Is it really the me whom both Vera and I loved?

This one and this one and this one?...

I ran from one canvas to the other, through the entire studio.

In all directions as they sat around me, painting, I saw myself.

Or did I not recognize myself from the back? From the side? In a three-quarter view, or a quarter. And directly in front...did I not recognize myself?

These are of someone else.

They are not ours.

Someone else's, someone else's.

Simply someone else's. This was not our beauty, not that which Vera owned.

Thirty-three abominations. Thirty-three abominations.

And they were all me. And not all me.

I burst into tears and began to curse like some jockey or stable-hand.

I went over to Vera. In her eyes there was a kind of blue despair burning... (her eyes are so incredible) and I saw myself once more. That real and unique

343

self which was already lost there on these canvases which had brought me into being.

Vera, all pale, like the pale-bluish fur on the color of her coat, silently led me to the door.

At home we did not speak.

Beginning with that evening she did not go to the theater.

I wept quietly, quietly kissing her hands with those lifeless fingers. In her eyes, large and wide, there was no dark crimson of the grape cluster.

Her eyes were like extinguished candle wicks, a murky black.

Walking side by side with her past the mirror (this happened to us on one of those days following that day) I saw that she was all black, all murky black: her thick hair was dull, her brows powerful and even, and those eyes where I could no longer be reflected in the murky impenetrability. But beside her I seemed strange, out of place, impossibly radiant, supple and vibrant and sparkling in every curl of my ash-blonde hair and in the gleam of my gray watery eyes.

It was terrible.

Vera noticed as well and suddenly smiled into the mirror at my reflection as she came to a halt.

I wept as I embraced her knees.

But on the following morning I secretly fled from her and went to them.

Several of them were there. They were painting me.

I stood there alone, naked, before them. For I belonged to them, to them, there on the canvas.

And I looked again.

I found that Vera and I had been very severe the day before and that I had shouted, swearing like...a prostitute.

I came there again another time. And I looked many times again. I was filled with consolation, with my consolation.

The thirty-three abominations were truthful. They were the truth. They were life. The sharp fragments of life, sharp, complete moments. Such are women. They have lovers.

Each of these thirty-three (or how many of them were there?) had painted his mistress. Excellent! I grew used to myself being in their presence.

Thirty-three mistresses! Thirty-three mistresses!

And I was all of them and yet all were not me.

I studied the abomination for a long while: before I modelled for them, as well as afterwards.

I modelled in order to study. This I felt so keenly. It seemed to me that I was learning about life by pieces, by separate pieces, fragments, but every fragment possessed all its own complexity and power.

The abominations began to divide in half. With every day this became clearer. One half became mistresses and the other half queens.

Each of the thirty-three created his mistress or his queen.

And I found amusement in taking count of the mistresses and the queens.

But each day they became confused again and when I would go away and would be resting on my elbows at home, I would try to remember every one of me, every fragment of myself there. The visages would become painfully confused and I would laugh like a silly fool, prance about and whisper loudly:

"Thirty-three mistresses. Thirty-three queens. And I am all of them and all are not me!"

I went to Vera who frequently sat for long periods on the floor with her arms around her knees and I said to her:

"All of them are not me there because I am all only in you. I cannot be me anywhere else."

Somehow I grew uncomfortable. I was searching for myself, but being lost I could not feel myself. I pressed closer to Vera. I encircled her unbending neck with my arms. I caressed her and peered into her eyes: I was searching. I felt an uncommonly painful and uneasy sensation in my chest. Vera's eyes no longer held my reflection.

They do not hold my reflection.

I wept. Then I became angry. I looked at Vera with hatred. With malicious joy I rushed from our height down the endless staircase and onto the street where everything was flashing and disembodied and I went there, to them...

* * * * * * * * * * * * ** * * * *

I was pleased with myself in their company. They begged me individually to go to one of the founders of the society of the thirty-three.

It was the one with the large balding head and lively childlike eyes. He lived in Paris and was going then to America for an exhibition.

I made arrangements with him through one of his pupils here, one of my "lovers." And I think that I will consent completely in a little while more.

I shall see Paris and America and life will be so much the richer for me. Poor, dear Vera! She is living and moving about in some kind of obliviousness. She reads parts to herself under her breath, without expression, muttering inaudibly. And her face, it has become like earth... She does not know that I am going out. She does not see me.

Or perhaps she does see me and already she is indifferent?

I sit there and hold her hand. I kiss her fragile fingers which bend only with difficulty, like a dead person's. I kiss...

But she does not smile. Even now I am no longer in her eyes.

My reflection is not there.

Poor Vera! Yesterday she said to me:

"You are right of course." So softly, not at all like her, she smiled.

Then, ever so slowly and incomprehensibly she added, arranging her words carefully and, so it seemed to me, after each word dying, dying:

"This is what I wished for."

Does it mean that after these words in her terrifying voice, the words to the effect that she must give me up, that I prayed to the Heavenly Queen in vain for salvation?

* * * * * * * * * * * * * * * * * * * **

Vera says that she will go nowhere, that she feels fine here, that she is quite content to go on living. Whether I leave or remain, this is all the same. I am there somewhere inside her. That eternal moment is within her.

But all this she utters very submissively, without the outburst which in the theater caused such a furor and distraction. But this submissiveness I found unpleasant. Unusual.

True I wanted to record everything, but I cannot, I feel sorry for Vera and I cannot understand anything.

What should I do?

Should I give up my plans?

But after all, that is madness. That is, Vera's despair is madness.

April

Vera has poisoned herself.

What should I do? How should I kill myself? Or should I?

Perhaps I will become accustomed to her death?

Vera always feared infidelity and habit.

But then when I used to sit for hours beside her, something would come over me. It was as though her thoughts, which she was no longer contemplating, would pass over into me, full and complete in themselves, and they were received unhesitatingly.

She was thinking:

Could it really be that this warm, fragile breath of mine whereby I imbibe life and which now, yes now, will be interrupted and which is innocent in all things, so involuntary and delicate, is it really not a habit in every breath and an infidelity in every expiration?

And I shall grow old.

Vera has aged already during these two months of agony.

* *

Everyone is saying that Vera was always disturbed. They visited us and began making arrangements. It turns out that there are relatives of some sort.

They will take care of the burial ceremonies...

I must leave.

Now I too believe that everyone who is genuine...neither gives into habit nor makes demands...

* *

Vera was a tragic figure. That is, she lived in the tragic element. So, in fact, she had written about herself. (Unfortunately I had not noticed that she burned all ner notes!)

I shall write down what I had copied from her at that time because it had seemed so fitting then.

"In every element only those creatures can exist who are adapted for breathing it in and who can be transformed within themselves. I share this belief.

Such is true even of the tragic element."

Vera was also the one who said:

"Whosoever can inhale the breath of tragedy throughout himself, that blessed person is my hero and appeaser."

* *

Now I have recopied her words once again, yet there are words of my own which seek utterance. I am writing them through tears.

Life is so fragile and irridescent like that stream of Vera's, like their caresses, like my sensuality, it is genuine and Vera did not want to accept it.

1907   *Translated by Samuel Cioran*

The Theater of the Soul

right—*Paraclete in the guise of Fortune Teller (McKay Morris). Photograph of the Theatre Guild production, New York, 1926.*

below—*Evreinov's own sketch of the set, for the benefit of the stage designer M. P. Bobyshev, for the premiere at Evreinov's Crooked Mirror Theater, 1912.*

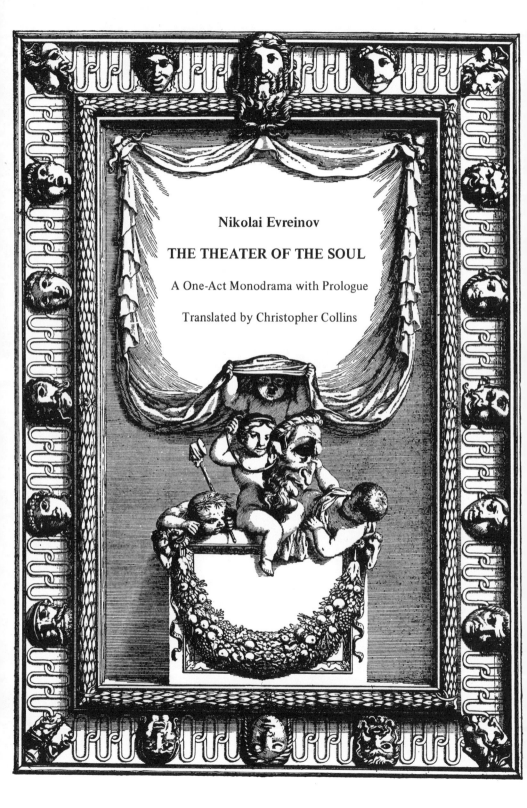

Nikolai Evreinov

THE THEATER OF THE SOUL

A One-Act Monodrama with Prologue

Translated by Christopher Collins

CHARACTERS

Professor

S_1 (The rational aspect of the Soul)

S_2 (The emotional aspect of the Soul)

S_3 (The subconscious aspect of the Soul)

Wife Image No. 1

Wife Image No. 2

Songstress Image No. 1

Songstress Image No. 2.

Conductor

*The action takes place in the Soul
within the space of thirty seconds.*

A blackboard and chalk have been set up in front of the lowered curtain.

PROFESSOR *(enters from the side, moves to the board, bows, and takes a piece of chalk in his hand).* Fellow citizens! The other day the author of the work being presented today came to me. I'm a specialist, you understand. I must confess I at first took a very dim view of this work, supposing it to be—as so often happens in the theater these days—some useless vaudeville, devoid of any deeper meaning or moral significance. So I was all the more pleased to find in The Theater of the Soul a strictly scientific work based on the latest developments in psychophysiology. The researches of Wundt, Freud, Theodule Ribot and others demonstrate that the human soul is not something indivisible, but consists of several *Selves.* Is that clear so far? *(Writes on the board:* $S_1 + S_2 + S_3 = S_n$.*)* Now Fichte argues that if the Self is the Self, then the world is not the Self. Perfectly clear, isn't it? Fine. But, according to the most recent data, although the world is not the Self, neither is the Self the Self. Perfectly clear? The Self is not the Self, because the Self consists of several Selves. In fact, the Self consists of three Selves. *(He writes on the board:* $S = x/3$.*)* Therefore, the true Self, the basic Self—what we used to call the Soul—may be broken down to Self sub one, the rational self, the thinking self—what we used to call Reason; Self sub two, the emotional Self, the romantic Self—what we used to call Feeling; and Self sub three, the subconscious Self, the psychical Self—what we used to call the Eternal. That's all clear now, isn't it? These three Selves together make up a larger entity, the Self. *(Writes on the board:* $s + s + s = S$.*)* Now, the ancients supposed that the Self was located in the liver. Descartes held that it was to be found in the brain, but the author of the present work believes—with no small justification— that the soul happens to be located in our body near the very spot on our chest that we strike instinctively when we wish to emphasize our good faith or when we say things like "my soul is filled with joy... My heart bleeds for you... My soul burns with indignation!" and so forth. And so, taking the above into account, the theater of the soul may be diagrammed as follows. *(With multicolored chalk draws a picture which he then explains.)* Here, above the diaphragm, we see a large heart suspended by the aorta and the superior vena cava, beating from 55 to 125 times per minute, surrounded right and left by the lungs, contracting and expanding at the rate of 14 to 18 times per minute. In the back, representing the spine and its attached ribs, is a small, garish, yellow colored telephone. Some pale threads, nerves, stretch upward from the diaphragm. We have then, so to say, a model of the stage for the Self to perform on. Now science, my fellow citizens, not only explains, but also gives a certain measure of consolation—for example, it is not sufficient to say that the Self has done something stupid! One has to determine which Self was the stupid one. If the emotional Self was stupid, it doesn't mean a thing. You don't have to worry about the subconscious either. But if the rational Self has been stupid, then it is time to be alarmed! But, my respected fellow citizens, whose Self clearly expresses itself in this insane day and time?.. At this point, I should like to conclude my speech and yield to the author, to the actors, and to you, a most worthy audience for this unusual presentation.

(The Professor retires. The blackboard is taken away. The curtain rises revealing a picture of the soul very much like that the Professor drew on the blackboard. On stage, that is, on the diaphragm, are all three Selves. They are quite similar, all are dressed in black, but in different kinds of clothes. S₁ wears a frock coat, S₂ wears an artist's smock, and a bright red bow, S₃ wears a travelling coat. They are further distinguishable in that S₁ has graying, neatly combed hair, he wears glasses, thin lips grace his pale face, and he is rather reserved. S₂ seems quite young, is dishevelled, has crimson lips and makes extravagant gestures. S₃, wearing a black half-mask, is sleeping downstage with one arm around his suitcase like some exhausted traveller on a train.)

S₂ *(on the telephone)*. What? Hello! You can't hear me? But I'm speaking loud enough... There's a loud hum? That's because your nerves are stretched extremely tight... Well, all right... A drink!.. I tell you, another drink!..

S₁ Don't forget you're the one that's forcing him to drink the third bottle for your own selfish pleasure. The poor heart!.. Look at it beat!..*

S₂ And so it's your opinion that it ought to be snoozing away all day like Subconscious over there?.. A fine way indeed to spend one's life...

S₁ If the heart keeps on beating like that, it won't go on much longer.

S₂ So, it'll stop sooner or later anyway.

S₁ You're using my very words.

S₂ Ah well, you don't talk nonsense all the time.

S₁ Don't pluck on the nerves!.. You've been told many times... *(The nerves resound each time they're plucked.)*

S₂ *(flaring up)*. By who? Who was told?.. What am I around here, a lackey or something? I'm a poet!.. I'm love!.. I'm fire!.. If it weren't for me this place would be full of mold and cobwebs... a classroom, a cemetery! Because where there's no passion, there's a cemetery...

S₁ Pure rubbish...

S₂ I'm speaking the honest truth... Whose fault is it he drinks, do you suppose?

S₁ You're the one demanding he drink more!

S₂ Sure, I demand it, so you and your boredom won't drive him to hang himself.

S₁ Pure rubbish... I think it's just the other way around, all his unhappiness

---

* Translator's note: In Evreinov's own production of the play at the Crooked Mirror Theater, the heart, lungs, the entire set moved rhythmically throughout the play, varying according to the mood and keeping time with the music.

and misfortunes are because you, the emotional Self, are such a debauched, lost soul! Don't you ever have the faintest interest, well, let's say, in intellectual pursuits, in the noble work of the mind, aren't you ever visited by any higher, moral considerations?

S2 You make me sick! You and your damned morality, you and your miserable catechism!

S1 I despise you, emotional Self!..

S2 And I despise you, rational Self! *(With his extravagant gestures he accidentally brushes the nerves.)*

S1 You scoundrel! Don't pluck on my nerves!..

S2 Shut up!.. Allow me to observe, Mr. Rational Self, that we have our nerves in common, and that when I pluck on your nerves, I'm also plucking on my own, and when, thanks to you, my nerves get numb, then I get stupid as a log, that is, like you. I'll pluck on the nerves any time I damn well feel like it. In fact, I'm quite happy they're strained so tightly, that gives me a chance to play a hymn of love and freedom on them!.. *(Plays his hymn, after which the heart commences beating still faster. On the telephone.)* Another drink!..

S1 *(tearing the receiver from S2)*. Valerian drops!

S2 *(tears it back)*. Another drink!

S1 *(tears it back and holds off S2)*. Valerian drops!.. You hear?.. None left? Go to the medicine cabinet... Valerian drops!.. Thirty in a glass of water. *(Leaves the telephone... Both pace around the stage. They meet face to face.)* Have you calmed down now?

S2 Have you?

S1 What do you think? *(Goes over to S3. Pause.)*

S2 How's Subconscious doing?

S1 Same as ever... Perfectly tranquil... Don't disturb him!.. It'll be worse for you if you do... *(On the telephone.)* Did you take the drops? Fine, I'll try one more time to talk some sense into him. *(Takes S2 by the arm and walks around with him.)* The truth of the matter is I don't understand the basic problem. Well, all right, this woman has captivated you with, so to say, the originality of her talent, if we can call it talent at all, but for a man on that account to desert his wife and children—forgive me for saying so—is not exactly a solution to the problem... at least not unless we're polygamists, that is, wild savages for whom soft thighs or round hips are of greater importance than a temple like this, that is, the soul...

S2 Oh, you and your damned logic!.. What is it all to me?!. She's beautiful!.. What's there to reason about?

S1 Animals don't reason, sure enough, but man, in whom a certain logical approach should obtain... *(Into the telephone as he walks past it.)* Light up a cigarette!

S2 God, but you're boring!.. It's perfectly awful to be eternally connected with anything so boring as all this sweetness and light of yours.

S1 You didn't use to talk that way.

S2 Sure, I even used to like you a lot, when you and I used to go arm in arm. I'll never forget, for instance, the service you rendered me when I was aflame with love for Anna. Convincing a distrustful girl and lulling the vigilance of her parents... When you put your mind to it you're a real clever rascal! But since then you've not only failed to get any sharper, but you've gotten quite dull, my good friend, like a rusty razor...

S1 Much obliged for the compliment... But I'm not going to be offended. You're just all worked up at the moment.

S2 Ah, but she's beautiful!.. Ye Gods!.. You've forgotten how beautiful she actually is, how unusual she is, so dainty, so piquant!.. Sure, she's a cafe singer, what does that prove?... You've forgotten what she looks like... You've forgotten! I'll call her. *(He leads out from stage left an image of the cafe singer, an extraordinarily seductive one. To her.)* Sing, sing, like you sang yesterday, the day before, last week, on that Sunday. *Chantez, je vous prie!* I beg you!.. *(To S1, who turns away from the image.)* Try to pick up a little French, will you, I really need it.

SONGSTRESS IMAGE NO. 1 *(singing and dancing in time to the joyfully beating heart).*

Est-ce vous le p'tit jeun'homme
Qu'était l'autre jour tantot
Pres d'moi dans l'metro?
A la station
De l'Odeon?
Je n'ai pas pu vous voir
Car il faisait trop noir
Mais j'voudrais savoir
Est—c'vous? est-c'vous?
Dont mon baiser si doux
M'a rendu amoureux fou?

L'autre jour j'étais dans le metro
Un monsieur s'assied pres de moi.
Je le regarde aussitot.
Mais la lumiere juste a ce moment
S'eteignit subitement.
Mon voisin effraye s'jette dans mes bras!
Affolee je l'embrasse et depuis c'jour la
Je le cherchais en vain et plein d'émoi.
J'dis a chaque homme, que j'apprecois:
Est-c'vous le petit bon homme etc.

S2 *(ecstatic).* Enchanting!.. This joy is worth more than the whole world!.. And those feet!.. My God, can there by anywhere in this world a carpet worthy of being trod upon by those feet, so tiny they make you want to cry... Dance on me!.. Dance in me!.. Oh, fragrant incense!.. *(Kisses her feet, then her hands and lips.)*

S₁ Oh, delusion!.. Leave her alone!.. Leave her... it's only your imagination!.. She's not like that at all! You're kissing her makeup, you're caressing her wig... She's forty years old... Leave her... It's all fake... Here's the reality. *(As his speech began Songstress Image No. 1 drifted off left, whence S₁ then leads in Songstress Image No. 2, a grotesque caricature.)* Look, if you want to know the truth... In-grown toenails on those divine feet and those "beloved" corns... Calf's head *au naturel*—without wig or makeup. *(Lifts off her wig revealing a bald head underneath.)* Let's take off the bust now! *(She removes her falsies.)* Let's take out the teeth now! *(She removes her false teeth.)* Now sing! *(She sings off-key, gumming the words and prancing around, with all the grace of some old nag sent off to the glue factory.)*

S₂ *(shouting).* It's not true, it's not true!.. She's not like that at all! *(To her.)* Get out of here!!! *(chases her off.)*

S₁ "You are angry, Jupiter, ergo you must be wrong."

S₂ Rubbish.

S₁ Oh, you know perfectly well that this grand passion of yours is not worthy to tie the shoelaces of the one you're prepared to betray... And for what? For what? *(Leads out from right a magnificent image of a wife, rocking a baby in her arms.)* For always being so dutiful, for caressing you, nursing your children?.. Oh, she can't sing, to be sure, like your cafe singer, but just listen to the way she sings a lullaby, if you still have ears for such pure sounds. True, she doesn't sing very well, but she's been singing without sleep the last three nights... She's been waiting for you...

WIFE IMAGE NO. 1 *(singing softly).*

> Sleep, oh darling baby boy,
> Sweetly dream, my little joy...
> Mommy's here so don't you cry,
> Lullaby, lullaby...

Sleep, little baby, go to sleep... Does 'a baby hurt? It'll go away, darling... You'll see, you precious... What?.. Dada?.. Where's Dada? Dada'll be here soon. Dada's working now and pretty soon he'll bring you a nice new toy. You want a horsie? Gallopy, gallopy... Want a horsie?.. Dada's so good...

S₂ *(rudely).* Enough of this comedy!.. That's not it at all... It's a crude idealization... *(Chases her off.)* Get out of here!.. Imagine what a heroine!.. All exaggerated... She's not like that at all... I know her... She's poisoned my entire life... Not a drop of poetry or joy, bores me to tears and acts like some damned heroine... A scullery maid!.. Here she is... *(Brings in Wife Image No. 2 and replaces Wife Image No. 1 with her. Wife Image No. 2 is a sharp-tongued petty bourgeoise with a slovenly chignon and dressed in a shabby dressing gown*

355

covered with coffee stains.)

WIFE IMAGE NO. 2 *(shrilly)*. Imagine, such happiness, a bookkeeper!..
If my mother and father only knew how I suffer with this wretched bastard...
It's a pure wonder he hasn't been fired by now!.. The drunken sot!.. His stupid
brain won't even operate without alcohol... Gave me all these kids and now la-
de-da... I'm in love, he says, with art, with the theater... This cafe singer a theater?
I wouldn't let painted sluts like that come anywhere near me! He'll infect all
the kids yet! Good-for-nothing idiot... Some breadwinner!.. If it hadn't been
for me he'd have hocked the kids' diapers long ago... Won't cross himself either,
the atheist... Stupid as a log, but he loves to philosophize... Freedom, he says,
a citizen's duty... Freedom to guzzle vodka?.. I'll freedom you, you wretch!..

S₂ There she is, your heroine... That's the one I dare not leave for *(leads
in from left Songstress Image No. 1)* this one, who, like some magic nectar in-
toxicates me, justifies my existence on earth... *(The Songstress sings and does
the can-can, forcing Wife Image No. 2 right and into the shadows, but then backs
up, stops singing as Wife Image No. 1, noble, majestic, aggrieved, advances on
her.)*

WIFE IMAGE NO. 1. Go away, I beg you, there is no place for you here.
S₁ Right.

WIFE IMAGE NO. 1. You don't love him anyway... You wouldn't sacrifice a thing for him. You've had dozens just like him before... Don't get him all
excited if you have the slightest shred of decency left. I need his presence, his
support... Don't take him away... Don't take him away from his family!..

SONGSTRESS IMAGE NO. 1 *(laughing gaily)*. Ha, ha, ha, ha! *(Speaking
deep in her throat with a French accent.)* Such big words!..

WIFE IMAGE NO. 1. Go away, I repeat, don't drive me too far...

SONGSTRESS IMAGE NO. 1. Are you threatening me? And why, pray
tell? Because my legs are beautiful, my breasts are firm, and happy words fly
from my mouth like doves, like champagne corks!..

S₂ *(applauding)*. Bravo, bravo...

WIFE IMAGE NO. 1 *(to her)*. All you need is money, you floozie for
sale!..

SONGSTRESS IMAGE NO. 1. What? I'm a floozie for sale, am I?.. You
take that back... *(Approaches threateningly.)*

WIFE IMAGE NO. 1. Get out!..*(They rush at each other and battle furi-
ously, while the quivering heart thumps loudly, seemingly in agony. We also hear
curses and bitter threats: "shameless hussy... floozie... parasite... idiot... whore...
slut... damn you to hell." They disappear into a dark corner, then come out again
even more furious, but now in the form of Images No. 2. The wife has her teeth
in the songstress' wig, the songstress has a firm grip on the wife's tresses. They
switch back again to their positive images and reveal the songstress' victory over
the wife. The wife is held flat on the floor by the songstress' powerful knee. The
unfortunate wife then runs off right with a wail amid the songstress' loud laughter and S₂'s applause. Meanwhile an enraged S₁ slaps the songstress loudly in the*

356

face, she shrieks pitifully as she backs off upstage like a wounded puppy. S2 is not going to stand for that! He hurls himself at S1 and strangles him. The heart stops for an instant, two or three overstrained nerves burst. S2, satisfying himself his enemy is dead, throws himself at the Songstress' feet.)

S2 You are now the ruler here!.. My queen!..

SONGSTRESS IMAGE NO. 1. Oh no, sweetheart, no indeed... I was just teasing... First the money, then the love... And you don't smell much like money to me... Where are you going to get any?.. No, no, I'm not yours... I was just teasing. *(She disappears left. S2 is paralyzed with despair. The Songstress' teasing singing drifts in from the left, far away. The infinitely sorrowful Wife Image No. 1 clutches her sick baby at right and fixes her enormous eyes on S2. She seems to be rocking her baby a little, or is it nodding her head reproachfully in S2's direction?)*

S2 *(unable to bear it any longer, rushes to the telephone).* Oh please... quick... It's all over now... I'm exhausted... The pistol's in the right back pocket... Hurry!.. Hurry!.. I can't bear it any longer... Don't miss!.. Between the third and fourth ribs!.. Go on, go on!.. What are you afraid of?.. It's just an instant. Quick!.. *(A pause. S3 awakes and uneasily looks around as if sensing impending disaster. A shot rings out, very loud, as if from a cannon, and the roar reverberates through the soul. An enormous, gaping hole appears in the heart, out of which roll red ribbons. Darkness descends. S2 falls convulsively to the floor beneath the heart, drowning in a sea of red ribbons. The heart stops. The lungs cease breathing. A pause. S3 trembles and stretches nervously a few times. The Conductor enters with a lighted lantern.)*

CONDUCTOR. Newville... Who's getting off here?.. Mr. Subconscious, hey, Mr. Subconscious!.. Here's where you change... Newville...

S3 Newville? All right... let's go! Newville!.. *(Puts on his hat, picks up his suitcase and yawns as he follows the Conductor.)*

CURTAIN.

ARTICLES

Denis Mickiewicz

APOLLO AND MODERNIST POETICS

In view of the amount of research devoted to various aspects of the Silver Age, it seems appropriate to call attention to the role of the journal *Apollo* (St. Petersburg, 1909-1917). In this most elegant of all Russian journals the final formulations of some of the leading tendencies in art and poetry were announced, the mature works of most of the pioneers of the "new trends" were published, and many important new poets and critics made their debuts. The name of the magazine appears in most sources which deal with Russian art and literary history, but usually only as a bibliographical reference, sometimes vaguely annotated as "another modernist journal," or, quite misleadingly, as an "organ of the Acmeists," an "anti-Symbolist" or "bourgois-decadent" publication. Despite the journal's unquestionably high artistic and scholarly standards, and its vitality, the lack of a more thorough treatment may have resulted from the editors' somewhat arrogant departure from the long revered norms of Russian publicists. It was customary, even among avant-gardists, to demonstrate a strong commitment to the causes of enlightening the public, by being highly partisan, sharply polemical, and perspicacious about "great issues." Lacking these features, *Apollo* was not identifiable with a particular cause. Avoiding "the path of devoted school-teachers" on the one hand, and that of autonomous art on the other, the editors stated that the concern for art, though primary, "will certainly lead us beyond the limits of specifically artistic tasks and themes." Similarly, while steering away from "lifeless academicism," they scorned the ephemeral "formless daring of a creativity which forgot the laws of cultural heritage."[1] Moreover, conceived as a creative accommodation of divergent views, *Apollo* maintained from its inception a distaste for "the intellectual impoliteness of convincing someone," and saw as the object of discourse "merely an articulate expression of one's point of view."[2] The absence of a more tangible, let alone extravagant, position, coupled with disinterest in persuading its public, annoyed even some of the journal's own noted contributors. It also makes it

360

difficult for historians to specify the influence of *Apollo* on Russian Modernism. Towards the end of this short survey, some implications of the positions outlined above will be touched on in relation to Modernism in general; the immediate purpose of this essay, however, is to align the history of *Apollo* with the development of Modernist poetry, specifically, with that of the isolation of Symbolist ideology and the emergence of Acmeism.[3]

Apollo began publication at the climax of the artistic and intellectual ferment which had been growing in Russia since the eighteen-nineties. Battles against the hegemony of civic thought had already been won. Artistic values, including those of the avant-garde, had been accepted as equal to any by the established press. A *juste milieu* had begun to form in Russia. The Modernist *maîtres* had reached out for world culture and had gained the reputation of authoritative scholars and intelligent craftsmen. Now, before the widening and deepening sensibilities of the younger generation, a variety of competing methods, manners and goals which germinated from mostly Symbolist sources unfolded with unprecedented swiftness. The new journal's appearance coincided with the rising need to order and evaluate the achievements of the movement and to promote works or authors whose influence would promise not only momentum, but also durability for the movement. The history of Modernism was always turbulent, but now the term "crisis" was heard more and more often in poetic circles. This crisis had significant external and internal manifestations. *The Scales (Vesy)* and *The Golden Fleece (Zolotoe Runo),* the two Symbolist strongholds, were about to close down, which meant that there would be no more avant-garde periodicals in Russia. This is not to say that, as some decades ago, there would not be any outlets for Modernist creativity. Now there were plenty of "thick" magazines and widely circulated papers which gladly accepted most of this work for publication; besides, the Symbolists' publishing houses Skorpion and Grif still intended to issue almanacs with their contributors' fiction. But there would be no other source that would constantly advocate a desired creative direction. In retrospect it may seem surprising that arguments about "directions" appeared to be so vitally important; but such was the nature of an avant-garde which sought to advance both realms: that of creative motivation and that of creative devices. The latter are, of course, more suited to objective discussion; they are easy to detect and to contrast.

But the former, muddled and far-reaching, only vaguely suggested by the artistic forms, provoked endless debates and required explanatory theories. This is why the leaders of contending schools never contested each other's techniques; only philosophy was subject to attack. In the years to come this trend was reversed, especially in scholarly criticism. *Apollo,* which was among the initiators of this reversal, was on the other hand determined to reject its extreme implications. Meanwhile, the internal vulnerability of the dominant school threatened the future of Modernism. The recent victory of Ivanov's brand of "the truest type of Symbolist creativity" over Bely's, which (with the tacit agreement of Blok) seemed to unite the most influential poets around the theory that "everyman's mythmaking" *(vsenarodnoe mifotvorchesto)* will be the overarching cultural goal, and will provide the inner resources for the canon of a Grand Style, did not produce a more effective stimulus for creativity than had the discarded esoteric individualism of Bely.[4] First, as Annensky points out in his article in the first issue of *Apollo,* Ivanov's myths had reached a stage of such complexity that they lost all hope of universality *(vsenarodnost').*[5] Over-complexity had generally begun to hamper Symbolist creativity on many levels. Then, as Tynyanov explains it, Symbolism "became entrapped in its own poetic culture . . . having recognized its themes as most important, as a propelling factor—it went after the themes—and went out of living poetry."[6] The tendency to transcend and escape from the limits of art always hounded international Symbolism, almost by definition. Now, however, there seemed to be no great talents forthcoming to fill its artistic ranks. It would be incorrect to assume that at the time a new set of principles had arisen to challenge or replace those of Symbolism. But there arose symptoms of fatigue from the efforts to specialize Symbolism more and more narrowly. The writings of the younger poets already indicated an impending rift in poetic feeling which, according to Zhirmunsky, was perhaps even more profound than the transition from the lyricism of the eighties to the art of the Symbolists.[7]

The editors of *Apollo,* too young to have been involved in and committed to the formulation of Symbolist tenets, while revering the high artistic standards of the *maîtres,* had a greater affinity with the less dogmatic youth, especially with the urbane and unfrenzied youth of St. Petersburg, and with the tastes and cosmopolitan *élan* of Diagilev's and Benois' *The World of Art*

(*Mir Iskusstva*) group. The legend of this first nucleus of organized Modernism in Russia is still very much alive in the West. For *Apollo* it represented a much needed antidote to the ponderous "daring" of the Moscow avant-gardists. In terms of values, tone, format, mode of operation, and effect on the cultural life of St. Petersburg, the group's journal, *The World of Art* (1898-1904), set a much appreciated example for the younger journal. Because poetry had made the most striking advances in Russia, the group around *Apollo* was initially drawn to poetry as the major issue. But *Apollo* began its activity neither as a successor to the still functioning *The Scales* and *The Golden Fleece* nor as their antagonist; it took into account the advances of Modernist scholarship since *The World of Art* and retained from the older journal the sense of clarity, emotional restraint, and a certain festive optimism. The design of *Apollo* (for which *The World of Art* artists Bakst, Dobuzhinsky and Mitrokhin were employed) surpassed in quality that of all Russian journals. It adopted and improved the typographical innovations introduced by *The World of Art.* It differed from *The Scales* not only in the quality of paper and print, but also in the style of its graphics. While *The Scales* leaned in its ornamentation and decoration mostly towards the style of *art nouveau, Apollo* in its stylization of Classical and Neo-Classical taste stressed the value of a more aristocratic appearance. Not as lavish as *The Golden Fleece, Apollo* was more reminiscent in its restrained *Schlichtheit* of the esthetics of the age of Pushkin.

The best available information on the founding of *Apollo* is provided by the memoirs of Sergei K. Makovsky, its founder, publisher, editor and a poet and art historian. Born in 1877, the son of a popular portraitist and historical genre painter, Konstantine E. Makovsky, he was naturally immersed in the cultural life of St. Petersburg. In his early career Makovsky was attracted to the trends set by *The World of Art,* whose Wednesday evenings he regularly attended. In areas besides Modernism Makovsky's tastes and activities were strikingly similar to those initiated by *The World of Art.* Because he was only an amateur artist, Makovsky did not develop the skills of the stylists Benois and Dobuzhinsky, but he was interested in the passéist directions they took, and like them he was a collector of art. In 1907 he founded the journal *Bygone Years (Starye gody),* which he edited until 1917; it was dedicated to the rediscovery of ancient art. From 1913 to 1914 Makovsky was the founder and editor of another journal exploring the history of art, *Russian Ikons (Russkie ikony).* Following the direction set by *The World of Art* Makovsky devoted much of his time to organizing and presenting exhibitions of art, not only in Russia, but also in Belgium, Germany, and France. They were of a very high caliber, though perhaps lacking the dash and luster of Diagilev's famous exhibitions. In January 1909 Makovsky introduced a new procedure in Russia, wherein an exhibition showed "all" of the contemporary artists instead of a particular artist or school; such was the "Salon of 1909."

It was in January 1909 at the "Salon" that the idea to found *Apollo* germinated; here Makovsky met the young poet Gumilev and discussed with him the ideas about a new Petersburg journal. Gumilev immediately offered to introduce Makovsky to Innokenty Annensky. Placing great hopes on Annensky's help to the writing youth *(pisatel'skaia molodezh'),* Gumilev spoke with the greatest enthusiasm about the author of *Quiet Songs (Tikhie pesni).*[8] Gumilev's idea resulted in the mutual satisfaction of the relatively inexperienced publisher and the unrecognized older poet, who seized the opportunity of literary recognition and stimulating association. At the "Salon" a wealthy dilettante impressed by Makovsky's efforts offered assistance for Makovsky's further enterprises. Thus, with his financial help, M. Ushkov became the co-publisher of *Apollo.*

Like Gumilev, who "basically did not belong to any literary school [at that time]" and who seemed to possess "not only talent, but also the freshness of some kind of original poetic truth," Makovsky did not want his new journal to join the movements of the Moscow or Petersburg Symbolists. Thus, long before any formal anti-Symbolist trends were articulated, the relatively young editorial board carried the sentiment of emancipation. This common tendency of emancipation and Gumilev's dedication to *Apollo* determined Makovsky's decision to ignore any doubts about Gumilev's intellectual ability to be the head of the poetry section of the journal. (These doubts were voiced especially by Vyacheslav Ivanov.)[9] A characteristic feature of the cultural scene of the time was the precondition for the founding of a journal to have "united" a group of like-minded authors in a "society."

To be published by a journal a writer had to establish contact with its "society" and conversely, for the editors of a prospective journal it was desirable to set up a society in order to ensure the necessary number of capable contributors. Makovsky was in a favorable position to attempt to establish a society because of his experience in journalism as editor of the art section of V. S. Mirolyubov's popular *Magazine for Everyone (Zhurnal dlia vsekh)* and as co-editor of *Bygone Years*—not to mention his excellent connections with influential artists and intellectuals. But if this enterprise was to become a leading national institution, the greatest possible prestige was necessary in order to distinguish the society from the many enthusiastic but short-lived circles which sprang up everywhere in Russia at this time. Makovsky and his friends got the help of Ivanov, whose prestige and willingness to work with young poets created both a workshop and a salon of the highest caliber. Ever since his return from the University of Berlin, Ivanov's erudition and instinct in matters of poetic craft made" Vyacheslav the Magnificent" the undisputed arbiter for the Petersburg Modernists. Of Ivanov, Makovsky wrote:

> Vyacheslav Ivanov was invariably the "soul" of these meetings, which the "Apollonians" called the "Poetic Academy". . .
>
> He was unusually broadminded in evaluating others' creativity. He loved poetry . . . not his own role in it as "mentor" (as we used to say), leader, teacher, ideologist, but the talent of every promising neophyte . . . . We all loved him for his temperamental [but] unselfish [ways], for his extravagant generosity, both in giving advice to his younger poet-brothers and in giving his views on art . . . and [for] his selfless attention to anyone who came to the temple of Apollo.

Another older *maître,* Annensky, exerted an influence on the whole enterprise. Makovsky recalls:

> It is doubtful that *Apollo* would have appeared if it were not for my meeting with Innokenty Fedorovich . . . Financial means were obtained. But I hesitated for a long time . . . Not because I did not envision the program of the journal, but because I lacked an experienced older adviser (who would be recognized by all of the members of the future editorial board) to lend authoritativeness to me, a beginning writer, in the difficult task of chief editor . . . From the day of our "alliance" [March 1909] Annensky set to work feverishly on articles and poems.... He proved to be exactly the kind of an older adviser I needed. I wanted to remain as objective as possible in the selection of materials, without being influenced by cliques, and even more, editorial nepotism— Annensky was exceptionally independent and tolerant.[10]

Annensky stood apart from the struggle for supremacy of the literary schools; he did not join any of the circles that formed around the various *maîtres* of Petersburg or Moscow Symbolism. Gumilev, who according to Makovsky was his most energetic and efficient helper, before he had made an arrangement with Annensky at Tsarskoe Selo, introduced Makovsky to his friends Alexei Tolstoy, Sergei Auslaender, and Sergei Gorodetsky; Makovsky had already met Mikhail Kuzmin.

The possibility of opening a major journal posed the problem of converting Ivanov's private salon into a professionally run organization. The first steps were described by Makovsky.

> Vyacheslav Ivanov was most concerned with the solution of this problem; he was already looking for another literary hearth to host the meeting of his "tower" (which demanded too much of his time and drained his financial resources). Here Gumilev with his youngsters helped a lot. Disregarding his disagreements with Vyacheslav Ivanov about the aim of poetry and the style of Russian verbal creativity *(slovotvorchestvo)*, he took an active part in creating the Academy of Verse...(soon re-named) the Society of Adepts of the Artistic Word.

Makovsky's connections with high governmental officials helped him to obtain permission to hold public meetings. *Apollo's* offices occupied luxurious suites which could also house small exhibits, concerts and lectures.

> Under the chairmanship of V. Ivanov the executive committee was elected by the founders: it included I. Annensky, S. Makovsky, M. Kuzmin, A. Blok, and N. Gumilev. When Annensky died (November 30, 1909), he was replaced by Professor F. F. Zelinsky, and somewhat later Professor Fedor Braun joined.

> The critic Valerian Chudovsky joined a year after *Apollo* was founded and after its secretary E. A. Znosno-Borovsky retired and was replaced by Mikhail L. Lozinsky who was also introduced by Gumilev.[11]

The society had as many as fifty-seven members, mostly poets, according to Leonid Strakhovsky. In addition to the staff members mentioned above, other members of the society who became regular contributors to the literature section of *Apollo* were M. Voloshin, A. Tolstoy, Johann von Guenther, V. Pyast (Pestovsky), S. Gorodetsky, F. Sologub, Ya. Verkhovsky, Kondratiev, Mandelstam, G. Ivanov, V. Narbut, and V. Borodaevsky. The society met formally once or twice a month.

In addition to lectures on the rhythmic subtleties of Russian versification, instrumentation of verse, and the application of classical meters to Russian rhythms (given respectively by Ivanov, Annensky, and Zelinsky), these meetings had three basic purposes: to present and discuss unpublished fiction of special thematic or methodological interest, to demonstrate "discoveries" in the history or theory of poetry, and (since the "society" boasted among its members such a number of prominent classical philologists) to read and discuss recent translations and original stylizations of classical sources. Compared with similar work performed in the days of *The World of Art* the level of scholarship and creative maturity was considerably higher. The pioneering Modernists welcomed every new effort on the part of their colleagues, and at the almost solemnly formal sessions of the "Academy" judgments were passed on each work after a punctiliously careful investigation—by standards which were not reached before nor after in Russia.

Perhaps most noteworthy for the wider public were the sessions at which the leading poets made formal speeches about their philosophy of poetry, intellectual and artistic allies. Such were the speeches "The Tenets of Symbolism" by Vyacheslav Ivanov on March 26, 1910; Blok's "On the Current State of Russian Symbolism" on April 8, 1910; and almost two years later on February 18, 1912, Ivanov's "Thoughts on Symbolism" and Bely's "On Symbolism." Historically, the latter occasion was more significant since it witnessed the first formal break with Symbolism on the part of the younger Modernist poets. D. V. Kuzmin-Karavaev, S. M. Gorodetsky, and Gumilev stated their principal disagreements with the objectives of Symbolism and the decision to part from that movement.

Since essentially it was this society that created the literary background out of which *Apollo* grew, it is revealing to examine the question which prominent figures of Modernist poetry did not participate in the society. The lists of the most prominent members of the "Society of the Adepts of the Artistic Word" reveals the conspicuous absence of such recognized poets as Balmont, Bely, Bryusov, Gippius, and Merezhkovsky. On the other hand, the participation of such Symbolists as Ivanov, Blok, Sologub, and Annensky indicates that *Apollo* was not intended as a counterforce to Symbolism, as is frequently suggested; nor did it reflect the geographical division between Petersburg and Moscow, as the absence of the Merezhkovskys and later of Blok demonstrates.

In terms of format of publications, *Apollo* was to publish ten numbers during the year; there would be no summer issues. Each issue would have approximately one hundred and twenty pages, and the entire journal would be divided into three major sections: a section of theoretical articles on art, literature, or music; a section called "Chronicle" devoted to surveys and criticism, both domestic and foreign, of the contemporary cultural scene; and a "literary almanac" section. In 1910 the literary almanac was placed in the second position in the journal, and in 1911 it was published separately as *The Literary Almanac of Apollo,* except for some poetry which was retained in the journal's first section. Later the sections called "Rossica," which was devoted to Russian cultural achievements abroad (such as concerts, exhibits, books, or Diagilev's productions); "Art and War," which recorded artistic activities pertaining to war (i.e. charity auctions, concerts, etc., the themes of war in art, and the destruction of monuments of art by war), and "Chronicle of the Revolution" (also dedicated to the preservation of art treasures) were added to the "Chronicle."

The first issue of *Apollo* appeared on October 15, 1909. Besides the customary introductory manifesto of the editor, an introductory article was written by Alexandre Benois, the former co-editor of *The World of Art.* It is a striking effort to make the vital task of the journal, the "Hymn to Apollo," as vivacious as possible, so that the curtain between art and life be transcended by a joyous dance. The editors also published a semi-humorous symposium of the leading members of *Apollo* in order to show the diversity of ways in which the group will serve Apollo. Also, they made it clear that their assertion of Apollo's continuous victory over Dionysus indicates *Apollo's* decision to "assert rather than to destroy norms."

The "stock taking" of all the achievements of Russian Modernist poetry was undertaken for *Apollo* by Innokenty Annensky. The author intended to write three articles under the general title *On Contemporary Lyricism:* "They" *(Oni,* published in Nos. 1 and 2 of *Apollo),* "Them" *(One,* in No. 3) and "It" *(Ono*—Annensky died before writing this third essay). The essays contain a peculiar blending of historical, critical and theoretical information. Annensky's tone with its intricate *causerie,* mannered humor, devious subtlety and elaborate irony, struck an unprecedented note in Russian criticism. His tone implied an equal amount of reverence to established as well as to beginning poets. Annensky stressed later that he intentionally characterized the vital issues of the present ("traditions, credo, hierarchy, egotisms, occupied positions") as "indifferently transient."[12]

Wandering in a sinuous way across the contemporary poetic scene, Annensky's essays are not so much an effort to explain what is good and what is not in Modernist poetry as an attempt to create a detached view, to extricate criticism from the norms of fashion and tradition. Annensky achieved this formally by fragmenting his thoughts into new patterns of associative digressions alternating between characterizations of poets, discussions on general poetics and historical information—while omitting value judgments. His avoidance of repetition demanded that the readers connect the various levels of discussion in an unusually rapid and lightfooted fashion. Perhaps not all members of the *Apollo* circle agreed with Annensky's treatment of the literary scene, but the commitment to discuss poetry purely aesthetically was consistently practiced by all the critics of *Apollo*. Only their tone became less and less mannered as the intended position of the pioneering article became more and more domineering. Whatever differences in aesthetic taste the younger critics developed, they rather superceded Annensky in his own directions than countered them. This important debt *Apollo* acknowledged posthumously. The third issue of *Apollo* carried an obituary in which the editors, besides lamenting the loss of the "brilliant...erudite...and enthusiastic" collaborator, promised to do anything in their power to make Russian society appreciate "one of the best representatives of Russian culture *(kul'turnost')*." Indeed, the January 1910 issue carried four essays, by Zelinsky, G. Chulkov, Voloshin, and Ivanov, examining Annensky as a classical philologist, lyricist, and writer of tragedies. These articles, consisting of not only praise, but also of serious criticism, belong to the most thoughtful literature so far published on Annensky.

Another assessment of modern poetry was given by Gumilev in the first of his series entitled *Letters on Russian Poetry.*[13] If Annensky's treatment appeared overly sinuous, Gumilev could certainly not be blamed for the lack of direct value judgments. For his first review Gumilev selected four younger poets who differed markedly from each other, and who can be analyzed as manifestations of four mutually opposed attitudes towards poetic creativity.[14] His first "letter" revealed Gumilev's impartiality to themes and partiality to manner. He attempts to combine the evaluation of a poet (the degree to which the author accomplished the tasks he set himself) with the assessment of what that poet's achievement may contribute to poetry in general. Although in the later reviews Gumilev displays, of course, an increasing mastery and skill, this first review is a good approximation of the type of column with which he became identified in *Apollo.* But most important, this review illustrates how the young generation will approach Modernist poetry. There is no longer any discussion of "true" Symbolism; Symbolism is not even mentioned. However, the debt to the lessons of Symbolism is manifest in what we may call "post-Symbolist awareness" in Gumilev's criticism, when he speaks for example of Gorodetsky's vital "morning mood" song, which renders words unnecessary, or the "surprises" in the solemn parts of Borodaevsky's "Byzantine spirit." On the other hand, Gumilev shows great appreciation of very modest themes, such as the humble realism in Sadovsky's poetry. At no point does Gumilev show an interest in formal innovations or an adherence to any particular school or technique. With great tolerance toward the choice of themes and styles, but insisting on artistic plausibility, he seems to look for poets rather than poetics.

The first issue of *Apollo* contained fourteen poems by nine leading poets.[15] It is a rare historical occasion for an impressive group of poets to publish simultaneously some of their best and most characteristic works, and address them to the same important subject: the source of their inspiration, Apollo. The theme gives room for a wide range of poetic and philosophical statements; thus, each poem in this collection is to some degree a *profession de foi.* These poems can serve as excellent references for a comparison of the artistic and philosophical merits of the direction of each master. Together the poems indicate the journal's high projected standards and its relatively low interest in artistic experimentation. The diversity of the nine poets is apparent, and thus *Apollo* enters the history of literature affirming diversity, stating the standards of a mature stage of Modernism. It is characteristic that none of the poems represent "searches" *(iskaniia).* All of the poets, even the younger ones, have found their philosophy, their poetic idiom, their style or "tone" and their specific sphere of images. Perhaps the most noteworthy common element among the poems (compared to those of the "second generation" Symbolists and their epigones) is the determined effort to achieve clarity and precision in spite of the complex nature of the theme. Space prevents detailed analyses of the poems, but it is my contention that as a set they are the best representation of Russian poetic achievements of that period.

The swiftly moving cultural developments of the time became more dramatic with the impending disappearance of Symbolist periodicals. In December 1909, *The Scales* and *The Golden Fleece* published a manifesto in their final issues.[16] *The Scales* spoke in an assured, satisfied tone of its role in aesthetics, and *The Golden Fleece* discussed its role in serving national causes. The editors of *The Golden Fleece* wrote that the aim of the journal—"to seek the Golden Fleece right here in the depths of the Russian spirit"—is opposed to that "reflected by *The World of Art*...[whose] formula of 'aestheticism' and 'historicism'...in literature and painting is bound to bring Russian art inevitably to a dead end." This notion is identical to that expressed in the articles by Chulkov and Gorodetsky which *The Golden Fleece* published about the first issue of *Apollo*.[17]

Apollo apparently saw little reason to comment extensively on the departure of *The Golden Fleece*.[18] Historically they were not connected, and the obvious ideological difference was not even that of a disagreement. Concerned almost exclusively with research about artists, the surviving journal avoided a stand on partisan Symbolist issues on one hand, and on the pursuit of the national spirit on the other. In terms of a national cause *Apollo* conceived its task as serving the enlightenment of Russia principally through that *juste milieu* which took Western aesthetical and ethical standards for granted.

The closing of the aesthetically more sophisticated *The Scales* produced a greater reaction in *Apollo*. By making "tomorrow" the symbol of a distinctly "different" process or phase of cultural growth, the admission is implied that *The Scales* sees its task only in "yesterday's" phase, which is now "successfully" accomplished. Accordingly, *Apollo* courteously acknowledged indebtedness to the older journal,[19] but did not make commitments to continue its policies. Especially because in the post-Bryusov period (1907-1909) *The Scales* stressed its "assertion of inseparable ties between aesthetics and mysticism," the debt which *Apollo* felt all Russian culture owed was to *The Scales'* earlier accomplishments: the authoritative guidance of Russian minds towards the current level of international standards in literature. Gumilev made two important points about the existence of *The Scales* and its place in the history of poetry, and his attitude may be regarded as representative of the attitude of *Apollo*. First, Gumilev says *The Scales* was successful in its role as a militant organ of Modernism:

> ...it also had the task of being the champion of cultural values which from Pisarev to Gorky have been treated rather irreverently. This task it fulfilled brilliantly and impressed upon the savages of the Russian press, if not respect for great names and ideas, at least . . . fear before them.

Gumilev then notes that regardless of the fate of the Symbolist journals or even Symbolism itself, in the history of art and in philosophy the modern artists have accepted Symbolism. Thus Gumilev, who soon became the noted leader of Acmeism, acknowledges the unquestionable heritage of Symbolism: "Now we can not avoid being Symbolists. This is not a challenge, or a wish, it is only a fact to which I attest."[20]

The Symbolists were not completely demobilized. While some of them joined *Apollo*, others busied themselves with the organization of new centers, of which three began to represent distinct directions. The mostly first-generation Aestheticists traditionally rallied around the publishing house Skorpion; in 1910 in Moscow the Transcendentalists founded their own publishing house, Musaget; and the "neo-populists," a carry-over of one of the principles of *The Golden Fleece,* headed by Blok, Pyast, and Chulkov, spent the 1910-1911 season in efforts to establish their own journal under the prospective names *The Symbolist, The Archer,* and *The Companion (Simvolist, Strelets,* and *Sputnik).* None of the currents produced a periodical, but a year later they all came out with representative almanacs, *Northern Flowers, A Musaget Anthology,* and *Sirin (Severnye Tsvety, Antologiia Musageta,* and *Sirin),* respectively. The "populist" current, representing merely an emotion rather than a professionally articulated political or aesthetic trend, soon dissolved between such diverse forces as the left-wing press, Musaget, and *Apollo*. Most of the old Aesthetes, by now classics of Modernism, felt no need to forge and defend a new common ideology. Consequently, Musaget emerged as the only organization besides *Apollo* dedicated to the advancement of Modernist culture.

The direction alternative to *Apollo* which was elaborated by the strong coalition of Bely and his circle, Vyacheslav Ivanov, E. Metner, and a group of professional philosophers headed by F. Stepun, N. Lossky, and B. Yakovenko, demands a deeper explication than the term "Transcendentalists" provides. Technically, like *Apollo,* Musaget was not only a publishing house but also a center for various activities: literary workshops, lectures, and other public presentations. Unlike *Apollo,* Musaget did not sponsor art exhibits and showed little interest in the visual arts; instead it emphasized its members' philosophic inclination by metaphysically approaching the "problem of culture which is the most complex problem of our days."[21] The traditional Modernist dichotomy became clear once more, only on a more advanced and perhaps more serious level. While in its approach to culture *Apollo* sought to discriminate among and to stimulate certain carefully selected achievements, Musaget sought to discover the very roots of culture in the depths of human spiritual experience. According to Musaget's ideologists the discovery of the basic cultural creative stimuli, which coincided with mankind's primary truths, would blaze a clear path for aesthetic creativity as well as effect the transformation of life by means of consciously elevating, universally relevant art. They argued that with its highly sophisticated formal dexterity contemporary art had become more suitable for expressing experiences than producing them, or finding their origins. Hence there was a need to go back to the primeval sources of such experiences. And these clearly lay beyond the reach of art.

In their efforts to reach the deepest sources of culture simultaneously on the philosophical, mystical, psychological and aesthetic levels, the leaders of Musaget did not neglect the value of direct communication through informal and formal speeches and lectures which they delivered in both capitals. The most important literary forum of the time, the Society of Adepts of the Artistic Word, which convened under the auspices of *Apollo,* was host to a number of such Musagetian excursions.[22] The drive to re-integrate poetry into culture which these speeches expressed achieved two historical results: Ivanov's and Blok's speeches on Symbolism given in March and April of 1910 revealed a gap in intellectual awareness between the second and the first "generations."[23] Later speeches by Pyast, Verkhovsky, Bely, and Ivanov, as already mentioned, effected a formal break with the third generation. *Apollo* published the first two speeches, and two responses: that of Bryusov and the reply to it by Bely.[24] This group of articles achieved great acclaim as *"the* debate on Symbolism conducted by its four leaders during the height of the crisis of the school."* Some critics see it as somehow the major literary achievement of *Apollo* and even connect it casually with the "rise of *Apollo's* Acmeism." To be sure, they were fine articles, but two of the "four leaders," Bryusov and Blok, would hardly agree with such a title; the "crisis" had already ended, since the second generation finally consolidated. As the only remaining journal *Apollo* harbored these articles more or less accidentally, out of personal respect to Ivanov and Blok. Bryusov's reply was published in order to be disassociated from, and lessen the impact of, the speeches. Bely's contribution was published in a backhanded if not insulting fashion, as will be seen below. Acmeism "arose" almost three years later, and was in no way influenced by this debate.

By the time of this debate, the alienation from Symbolist theories had proceeded far enough for *Apollo* to stay completely aloof from the issue. Not a single remark appeared in *Apollo* for or against either interpretation of Symbolism. Gumilev's second article about *The Scales,* which appeared in the same issue as Bryusov's contribution to the debate, clearly implied that the debate on Symbolism was irrelevant to the present reality of art, since "the movement . . . is sufficiently clarified," its historic course ended with *The Scales,* and "the very arguments about Symbolism show that the poets are no longer satisfied with the term."[25] Bely's contribution was put in small print in the "Chronicle" sections with an editorial footnote explaining that for "lack of space" this "important" debate would be continued outside the main section. But no further contributions appeared in *Apollo* to justify the editors' concern about space.

One may speculate that despite closer contact with Ivanov and Blok than with Bryusov, the sympathies of *Apollo* were on the side of the latter—not because Bryusov represented a "truer" Symbolism, but because he refrained from ideologizing, and treated the movement as if it were an academic matter of the past. It is also not insignificant that in the main section of the same issue as Bely's essay the editors printed an annihilating criticism of Bely's book *Symbolism* by Bryusov.[26]

The combat among the Symbolists did not cease after the debate in *Apollo.* In view of the alienation from its host, *Apollo,* and to accommodate Ivanov's idea to publish intimate, diary-like theoretical notes of the leading Symbolists, Musaget decided to publish their own bi-monthly *Works and Days (Trudy i Dni),* an intimate diary (Moscow, 1912-1916). It began as a direct continuation of the debate but gradually turned against the younger generation of poets, applying terms "consciously designed to repel" the epigones and the heretics. As a parallel development *Apollo* published a letter to the editors[27] in which Kuzmin presents a number of reasons why he decided to break with the "renewed Symbolism as it is expressed in *Works and Days.*"

If the rift between the poets of the second and third generations was clearly apparent, *Apollo's* position remained courteous, but circumspectly specific. In a review of *Works and Days*[28] Valerian Chudovsky, one of *Apollo's* most thoughtful columnists, undertook the task of defining his journal's relation to the last and purest stronghold of Russian Symbolism. Chudovsky stresses that taken separately all the articles in *Works and Days* are "good and even magnificent; in many [of them] I felt the genuine vision of the truth by which I live myself." But together, he says, these articles reflect the underlying intention of *internally uniting* poetry, art and religious philosophy. Chudovsky admits that integration of all culture and life is a profound and beautiful wish, but to him the tendency to resist the diffusion of atomization of culture found in individual "formalist" searches of most contemporary artists, is dangerous and unnecessary. *"Apollo feels that such a tendency is dangerous"* because it will turn life, as well as art, into an abstract speculative gnosticism and thus isolate these areas from the nature of man. It is an unnecessary trend because:

> ...artistic life will acquire its unity from within itself . . . . Our task, the task of *Apollo,* is to demonstrate that the seeming diffusion of the artistic searches . . . has its own synthesis, distinct from that which religion calls the One *(Edinyi),—* [it is] the synthesis of pure Beauty. We do not argue with them [the Transcendentalists] if they tell us: "There is only one God," we will reply: "Yes, but for art his name is Sun."

Chudovsky fears that the heterodoxy of *Works and Days* is of a greater danger than if it had been a plain heresy, which would have perished automatically: "the heterodoxy of [our] brother may eventually corrupt our own faith."

Thus, officially *Apollo* maintained an affinity with "our beloved" individual masters, rejecting only their collective ideology. But the individual members of *Apollo* became critical not only of the ends of "true" Symbolism but of the means of its representatives as well. For example, one might have expected that the decision of the former publishers of *The Scales* and *The Golden Fleece* to issue Symbolist verse in almanacs without polemical essays, would have caused universal acclaim, but neither the *Anthology* of Musaget nor the *Northern Flowers* of Skorpion created any enthusiasm on the part of the third generation. Gumilev, who appeared in and reviewed both of these volumes,[30] blamed Musaget for being unrepresentative and unselective and for making no editorial effort to order the material in a way that would demonstrate an hierarchical concept or point in some direction.

The most interesting point in his review is the observation that Symbolism is ineffectual when relieved from ideologizing, at least in a collection isolated from the total environment of their authors' works. "What was good six, seven years ago in *The Scales* with the support of articles and reviews now appears helpless and unconvincing."

But even on the level of individual artistic standards, aside from schools and ideologies, the third generation began to "outgrow" the aesthetics of the still respected veterans of Modernism. It is beyond the scope of this survey to elaborate on the individual cases. Roughly summarized, it was neither a matter of better verse-making nor of philosophizing; it was a case of a different psychic reaction to a different stage of modernity. The creativity of the *maitres* made increasingly less impact on the younger poets, although both their poetry and articles continued to appear in *Apollo*.

Apollo's policy of "observing the ties with the cultural past" included the recent past. Unlike the tiny but notorious group of radical Futurists, the third generation Modernists in *Apollo* sought to abolish as few as possible of the Modernist tendencies—only those which seemed to actively hamper creative processes. Thus the *Apollo* circle never lost respect for the achievements of Symbolism; it also regarded the styles of other cultural epochs as vital and suggestive creative possibilities. Despite great discrimination and restraint, the Apollonians were inspired by such "thematic" possibilities in much the same way as were the members of *The World of Art,* who had dedicated their art to the rediscovery of these sources.

Apollo's taste for graphic sharpness, which was also inherited from *The World of Art,* reflected the movement towards objectivity discussed earlier. Gradually this direction became recognizable as a post-Symbolist orientation indicated by the tendency to stress the delineations of objects rather than to project any ties from the objects to absolutes. The drive for delineation extends to the area of expression of lyrical notions as well as to the depiction of concrete reality. The premium now placed on clarity and vividness above the power of symbolization released a greater energy and incisiveness of the artistic gesture. Accordingly, the liberation from the intellectual demands of Transcendentalism shifted the process of creative perception from the "viewing with the mind" to a greater employment of the senses; the artistic objects now created, stripped of their intellectually symbolic functions, acquired a stark nakedness revealing their intrinsically colorful and multiform suggestiveness. Authors were now challenged by the "manly" task of mastering the temptation to diffuse their images and meanings by observing firmly the factual perimeter of each object. Such an outlook, which in poetic circles in 1912 was called "Adamism," complemented the prominence allotted to the treatment of primeval themes in painting, music, ballet, and prose. The "Adamistic" outlook revitalized stylization by keeping it from being predominantly decorative; this practice now assumed the full-blooded kinetic function of a gesture. Taste in objects of beauty also shifted from enjoying "discoveries" and longing to imbue them with extra meaning, to the gusto of possessing concrete items. The range of possibilities of expression within this attitude was extremely wide: from a primitivist enjoyment of the most elemental forms of a Gothic complexity to increasingly refined delineation. The treatment of taste as a more reliable standard for convention than profundity encouraged a lively practice of collaboration and cooperation among the arts.

The issue of retrospectivism is featured already in the first number of *Apollo.* Voloshin's article entitled "Archaism in Russian Painting" *("Arkhaizm v russkoi zhivopisi")* is an interpretation of the use of symbols by three of *The World of Art* artists, Bakst, Bogaevsky, and Roerich. Voloshin describes what the artists saw as the historic past of mankind, but more importantly, he discusses the stimulus which the discovery of the past may have on art. "Painters and poets turn the many-faceted mirror of world history in order to find in each prism a fragment of their own face."[31]

This article is a specific articulation of the trend called historical retrospectivism that was discussed earlier in connection with *The World of Art*. But here the discussion of the treasures of history for the creative artist is extended further back to classical times and to the prehistoric past. Voloshin himself was an artist, art critic, poet, and amateur archeologist, and thus he provided a personal example of that peculiar syncretizing artist of *Apollo*.

In the next two issues of *Apollo* Bakst himself wrote an article called "The Paths of Classicism in Art" *("Puti klassitsizma v iskusstve")*. Bakst takes a kind of Neo-Classicist position that is more advanced for Russian Modernism than the positions discussed heretofore. By "advanced" we mean that as these positions are applied to poetry they presage what the "Adamists" or "Acmeists" would later advocate in the Guild of Poets. The set of positions Bakst enunciates in this article bespeaks a considerable evolution away from his association with *The World of Art* a decade earlier. Then he had been among the first to advocate the emancipation of art from heteronomous purposes and immersion in the joy of stylization. Now in the *Apollo* article he examines the pitfalls of Modernism.

Artists became isolated from each other; they had lost interest in and attachment to the past, and therefore had no common heritage; the loss of this bond led to great interest in themselves, and hence to increasing individualism. For Bakst individualism is the loss of tradition and the loss of the sense of pure craft. As such, individualism is the most frightening enemy not only of art in general, but also of schools of art. As Bakst recognized here, it is only when many artists share recognized values that an important style can be created. A solution might well be a return to Classicism, which might serve as the unifying factor, if not for art as a whole, at least for the formation of a school of art. Such a return would also serve to strip away the many cumbersome features added by artists posing as stylists or mystics. Bakst sees the future art as pure: "Future art will burn toward the cult of man, his nakedness." This bareness of the new man is strikingly similar to what Gumilev, Gorodetsky, and Zenkevich will describe as the outlook of the newly awakened man who sees reality again, as if for the first time, and reminiscent of the poems of Voloshin in the first issue of *Apollo*. Speaking of what constitutes content in art, Bakst writes: "Elements of recent art—are air, the sun, greenery; the elements of the future are stones and men."[32] This prediction is also closely related to a trend in Acmeist poetry, especially prominent in Mandelstam's collection *Stone* (1913).

The first pronouncements to strike a new chord in Russian literary thought appeared in the fourth issue (January 1910) of *Apollo*. They were essays by Kuzmin and Voloshin. The latter's article on Henri de Régnier states directly, and officially for the first time, that Symbolism has been overcome. Voloshin uses the work of De Régnier as a vehicle for his argument: "The creativity of Henri de Régnier represents the transition from Symbolism to new Realism. For us who have outlived Symbolism and who enter a new organic epoch of art this example of the harmonious, strict and consistent metamorphosis is infinitely important."[33]

Kuzmin's essay[34] did not even mention the issue of schools and "isms"; it defined three contemporary approaches to style. But the now famous essay presented a challenging contrast to Symbolism and to non-Modernism by its very appearance and by its spirit. In every line its aloof tone, its own easy-going but precise working, and a deceptively simple language which is soft and polite but merciless to the uncultured (if they are cultured enough to catch the arguments) represent a conscious articulation of a new sensibility. To diminish any possibility of controversy this essay was modestly subtitled "notes on prose" *(zametki o proze)*, and it ended with the deprecatory remark that all the lecturing was done for the author's own benefit. But his article did have a great effect, especially on poetry, due to several well-calculated features; it contained nothing that did not apply to poetry; its unusual tone, reminiscent of, but not as esoteric as Annensky's criticism, applied indisputable terms which even when ironic lacked the usual dogmatic offensiveness. Most importantly, this unpedantic call for clarity re-introduced Annensky's practice of discussing aesthetic values without referring to all current doctrines.[35] Achieved only by omission, this was apparently not quite fully perceived by the readers. Kuzmin made it more emphatically a year later in a historical essay entitled "Gluck's *Orfeo ed Euridice.*" After discussing Gluck's revolutionary position at the time of one of history's great debates among musical schools on creating operas, which by definition include extra-musical creativity, Kuzmin concludes his essay:

> We do not wish hereby to diminish the trust in, and dampen the tendency to found schools, [not to attack] conscious adherence to principles in creativity; we only wish to remind [you] that these are not the

[factors] that should be regarded as the principal virtues when a work of art is evaluated, and that in the historic perspective [such] reformatory activity of artists retreats to a very distant plane.

But Kuzmin's "beautiful clarity," which was alien to the problematic approaches of the metaphysicists, stands as a historically tested value, distinctly in the foreground of other artistic merits. For that reason Kuzmin places at the beginning of his essay the words of Gluck: "My efforts have to be directed to find beautiful simplicity, and I consciously avoided the ostentatious trickiness which would harm it..."[36] This quotation enabled Kuzmin to show the "Orfeists" and theoreticians of Musaget that his own views were identical to those of a venerable master who still holds the reputation of one of the finest interpreters of the Orpheic spirit and myth.

If Voloshin and Kuzmin proposed new, post-Symbolist directions and titled them "Neo-Realism" and "Clarism," Gumilev does not yet announce a new school in his essay "The Life of Verse,"[37] although his interpretation of the topic also differs considerably from that given in the standard Symbolist writings. Perhaps unknown to Gumilev himself at the time, and unnoticed by literary historians, this essay embodied the essential point of departure for the future Acmeists. This fact is verified by Mandelstam's argument twelve years later, that "verbal images may be regarded not only as objective facts of consciousness, but also as organs of human senses . . . which permits the construction of an organic poetics which has a biological character rather than a canonic one."[38]

According to Gumilev "gesture" becomes the prime means of communication because the reader, by "the suggestive means of his own body, experiences the same [impulses] as the poet, so that the uttered thought becomes no longer a lie, but truth." Like many Symbolists he realizes the necessity of extraverbal means to reveal psychological reality or "to give himself; but it is a mysterious [figure] not known to himself that the poet lets the reader guess." However, this aim can better be achieved through the channels of sensual perception by means of lucid imagery and physical properties of language than it can through devious intellectual correspondences, abstract schemes and obscure myths.

But more directly than in the theoretical part of this essay or in his Acmeist "manifesto," the intentions of Gumilev and his trend are revealed in practical criticism, or in what T. S. Eliot calls "workshop criticism," in which the poet's evaluation of the work of others represents a thorough examination and ordering of his own artistic values. In the latter part of "The Life of Verse" Gumilev cites and comments on "living" poems of four Symbolists which "like live beings enter the circle of our life."[39] Such a "downward directed" role was probably not the intention of most Symbolists, who sought to transform or at least elevate life rather than to adorn it. But Gumilev selected what he needed.

More than the refined but easy-going Kuzmin, Gumilev urges that in poetry "gesture"[40] be used to create a stronger linkage between verse and reality. Stressing such "bodily" vividness of verse, Gumilev approaches a formal stylistic category defined later as *skaz* (the narrative manner designed to imitate oral speech). In 1915 Valerian Chudovsky, Gumilev's fellow critic in *Apollo,* saw in this category the possibility of applying objective units for the observation of each line of verse.[41] Thus, "gesture" appeared as the most successful method for revealing the author's individuality —and to Gumilev this was the main task of poetry. The "complete harmony of all details" became essential in order to make the poem "ring" and "ring true" *(zvenet' istinno).* This point emphasizes what Tynyanov termed the functional character of elements within the dynamic system of a literary work. It is in this sense that I would interpret his ambitious requirement that a modern poem has to "satisfy all demands." Methodologically, the "functional" view assumes a close analysis of verse, and at least theoretically it points at the possibilities of quantification. Although the circles around Gumilev foresaw little practical results from the statistical efforts of Bely, the purely objective aspects of the poetic craft attracted the "younger generation of poets," who eagerly analyzed the ingredients and the rules of poetic gesture.

Gumilev's and Mandelstam's morphogenetic outlook on the "life of verse" refers to the departure in *taste* from the *intellectual* aesthetics of Symbolism, with the ensuing differences in perceiving, selecting and ordering artistic imagery. This departure in views, which eventually grew more pronounced, may be said to represent (in varying degrees), the entire post-Symbolist generation's orientation, regardless of schools and "isms." The same may be said about the adoption of Annensky's and Kuzmin's value of delineation *(razdel'nost'),* which sought to exhibit maximally the individuality of images and gestures with ever-increasing logical and

pictorial gaps between them. Besides various psychological implications, the new premium on the discontinuity of design (pointed
out in *Apollo* by Chudovsky)[42] affected the syntactic structure,
strophic form (greater semantic distances between lines of verse
diminish the importance of strophic division), and possibly due to
increasing abruptness of speeds—the rhythmic structure within
lines is also affected.[43]

More importantly, the concentration on separate objects
rather than on the halo of their context affords a wider range of
outside associations evoked by that object and requires a smaller
number of parts for unifying the composition, by eliminating, so
to speak, the connective tissue. This fact explains why the comparatively frugal (or as Vinogradov says, "impoverished"[44]) language
of the post-Symbolists is still capable of extraordinary emotional
intensity and startling "resurrections" of worn-out verbal formulas.
The artist is also free to make the most abrupt changes of tone or
direction of thought at any point in the composition. It follows
that the requirement of the Symbolists to create and sustain a
mood to hypnotize the audience is now replaced by a new criterion—unexpectedness[44] is now the carrier of interest and the
navigator of composition. Thirdly, the employed objects may retain their exactness if structured into a "gothic complexity." Or,
if one links them by irrational associations, all members remain
fully tangible to the senses. Finally, and I think this is characteristic for the last phase of all artistic Modernism, the dynamics of the
work proceed by contrasts or "leaps" between images or object-
clusters rather than by smooth, chromatic continuity. It follows
that such concepts as melody or any chain of event linearity are
no longer indispensible for the plot which in fact will eventually
introduce manipulations of time such as flashbacks, lapses, multi-
exposures of events into lyricism.

The well-known investigations of various aspects of post-Symbolist poetics have never been able to provide definitive concepts
for the dynamics of the events within Modernism. Most often one
hears about "the rebellion against Symbolism" and the moving
back to "Classicism" or "Neo-Classicism,"—which has little in
common with the direction just outlined. It also follows from the
preceding pages that there was no "rebellion" and that there was
no monolithic Symbolist school to rebel against. The forces that
eventually led to the emancipation from certain extreme tendencies sprang from individual Symbolists themselves and were developed by their respectful pupils. These further developing trends

have been pinpointed by historians who were under the impression of the new poets' earliest works; then, disregarding chronology, literary historians link these with the poets' more striking pronouncements and manifestos.

Meanwhile, long before any post-Symbolist manifestos, *Apollo* published Vyacheslav Ivanov's reaction against the new outlook. Ivanov articulated his scorn for the circle of *Apollo* in one of the poems of his collection *Tender Secret (Nezhnaia taina)* which he dedicated to Kuzmin. One stanza reads:

> My ally on Helicon
> Alien amid society scrapes,
> My brother in the Delphic Apollo,
> But then, on the Moika, almost an enemy!

In the April 1910 issue of *Apollo* Ivanov discussed Gumilev, Voloshin, and Kuzmin. By stressing the quality of Kuzmin's content, Ivanov avoided the discussion of form and style, thus bypassing the topic of concern to the younger generation. Voloshin and Gumilev received a much more critical review than did Kuzmin. Writing about Voloshin's poetry Ivanov pointed out a sound set of values, fine technique, and a solid course of apprenticeship. However, Ivanov's serious reservations arise from his conviction that Voloshin, in his wanderings, failed to learn one paramount element—the mystery of life. Ivanov cautions that even though one may enjoy the book, one would not wish it to influence young poets.

Ivanov was still harder on Gumilev. Reviewing *Pearls* Ivanov begins by saying that Gumilev is a promising pupil of Bryusov—but still a pupil. He is imitative in pose, style and themes; he blows up the exotic Romanticism of the young Bryusov, naively revealing sometimes a secret Symbolism which allows him to confuse life and dreams. This, writes Ivanov, is natural because Gumilev is unable to find an authentic experience. The "restrictedness of his poetic scope and the lack of responsiveness to anything which lies outside of his dreams, bordering at times on a naive lack of comprehension, causes the dissimilarity with [Pushkin's] poet-echo..." At times Gumilev, like the "silly 'parrot of the Antilles islands' leans towards Aestheticism, revealing the dilemma of his consciousness." Who is right—the romantic eagle or the aesthetic parrot? "And of course at this stage the poet does not yet know [where to find] Jacob's Ladder." Compared to other reviews by Ivanov this one is very harsh; it must be explained as a sortie against an enemy who probably struck the author as a more formidable foe than the review acknowledges.

It was not so much the older masters, Ivanov and Annensky, as their respective pupils, Kuzmin and Gumilev, who attracted a number of young talents to augment the original circle of *Apollo*. Besides Chudovsky, Mikhail Lozinsky, and the sixteen-year-old Georgy Ivanov, new forces appeared when in its ninth issue (July 1910) *Apollo* launched the poems of Mikhail Zenkevich, Nikolai Karpov, and five "astonishing" poems of the nineteen-year-old Osip Mandelstam. In 1910, after a fairly successful publication of his first collection of poems, Vladimir Narbut was invited to contribute to *Apollo*. That same year Gumilev introduced his young wife, Anna Akhmatova. The circle of young poets at *Apollo* also included Count Vasili A. Komarovsky, highly esteemed by his contemporaries but now relatively unknown because of his early death in 1914, a secluded life, and a relatively small output. Komarovsky left behind only one collection[46] and some posthumous poems in the journal.

Contrary to standard critical opinion, this "generation" displayed a strong tendency towards Primitivism. On the linguistic level this meant a greater employment of the senses as a vehicle for perception, as opposed to the primarily intellectual mode of the Symbolists. If Akhmatova perceived her word-image-objects very keenly with the monochrome eyes of the "Grey-eyed King" of her first poem published in *Apollo,* other poets of her group sought to employ even less complicated materials. Gumilev applauded Zenkevich, whose poetry is a "reminder of an important but forgotten knowledge, that of primitive perceptions."[47] Gumilev quotes lines which present this idea in its extreme form:

> And learn dark insight
> From the slimiest of beasts.

Such a "dark insight" provides means of extra-verbal communication unlike the elaborate "instrumentational" devices or abstract "hints" of the Symbolists. It involves perceiving the "gesture" of things by means of maximal rapport with the referents. Gumilev also quotes the other young Primitivist, Narbut:

> Now I know that I will understand
> The mute speech of animals.

The Primitivist direction also had a wider application. Gumilev describes the process:

> The first generation of Russian Modernists was captivated among other things by Aestheticism. Their poems abounded in beautiful, sometimes contentless words, [ornamental] labels. The reaction against that appeared in the second generation (with Blok and Bely), but it was somehow undecisive and short-lived. The third generation went all the way in this direction. Zenkevich, and even more, Vladimir Narbut grew to hate not only meaningless beautiful words, but all beautiful words, not only cliché elegance but any elegance in general. Their attention was attracted by all that was really rejected slime, dirt, and soot of this world.[48]

But anti-Aestheticism was only one of the post-Symbolist directions in *Apollo*. In the preceding issue of the journal Gumilev had praised the virtuosity and good taste of Georgy Ivanov. But it is important to distinguish this assimilated Aestheticism from that of the early Modernist "discoveries." "It is rare that young poets have a refined verse which can be either precipitating and swift or retarded, always in correspondence with its themes. This is why reading each poem creates an almost physical feeling of satisfaction. Upon closer reading we find other major virtues . . . unexpectedness of themes and a kind of graceful 'intellectual guilelessness' *(glupovatost')* in the degree demanded by Pushkin."[49]

Towards the fall of 1911 the younger poets from the *Apollo* circle had become aware of a newer brand of Modernism, and they founded a society which they named the "Guild of Poets" *(Tsekh poetov)*. As the stylized title implies, this organization was intended as a professional workshop-association "for poets of different orientation who [wished to] work together on perfecting their verse."[50] The intellectual strength of this "society" lay not in scholarly presentations that could match those offered by the Society of Adepts, nor in a common philosophy, or even in common tastes; the leaders of the Guild adopted a more uncontroversial approach. They concentrated on the discussion of form and technique in individual works without forgetting that form and technique were only a common means to the individual poet's ends—which were left respectfully alone. As Akhmatova recalls:

> The meetings of the Guild of Poets [began] in November 1911 and lasted until April 1913 (i.e. our departure to Italy): approximately 15 meetings were held . . . from October 1912 until April 1913

approximately 10 meetings . . . Gumilev and Gorodetsky were the trustees; Dimitri Kuzmin-Karavaev the business manager, Anna Akhmatova secretary; [among the members were] Osip Mandelstam, Vladimir Narbut, N. Zenkevich, N. Bruin, Georgy Ivanov, Georgy Adamovich, V. V. Gippius, M. Moravskaya, Elena Kuzmina-Karavaeva, Chernyavsky, M. Lozinsky. The first meeting was held at the Gorodetskys' . . . it was attended by Blok and [some] French [visitors].[51]

It was during this period at the Society of Adepts that the Musaget Symbolists gave their lectures on Symbolism, lectures "designed to repel the epigones and heretics." Gumilev, Gorodetsky and Kuzmin-Karavaev opposed the speakers; Nedobrovo and Chudovsky supported the speakers. But there was no dialogue between the lecturers and the audience; the interests were too diverse. However, the Guild maintained a cordial relation and solidarity with the older Society.[52] On the other hand, as the younger group began to acquire a more distinct character, it began to lose its more peripheral members such as Blok and Nedobrovo. With his group the latter joined the Society of Adepts, weakened also by Ivanov's departure for Moscow and now referred to as the Academy of Verse. In the meantime the Guild moved towards closer consolidation. Ideologically the official principles were still defined only as "honesty [fidelity to real experiences] of poetry" and pursuit of "the line of the greatest resistance."

Akhmatova says that at one of the December 1912 meetings of the Guild, in Gumilev's house in Tsarskoe Selo, it was decided to name the emerging school "Acmeism."[53] Many aspects of Acmeism are dealt with elsewhere in this volume. The range of its meaning extends from a small club of poets to part of an international movement. It had no metaphysical system. In fact, the intent of Acmeism, to detect and define things at the peak of their manifestation, and to discover and name living reality by its most vital characteristics, excluded the possibility of any systems. Acmeism was by its nature anti-theoretical. *Apollo* welcomed the taste of the Acmeists, seeing in their school a potential for vigorous criticism unburdened by ideologies.

On December 19, 1912 Gorodetsky gave a lecture in The Vagabond Dog (a cafe) which provoked a lively debate and might have been the first public announcement of Acmeism.[54] A written definition had been published one month earlier by Gumilev in a review of Gorodetsky's *Flowering Staff*. In it Gumilev remarked that the poet understood that he must adopt the Acmeist outlook in order to make his myth work.[55] But formal attempts to describe the new departure did not appear until 1913 in the January and February issues of *Apollo.* These essays have generally been received as somewhat incongruous programmatical statements, but it seems wiser to regard them as descriptive surveys by writers who show different degrees of critical sophistication.

Gumilev's article "Symbolism's Legacy and Acmeism"[56] presents no observations and norms that would be new to the readers of his *Letters on Russian Poetry.* It is, however, the first formal attempt to embrace all the major features of the latest Modernist poetry. For Gumilev, who knew the creative problems of his colleagues professionally and intimately, it must have been plain that in the second decade of this century no pure "isms" could provide first-rate poetry. If the swing toward Objectivism went as far as concreteness of word-objects, then a demand to project the individuality of the author in lyricism calls for a proportionately greater effort. The variety of solutions made it obvious to Gumilev that it was a matter of choosing a personal "balance of forces," whereas for the Symbolists it was a matter of increasing the range of isoclinal forces.

The virtues of Gumilev's article proved also to be its faults. Like Annensky's misunderstood article "On Contemporary Lyricism" and like the Kuzmin essay, this article refrained from the usual value judgments, but it also refrained from "pulling punches." Its vigorous nature, brevity, and the term "Acmeism" endowed this dense essay with the character of a manifesto. The latter fact did Gumilev and Acmeism a disservice because it prompted the readers to search vainly for a "clear theoretical foundation of a new school" in what was a restrained attempt to describe approvingly a multifarious artistic development.

Gorodetsky's more flamboyant essay "Some Currents in Contemporary Russian Poetry"[57] includes a very partial comparison of Symbolist and Acmeist poets. Gorodetsky summarized his survey of the first group in the statement that the "catastrophe" of Symbolism indicates that it failed to be an agent expressive of the spirit of Russia, but he strongly implied that Acmeism would master that task.

Mandelstam's essay "On the Interlocutor"[58] does not mention Acmeism; it is a vigorous attack on the latest Symbolist theory about communication with the reader. One can assume that this article was written several months before it was published, because the argument seems to be directed specifically against Ivanov's speech "Thoughts on Symbolism" which was published a year earlier in *Works and Days*. Mandelstam concludes acmeistically that "poems exist as events and not as traces of experiences," as is implied by Ivanov's theory of echo.

Far more revealing of the nature of Acmeism than these essays are the nine poems of Gumilev, Gorodetsky, Narbut, Zenkevich, Akhmatova and Mandelstam published in the following issue of *Apollo*.[59] The editor's notice said that these poems were printed to illustrate the ideas expressed in the articles by Gumilev and Gorodetsky. "The verses belong to poets who are united by these ideas . . ." The words "Acmeism" and "Adamism" are not mentioned. The degree of "unity" of the authors remains the same as it was before the appearance of the new names. But like the sets of poems in the first issue of *Apollo* they can be rewardingly read as the lyrical creeds of the six poets. All of them are highly individualistic, but they can stand together as a milestone in the advancement of Modernist poetry in the direction outlined on the preceding pages.

Apollo shared the aesthetic views of most Acmeists, but did not identify itself with them as an organization. Most of the officials of *Apollo* did not become Acmeists. Makovsky did not join the new school, though he retained close personal and professional contact with its members. Retrospectively, he too doubted the existence of positive Acmeist features.

Gumilev never used his office in *Apollo* to promote his school. His column in *Apollo* surprised his colleagues with virtues they would not have suspected from his oral performances. The arrogant leader of Acmeists never allowed his school's ideology to interfere with his job as a critic for *Apollo*. All of his own reviews are attempts to combine the judgment of a poet on his own grounds with the general current standards of the field. Gumilev's avoidance of "going beyond the limits of only poetry" made his remarks practical and uncontroversial.

Between 1912 and 1914 the Acmeists were very active. In 1912 they founded their own journal of poetry *(Hyperborei)* and a Guild of Poets publishing house; neither was officially "Acmeist," but the listed names almost exactly matched those which appeared in association with Acmeism. As their reputation grew they were invited to publish in various other journals. According to G. Struve, Gumilev and Akhmatova became permanent contributors to *Russian Thought (Russkaia mysl')*. While the aesthetics of Acmeism persisted, after Gumilev joined the armed forces in 1914 it began to lose momentum as an organization. But throughout the war the Acmeists, including Gumilev, maintained their ties with *Apollo*—which preceded and outlived Acmeism as an organized group. It must also be mentioned that by the time World War I had broken out, *Apollo,* although it continued publishing poetry, became less interested in poetry criticism (the issues had become more or less clarified) and displayed greater attention to the problem of contemporary visual arts.

Not much needs to be said about the relation of *Apollo* to left-wing extremist groups such as Futurism and Ego-Futurism which sprang up at about the same time as Acmeism. These groups, especially the Moscow Futurists, based their entire thrust on the categorical rejection of all culture (including Pushkin). While the talent of many Futurists was undeniable and some of their positions logically supportable, even if it wanted to welcome the radicals, *Apollo* was too sophisticated and deeply committed to traditional culture to be able to share any negative goals with the Futurists. According to Vladimir Markov, most of the attacks came from the radicals. At first *Apollo* was simply amused by the considerable humor of such things as the collection *A Trap for Judges (Sadok Sudei),* excerpts of which *Apollo* printed in the section "The Bees and Wasps of *Apollo*." Boris Eikhenbaum interpreted the post-Symbolist condition as a dilemma: "It became necessary either to create a new *koznoiazychie,* a new primitive lingo, or to liberate the traditional poetic language from the chains of Symbolism and bring it to a new balance. In other words there arose the question of a revolution or evolution."[60] From its inception *Apollo* took the latter direction and announced in 1910 that it had a double role: to examine contemporary artistic developments, and to maintain and strengthen the ties with the past.

However, by the fall of 1913 the "left" had made considerable advances. On one hand some radical artists, especially painters, moved from the religious and chap-book *(lubochnaia)* tradition towards folksy Primitivism and from Symbolism towards Expressionism. Another current began to develop in the direction of "scientism." At this point *Apollo* saw it necessary to respond, and Chudovsky wrote an article entitled "Futurism and the Past." At the outset he concedes that the young tempestuous movements, which at first seem like foreign news items, are here to stay:

They are a very significant phenomenon more than a school; their unquestionable novelty lies in their total, basic, complete, unequivocal, rejection of the past. Of course the idea of Futurism is ancient; the reverencing of the future. Spiritually these notions emerged with the Encyclopedists. They became more actual in 1848 when "men without pasts" replaced those with pasts. The idea of "art for art's sake" germinated from the psyche of the alienated worker. For the artist who does not care about the significance and meaning of his art, work becomes an end in itself. It follows logically that the means of production become the expression. Thus, Futurism only seems new; the Futurists are only the last link of a progression, and they are deceived by their personal physiological youth. So they think they are creative, but we know that this orientation long had ceased to be creativity.

Chudovsky concludes with the statement that, "Alas, these young people do not know what a pure, lofty, holy fortune it is to carry ideas which were nurtured through millenia . . . by so many demi-gods and heroes."[61]

Guarding Modernism against excesses, transcending the proliferating "isms," *Apollo* descried the new tendency of the extreme Objectivist Futurists to espouse "scientism." In a formal article called "The 'New' Art and the 'Fourth Dimension' " Makovsky voiced his grave concern about this trend; to him it represented a mixture of powerfully innovative talent, outrageous illiteracy, partly understood modern mathematics and most dangerous of all, a real affinity for the pace of contemporary civilization. Makovsky concludes that there is hope that nature (human, artistic, or spiritual) will ultimately reject the attempts to fuse art and science; otherwise "scientific metaphysics" will "devour Apollo" which would mean *finis artis.*[62]

Extreme anti-intellectual trends such as Suprematism, or, in poetry, transsense *(zaum')* produce at best extreme stylization of extreme primitivism;[63] and excessive "stylizationism" *(stilizatorstvo)* whether carried out by artists of *The World of Art* or Futurism is bound to either obscure the identity of the author and the work of art, or to divorce the artist's method from his original purpose.

It is well-established that in the course of greater and greater objectivization, international Modernism advanced consistently towards the idea that an artistic device may well be divorced from the author's motivation (by the author himself) and that such a device may become a value in itself.[64] In such cases the effect could be created of a comical grotesque, a grandiose and compelling buffoonery, or a tragic absurdity; and the device may seem more artistic and more original than one that is subservient to lyrical motivation. That path was legitimate, logical, and triumphant in Modernism; only it lead to the end of Modernism as a historical phenomenon. Random composition "happenings," *art povera,* or the "put on" have liberated the artist from premeditating the effects of his design. The elimination of that aspect of creativity together with the author's indifference to the durability of the finished work of art represent a step beyond the boundaries of what was known as Modernist, psychology-bound creativity. Thus the demise of Western Modernism, which was not caused externally, was brought about not (as Edmund Wilson or Irving Howe have speculated) by the Modernists' separation from social causes,[65] but by a far more extreme Aestheticism, the maximal effacement of the work's cultural value.

In its quest for balance and proportion *Apollo* eschewed this extreme position, as well as that of Transcendentalism or Utilitarianism. For that reason politics, the humanistic "sister of aesthetics," was neither expelled from nor particularly honored in the Apollonian circle of considerations. Because such an attitude seemed almost incomprehensible to a large portion of the intelligentsia, in 1913 *Apollo* published two "once-and-for-all" statements about politics to that effect.[66]

For *Apollo* the balance between formal perfection and thematic weight was a clear enough criterion for the admission of a work to Apollo's temple. As Russians, for a practical way of looking up towards Phoebus, the poets and theorists of *Apollo* unanimously turned to Pushkin, "the idle reveller *[guliaka prazdnyi],* whose name is the symbol of sunny rebirth, bright briskness, 'young life'."[67]

Apollo closed in 1918. Its last issue appeared after the October Revolution under the editorship of the former secretary, Mikhail Lozinsky; Makovsky had already left Petrograd.[68] It was clear by then that Russian Modernism would not survive unless it abandoned its two defining characteristics: Aestheticism and Transcendentalism. *Apollo,* the most accomplished bearer of these two trends, found itself almost automatically thrown overboard from "the ship of contemporaneity."

NOTES

[1] Editor's opening manifesto, *Apollon,* 1 (1909), 3.

[2] "Pchely i osy Apollona," *Apollon,* 1 (1909), 84.

[3] In the span of nine years (a longer life than any other Russian Modernist journal) a good magazine obviously published more important material than can be cited, let alone analyzed, in an article. Thus all foreign contributors, whose calibre and number could be the envy of any journal, plus many domestic contributions related to our theme will have go to unmentioned.

[4] This was a bitter, almost two-year-long feud which finally took the form of Universalism versus Individualism. Bely finally capitulated and announced that *"The Scales* realizes that 'extreme individualism'has now outlived its age, and will join in the searching for new horizons of the spirit." [*Vesy,* 1 (1909), ii.] This passage was quoted triumphantly in "Melkie svedeniia," *Zolotoe Runo,* 3 (1909), 120.

[5] Innokentii Annenskii, "O sovremennom lirizme," ("Oni"), pp. 16-17.

[6] Iurii Tynianov, "Promezhutok," *Russkii sovremennik,* 4 (1924), 215.

[7] V. Zhirmunskii, "Dva napravleniia sovremennoi liriki," *Voprosy teorii literatury,* reprint (The Hague, 1961), 183.

[8] Sergei Makovskii, "Nikolai Gumilev. Po lichnym vospominaniiam," *Novyi zhurnal,* 77 (1964), 162.

[9] S. Makovskii, *Na parnase serebrianogo veka* (Munich, 1961), 197-98, and 199-200.

[10] S. Makovskii, *Portrety sovremennikov* (New York, 1955), 274-75 and 252-53.

[11] Makovskii, "Nikolai Gumilev...", p. 166.

[12] I. Annenskii, "Pis'mo v redaktsiiu," *Apollon,* 2 (1909), 34.

[13] This was Gumilev's principal and regular assignment for *Apollo.* When his own poetry was under review, and during some of his absences (military duty), his letters were replaced by those of Kuzmin, Vyacheslav and Georgy Ivanov, Chudovsky, and Maria Tumpovskaya. Similarly, Kuzmin was appointed to survey current Russian fiction regularly in his column "Notes on Russian Belles-lettres." Voloshin was in charge of describing the literary life of Moscow ("Literaturnaia zhizn' ").

[14] Gumilev discusses Gorodetsky *(Rus'),* Borodaevsky *(Stikhotvoreniia),* Sadovskii *(Pozdnee utro),* and Ivan Rukavishnikov. "Pis'ma...", *Apollon,* 1 (1909), 22-23 (2nd pagination).

[15] Besides an "editorial" paean by Makovsky, the collection includes V. Ivanov's sonnet "Apollini," Balmont's "Kupina" and "Posledniaia zaria," Bryusov's "Aleksandriiskii stolp," Kuzmin's "Ty imianem monasheskim ovеian" and "Kak stranno v golose moem slyshen golos," Voloshin's "Delos," "Sozvezdiia" and "Polden'," Gumilev's "Kapitany," Annensky's "Ledianoi trilistnik," and Sologub's "Ia opiat' kak prezhde molod."

[16] "Ot redaktsii," *Zolotoe Runo,* II, 12 (1909). S. Ia. Poliakov, "K chitateliam," *Vesy,* 12 (1909), 185-91.

[17] Empirik [Chulkov], "O Peterburgskom Apollinizme," *Zolotoe Runo,* 10 (1909), 136-38. Gorodetskii, "Formotvorchestvo," *Ibid.,* 58.

[18] Only one note appeared: A. Rostislavov, "Zolotoe Runo," *Apollon,* 9 (1910), 42-44 (2nd pagination).

[19]See Kuzmin, "Zametki...", *Apollon*, 7 (1910), 45; Chulkov, "Vesy," *Ibid.*, 16-17. The editor's apology for having injudiciously placed Chulkov's vindictive response among the first of the series, "Ot izdatelei," *Apollon*, 8 (1910), 71; N. Vrangel', "Iskusstvo v *Vesakh*," *Apollon*, 10 (1910), 17; and mainly, see Kuzmin, "Khudozhestvennaia proza *Vesov*," *Apollon*, 9 (1910), 35-41 and Gumilev, "Poeziia v *Vesakh*," *Apollon*, 9 (1910), 42-44.

[20]Gumilev, "Zhizn' stikha," *Apollon*, 7 (1910), 14, 13.

[21]Belyi, "Orfei," *Trudy i dni*, 1 (1912), 60.

[22]See for example N. V. Nedobrovo's account, "Obshchestvo revnitelei khudozhestvennogo slova," *Trudy i dni*, 2 (1912), 24-25. At this event V. Ivanov and Nedobrovo, after hearing Bely's report on the work of his "Circle of Rhythmists," objected convincingly to Bely's failure to take into account the rhythmical role of permanent and ambulatory caesura in his statistical treatment of the iambic pentameter. Also see the review of Chudovsky's lecture on that "new school" of criticism, published in *Apollo's* supplement *Russkaia khudozhestvennaia letopis'*, 16 (1911).

[23]See Merezhkovskii, "Balagan i tragediia," *Russkoe Slovo*, No. 211 (September 14, 1910) and Briusov, "O 'rechi rabskoi' v zashchitu poezii," *Apollon*, 9 (1910), 31-33. See the entry in Blok's diary, March, 1913 in *Sud'ba Bloka*, ed. Nemerovskaia and Vol'pe (L. 1930), p. 140.

[24]V. Ivanov, "Zavety simvolizma," *Apollon*, 8 (1910), 5-20; Blok, "O sovremennom sostoianii russkogo simvolizma," *Apollon*, 8 (1910), 21-30; Briusov, "O 'rechi rabskoi'..." and Bely, "Venok ili venets," *Apollon*, 11 (1910), 1-4 (2nd pagination).

[25]Gumilev, "O poezii v *Vesakh*," p. 43.

[26]Briusov, "Ob odnom voprose ritma," pp. 52-60.

[27]Kuzmin, "Pis'mo v redaktsiiu," *Apollon*, 5 (1912), 56-57.

[28]Chudovskii, "Trudy i dni," *Apollon*, 2 (1912), 55-56.

[29]Both almanacs appeared in Moscow in 1911.

[30]Gumilev, "Pis'ma...", *Apollon*, 8 (1911), 67-68.

[31]Voloshin, "Arkhaizm v russkoi zhivopisi," *Apollon*, 1 (1909), 43.

[32]Bakst, "Puti klassitsizma v iskusstve," *Apollon*, 3 (1909), 60.

[33]Voloshin, "Anri de Renie," *Apollon*, 4 (1910), 25.

[34]Kuzmin, "O prekrasnoi iasnosti," *Apollon*, 4 (1910), 5-10.

[35]See Znosko-Borovskii, "O tvorchestve M. Kuzmina," *Apollon*, 4-5 (1917), 27.

[36]Kuzmin, "*Orfei i Evridika* Kavalera Gluka," *Apollon*, 10 (1911), 19 and 9. This quote must have been taken from the conclusion of Gluck's preface to the Italian version of *Alceste*, written in 1767.

[37]Gumilev, "Zhizn' stikha," *Apollon*, 7 (1910), 5-14. Because an appendix of the article is devoted to the "recently closed" journal *The Scales*, one assumes that it was written no later than the articles by Kuzmin and Voloshin.

[38] O. Mandel'shtam, "O prirode slova" (1922) in *Sobranie sochinenii* (New York, 1955), p.348.

[39] Gumilev, "Zhizn' stikha," pp. 8, 9.

[40] It is difficult to pinpoint the exact sources of Gumilev's use of this concept. Its origins may stem from Wilhelm von Humboldt's generative theory of lingual creativity. [See Noam Chomsky, *Current Issues in Linguistic Theory* (The Hague, 1964), pp. 17-22 and his *Cartesian Linguistics* (New York, 1966), pp. 19-28.] Humboldt's theories became best known in Russia through the writings of Potebnia. The term itself *(Lautgelarde)* was introduced by Wilhelm Wundt [see *Volkerpsychologie* (Leipzig 1908 and 1912)]. Gumilev may have heard about this concept from his philologist friends at the University of St. Petersburg. It is interesting to compare Gumilev's view with the almost identical notions in R. P. Blackmur's *Language as Gesture.* See also A. L. Pogodin, "Iazyk kak tvorchestvo," *Voprosy po teorii i psikhologii tvorchestva,* IV (Kharkov, 1913), p. 29.

[41] V. Chudovskii, "Neskol'ko myslei k vozmozhnomu ucheniiu o stikhe," *Apollon,* 8-9 (1915), 55-94.

[42] V. Chudovskii, "Po povodu stikhov Anny Akhmatovoi," *Apollon,* 7 (1912), 46-48. Chudovsky imaginatively compares Akhmatova's breaking of composition to Hiroshige's synthetic perception.

[43] Alexis Rannit describes this feature as "a move toward the dynamics of expressionism." See "Anna Akhmatova Considered in the Context of Art Nouveau," in Akhmatova, *Sochineniia* (Inter-Language Literary Associates, 1968), II, 25.

[44] A. Akhmatova, "O stikhakh N. L'vovoi," (1913), *Sochineniia,* II, 280. Also O. Mandel'shtam, "Utro akmeizma," *Literaturnye manifesty* (M. 1919), p. 48.

[45] See V. Ivanov, "Pis'ma...", and "O proze M. Kuzmina," *Apollon,* 7 (1910), 38-40, 46-51.

[46] Graf V. A. Komarovskii, *Pervaia pristan'* (St. Petersburg, 1913).

[47] Gumilev, "Pis'ma...", 3-4 *Apollon* (1912), 100.

[48] Gumilev, "Pis'ma...", *Apollon,* 6 (1912), 53.

[49] Gumilev, "Pis'ma...", *Apollon,* 3-4 (1912), 101.

[50] See Note 2 above and the preface to the Guild of Poets.

[51] Akhmatova, "Mandelstam," *Vozdushnye puti,* IV (New York, 1965), p. 30.

[52] Makovskii, *Portrety...,* p. 276.

[53] Akhmatova, "Mandelstam," p. 31.

[54] For the description of Gorodetsky's lecture see "Smes'," *Apollon,* 1 (1913), 70-71.

[55] Gumilev, "Pis'ma...", *Apollon,* 9 (1912), 53.

[56] Gumilev, "Nasledie simvolizma i akmeizm," *Apollon,* 1 (1913), 42-45.

[57] Gorodetskii, "Nekotorye techeniia v sovremennoi russkoi poezii," *Apollon*, 1 (1913), 46-50.

[58] Mandel'shtam, "O sobesednike," *Apollon*, 2 (1913), 49-54.

[59] *Apollon*, 3 (1913), 31-39. The poems include Gumilev's "Piatistopnye iamby," Gorodetsky's "Adam" and "Zvezdy," Narbut's "Ona nekrasiva..." and "Kak bystro vysykhaiut kryshi," Akhmatova's "Ia prishla tebia smenit', sestra..." and "Cabaret Artistique," Zenkevich's "Smert' losia," and Mandelstam's "Aiia-Sofiia" and "Notre Dame."

[60] B. Eikhenbaum, *Poeziia Anny Akhmatovoi* (Petrograd, 1923), p. 19.

[61] Chudovskii, "Futurizm i proshloe," *Apollon*, 6 (1913), 30.

[62] S. Makovskii, " 'Novoe' iskusstvo i 'chetvertoe izmerenie'," *Apollon*, 7 (1913), 58-59.

[63] See Z. Ashkinazi, "Leipzig 1914g.", *Apollon*, 3 (1915), 70-71.

[64] V. Zhirmunskii, "Dva napravleniia..." p. 183.

[65] In connection with the Franco-English brand of Symbolism, in 1931 Edmund Wilson came to the conclusion that there "are in our contemporary society, for writers who are unable to interest themselves in it . . . only two alternative courses to follow—Axel's [from Villiers de l'Isle Adam's tragedy] or Rimbaud's. If one chooses the first of these, the way of Axel, one shuts oneself up in one's own private world . . . ultimately mistaking one's chimeras for reality [plus suicide] . If one chooses the second, the way of Rimbaud, one tries to leave the twentieth century behind . . . and follow that hysterical excitement over modern 'primitives' [and give up creativity] ." See E. Wilson, *Axel's Castle* (New York, 1931), pp. 287-88 and Irving Howe, "The idea of the Modern," *Literary Modernism* (Greenwich, Conn., 1967), pp. 11-40.

[66] See V. Chudovskii, "O Merezhkovskom, Nekrasove i o politike v iskusstve," *Apollon*, 7(1913), 47-52 and S. Makovskii, "Dusha reaktsii i sviatoe bespokoistvo," *Apollon*, 6 (1913), 44-47.

[67] See such articles as P. Morozov, "Pushkin i angliiskaia poeziia," *Apollon*, 1 (1917), 44-52; Vladislav Khodasevich, "Peterburgskie povesti Pushkina," *Apollon*, 3 (1915), 33-50; B. Tomashevskii, "Frantsuzskie poety XVIII veka," *Apollon*, 6-7 (1915), 63-85. One may recall the authoritative opinions of Eikhenbaum or Zhirmunsky, who believed that of all Modernists the poets of *Apollo* have come closest to the Apollonian limpidity of Pushkin.

[68] Makovskii, *Portrety...*, p. 253, p. 412.

Міръ Искусства

1902
№ 3.

...for them the call of the past was stronger than the call of the future.
Berdyaev, 1914

John E. Bowlt

THE WORLD OF ART

The last decade of the nine-teenth century was a time of tension and search in all areas of Russian culture, and in painting and literature particularly it marked the beginning of a renaissance which was to last for the next thirty years. The 1890s witnessed not only the intense development of the neo-nationalist style nurtured by the art colonies, Abramtsevo and Talashkino, but also, of course, the birth of Russian Symbolism. Both esthetic directions found common ground within the perimeter of the *World of Art,* contributing both to its cultural eclecticism and to its internal contradictions. Thus, the *World of Art* deserves our attention as a meeting-place of ideas essential to the genesis and evolution of Russian Modernism, although, in fact, it can scarcely be considered as an avant-garde or Decadent group.

Behind its Alexandrine facade the *World of Art* formed a platform for a ceaseless struggle of extremes: Russian culture vs. that of the West, art for art's sake vs. art for the individual, art of the past vs. art of the present. It was logical, therefore, that Bryusov's description of the contemporary intelligentsia as "the crest of a wave"[1] should have appeared in the *World of Art* magazine, since nowhere else did such eschato-logical parallelisms as "reality and l'azure," "flowers and the tomb," "The Russian peasantry and the primordial chaos" appear more frequently and more succinctly. Poised between two centuries, torn between Russia and Europe, the *World of Art* could well contain such apparent contrasts and thus, as Gippius said, "could have been born only in St. Petersburg."[2] Its wide diapason accomodated the views of most leading Russian intellectuals of the time and hence formed a positive and erudite contribution to the development of the Russian Silver Age. Yet despite its artistic output, its cultural synthesism and its organiza-tional ability, the *World of Art* has not received the attention of Western scholars or, until very recently, that of their Soviet col-leagues. This is to be regretted, the moreso since adequate scope has already been given to the achievements of Diaghilev's *Ballets Russes* in the West (as the recent spate of auctions and exhibitions has proved) and to certain writers closely connected with the *World of Art* such as Gippius and Vyacheslav Ivanov. In spite of this, the early, Russian phase of Diaghilev's enterprise has remained unexplored or, at best, has been relegated to secondary comment. The aim of this essay, then, is to examine the *World of Art* as a source both of artistic creation and of intellectual judgment. In this way a modest tribute will be offered to Diaghilev in this, the one hundreth anniversary of his birth.

To formulate a definition of the *World of Art* in a few pages is difficult since a multiplicity of names and activities can be placed quite logically under this one rubric. The title, the *World of Art,* was applied to a group of esthetes, artists, literati and musi-cians, to an art journal and to a series of art exhibitions: but even if we were to take each of these aspects singly, we would still encoun-ter numerous difficulties in trying to analyze them, since, for ex-ample, the name was used for two separate cycles of exhibitions (1899-1906 and 1910-1924) and for two distinct societies (the original group led by Diaghilev and Benois in the late 1890s and early 1900s and the exhibition society which sponsored the second cycle of exhibitions). Again, if we try to limit ourselves to the acti-vities of the first World of Art society and its journal, we will be forced still to touch on a plethora of names associated with it: un-like the Knave of Diamonds or the Union of Youth, the World of Art was not a formal society and had no definitive list of members or club code, so our usage of the word "member" should not be taken too literally in this context. The boundaries of the *World of Art* are blurred still more when we remember that many of the artists and literati associated with it contributed to other artistic literary camps, including the Scorpion fraternity, the *Golden Fleece, Art* and *Apollon.* Despite such obstacles, the original group and the journal do present a basis on which to form a factual description, a critical premise and a general evaluation of the role and achievement of the *World of Art* within the Russian Parnasse.

The guiding force of the *World of Art,* both as a group and as a journal, was S. P. Diaghilev (1872-1929), the "man with an eye,"[3] and it was his ability to arrange exhibitions of lasting importance, to appreciate the good and bad features in a work of art that earned him his initial fame. Diaghilev was not an artist (reputedly, he never put brush to canvas), but a critic and esthete of extraordinary taste and wide culture. Because of his substantial knowledge of art, both Russian and Western European, both ancient and modern, and because of his natural inclination to dominate, to use people ruthlessly and autocratically, he was able to enlist material and spiritual support for his various undertakings, the journal, the exhibitions and the ballet among them. And it was the forcefulness of Diaghilev, "uncouth and charming, a lackey and a minister"[4] which both founded the group as a titled group in the late 1890s and contributed to its disruption after 1903. In a letter to his step-mother, E. V. Panaeva-Diaghileva, he summed up his character: "...firstly, I'm a great charlatan, albeit a brilliant one, secondly, I'm a great charmer, thirdly a great lout, fourthly, a man with a great amount of logic and with few principles, and fifthly, it would seem, untalented; anyway, it would seem, if you like, that I've found my real objective—art patronage. Everything is available except money, *mais ça viendra.*"[5]

Before the establishment of the journal called *World of Art* in the fall of 1898, the group of artists, musicians and critics who were to form the editorial and intellectual basis of the group had, for the most part, already been in contact for several years. This was because the leading members were all from St. Petersburg, because (with the exception of Diaghilev) they attended the same Gymnasium and/or art schools and because they remained together even while studying in Germany and France: L. S. Bakst (1866-1924), A. N. Benois (1870-1960), Diaghilev, D. V. Filosofov (Diaghilev's cousin, 1872-1942), E. E. Lanceray (1875-1946), A. P. Nourok (Nurok, pseudonym—Silen, 1863-c.1945), Walter

Nouvel (V. F. Nuvel', 1871-1949), N. K. Rerikh (1874-1948) and K. A. Somov (1869-1939) were all inhabitants of St. Petersburg (although Diaghilev was born in the provinces) and of these Benois, Filosofov, Nouvel, Rerikh and Somov attended the same Gymnasium simultaneously. Hence, early on, between 1884 and the early 1890s, a close bond was established between the future esthetes which soon evolved into their self-styled Pickwickians' Club, an esoteric group which even at school began to cultivate its knowledge of Hellenism, Egyptology, the Italian Primitives, Far Eastern art, the French seventeenth and eighteenth centuries. And, as Filosofov wrote, although the list might be extended to include "Gainsborough and Beardsley, Levitsky and Bryullov, Velasquez and Manet, German woodcuts of the sixteenth century and Goya's prints, steel engravings and lithographs of 1830, Orlov's sketches and those of Daumier,"[6] the climaxes of global culture were seen to be Egypt, Greece and the Middle Ages. As Diaghilev indicated in his introductory essay in the first issue of the journal, these stages of art formed the esthetic foundation of the *World of Art* artists, a concept shared, of course, by many of their literary colleagues. Despite, or perhaps because of, their vast collective knowledge and refined critical sensibility, a rarified atmosphere was created within the group which allowed no vulgarity, no provincialism, no civic or social tendentiousness. Such a tone was maintained, even intensified, when the initial group was joined by the contingent of literati, Z. N. Gippius (pseudonym—Anton Krainy, 1869-1945), D. S. Merezhkovsky (1865-1941), N. M. Minsky (pseudonym of Vilenkin, 1855-1937), V. V. Rozanov (1856-1919) in the late 1890s and by Bely and Bryusov in 1902. Despite the weight of such names, the *World of Art* remained oriented primarily towards the visual arts, rather than towards literature, an inclination which became more pronounced during the last two years of the journal's existence (1902-1904). This is not to say that the non-literary members were ignorant of literary trends, in fact, as Bryusov said, Nouvel and Nourok, among others, had a sound knowledge of modern French and German poetry.[7] The antagonism felt between the artistic and literary camps within the World of Art, particularly within the framework of the journal, was irritated both by the tendency of the non-literary members to "lightheartedly leave aside religious questions"[8] and by the egocentricity of Diaghilev which Bely and Bryusov could not endure. The division between the literary/philosophical members and the "retrospective dreamers"[9] reached its culmination in 1903 when Filosofov, Gippius and Merezhkovsky left to form their own journal, *New Path* (1903-1904). Diaghilev did not intend to close down the literary section of the journal because of this withdrawal, but on the contrary, went so far as to ask Chekhov to become literary editor. Although Chekhov refused, the literary section was kept open and despite the journal's proclivity for articles on art history during 1904, important literary contributions were made, including Bely's "Symbolism as World-Conception."

The neglect of "religious questions" on the part of the artists and their concentration on art as an exquisite craft aligned them with certain members of the so-called first generation of Russian Symbolists, especially Balmont and Bryusov who were frequenters of their meetings and contributors to the journal. The estheticism of the *World of Art* artists, their alienation from social and political reality—reflected in their retrospective depictions of Versailles executed with unfailing technical finesse—indicated their tentative acceptance of "art for art's sake." Just as the verse of Balmont and Bryusov was opposed to that of Nekrasov, so the artistic output of such painters as Benois and Somov was alien to the art of the Realist Wanderers with their imitative presentations of social disorders. Diaghilev, writing in 1897, described their reaction to the Realists: "It's time for these anti-artistic canvases to stop appearing—with their militia-men, police-officers, students in red shirts and girls with cropped hair."[10] The motto which appeared on some *World of Art* publications epitomized their attitude towards the function of art: "Art is Free, Life is Paralyzed" ("Svobodno iskusstvo, skovana zhizn' ")—in other words, art was something too ethereal, too mobile to be anchored to depictions of the realities of life. Indeed, not until the 1905 revolution did some of the World of Art painters and writers turn their attention to the burning social questions of the day, and even then only a few, including I. Ia. Bilibin (1876-1942), M. V. Dobuzhinsky (1875-1957), Lanceray and V. A. Serov (1865-1911), worked at all effectively in this area by producing illustrations for satirical magazines. Most World of Art artists confined their political involvement to the signing of a joint communique or to private statements welcoming the 1905 revolution and condemning the status quo.[11] But for the most part their efforts were abortive, and they retired to the calm world of their epicurean dreams at least until 1917. This clarity of artistic vision distinguished them from the second generation of Russian Symbolists, among whom one might include the Saratov/Moscow Blue Rose movement—this group of artists regarded art as far more than an exercise in craftsmanship, and like their confreres Bely, Blok and Ivanov, treated it as a theurgic force by which to move *ab realia ad realiora.* The apolitical, asocial, even aphilosophical behavior of many of the World of Art members, however, should not allow us to apply the label "art for art's sake" as a general term for the direction favored by all of them. Indeed, together with its advocation of Symbolist heroes, Ibsen, Nietzsche and Vladimir Solovyov, the World of Art tolerated, even publicized, such names as Dostoevsky, Repin, Ruskin and Tolstoi; in this way it acted as a junction of interests rather than as the champion of a single trend. As Filosofov remarked, "The World of Art never had a definite program . . . . It was a cult of dilettantism in the good and true sense of the word."[12] Although it was precisely for its "dilettantism" that the World of Art was attacked,[13] its amateur enthusiasm, haphazard methods and youthful extremism were characteristic of it from the first meetings of the Pickwickians' Club to the last business entanglements of Diaghilev's *Ballets Russes.* And nowhere were they more obvious than on the pages of the journal *World of Art*.

The journal called *World of Art* (1898-1904) was the vehicle of the literary and painterly ideas favored by the group's central and peripheral members. It was born in 1898, the year in which the progressive review entitled *Northern Messenger* had died—after a decade of important literary activity.But just as its predecessor had concentrated on literature, *World of Art* inclined towards the visual arts, especially painting and graphics; and its service as a propagator of both Western European and national art was perhaps its most enduring work. At first the journal was subsidized by S. I. Mamontov (1841-1918), owner of Abramtsevo, and Princess M. K. Tenisheva (1868-1928), owner of Talashkino, but Mamontov withdrew his support after his financial collapse and imprisonment in 1899 and Tenisheva did the same in 1900—owing to her strained relations with Benois, Diaghilev and Mamontov and her uncomfortable position as a Maecenas which was caricatured twice by the press.[14] The life of the magazine, the luxurious presentation of which consumed exceedingly large sums, was saved in 1900 only by an annual grant of 10,000 rubles from the Tsar's private funds, an act prompted by the intercession of Serov. Because of its progressive outlook and encouragement of Modernism, *World of Art* was labelled as "tasteless affectation,"[15] and during the five years of its existence it was never a popular journal (subscribers rarely numbered more than one thousand). Although the magazine was an artistic success, it was doomed to a premature collapse not necessarily through lack of financial support (which is suggested frequently as the main reason for its failure), but through the unsympathetic domination of Diaghilev and his loss of interest in his brainchild shortly after 1900. Within four years Diaghilev's position as editor and arbiter of the journal was being threatened by personal and professional hostility from his colleagues, especially Bakst and Somov and the newcomers Bely and Dobuzhinsky. By the end of 1904, when Nicholas II withdrew his annual subsidy because of the Russo-Japanese War, the enterprise was enfeebled enough to collapse even though specific contents for 1905 had already been advertized and even though other finances were offered. In any case, Diaghilev had already begun to expand his cultural endeavors: in 1905 he organized the famous Tauride Palace Exhibition of Russian Portraits; in 1906 he went to Paris to arrange the Russian section of the Salon d'automne; in 1907 he arranged a season of Russian music in Paris. Even before moving westward, Diaghilev had cooled towards the magazine, and at the beginning of 1904 put its general editorship into the hands of Benois, as a result of which it became even more concerned with art history. Despite its brief period of activity the *World of Art* journal, like its contemporaneous exhibitions, deserves to be remembered for the way in which it familiarized Russians with their own culture and that of the West—particularly with the art and literature of the preceding twenty years. Its communication via both critiques and illustrations of the Paris school, the German Simplicissimus group, European and Russian Symbolism, the neo-nationalist movement and the World of Art itself exerted a profound and permanent influence on the development of Modernist Russian culture.

The first numbers of the *World of Art* were projected in the mid-1890s and began to appear in November, 1898 after innumerable conferences in Diaghilev's apartment at the corner of Liteiny Prospect and Semeonovskaya Street (shortly after he moved to the Fontanka). It was here at the editorial "Tuesdays" and "Sunday teas" that Diaghilev (general editor), Benois (art editor) and Filosofov (literary factotum) planned the forthcoming issues with fellow members of the club and invited colleagues. The atmosphere of this office-cum-apartment summarized aptly the mixture of dilettantism and professionalism, naivete and wisdom which pervaded the pages of the *World of Art;* as Benois wrote: "The place of honor was occupied by three portraits by Lenback . . . two drawings by Menzel, some water-colors by Hans Herrman and Bartels, a pastel portrait by Puvis de Chavannes and several sketches by Dagnan-Bouveret . . . a handsome, large, black, sixteenth-century table served as the "editor's desk" . . . In front of him lay writing materials and among them a pot of glue and a large pair of scissors which served as a favorite distraction for him—Diaghilev was passionately fond of cutting out photographs from which reproductions were made in the review . . . The meetings of the editorial staff invariably took place in the dining room, but they were entirely unlike those of other papers. The mere fact that they took place during tea-time, to the accompaniment of the hissing samovar, gave them a very homely, unoffical character . . ."[16] Diaghilev's love of juxtaposing the familiar with the unfamiliar, the sentimental with the bizarre, was expressed above all in the dramatic contrast between his old nanny in charge of the samovar and his exotic chandelier of wood cut in the form of a many-headed dragon, of which, amusingly, Rozanov was "suspicious."[17] Perhaps such an esthetic dichotomy would account for the conflict of ideas encountered even in the very first issue of the journal and made more evident as the years passed. In design and content the journal was modern and professional, and its first issue gave rise immediately to comparison with the Berlin journals *Insel* and *Pan* and with *The Yellow Book* and *The Savoy.* The cover, head-pieces and decorations were by World of Art artists, the type was chosen from a range of nineteenth-century matrices in the letter foundry of the St. Petersburg Academy, and the illustrations were of first-rate quality, for the excellent monochrome and color reproductions incorporated the latest achievements of European polygraphy—the heliogravure and phototype were executed in Germany, the autotype in Germany and Finland.

The first number was devoted mainly to the work of V. M. Vasnetsov (1848-1926) and the Abramtsevo group and was prefaced by the first part of Diaghilev's essay "Complicated Questions" ("Slozhnye voprosy"). The choice, however, was not altogether fortunate since Vasnetsov was not favored by all parties concerned, Benois among them. On the other hand Vasnetsov's excessively stylized depictions of scenes from Russian mythology were accepted by the conventional public and critics, and even by such dieverse intellectuals as Blok and Filosofov.[18] Paradoxically, this was the reason why reproductions of V. Vasnetsov's work should have appeared simultaneously in N. P. Sobko's rival magazine *Art and Art Industry* (1898, No. 1), which saw Vasnetsov's prowess not in his esthetic stylization and proximity to Art nouveau, but in his maintenance of nineteenth-century Realist traditions. Benois, who was in Paris when the first number came out, argued that Vasnetsov did not deserve this publicity when such great landscapists as I. I. Levitan (1861-1900) were still not appreciated adequately, an opinion which he advanced in the second part of his *History of Russian Painting in the Nineteenth Century* (1902). The choice of materials also worried such astute connoisseurs as P. M. Tretyakov (1832-1898), as he explained in a letter to his son-in-law, the collector, S. S. Botkin: "The outside is alright, but it's been put together in a terribly muddled manner . . . why have photographs of Vasnetsov been put in?"[19] But whatever the polemics concerning Vasnetsov, it was significant that Diaghilev should have concentrated on the latest Moscow/Abramtsevo trends (perhaps under some pressure from Mamontov) rather than on the stylists of St. Petersburg or on Western European movements. Indeed, the idea that the World of Art was a cosmopolitan group more appreciative of Germany and France than of Russia should at least be mollified in view of its evident interest in national cultural traditions. Not only did it admire the neo-nationalist artists, contributing substantially to the propagation of such names as A. Ia. Golovin (1863-1937), K. A. Korovin (1861-1939), S. V. Malyutin (1859-1937), V. Vasnetsov and M. A. Vrubel' (1856-1910), but it also valued its nineteenth-century heritage of Russian literature; it was one of the many paradoxes about the *World of Art* that despite its condemnation of Tolstoy as a writer who almost dismissed "beauty" from his work,[20] it encouraged such positive appraisals of the "critical realists" as Merezhkovsky's "Lev Tolstoy and Dostoevsky" (1900, No. 1-6) and Shestov's "Dostoevsky and Nietzsche (1902, No. 3-4). But in general the *World of Art* did censure all those who considered didacticism more important to art than formal beauty, and they conveniently found confirmation of this in the aphorisms of one of their favorite Symbolist writers, S. Przybyszewski: "The artist is neither a servant, nor a guide, does not belong to the people or to the world, does not serve any idea or any society."[21] Such a radical attitude was bound to cause conflict even within the ranks of World of Art itself and lost it the initial sympathy of such august figures as Repin and Stasov within the first year of the journal's existence. Diaghilev's article "Complicated Questions" in the first two issues, together with the continual attacks on the Wanderers and on the Academy (these appeared concisely and forcefully in the regular Chronicle section) brought forth protests from the leading Realists, especially from Repin, whose angry letter of resignation from the *World of Art* was published in No. 10 of 1899. It is amusing to contrast Repin's description of Diaghilev written in 1898—"Yes, he's really on the move, he's what our time really needs—he's a damn good fellow"— with that of 1901—"No, God didn't give Diaghilev a sense of measure. He spoils everything—possessed by excessive love of power . . ."[22] Such a reversal of attitudes was experienced by many of Diaghilev's acquaintances, Bakst, Benois, and Somov among them.

Despite its evident support of the neo-nationalist movement— and a cursory examination of the journal finds illustrated contributions on E. D. Polenova (1899, No. 1-4), M. V. Nesterov (1900, No. 1-2), Talashkino (1903, No. 4), M. V. Yakunchikova (1904, No. 3),—the *World of Art* did not remain blindly national, and brought its readers into contact with the Modernist culture of Western Europe. Although in this a distinct predilection for the graphics of Beardsley and Valloton was evident, the journal did explore other areas such as exterior and interior decoration of buildings and acquainted its readers with the latest designs of Simpson, Mackintosh, Golovin and Vrubel for facades, ironwork, friezes, etc. However, literary presentations by non-Russian writers were comparatively few, including articles by Huysmans, Maeterlinck, Nietzsche and Ruskin between 1899 and 1900. The reproduction of graphics by Beardsley, Diez and T. Heine exerted an undoubted influence on many young Russian artists and contributed to the renaissance which Russian graphic art enjoyed in the 1900s: in this respect the last numbers of the magazine for 1904 were particularly interesting since instead of reproductions of Western graphists, readers saw decorations by the subsequent Blue Rose member, N. P. Feofilaktov (1878-1941) in No. 8-9, Benois' illustrations to Pushkin's *Bronze Horseman* (No. 1) and Lanceray's drawings to Balmont's *Poetry of the Elements* (no. 12). Not all graphic decorations of literary pieces were, however, successful and there were occasional ornamental non-sequiturs such as the Bilibinesque cockerel, sunflower and ears of corn which interpolated Bely's "Symbolism as World-conception" (No. 5). Benois' illustrations to Pushkin and Lanceray's to Balmont were indicative of the close association between the visual arts and literature observed within the framework of the *World of Art.* However, the collaboration between the artists and literati of the editorial board itself was never complete and a formal split occurred when Merezhkovsky established the separate literary/philosophical organ, *New Path,* in 1903. As Grabar recalled, "There was never . . . a moment when the *World of Art* presented a common, united front, whether political, social or even purely artistic."[23] But despite internal differences, the *World of Art* attempted to examine all areas of art within the orbit of a single journal and serious (although sometimes misguided) endeavors were made in the field of comparative criticism, e.g. Balmont wrote on Goya (1899, No. 11-12), Filosofov argued with Benois on A. Ivanov and V. Vasnetsov (1901, No.6), and Benois wrote on Palestrina and Rossini (1899, No. 11-12). In addition, reports and reviews were presented within the covers of a single issue on art, music and literature, so that an overall view of Modernist developments—whether of Vrubel or Bryusov, Somov or Debussy, Sologub or Reger—could be achieved with a minimum of effort. This aspiration towards synthesism was perhaps the greatest legacy of the *World of Art* and in this it preceded the later Symbolist journals, *The Scales* and *The Golden Fleece.*

The association between representatives of art and literature led to the fine series of portraits of World of Art members and associates executed by such painters as Bakst and Somov. True, the most famous of these, the cycle of "heads" commissioned in 1906 by N. P. Ryabushinsky, editor of *The Golden Fleece,* were produced after the disintegration of the World of Art, but for obvious reasons they can still be classed as part of the World of Art endeavor: among them figured Bakst's portrait of Bely, Vrubel's unfinished portrait of Bryusov and, perhaps the most remarkable, Somov's portrait of Blok. Somov's small crayon and gouache rendering of Blok's head must surely rank as one of the most successful interpretations of a Symbolist character by a contemporaneous artist. Blok's head appears as if carved from a piece of stone, an impression emphasized by the symmetrical hairstyle, the Roman nose and the empty background; gazing out from this cold, pale montage are the eyes: "In Blok's eyes, so clear and seemingly beautiful, there was something lifeless—and it was this, probably, which struck Somov."[24] It was a fortunate coincidence that both the poet and the painter should have shared a similar world-view at this time. Blok, plunged into despair and urban decadence, breathed the same vapid air as Somov whose pictures of fireworks at Versailles and depictions of erotic play served only to hide the deep cynicism and sense of isolation felt by him throughout his life. His insertion of a pale vacuum as the background to the Blok portrait was therefore in keeping with the spiritual state of both and brought to mind immediately the ending of Blok's *Balaganchik:* "(Harlequin) jumps through the window. The distance visible through the window turns out to be drawn on paper. The paper burst. Harlequin flew head over heels into emptiness."[25]

The pessimistic conclusion both in Blok's play and in Somov's portrait was to a certain extent the direct result of an artistic style founded on morbid subjectivism (a transient mood with Blok, but constant with Somov), a faith of futility. Within the sphere of the World of Art several such parallel positions can be perceived, i. e. between writers and painters, and form specific esthetic patterns within its overall prism. Somov's introspection and preoccupation with sex and death had much in common with Diaghilev's fundamental notion that art should be the summation of the ego: ". . . . the meaning of (a work of art) consists of the highest manifestation of the creator's individuality and in the closest possible relationship between this individuality and that of the perceptor."[26] At its face value such a statement was a virile, assertive plea for the artist's liberation from civic duty and, in turn, recalled the egocentric, yet dynamic and elemental verse of the early Balmont. But just as this conception turned "inward" and led directly to the emotional disintegration and contrived confusion of some of Bryusov's verse in the early 1900s, or in much of Blok's work between 1904 and 1910, so at least thematically, much of Somov's work reflected the same *taedium vitae* and served as a practical extension of Diaghilev's argument. In contrast to Bakst, Benois or Serov who turned to past cultures as embodiments of social and moral cohesion, Somov regarded his subjects, normally from 18th century France, with bitter irony depicting them as equally corrupt and artificial as his own age. In this way, he might be compared with Bryusov parodying Classical values in *Tertia Vigilia* or with Blok raising the cardboard sword of the Middle Ages in *The Rose and The Cross.* It was logical, therefore, that Bryusov should have been an admirer of Somov's work and of his imitator, Feofilaktov, the "Moscow Beardsley." Somov's "People-ghosts playing at being people"[27] were, however, the consequence of only one intellectual premise among several found within the World of Art. Benois, Diaghilev's closest colleague and, at one time, mentor, was opposed to such a philosophy of introspection as he indicated in a long and sensitive article in *The Golden Fleece,* "Artistic Heresies." "Does not individualism, the cornerstone of contemporary artistic life—teach us that only that has value which has arisen freely in the artist's soul and has poured freely into his creation? ... Artists have scattered into their own corners, they amuse themselves with self-admiration, they beware of mutual influences and at all costs try be only themselves. Chaos reigns, something turbid which has scarcely any value and which, strangest of all, has no physiognomy . . .Individualism is a heresy mainly because it denies communication...."[28] Benois had sensed emergent artistic chaos as early as 1902 when he had made the plea for the discovery and maintenance of a definite artistic style,[29] but only stylization had been found at least within the framework of the *World of Art.* To a considerable extent it was this awareness which prompted Benois to look back to the rationality and integration of 18th century France and to Classical culture since for him it presented a panacea to social ills, a source of spiritual inspiration, which for Somov it was not. Benois' naive and often humorous depictions of Versailles emerged almost as evocations of some distant, yet fondly remembered childhood. His admiration for, and erudition in, this "enchanting lie"[30] was matched only by V. Ivanov's love and knowledge of Greece and Rome.

The retrospectivism favored by the *World of Art* was not confined to praise of specific historical periods such as Classical Greece or Versailles. A profound interest in popular myth and in the primordial state of Man also occupied painters such as Bakst, as well as several writers. It has already been mentioned that in the first number of the journal, alongside Diaghilev's advocation of subjective art, there was an illustrated contribution on V. Vasnetsov. Vasnetsov's work, like that of Vrubel, was seen by the World of Art members as the incarnation of an archaic, barbaric force, a world of ancient legend and elemental unity. It is, therefore, not surprising that Blok, with his ideas of the "Elements and Culture" (essay of 1908), should have liked Vasnetsov's painting. As early as 1901 in his series of "Philosophical Conversations," Minsky had defined the predicament of his contemporary culture as one which lacked the "wholeness and harmony of the child's soul,"[32] a statement which anticipated V. Ivanov or even the Neo-primitivists with their conscious recourse to naive art. V. Ivanov, of course, extended Minsky's thesis to conclude that "True Symbolism must

28 XI
914 рисовал М. В. Добужинский

reconcile the poet and the mob in a great, universal art . . . We are taking the path of the symbol to the myth . . ."[32] Within such a world-view it was easy to accommodate the work of Bakst and on a different level, that of the mystical Lithuanian painter, M. K. Chiurlienis (1875-1911), recognized and propagated by the World of Art circle. Bakst's depiction of Grecian landscapes which combined ethnographical accuracy and intense imagination were bound to appeal to the Hellenism of V. Ivanov. In the light of this we can forgive V. Ivanov's panegyric of Bakst's *Terror Antiquus*[33] in which the painter juxtaposed Aphrodite and her dove with primal chaos to form a "cold, contrived symbol," a "geographical map in relief, seen from an airplane."[35] While Bakst's picture was exaggerated, and in extremely bad taste, it summarized his belief in the need to return to a barbaric, elemental state, a concept which he later developed in his highly important article, "The New Paths of Classicism: "Painting of the future calls for a lapidary style, because the new art cannot endure the refined . . .Painting of the future will crawl down into the depths of coarseness . . ."[36] Although this statement was directly relevant to the emergence of the Neo-primitivist painting of N. S. Goncharova, M. F. Larionov, A. V. Shevchenko, D. D. Burliuk and others, it also had wider implications, especially when examined through the lens of Ivanov's terminology—"Dionysus...anarchy...the mob." A similar esthetic and philosophical resemblance can be seen between the peripheral World of Art members, M. A. Voloshin (1877-1932) and K. F. Bogaevsky (1872-1943). Voloshin's assertion that the "art of the future can arise only out of the new barbarism"[37] did much to explain his admiration for the stylized, arid, primeval landscapes of Bogaevsky with their deserted mountains and valleys, reminiscent, as it happens, of Voloshin's own water-colors. Such titles as *From the Past of the Crimea, Recollection of Mantegna* and, perhaps coincidentally, *Terre Antique,* would indicate Bogaevsky's sympathies for Bakst, Benois and Rerikh, rather than for Somov.

The quest for synthesism undertaken by so many of the World of Art painters and writers was, of course, evident from their discovery and support of Wagner and the operatic drama. Although he was admired by all associates of the World of Art, the reasons for his popularity differed among them. In the case of Benois and Diaghilev it was an admiration for the way in which Wagner had combined musical and visual forces to produce an expressive and emotive whole differing so profoundly from the light Italian and

415

French operas frequented by their forebears. Their appreciation, however, was not limited to passive observation; as early as 1893 Diaghilev had given a formal concert on the Filosofovs' estate when he had performed two arias from *Parsifal* and *Lohengrin* and in 1902 Benois realized one of his first stage sets by designing the Imperial Theater's presentation of *Götterdämmerung.* In the case of both men Wagner remained a lifetime interest and his name was mentioned frequently on the pages of the *World of Art.* The principal essay on the composer, B. Lichtenberger's "Wagner's Views on Art," expressed many thoughts similar to those of the Russian Symbolist philosophers. Such statements as "Drama is nothing but myth" or that Greek drama was "collective" ("sobiratelnaya") because it included not only many people, but also a union of the arts"[38] were to find parallels in the writings of Bely and Ivanov. According to many of the World of Art members Rimsky-Korsakov and Skriabin, like Wagner, had at times succeeded in creating a synthetic art. Rimsky-Korsakov's equation of notes with colors ("svetozuk")[39], and his own mastery of operatic form endeared him to Diaghilev who at one time took lessons from him and propagated his operas so successfully in West. Skriabin's attempts to create synthetic music and raise musical performance into a grand *Poem of Ecstasy* in which all took part were seen by most of the Symbolists, especially Balmont and Ivanov, as experiments in artistic wholeness pointing back to the Greek drama. Ivanov said: "The theater must stop being 'theater' in the sense of spectacle— *zu schaffen, nicht zu shauen.* The crowd of spectators must fuse into a choral body, like the mystical community of ancient 'orgies' and 'mysteries' . . ."[40] To Diaghilev "heathen and hedonist"[41] Skriabin meant much, as shown by his invitation for Skriabin to appear as a soloist at the season of Russian music in Paris in 1907. Skriabin's efforts to draw distinct parallels between the seven colors of the spectrum and the seven notes of the European scale acted as a pseudo-scientific basis for his investigations into the possibilities of total art; but in his attempt to create "visual music" he was not alone as he had certain affinities with N. K. Metner (Medtner), Rachmaninov and above all Chiurlienis.

When Chiurlienis moved from Lithuania to St. Petersburg in 1909, he was treated immediately as a long lost relative by the Symbolists, especially Ivanov. Inevitably he came into contact with the associates of Makovsky's new journal *Apollo,* and in this way met former members of the World of Art such as Bakst,

Benois and Grabar. For the Symbolists Chiurlienis was perhaps the most synthetic artist of all since his search for wholeness was undertaken on two levels—on the one hand his interest in European and Eastern folklore associated him with Bakst, Bogaevsky and Ivanov, and on the other hand his attempts to "paint music," i.e. to unite two art forms, merited him comparison with Wagner and Skriabin. But it was not only his retrospectivism and visual music which linked him with the World of Art and post-World of Art intellectuals, but also his familiarity with the work of Beardsley, Puvis de Chavannes, Ibsen, Nietzsche and Wilde; structurally too his pictures had much in common with those of the St. Petersburg painters, particularly in the elements of linearity and symmetry (see for example *Sonata of the Stars, Allegro* [1908] and the *Victim* [1909]). It was this which prompted Ivanov to speak of the "geometrical transparency"[42] of Chiurlienis' pictures and Chudovsky to observe that "one of the main peculiarities of Chiurlienis' composition is the dominance of the vertical line. He is the poet of the vertical . . . . Every vertical is a denial of earthly life."[43] The "transparency" of Chiurlienis' work, by which Ivanov must have meant the fusion of shapes and absence of strict delineation, was however a quality alien to the graphic clarity of Bakst, Benois or Somov; the consequent tendency towards abstraction in his painting linked him more closely with V. E. Borisov-Musatov (1870-1905) and the second generation of Symbolist painters, the Blue Rose.

Wagner and music was a topic favored by Bely in one of the later contributions to the World of Art, and he expanded the meaning of music far beyond its tonal basis. In "Forms of Art" Bely defined the essence of reality as music: "Movement is the basic feature of reality . . . . Only music goes to the heart of images, i.e. movement. Every artistic form has as its starting-point reality and as its finishing-point music . . . . In music images are absent."[44] This broad conception of music was not shared by the central members of World of Art, and in fact was more identifiable with the second generation of Symbolists, many of whom grouped around *The Golden Fleece,* than with the first; indeed, it is difficult to envisage the practical Diaghilev, the modest Benois and the retiring Somov (or for that matter Balmont and Bryusov) considering opera and poetry in such terms, despite their debt to Wagner and Verlaine. Of course, Bely's comprehension of music as the fundamental and absolute form of reality was but another symptom of the general aspiration towards monism; but his development of the basic concept into a theoretical premise—and hence his attribution of art with a philosophical purpose—was something rather outside the World of Art framework and closer to Blok or the Blue Rose.

The fact that one of the last literary contributions to the *World of Art* was by Bely forms a convenient bridge from the Bryusov/Benois generation to that of Blok/Borisov-Musatov. In fact, in this article ("Symbolism as World-conception") Bely continued to talk of the intensity of "musical symbols" and the "approach of inner music to the surface of the consciousness."[45] Such abstract metaphysical thinking would explain his recognition of the musical canvases and evocative allusions of such painters as Borisov-Musatov and P. V. Kuznetsov (1878-1968), already far removed from the formal accuracy of the World of Art painters. In the *World of Art* Bely wrote: "In painting we are concerned with the projection of reality onto a plane . . . It is not the picture itself which should come to the foreground, but the veracity of the emotions and moods being experienced which this or that picture of nature evokes in us."[46] The idea that evocation of mood was more important in art than the representation of a given part of reality was especially relevant to the Blue Rose artists who in some measure reacted against the rigidity and "frozen poses"[47] of the World of Art painting. The delicate, azure canvases of Kuznetsov and P. S. Utkin (1877-1934) expressed Bely's argument convincingly and developed it almost to the point of non-representationalism:" . . . the artists . . . acknowledge emotion and replace thought, form and in fact even reason itself by it."[48] Indeed, it was the interfusion of masses, the subtle gradations of pastel colors and loss of control and outline which recalled the musicality of Chiurlienis' work and the cosmic artistic synthesism of Skriabin and Kandinsky.

Despite the interest in absolute art by the World of Art, the group was still very conscious of artistic boundaries and esthetic canons peculiar to each artistic disipline. Paradoxically, it was their observation of these specific limitations and not their dismissal of them which contributed to the success of Diaghilev's presentations of ballet—like opera one of the most striking examples of a synthetic art form. Diaghilev's opera and ballet productions remained purely artistic, with no religious or theurgical aim. They remained, as Ivanov said, "spectacles" rejecting any notion of audience participation, and the very idea of the "front row of the dress-circle . . . . beauty, diamonds and bare shoulders"[49] participating in an orgiastic romp of the Polovtsian Dances was to say the least unbecoming. The success of the Ballets Russes was very much the result of the general approach to art observed by Bakst, Benois and Diaghilev: that it was a supreme human expression which depended, nevertheless, on severe rules of technique, esthetic balance and thematic resemblance. The attention to fine detail demanded by Diaghilev in the dance, stage design and musical performance was therefore symptomatic of the World of Art's emphasis on the "how" rather than the "what," on technical precision rather than mimetic representation. In this respect the initial World of Art painters moved on the same artistic level as Bryusov and Balmont considering art primarily an exercise in the use of the intrinsic properties of a given medium. The sense of form, composition and emotional restraint identifiable with much of the World of Art output—in Somov's water-colors or Bryusov's verse—reached its creative apotheosis in the graphics of Bakst, Benois, Bilibin, Dobuzhinsky, A. P. Ostroumova-Lebedeva (1871-1955) and Somov. Their unfailing sense of line, in itself indicative of their innate artistic discipline, demonstrated a technical prowess so lacking in the Realist works of the preceding decades.

The renaissance of the artist's carft to which the World of Art contributed so much resulted from several factors: firstly, at at early age many of them were urged to draw and paint and were surrounded by works of art in their well-to-do homes; secondly, they were for the most part born within the severe persepctives and planes of St. Petersburg; thirdly, they received expert tuition from the leading art teachers of the day both in Russia (P. P. Chistyakov and Repin) and in the West (Azbe and Whistler); fourthly, they looked to the Neo-classicism of the late seventeenth and eighteenth centuries as the apex of Western man's cultural development and saw the symmetry and linearity of Versailles—one of their more frequent subjects—as their artistic ideal. It was their inclination towards stylization, towards what was termed the "theatralization of Nature" that oriented them towards the theatrical decor and costume designs for which many of the World of Art painters became so famous in the West. Their technical mastery in graphics was well demonstrated in their many studies for stage productions as well as in miniatures, embroidery and fashion designs, and above all, in book illustration where an abundance of detail had to be included within strictly curtailed boundaries. The exquisite covers, title-pages, head- and tail-pieces which we find on the pages of the *World of Art* and contemporaneous publications established a decorative tradition which was maintained without loss of brilliance until the late twenties by the original members of World of Art and a second generation of similar stylists, S. V. Chekhonin (1878-1935) and D. I. Mitrokhin (b. 1880) among them. Perhaps the greatest book illustrator of the time was Somov, whose love of the *Commedia dell' arte* enabled him to produce such a striking cover for the first edition of Blok's dramatic works in 1907 (though Blok did not care for it). In the same year he executed his equally famous covers to Ivanov's *Cor Ardens* and Balmont's *Fire-bird* (which Kuzmin called "nothing more than a divine rag doll"[50]). Mention might also be made of Bilibin's fine covers and illustrations for the series of Russian fairytales published in 1899 and after, and the edition of Pushkin's "The Queen of Spades" (1911) with illustrations by Benois. The graphic expertise in the decorative pieces of these artists might be seen, in broader terms, as the result of their non-philosophical approach to art; because without definite ideological justification their art was left to turn in on itself, to manipulate to the fullest extent its own properties of line, color and mass. Bely said that schematization (stylization) points to the "inability to cope with reality"[51] and the elegant yet brittle examples of technical bravura seen in much of Somov or the early Lanceray (or for that matter Annensky and Bryusov) speak ironically of the dark abyss beyond. It is significant therefore that the work of the Blue Rose artists between 1904 and 1907, at least, should have often been the product of only fair or even mediocre technique—and that it captivated the spirit rather than the intellect. The reason was that just as Blok's poetry to the Beautiful Lady was metaphysical rather than rational, so were the pictures of Kuznetsov and Utkin "like prayers . . . a spring flower of mystical love . . . . not physical, but psychological."[52] Thus it was to be expected that the leaders of the Blue Rose would neglect the decorative arts and virtually ignore stage design, at least until after their Symbolist phase.

The critical achievements of the non-literary members of the *World of Art* have been sadly underrated. It was this capacity perhaps more than any other which separated the group from subsequent artistic collectives such as the Blue Rose and Knave of Diamonds; because while the members of these groups were artists (and as such were probably more important than their World of Art colleagues), they had little of the cultural universality or critical sensibility which Bakst and Benois possessed. Diaghilev himself contributed much of critical value; his book on Levitsky (St. Petersburg, 1902, decorated by Somov), one of a series of similar monographs projected by Diaghilev, was a work of sound organization and lucid presentation, while his short articles on the art of his time showed his immediate awareness of negative or positive artistic innovation. A more scholarly and articulate art critic than Diaghilev was Benois. Apart from large-scale works such as *The History of Russian Painting in the Nineteenth Century* (St. Petersburg, 1901-1902) and *The Russian School of Painting* (St. Petersburg, 1904), his reviews and articles (regular contributions to the newspapers *Word* and *Speech* and to *The World of Art, The Golden Fleece* and *Apollo)* were valuable although sometimes debatable contributions to art criticism. In addition Benois performed the exacting duties of editor of *Art Treasures of Russia* from 1901 until 1903 and was editorial assistant of *Old Years* from 1907 until 1916. Bakst, Bilibin, Rerikh and peripheral artists of the World of Art such as I. E. Grabar (1871-1960) and S. P. Yaremich (1869-1939) had perceptive critical minds as well as creative talent. The gift of meaningful criticism which the World of Art members had was partly the result of their eclecticism, their broad cultural interests, inspired by regular meetings with representatives of national and international art movements at a host of cultural events—at Diaghilev's own "Tuesdays" and "Sundays," at Nouvel's and Nourok's "Evenings of Contemporary Music" and after 1905 at Vyacheslav Ivanov's "Wednesdays" held in his celebrated "Tower." This high level of intellectuality was found in Moscow and the provinces only on a much smaller scale; and although the quest for artistic syntehsism was pursued there perhaps even more avidly than in Petersburg, the critical and theoretical accomplishments of such radicals as the Burlyuk brothers, Larionov, Malevich or for that matter Kruchenykh and Mayakovsky, betrayed ignorance of cultural history, faulty reasoning and little sense of measure. Yet Moscow and the provinces retained an energy which the World of Art members lacked: "We are enfeebled, sick right through and deprived of a fundamental, vital force," wrote Benois.[53] K. S. Petrov-Vodkin (1878-1939), one of the new provincial artists, expanded this statement: "They know the end of the past is inevitable—therein lies the fascination of the

БАКСТ
1906

ЛОЖНЫЕ ВОПРОСЫ.

В. Васнецовъ

Нашъ Мнимый Упадокъ

mood of the World of Art and therein lies the old age of their esthetic belief."[54] It was the youth of new writers and artists in Moscow and the provinces, their passion for painting and poetry and their contempt for old artistic norms which ensured the dynamic development of Russian culture after 1904 and turned Moscow into the center of avant-garde activity until well after the Revolution.

The role of the World of Art as an exhibition society has been reserved for the closing pages of this essay because while it is a crucial field for the art historian, it has little significance for the literary scholar. The cycle of exhibitions entitled World of Art (1899 to 1906) did share certain features with the other activities of the "club" and journal. The series was begun by Diaghilev and also ended by him—indirectly, because of his changing interests and stubborn character. As an organizer of exhibitions he was unsurpassed even by Ryabushinsky or Makovsky, because he mounted shows of both national and Western European art, at home and abroad. These included the famous Tauride Palace Exhibition of Russian Portraits (St. Petersburg, 1905) and the highly successful Russian section at the Salon d'automne (Paris, 1906). The first World of Art exhibition opened in St. Petersburg early in 1899, presenting Russian painters such as Bakst, Benois, Golovin, Korovin, Serov and Somov—and contemporary European artists such as Degas, Monet and Puvis de Chavannes. Diaghilev's bringing together leading artists of Europe under the umbrella of a single exhibition was an unprecedented event for the Russian public. Although the ensuing exhibitions of 1900, 1901, 1902, 1902/ 1903, 1903 and 1906 were purely national affairs, their impact on the Russian art world was great, because they helped disseminate the newest Russian art. But they were not truly representative of the art scene until the last show, earlier ones having an obvious bias for St. Petersburg. In fact, only at the end of 1902 did Diaghilev allow a World of Art exhibition to travel to Moscow. The 1906 session, although held in Petersburg, had the most impressive contingent of Muscovites. Because of this diversity the 1906 exhibit was the most interesting; it included Bakst's portraits of Gippius and Bely, several works by Blue Rose artists and notable contributions from Larionov and Jawlensky. The exhibition was in fact dominated by artists from outside the World of Art, and the mystical canvases of Kuznetsov together with the new color harmonies of Larionov and Jawlensky indicated that the classical severity and symmetry of the World of Art painters had already yielded to the more dynamic trends of the provincial artists. The disintegration of the World of Art which this last exhibition demonstrated so clearly had been preceded by an internal rift in the World of Art committee early in 1903. The ostensible reason for disagreements was the proposal to merge or not with the new Moscow exhibition society called the Union of Russian Artists; Diaghilev was against such a move, but Benois was for it—as Grabar recalled: "I was silent and began to realize that an open fight between Moscow and St. Petersburg was on . . . . But what was most unexpected was that some of the Petersburgians who had grounds for feeling offended took the side of Moscow. Still more unexpected was Benois' speech—he also declared himself in favor of the organization of a new society. Diaghilev and Filosofov exchanged glances. The former was very worked up, the latter sat calmly, smiling sarcastically. With that it was decided. Everyone stood up. Filosofov loudly announced, 'Well, thank God, that's it—the end'."[55] But this apparent revolt against Diaghilev's pride was the outcome not of arguments at one meeting; it came from the atmosphere of tension and potential disruption which had been felt from the early days. As Benois wrote, "All felt that we ought to finish."[56] With the withdrawal of Filosofov, Gippius and Merezhkovsky a few months later, and with the discontinuation of the journal in the following year, the breach was final.

Even if the World of Art had continued to exist as a society and as a journal, it would have been no match for the flamboyance and ebullience of the next movements such as Futurism. For Benois, steeped in the traditions of the eighteenth century, the Futurists embodied "The Coming Huns" of Bryusov's poem—they championed the "cult of emptiness, darkness and nothingness."[57] Despite its propagation of Modernism during the early phase, the World of Art remained at heart aristocratic and conservative, and in this lay its tragic flaw. It was fitting, therefore, that Diaghilev's last major undertaking in Russia was the Tauride Palace Exhibition; because this grand assemblage did not espouse the cause of Symbolist poetry or art nouveau, but the noble Russian portraiture of the eighteenth and nineteenth centuries. In a speech after the opening Diaghilev acknowledged the imminent collapse of his own era (alluded to by this illustrious collection of historical symbols) and also, perhaps unwittingly, expressed the very ethos of the World of Art: "Plunged into the depths of the history of artistic images and thereby invulnerable to reproaches of extreme artistic radicalism, I can say boldly and with conviction . . . that we are the witnesses of a great historical moment of reckoning and ending in the name of a new, unknown culture—a culture which has arisen through us but which will sweep us aside. And hence with neither fear nor unbelief I raise my glass to the ruined walls of the beautiful palaces, as I do to the new behests of the new esthetics. And all that I, an incorrigible sensualist, can wish for is that the impending struggle would not abuse the esthetics of life and that death would be as beautiful and as radiant as the Renaissance!"[58]

NOTES

1. V. Briusov, "Bal'mont," *Mir Iskusstva,* No. 7/8 (1903), 29.

2. Z. Gippius, "Poliksena Solov'eva," *Vozrozhdenie,* No. 89 (1959), 118-24. Quoted in T. Pachmuss, *Zinaida Gippius* (Carbondale, 1971), 8.

3. Serov's words quoted in M. Kopshitser, *Valentin Serov* (M. 1967), 175.

4. A. Belyi, *Nachalo veka* (M.-L. 1933), 195.

5. IRLI. Manuscript Section, f. 102, ed. 88, l. 446. Quoted in N. Lapshina, "Mir iskusstva," *Russkaia khudozhestvennaia kul'tura kontsa XIX-nachala XX veka* (M. 1969), Book 2, 133.

6. D. Filosofov, "Tozhe tendentsiia," *Zolotoe runo,* No. 1 (1908), 73.

7. V. Briusov, *Dnevniki, 1891-1910* (M. 1927), 115.

8. N. Sokolova, *Mir iskusstva* (M.-L., 1934), 61.

9. S. Makovsky's term. See S. Makovskii, "Retrospektivnye mechtateli," *Stranitsy khudozhestvennoi kritiki* (St. P., 1909), Book 2, 114-41.

10. S. Diaghilev in *Novosti,* No. 67 (1897), quoted in N. Sokolova, p. 33.

11. See A. Benois, M. Dobuzhinskii, E. Lanceray, K. Somov, "Golos khudozhnikov," *Syn otechestva* (November 12, 1905) and reprinted in *Zolotoe runo,* No. 1 (1906), 132-33.

12. Quoted in A. Grishchenko, N. Lavrskii, *A. Shevchenko* (M. 1919). Ch. 1.

13. I. Repin, "Po adresu 'Mira iskusstva'," *Niva,* No. 15 (1899), 298-300.

14. A. Savinov, *P. E. Shcherbov* (L. 1969), 60-61 and 71.

15. S. Makovskii, *Portrety sovremennikov* (New York, 1955), 202.

16. A. Benois, *Reminiscences of the Russian Ballet* (London, 1941), 187-89.

17. P. Pertsov, *Literaturnye vospominaniia* (M.-L. 1933). Ch. 8

18. It has been asserted that Blok's poems "Gamaiun, ptitsa veshchaia" (1899) and "Sirin i Alkonost' " (1899) were inspired by Vasnetsov's paintings. See G. Sternin, *Khudozhestvennaia zhizn' Rossii na rubezhe XIX-XX vekov* (M. 1970), 180.

19. GTG, f. 48/931, ll. 1/1 gen. Quoted from Sternin, p. 187.

20. See for example S. Volkonskii, "Iskusstvo," *Mir iskusstva,* No. 3/4 (1898/1899), 63-66.

21. S. Przybyszewski, "Na putiakh dushi," *Mir iskusstva,* No. 5/6 (1902), 102.

22. From letters of Repin to A. A. Krennyi (Sept. 13, 1898) and I. S. Ostroukhov (Nov. 25, 1901), respectively. Quoted in I. Brodskii (sost.), I. Repin, *Izbrannye pis'ma v dvukh tomakh* (M. 1969), II, 142 and 167.

23. I. Grabar', *Moia zhizn'*. *Avtomonografiia* (M.-L. 1937), 178.

24. G. Chulkov, *Gody stranstvii* (M. 1930), 125.

25. A. Blok, "Balaganchik," *Sobranie sochinenii* (M.-L. 1962), IV, 20.

26. S. Diagilev, "Osnovy khudozhestvennoi otsenki," *Mir iskusstva,* No. 3/4 (1898/1899), 57.

27. V. Dmitriev, "Konstantin Somov," *Apollon,* No. 9 (1913), 35.

28. A. Benois, "Khudozhestvennye eresi," *Zolotoe runo,* No. 2 (1906), 80-81.

29. A. Benois, *Istoriia russkoi zhivopisi v XIX veke* (St. P. 1902), 274.

30. A. Benois, *op. cit.* , I, 12.

31. N. Minskii, "Filosofskie razgovory," *Mir iskusstva,* No. 7 (1901), 3.

32. V. Ivanov, "Poet i chern'," *Po zvezdam* (St. P. 1909), 41-42.

33. V. Ivanov, "Drevnii uzhas. Po povodu kartiny L. Baksta," *Zolotoe runo,* No. 4 (1909), 51-65.

34. Benois quoted in Sokolova, p. 125.

35. Mamontov quoted in Sokolova, p. 125.

36. L. Bakst, "Puti klassitsizma," *Apollon,* No. 3 (1909/1910), 60.

37. M. Voloshin, "Mysli o teatre," *Apollon,* No. 5 (1909/1910), 39.

38. G. Lichtenberger, "Vzgliady Vagnera na iskusstvo," *Mir iskusstva,* No. 7/8 (1898/1899), 107, 108.

39. See Bal'mont, *Svetozvuk v prirode i svetovaia simfoniia Skiabina* (M. 1917).

40. V. Ivanov, "Novaia organicheskaia epokha i teatr budushchego," *Po zvesdam,* p. 205.

41. Gippius's words. See Pachmuss, 414.

42. A letter from Ivanov to Makovsky, quoted in S. Makovskii, "N. K. Churlianis," *Apollon,* No. 5 (1911), 25.

43. V. Chudovskii, "N. K. Churlianis," *Apollon,* No. 3 (1914), 30.

44. A. Belyi, "Formy iskusstva," *Mir iskusstva,* No. 2 (1902), 347.

45. A. Belyi, "Simvolizm kak miroponimanie," *Mir iskusstva,* No. 5 (1904), 176.

46. Belyi, "Formy iskusstva," 351.

47. Sokolova's term. See N. Sokolova, p. 117.

48. A. S[kalon] , "Vystavka Golubaia roza," *Russkie vedomosti* (March 25, 1907).

49. R. Buckle, *Nijinsky* (London, 1971), 80.

50. M. Kuzmin, Preface to *K. A. Somov* (Pg. 1916), p. 2 (unpaginated preface).

51. Belyi, "Formy iskusstva," 343.

52. S. Makovskii, "Golubaia roza," *Zolotoe runo,* No. 5 (1907), 25.

53. N. Sokolova, "Iskusstvo na rubezhe XIX-XX," *Ocherki po istorii russkogo iskusstva* (M. 1954).

54. K. Petrov-Vodkin, *Zapisnaia knizhka. Fragmenty vospominanii.* GRM, R. O. f. 105, ed. 15. Quoted in L. D'iakonitsyn, *Ideinye protivorechiia v estetike russkoi zhivopisi kontsa 19-nachala 20 vv.* (Perm', 1966), 144.

55. I. Grabar', 188.

56. A. Benois, *Voznikonovenie "Mira iskusstva"* (L. 1928), 53.

57. "Posledniaia futuristicheskaia vystavka," *Rech',* No. 8 (Jan. 9, 1916).

58. S. Diagilev, "V chas itogov," *Vesy,* No. 4 (1905), 45-46.

APPENDIX — RUSSIAN TEXTS

ДВЕНАДЦАТЬ

1

Черный вечер.
Белый снег.
Ветер, ветер!
На ногах не стоит человек.
Ветер, ветер —
На всем божьем свете!

Завивает ветер
Белый снежок.
Под снежком — ледок.
Скользко, тяжко,
Всякий ходок
Скользит — ах, бедняжка!

От здания к зданию
Протянут канат.
На канате — плакат:
«Вся власть Учредительному Собранию!»
Старушка убивается — плачет,
Никак не поймет, что значит,
На что такой плакат,
Такой огромный лоскут?
Сколько бы вышло портянок для ребят,
А всякий — раздет, разут...

Старушка, как курица,
Кой-как перемотнулась через сугроб.
— Ох, Матушка-Заступница!
— Ох, большевики загонят в гроб!

Ветер хлесткий!
Не отстает и мороз!
И буржуй на перекрестке
В воротник упрятал нос.

А это кто? — Длинные волосы
И говорит вполголоса:
— Предатели!
— Погибла Россия!
Должно быть, писатель —
Вития...

А вон и долгополый —
Сторонкой — за сугроб...
Что нынче невеселый,
Товарищ поп?

Помнишь, как бывало
Брюхом шел вперед,
И крестом сияло
Брюхо на народ?..

Вон барыня в каракуле
К другой подвернулась:
— Ужь мы плакали, плакали...
Поскользнулась
И — бац — растянулась!

Ай, ай!
Тяни, подымай!

Ветер веселый
И зол, и рад.
Крутит подолы,
Прохожих косит,

Рвет, мнет и носит
Большой плакат:
«Вся власть Учредительному Собранию»...
И слова доносит:

...И у нас было собрание...
...Вот в этом здании...
...Обсудили —
Постановили:
На время — десять, на́ ночь — двадцать
                                   пять...
...И меньше — ни с кого не брать...
...Пойдем спать...

Поздний вечер.
Пустеет улица.
Один бродяга
Сутулится,
Да свищет ветер...

Эй, бедняга!
Подходи —
Поцелуемся...

Хлеба!
Что́ впереди?
Проходи!

Черное, черное небо.

Злоба, грустная злоба
Кипит в груди...
Черная злоба, святая злоба...

Товарищ! Гляди
В оба!

2

Гуляет ветер, порхает снег.
Идут двенадцать человек.

Винтовок черные ремни,
Кругом — огни, огни, огни...

В зубах — цыгарка, примят картуз,
На спину б надо бубновый туз!

    Свобода, свобода,
  Эх, эх, без креста!

    Тра-та-та!

Холодно, товарищи, холодно!

— А Ванька с Катькой — в кабаке...
— У ей керенки есть в чулке!

— Ванюшка сам теперь богат...
— Был Ванька наш, а стал солдат!

— Ну, Ванька, сукин сын, буржуй,
  Мою, попробуй, поцелуй!

    Свобода, свобода,
  Эх, эх, без креста!
  Катька с Ванькой занята —
  Чем, чем занята?..

    Тра-та-та!

Кругом — огни, огни, огни...
Оплечь — ружейные ремни...

Революцьонный держите шаг!
Неугомонный не дремлет враг!

Товарищ, винтовку держи, не трусь!
Пальнем-ка пулей в Святую Русь —

    В кондову́ю,
    В избяну́ю,
  В толстозадую!

Эх, эх, без креста!

3

Как пошли наши ребята
В красной гвардии служить —
В красной гвардии служить —
Буйну голову сложить!

Эх ты, горе-горькое,
Сладкое житье!
Рваное пальтишко,
Австрийское ружье!

Мы на горе всем буржуям
Мировой пожар раздуем,
Мировой пожар в крови —
Господи, благослови!

4

Снег крутит, лихач кричит,
Ванька с Катькою летит —
Електрический фонарик
      На оглобельках...
      Ах, ах, пади!..

Он в шинелишке солдатской
С физиономией дурацкой
Крутит, крутит черный ус,
      Да покручивает,
      Да пошучивает...

Вот так Ванька — он плечист!
Вот так Ванька — он речист!
Катьку-дуру обнимает,
      Заговаривает...

Запрокинулась лицом,
Зубки блещут жемчугом...
      Ах ты, Катя, моя Катя,
      Толстоморденькая...

У тебя на шее, Катя,
Шрам не зажил от ножа.
У тебя под грудью, Катя,
Та царапина свежа!

Эх, эх, попляши!
Больно ножки хороши!

В кружевном белье ходила —
Походи-ка, походи!
С офицерами блудила —
Поблуди-ка, поблуди!

Эх, эх, поблуди!
Сердце ёкнуло в груди!

Помнишь, Катя, офицера —
Не ушел он от ножа...
Аль не вспомнила, холера?
Али память не свежа?

Эх, эх, освежи,
Спать с собою положи!

Гетры серые носила,
Шоколад Миньон жрала,
С юнкерьем гулять ходила —
С солдатьем теперь пошла?

Эх, эх, согреши!
Будет легче для души!

6

...Опять навстречу несется вскачь,
Летит, вопит, орет лихач...

Стой, стой! Андрюха, помогай
Петруха, сзаду забегай!..

Трах-тарарах-тах-тах-тах-тах!
Вскрутился к небу снежный прах!..

Лихач — и с Ванькой — наутек...
Еще разок! Взводи курок!..

Трах-тарарах! Ты будешь знать,
. . . .
Как с девочкой чужой гулять!..

Утек, подлец! Ужо, постой,
Расправлюсь завтра я с тобой!

А Катька где? — Мертва, мертва!
Простреленная голова!

Что́, Катька, рада? — Ни гу-гу...
Лежи ты, падаль, на снегу!

Революцьонный держите шаг!
Неугомонный не дремлет враг!

7

И опять идут двенадцать,
За плечами — ружьеца.
Лишь у бедного убийцы
Не видать совсем лица...

Всё быстрее и быстрее
Утораплпвает шаг.
Замотал платок на шее —
Не оправиться никак...

— Что, товарищ, ты не весел?
— Что, дружок, оторопел?
— Что, Петруха, нос повесил,
Или Катьку пожалел?

— Ох, товарищи, родные,
Эту девку я любил...

Ночки черные, хмельные
С этой девкой проводил...

— Из-за удали бедовой
В огневых ее очах,
Из-за родинки пунцовой
Возле правого плеча,
Загубил я, бестолковый,
Загубил я сгоряча... ах!

— Ишь, стервец, завел шарманку,
Что ты, Петька, баба что ль?
— Верно, душу напзнанку
Вздумал вывернуть? Изволь!
— Поддержи свою осанку!
— Над собой держи контроль!

— Не такое нынче время,
Чтобы няньчиться с тобой!
Потяжеле будет бремя
Нам, товарищ дорогой!

И Петруха замедляет
Торопливые шаги...

Он головку вскидавает,
Он опять повеселел...

Эх, эх!
Позабавиться не грех!

Запирайте етажи,
Нынче будут грабежи!

Отмыкайте погреба —
Гуляет нынче голытьба!

8

Ох ты, горе-горькое!
Скука скучная,
Смертная!

Ужь я времячко
Проведу, проведу...

Ужь я темячко
Почешу, почешу...

Ужь я семячки
Полущу, полущу...

Ужь я ножичком
Полосну, полосну!..

Ты лети, буржуй, воробышком!
Выпью кровушку
За зазнобушку,
Чернобровушку...

Упокой, господи, душу рабы твоея...

Скучно!

9

Не слышно шуму городского,
Над невской башней тишина,
И больше нет городового —
Гуляй, ребята, без вина!

Стоит буржуй на перекрестке
И в воротник упрятал нос.
А рядом жмется шерстью жесткой
Поджавший хвост паршивый пес.

Стоит буржуй, как пес голодный,
Стоит безмолвный, как вопрос.
И старый мир, как пес безродный,
Стоит за ним, поджавши хвост.

10

Разыгралась чтой-то вьюга,
    Ой, вьюга́, ой, вьюга́!
Не видать совсем друг друга
    За четыре за шага!

Снег воронкой завился,
Снег столбушкой поднялся...

— Ох, пурга какая, спасе!
— Петька! Эй, не завирайся!
От чего тебя упас
Золотой иконостас?
Бессознательный ты, право,
Рассуди, подумай здраво —
Али руки не в крови
Из-за Катькиной любви?
— Шаг держи революцьонный!
Близок враг неугомонный!

    Вперед, вперед, вперед,
    Рабочий народ!

11

...И идут без имени святого
    Все двенадцать — вдаль.
    Ко всему готовы,
    Ничего не жаль...

Их винтовочки стальные
На незримого врага...
В переулочки глухие,
Где одна пылит пурга...
Да в сугробы пуховые —
Не утянешь сапога...

    В очи бьется
    Красный флаг.

Раздается
Мерный шаг.

Вот — проснется
Лютый враг...

И вьюга́ пылит им в очи
Дни и ночи
Напролет...

Вперед, вперед,
Рабочий народ!

12

...Вдаль идут державным шагом...
— Кто еще там? Выходи!
Это — ветер с красным флагом
Разыгрался впереди...

Впереди — сугроб холодный,
— Кто в сугробе — выходи!..
Только нищий пес голодный
Ковыляет позади...

— Отвяжись ты, шелудивый,
Я штыком пощекочу!
Старый мир, как пес паршивый,
Провались — поколочу!

...Скалит зубы — волк голодный —
Хвост поджал — не отстает —
Пес холодный — пес безродный...
— Эй, откликнись, кто идет?

— Кто там машет красным флагом?
— Приглядись-ка, эка тьма!
— Кто там ходит беглым шагом,
Хоронясь за все дома?

— Всё равно, тебя добуду,
Лучше сдайся мне живьём!
— Эй, товарищ, будет худо,
Выходи, стрелять начнём!

Трах-тах-тах! — И только эхо
Откликается в домах...
Только вьюга долгим смехом
Заливается в снегах...

    Трах-тах-тах!
    Трах-тах-тах..,

...Так идут державным шагом —
Позади — голодный пес,
Впереди — с кровавым флагом,
  И за вьюгой невиди́м,
  И от пули невредим,
Нежной поступью надвьюжной,
Снежной россыпью жемчужной,
  В белом венчике из роз —
  Впереди — Исус Христос.

Январь 1918

ЧАСТЬ ПЕРВАЯ

ДЕВЯТЬСОТ ТРИНАДЦАТЫЙ ГОД

Петербургская повесть

ГЛАВА ПЕРВАЯ

С Татьяной нам не ворожить...
Пушкин

Новогодний праздник длится пышно,
Влажны стебли новогодних роз.
1914

In my hot youth when George
the Third was king...
Don Juan *

Новогодний вечер. Фонтанный Дом. К автору, вместо того, кого ждали, приходят тени из тринадцатого года под видом ряженых. Белый зеркальный зал. Лирическое отступление — «Гость из Будущего». Маскарад. Поэт. Призрак.

Я зажгла заветные свечи,
    Чтобы этот светился вечер,
        И с тобой, ко мне не пришедшим,
        Сорок первый встречаю год.
Но...
    Господняя сила с нами!
    В хрустале утонуло пламя
        «И вино, как отрава, жжет» [1].
Это всплески жесткой беседы,
    Когда все воскресают бреды,
        А часы все еще не бьют...
Нету меры моей тревоге,
    Я сама, как тень на пороге,
        Стерегу последний уют.
И я слышу звонок протяжный,

---

   * В дни моей пылкой юности, когда Георг Третий был королем... *Дон-Жуан, (англ.).*

И я чувствую холод влажный,
Каменею, стыну, горю...
И, как будто припомнив что-то,
Повернувшись вполоборота,
Тихим голосом говорю:
«Вы ошиблись: Венеция дожей —
Это рядом... Но маски в прихожей,
И плащи, и жезлы, и венцы
Вам сегодня придется оставить.
Вас я вздумала нынче прославить,
Новогодние сорванцы!»
Этот Фаустом, тот Дон-Жуаном,
Дапертутто, Иоканааном;
Самый скромный — северным

         Гланом
Иль убийцею Дорианом,
И все шепчут своим Дианам
Твердо выученный урок.
А какой-то еще с тимпаном
Козлоногую приволок.
И для них расступились стены,
Вспыхнул свет, завыли сирены,
И, как купол, вспух потолок.
Я не то что боюсь огласки...
Что́ мне Гамлетовы подвязки,
Что́ мне вихрь Саломеиной пляски,
Что́ мне поступь Железной

         Маски,
Я еще пожелезней тех...
И чья очередь испугаться,
Отшатнуться, отпрянуть, сдаться
И замаливать давний грех?..
Ясно все:
    Не ко мне, так к кому же! [2]
Не для них здесь готовился ужин,
И не им со мной по пути.
Хвост запрятал под фалды фрака...
Как он хром и изящен...
        Однако
Я надеюсь, Владыку Мрака
Вы не смели сюда ввести?
Маска это, череп, лицо ли —
Выражение злобной боли,
Что лишь Гойя мог передать.

Общий баловень и насмешник,
  Перед ним самый смрадный грешник —
    Воплощенная благодать...

Веселиться — так веселиться,
  Только как же могло случиться,
    Что одна я из них жива?
Завтра утро меня разбудит,
  И никто меня не осудит,
    И в лицо мне смеяться будет
      Заоконная синева.
Но мне страшно: войду сама я,
  Кружевную шаль не снимая,
    Улыбнусь всем и замолчу.
С той, какою была когда-то,
  В ожерелье черных агатов,
    До долины Иосафата [3)]
      Снова встретиться не хочу...
Не последние ль близки сроки?..
  Я забыла ваши уроки,
    Краснобаи и лжепророки! —
      Но меня не забыли вы.
Как в прошедшем грядущее зреет,
  Так в грядущем прошлое тлеет —
    Страшный праздник мертвой

          листвы.

Б   *Звук шагов, тех, которых нету,*
Е   *По сияющему паркету*
Л   *И сигары синий дымок.*
    И во всех зеркалах отразился
Ы   *Человек, что не появился*
Й   *И проникнуть в тот зал не мог.*
    Он не лучше других и не хуже,
    Но не веет летейской стужей,
З   *И в руке его теплота.*
А   *Гость из будущего! — Неужели*
    Он придет ко мне в самом деле,
Л   *Повернув налево с моста?*

С детства ряженых я боялась,
  Мне всегда почему-то казалось,
    Что какая-то лишняя тень
Среди них «без лица и названья»
  Затесалась...

Откроем собранье
В новогодний торжественный день!
Ту полночную Гофманиану
Разглашать я по свету не стану
И других бы просила...
                         Постой,
Ты как будто не значишься в списках,
В калиострах, магах, лизисках [4],
         Полосатой наряжен верстой, —
Размалеван пестро и грубо —
Ты...
         ровесник Мамврийского дуба,
Вековой собеседник луны.
Не обманут притворные стоны,
   Ты железные пишешь законы,
      Хаммураби, ликурги, солоны
         У тебя поучиться должны.
Существо это странного нрава,
   Он не ждет, чтоб подагра и слава
      Впопыхах усадили его
         В юбилейные пышные кресла,
      А несет по цветущему
                              вереску,
      По пустыням свое
                         торжество.
И ни в чем не повинен: ни в этом,
   Ни в другом и ни в третьем...
                              Поэтам
      Вообще не пристали грехи.
Проплясать пред Ковчегом Завета
   Или сгинуть!..
                    Да что там! Про это
      Лучше их рассказали стихи.
Крик петуший нам только снится,
   За окошком Нева дымится,
      Ночь бездонна и длится, длится —
         Петербургская чертовня...
В черном небе звезды не видно,
   Гибель где-то здесь очевидна,
      Но беспечна, пряна, бесстыдна
         Маскарадная болтовня...
Крик:
   «Героя на авансцену!»

Не волнуйтесь: дылде на смену
Непременно выйдет сейчас
И споет о священной мести...
Что ж вы все убегаете вместе,
Словно каждый нашел по невесте,
Оставляя с глазу на глаз
Меня в сумраке с черной рамой,
Из которой глядит тот самый,
Ставший наигорчайшей драмой
И еще не оплаканный час?

Это все наплывает не сразу.
Как одну музыкальную фразу,
Слышу шепот: «Прощай! Пора!
Я оставлю тебя живою,
Но ты будешь м о е й вдовою,
Ты — Голубка, солнце, сестра!»
На площадке две слитые тени...
После — лестницы плоской ступени,
Вопль: «Не надо!» — и в отдаленье
Чистый голос:
            «Я к смерти готов».

*Факелы гаснут, потолок опускается. Белый (зеркальный) зал
снова делается комнатой автора. Слова из мрака:*

Смерти нет — это всем известно,
Повторять это стало пресно,
А что есть — пусть расскажут мне.
Кто стучится?
            Ведь всех впустили
Это гость зазеркальный? Или
То, что вдруг мелькнуло в окне...
Шутки ль месяца молодого,
Или вправду там кто-то снова
Между печкой и шкафом стоит?
Бледен лоб, и глаза открыты...
Значит, хрупки могильные плиты,
Значит, мягче воска гранит...
Вздор, вздор, вздор! — От такого вздора
Я седою сделаюсь скоро
Или стану совсем другой.
Что ты манишь меня рукою?!

За одну минуту покоя
Я посмертный отдам покой.

TRISTIA

1

Я изучилъ науку разставанья
Въ простоволосыхъ жалобахъ ночныхъ.
Жуютъ волы, и длится ожиданье,
Послѣдній часъ веселій городскихъ,
И чту обрядъ той пѣтушиной ночи,
Когда, поднявъ дорожной скорби грузъ,
Глядѣли въ даль заплаканныя очи,
И женскій плачъ мѣшался съ пѣньемъ музъ.

2

Кто можетъ знать при словѣ — разставанье,
Какая намъ разлука предстоитъ,
Что намъ сулитъ пѣтушье восклицанье,
Когда огонь въ Акрополѣ горитъ,
И на зарѣ какой то новой жизни,
Когда въ сѣняхъ лѣниво волъ жуетъ,
Зачѣмъ пѣтухъ, глашатай новой жизни,
На городской стѣнѣ крылами бьетъ?

3

И я люблю обыкновенье пряжи,
Снуетъ челнокъ, веретено жужжитъ.
Смотри, навстрѣчу, словно пухъ лебяжій,
Уже босая Делія летитъ.
О, нашей жизни скудная основа,
Куда какъ бѣденъ радости языкъ!
Все было встарь, все повторится снова,
И сладокъ намъ лишь узнаванья мигъ.

4

Да будетъ такъ: прозрачная фигурка
На чистомъ блюдѣ глиняномъ лежитъ,
Какъ бѣличья распластанная шкурка,
Склонясь надъ воскомъ, дѣвушка глядитъ.
Не намъ гадать о греческомъ Эребѣ,
Для женщинъ воскъ, что для мужчины медъ.
Намъ только въ битвахъ выпадаетъ жребій,
А имъ дано гадая умереть.

1918

СОЛОМИНКА.

I

Когда, соломинка, ты спишь въ огромной спальнѣ
И ждешь, безсонная, чтобъ, важенъ и высокъ,
Спокойной тяжестью — что можетъ быть печальнѣй —
На вѣки чуткія спустился потолокъ,

Соломка звонкая, соломинка сухая,
Всю смерть ты выпила и сдѣлалась нѣжнѣй,
Сломалась милая соломка неживая,
Не Саломея, нѣтъ, соломинка скорѣй.

Въ часы безсонницы предметы тяжелѣе,
Какъ будто меньше ихъ — такая тишина —
Мерцаютъ въ зеркалѣ подушки, чуть бѣлѣя,
И въ кругломъ омутѣ кровать отражена.

Нѣтъ, не соломинка въ торжественномъ атласѣ,
Въ огромной комнатѣ надъ черною Невой,
Двѣнадцать мѣсяцевъ поютъ о смертномъ часѣ,
Струится въ воздухѣ ледъ блѣдно-голубой.

Декабрь торжественный струитъ свое дыханье,
Какъ будто въ комнатѣ тяжелая Нева.
Нѣтъ, не Соломинка, Лигейя, умиранье —
Я научился вамъ, блаженныя слова.

II

Я научился вамъ, блаженныя слова,
Леноръ, Соломинка, Лигейя, Серафита,
Въ огромной комнатѣ тяжелая Нева,
И голубая кровь струится изъ гранита.

Декабрь торжественный сіяетъ надъ Невой.
Двѣнадцать мѣсяцевъ поютъ о смертномъ часѣ.
Нѣтъ, не соломинка въ торжественномъ атласѣ
Вкушаетъ медленный, томительный покой.

Въ моей крови живетъ декабрьская Лигейя,
Чья въ саркофагѣ спитъ блаженная любовь,
А та, соломинка, быть можетъ Саломея,
Убита жалостью и не вернется вновь.

1916

1

Въ Петербургѣ мы сойдемся снова,
Словно солнце мы похоронили въ немъ,
И блаженное, безсмысленное слово
Въ первый разъ произнесемъ.
Въ черномъ бархатѣ совѣтской ночи,
Въ бархатѣ всемірной пустоты,
Все поютъ блаженныхъ женъ родныя очи,
Все цвѣтутъ безсмертные цвѣты.

2

Дикой кошкой горбится столица,
На мосту патруль стоитъ,
Только злой моторъ во мглѣ промчится
И кукушкой прокричитъ.
Мнѣ не надо пропуска ночного,
Часовыхъ я не боюсь:
За блаженное, безсмысленное слово
Я въ ночи совѣтской помолюсь.

3

Слышу легкій театральный шорохъ
И дѣвическое „ахъ" —
И безсмертныхъ розъ огромный ворохъ
У Киприды на рукахъ.
У костра мы грѣемся отъ скуки,
Можетъ быть вѣка пройдутъ,
И блаженныхъ женъ родныя руки
Легкій пепелъ соберутъ.

4

Гдѣ то грядки красныя партера,
Пышно взбиты шифоньерки ложъ;
Заводная кукла офицера;
Не для черныхъ душъ и низменныхъ святошъ...
Что жъ, гаси, пожалуй, наши свѣчи
Въ черномъ бархатѣ всемірной пустоты,
Все поютъ блаженныхъ женъ крутыя плечи,
А ночного солнца не замѣтишь ты.

25 Ноября 1920 г.